SEARCHING & RESEARCHING ON THE INTERNET & THE WORLD WIDE WEB

FOURTH EDITION

KAREN HARTMAN

ERNEST ACKERMANN

Mary Washington College

FRANKLIN, BEEDLE & ASSOCIATES, INCORPORATED
8536 SW ST. HELENS DRIVE, STE. D
WILSONVILLE, OREGON 97070
503/682-7668
WWW.FBEEDLE.COM

Dedication

To Jack, Tracy, and Hilary

—K. H.

To my family—Lynn, Karl, and Oliver—and to the memory of my parents

Henry Ackermann (1904 – 1977)

Marie Ackermann (1914 – 1997)

always encouraging, always loving.

—E. A.

President and Publisher	Jim Leisy (jimleisy@fbeedle.com)
Production	Tom Sumner
	Jeni Lee
	Dean Lake
Cover	Neo Nova
Marketing	Chris Collier
Order Processing	Krista Brown

Printed in the U.S.A.

Names of all products herein are used for identification purposes only and are trademarks and/or registered trademarks of their respective owners. Franklin, Beedle & Associates, Inc., makes no claim of ownership or corporate association with the products or companies that own them.

Rights and Permissions
Franklin, Beedle & Associates, Incorporated
8536 SW St. Helens Drive, Suite D
Wilsonville, Oregon 97070

ISBN: 1-59028-036-9 (paperback)
       1-59028-041-5 (hardback)

Library of Congress Cataloging-in-Publication data is available from the publisher.

CONTENTS

Preface vii

chapter 1 ◆ INTRODUCTION TO THE INTERNET AND THE WORLD WIDE WEB   1

About This Book 2
The World Wide Web as an Information Resource 2
Hypertext and Hypermedia 4
Activity 1.1: Using a Search Engine 5
Key Terms and Concepts 13
Information Sources Available on the Web 16
Browser Essentials 18
Summary 27
Selected Terms Introduced in This Chapter 29
Review Questions 29
Exercises and Projects 30

chapter 2 ◆ MANAGING AND USING INFORMATION FROM THE INTERNET AND THE WORLD WIDE WEB   33

Common Types of Files on the Internet and the Web 34
Considering Copyright Guidelines Before Sharing and Copying Information 38
Capturing and Using Text, Images, and Data from the Web and the Internet ... 39
Activity 2.1: Capturing and Downloading Images
    into a Word-processing Document 45
End of Activity 2.1 49
Using Favorites to Keep Track of Resources 49
Procedures and Steps for Managing Internet and Web Information 52
Summary 55
Selected Terms Used in This Chapter 56
Review Questions 56
Exercises and Projects 58

chapter 3 ◆ USING THE WEB FOR RESEARCH   60

The First Step: Evaluating Your Information Needs 61
Choosing the Best Search Tool to Start With 63
Browsing the World Wide Web: Using Directories 64
Activity 3.1: Using a Directory to Browse for Information 65
Finding Information Gems in Virtual Libraries 69
Activity 3.2: Finding Resources in a Virtual Library 72
Searching the World Wide Web: Using Search Engines 77
Activity 3.3: Using Boolean Search Operators 79
Activity 3.4: Using Phrase Searching to Find Information 83
Using Several Search Engines
    Simultaneously: Meta-search Tools 87
Activity 3.5: Using a Meta-search Tool to Find Information 89

Content Issues: Pornography, Free Speech, Censorship, and Filtering 91
Summary 92
Selected Terms Introduced in This Chapter 93
Review Questions 94
Exercises and Projects 95

chapter 4 ⬥ A RESEARCHER'S TOOLKIT: DIRECTORIES AND VIRTUAL LIBRARIES　　98

Characteristics of Directories 99
Browsing and Searching Directories 101
Activity 4.1: A Major Directory and How to Use It 102
Virtual Libraries: Directories with a Difference 108
Activity 4.2: Using a Virtual Library 109
A Researcher's Toolkit 114
Summary 122
Selected Terms Introduced in This Chapter 122
Review Questions 123
Exercises and Projects 124

chapter 5 ⬥ SEARCH STRATEGIES FOR SEARCH ENGINES　　126

Search Engine Databases 127
Search Features Common to Most Search Engines 129
Output Features Common to Most Search Engines 133
A Basic Search Strategy: The 10 Steps 133
Activity 5.1: Search Strategies in AltaVista 135
Activity 5.2: Search Strategies in Google 139
Activity 5.3: Search Strategies in Vivisimo 143
Summary 146
Review Questions 147
Exercises and Projects 149

chapter 6 ⬥ SPECIALIZED DATABASES　　152

Overview of Specialized Databases 153
Information in Specialized Databases
    Is Often Not Accessible Via Search Engines 154
How to Find Specialized Databases 154
Using Specialized Databases 156
Activity 6.1: Searching MEDLINE 156
Activity 6.2: Finding Company Information 164
Activity 6.3: Searching for United States Supreme Court Opinions 169

Activity 6.4: Finding an Individual's Email Address,
Mailing Address, and Phone Number 174
Activity 6.5: Searching for a Business Address, a Phone Number,
a Map, and Driving Directions 179
Summary 182
Selected Terms Introduced in This Chapter 182
Review Questions 182
Exercises and Projects 184

chapter 7 ⬥ SEARCHING FOR NEWS AND MULTIMEDIA 187

Searching for News 188
Weblogs and E-Zines 189
News Tracking and Alerts 192
RSS and News Aggregation 194
Activity 7.1: Setting Up a Personal Newsreader, or Aggregator 195
Searching for Multimedia 202
Summary 208
Selected Terms Used in This Chapter 209
Review Questions 209
Exercises and Projects 211

chapter 8 ⬥ SEARCHING LIBARY CATALOGS 213

Overview of the Development of Online Catalogs 214
Characteristics of Online Library Catalogs 214
Ways to Find Library Catalogs 216
Activity 8.1: Using Libweb to Find a National Catalog 216
Activity 8.2: Using LIBCAT to Find Special Collections 222
Summary 228
Selected Terms Introduced in This Chapter 228
Review Questions 228
Exercises and Projects 230

chapter 9 ⬥ SEARCHING EMAIL DISCUSSION GROUPS & USENET NEWS 232

Email Discussion Groups 233
Activity 9.1: Finding a Discussion Group 238
Usenet Newsgroups 241
Activity 9.2: Searching Usenet News Using Google Groups 247
Etiquette in a Discussion Group or a Usenet Newsgroup 251
Summary 252
Selected Terms Introduced in This Chapter 254
Review Questions 254
Exercises and Projects 256

chapter 10 ▲ SEARCHING ARCHIVES, DOWNLOADING FILES & FTP   258

Understanding the URL Format for FTP 259
Downloading a File by Anonymous FTP 260
Locating FTP Archives and Other Sites for Finding Software 261
Downloading and Working with Files from Software Archives 262
Activity 10.1: Downloading and Installing Software from a Software Archive .. 266
Using an FTP Client Program 271
Summary 274
Review Questions 275
Exercises and Projects 277

chapter 11 ▲ EVALUATING INFORMATION FOUND ON THE WORLD WIDE WEB   279

Reasons to Evaluate 280
Guidelines for Evaluation 281
Activity 11.1: Using a URL and Search Engines to Investigate a Resource 284
Activity 11.2 Applying Guidelines to Evaluate a Resource 291
Information About Evaluating Resources on the World Wide Web 294
Summary 295
Review Questions 296
Exercises and Projects 298

chapter 12 ▲ CITING WEB AND INTERNET SOURCES   300

Guidelines for Citing Internet and Web Resources 301
Citation Examples 305
Information on the Web About Citing Electronic Resources 312
Summary 313
Review Questions 313
Exercises and Projects 315

Appendix A: Ways to stay current 317

Appendix B: Privacy and Security on the Internet and the Web 259

Appendix C: Internet Explorer Details 331

Glossary 337

Index 348

PREFACE

Searching and Researching on the Internet and the World Wide Web, Fourth Edition gives a straightforward and accessible approach to using the World Wide Web and the Internet for finding information. It is primarily designed for students in college-level courses or for self-study. The topics address the research needs of students in a broad range of disciplines, as well as college-level instructors, researchers, prospective and in-service K–12 teachers, librarians, and others interested in tapping the Web and the Internet for information. It also serves as a guide to the appropriate methods to acquire, evaluate, and cite resources. People with experience working with the Web and those who are first learning will find it beneficial.

Certain assumptions are made about the reader of this book. We expect the reader to be acquainted with the fundamental operations of a personal computer, in particular the ability to launch and use applications software. Access to the Internet is equally important to successfully completing the activities and exercises. The reader must have an Internet account either at his or her college or with an Internet service provider.

Important Features of the Book

In the course of this book, you'll learn how to find answers to research and reference questions, as well as how to find email and street addresses, maps, and shareware programs. We discuss several different types of information resources—directories, virtual libraries, search engines, and specialized databases. The main topics are formulating search strategies, understanding how to form search expressions, evaluating information, and citing resources. We carry these themes throughout the book. The 10-step search strategy developed in Chapter 5, for example, is applied to activities and exercises in many of the subsequent chapters. This strategy, combined with the numerous activities throughout the book, provide a variety of techniques and concepts that are useful to the beginner and the more advanced researcher. In reading the text and working through the activities and projects, you'll come to understand that for every research question you ask, you will need to go through a process to create the most appropriate search strategy. You also need to decide whether to use a directory, search engine, or other type of resource. You'll see that this search formation process or methodology guarantees a more precise result and is applicable to any search engine or database.

The step-by-step activities in the text were developed using Microsoft Internet Explorer. You'll find, however, that the essential search skills, the ways to determine which types of resources to use, and the ways to evaluate and cite resources that we cover in the book depend very little on the specific Web browser and computer system you use. After reading the text and working through the activities you'll be better prepared to effectively find what you need, determine the appropriate tools and resources to use, and evaluate what you have found.

Using the World Wide Web for Research

The Internet and the World Wide Web have had a profound effect on the way we find information and do research. Part of this is due to the astounding increase in the amount of information available and the tools we have at our disposal for finding it. The information explosion raises a number of important issues. We really do need to know how to search the Web *effectively*.

Sometimes we may get frustrated with the Internet or the Web because there appears to be too much extraneous information, yet we are anxious to get as much good information as we can. We need to know how the different search engines are constructed so that as new search engines appear we will have developed skills that enable us to search any database. We also need to know when a search engine isn't the most appropriate resource to use. In some cases we'll want to use a virtual library or a Web directory. With all the information making up the Web, we also need to know how to evaluate sources we find.

In addition to these issues, the student also needs to keep in mind the ethical issues surrounding Internet use. This includes knowing the etiquette of an email discussion group, asking permission to use an image on a Web page or research paper, and citing Web research properly in a paper or project.

Organization and Content

Throughout the book we emphasize effectively using the resources and tools on the Internet and the Web for searching and researching. We discuss some technical details of how the resources are organized and how the tools do their work, but always within the context of getting more precise results. This emphasis, combined with the numerous step-by-step activities throughout the book, gives what we feel is a good blend of techniques and concepts that are useful and beneficial to students.

The arrangement of the chapters lays out a specific path through the material. The book is organized as follows:

Chapters 1 and 2	Introduction to the Internet and the Web; managing and using Web information, learning about file types and copyright guidelines
Chapter 3	Introduction to research skills and tools on the Web
Chapter 4	Overview of directories and virtual libraries; a list of reliable academic Web sites by subject
Chapters 5, 6, 7, and 8	Search strategies and tools—search engines, meta-search tools, specialized databases, searching for news and multimedia, and library catalogs
Chapters 9 and 10	FTP archives, email discussion groups, and Usenet news archives
Chapter 11	Evaluating information found on the Internet and the Web
Chapter 12	Citing information for research
Appendix A	Ways to keep up to date with Web research tools
Appendix B	Learning about privacy and security on the Internet
Appendix C	An overview of Internet Explorer

We start with an introduction to the Internet and the Web, covering the essentials of using a browser and some other technical details, such as how to manage and use information found on the Internet. We then move to using the Web for research, where we introduce a number of fundamental concepts and tactics for finding information on the Web. From there we move to the resources we can browse: directories and virtual libraries. Next we cover developing a search strategy, constructing search expressions, and using the common features of various search engines and other searchable databases. This is followed by numerous examples of using search engines and discussions of using specialized databases. A chapter devoted to searching for news and multimedia includes an overview of weblogs and RSS (Really Simple Syndication) technology and more. There are other resources to use to find information: library catalogs, FTP, email, discussion groups, and Usenet newsgroups; we take them up in the next three chapters. Evaluating resources and citing resources are considered next. Appendix A addresses some of the privacy and security issues related to using the Internet and the Web.

There are other paths through this material; however, we feel you should go through Chapter 3 before moving on to other chapters in the book. You may skip or select certain topics from the first three chapters if you feel a complete introduction to the Internet and the Web and tips on managing information aren't necessary. Chapter 5 is essential to the discussions about searching in the remainder of the text. If using library catalogs doesn't fit into your plans, you may skip Chapter 8. If you're pressed for time and need to concentrate on research skills then you can skip Chapters 9 and 10. Evaluating resources can be considered any time after you have become experienced with the nature of information on the Internet.

Each of the chapters contains at least one step-by-step activity that demonstrates fundamental skills and concepts. Some of the text depends on the reader becoming a participant in the activities or having other experiences using the Internet and the World Wide Web. By following the activities and trying them out, the student may gain some first-hand, guided experience. Including these activities is a bit of a risk because of the dynamic nature of the Internet and the World Wide Web. Nothing is frozen in place, and it may be that when you work with these you'll see differences in the way information is displayed. Don't let that deter you. Using the World Wide Web and the Internet means adapting to changes. Be persistent and use your skills to make accommodations to a changing, but important, environment. The dynamic nature of the Web is one of its most exciting features.

New in This Edition

The fourth edition builds on the successful features of the earlier editions. The approach and layout has been maintained. Activities and exercises have been updated to make them fresher and to meet the challenge of the evolving Internet and World Wide Web, and to be more relevant to students' needs. The text examples and activities all use Internet Explorer as the browser, which is a change from the third edition. Content rearrangement included moving browser details from its own chapter to an appendix, and moving strategies for finding people and maps to the chapter on specialized databases. New content in this edition includes a discussion of browsers other than Internet Explorer, including Mozilla and Opera; and a list of annotated academic Web sites arranged by subject in Chapter 4, "A Researcher's Toolkit: Using Directories and Virtual Libraries." The proliferation of weblogs and growth of RSS technology prompted the creation of a new chapter that covers these topics in the context of searching for news.

Supplemental Materials

For those teaching courses with this book, an instructor's guide is available from the publisher. The book has an accompanying Web site, "Searching and Researching on the Internet and the WWW," with the URL **http://webliminal.com/search-web.html**. Hyperlinks on that site will take you to individual Web pages for each chapter and appendix. These contain up-to-date links to all the resources mentioned in the book. They are periodically updated to keep the activities current. Furthermore, since the material at Web sites can change, this site gives access to the most recent versions of information on the Web.

About Us

The material in this book is derived directly from our experiences. During the past several years we've been involved in teaching students about using the Internet and the Web as resources for research. We also lead workshops for librarians, teachers, and other groups of professionals interested in using the resources on the Internet in their work; and we give presentations about finding, evaluating, and citing resources on the Web. As a librarian and a professor of computer science, we work as researchers ourselves.

Acknowledgments

There are many people to thank for the encouragement, friendship, support, and help that carried us through the many months of work on this project. We owe our greatest thanks, as always, to our immediate and extended families. They, more than anyone else, have made it possible for us to complete this work. Karen wishes to especially thank her husband, Jack, and their daughters Tracy and Hilary for their patience and support throughout the many years while she's worked on all the versions of this book. They have never complained that she was unavailable for conversation and help on many weekends and evenings. Ernie wishes to thank his wife Lynn for all her help, love, and support—reading drafts and making improvements, being encouraging and supportive always, and (as she says) keeping herself amused. He also wants to thank his children, Karl and Oliver, for their special encouragement, interest, and advice, and for giving him the most important reasons for writing.

We want to thank all the people who fall into the categories of friends, colleagues, and students in Fredericksburg, Virginia, and at Mary Washington College who've given us their support, encouragement, help, and understanding. We'd like to especially thank Jack Bales for allowing us to use a piece of his writing in an example of citing Web pages in Chapter 12, and we want to thank Alexander Jacobsen for his excellent work in checking and suggesting URLs.

We especially want to thank Ann L. Watts, librarian for the Boone Campus Library, Des Moines Area Community College, for the work she's done on carefully preparing exercises for this edition. She's also shared with us her experiences teaching courses using our books. We appreciate her friendship and her encouraging correspondence.

Franklin, Beedle & Associates has been a very supportive and cooperative publisher and has helped us greatly throughout this project. We'd like to especially thank Jeni Lee, Dean Lake, and Tom Sumner, production; Jim Leisy, Chris Collier, and Krista Hall.

This book has been through several reviews and we want to thank our reviewers—Mimi Will, Kris Chandler, Bill O'Connor, Lois Davis, Kathy Finney, and Dave Bullock—for their helpful, insightful, and frank comments and suggestions.

We hope you like this book and find it useful. Feel free to send us email letting us know your opinions, suggestions, or comments about our work. When you have the time, visit our home pages on the Web.

Karen Hartman
kphartman@fastmail.fm
http://webliminal.com/khartman

Ernest Ackermann
ernie@umw.edu
Department of Computer Science
University of Mary Washington
http://webliminal.com/ernie

INTRODUCTION TO THE INTERNET AND THE WORLD WIDE WEB

1

Every day, millions of people around the world use their computers to access the information on the Internet that makes up the World Wide Web. They search for and retrieve information on all sorts of topics in a wide variety of areas. The information can appear in a variety of digital formats, such as text, images, audio, or video. Individuals, companies, research labs, libraries, news organizations, television networks, governments, and other organizations all make resources available. People communicate with each other, sharing information and making commercial and business transactions, using electronic mail. All this activity is possible because tens of thousands of networks are connected to the Internet and exchange information in the same basic ways. The World Wide Web is part of the Internet, but it's not a collection of networks. Rather, it's the information that is connected or linked in a sort of web. Never before has so much information from such a wide variety of sources and in so many formats been available to the public.

Using a Web browser—the computer program or software that lets you access the World Wide Web—you can find information on almost any topic with just a few clicks of your mouse button. Some of the resources on the Web have been classified into directories that you can easily browse by going from one category to another. Several search tools (programs that search the Web for resources) are readily available. When you type a keyword or phrase into a form and click on a button or icon on the screen, a list of items appears. You simply click on the ones you want to retrieve. The amount and variety of information available are astounding, but sometimes it's difficult to find appropriate material.

This chapter covers some of the basic information and concepts you need to begin finding information on the World Wide Web. The sections in this chapter are as follows:

✦ The World Wide Web as an Information Resource

✦ Hypertext and Hypermedia

✦ Key Terms and Concepts

✦ Information Sources Available on the Web

✦ Browser Essentials

About This Book

This book is designed to help anyone who uses the World Wide Web and the Internet to find information or research a topic. We'll cover the tools and methods with which you search for resources on the Web, and we will explain how to access and use those tools. We'll go over the methods and techniques that will help you be effective and efficient in your searching and researching. We'll also talk about how to evaluate and cite resources within the context of a research project. The text and activities are designed to give you the experience you need to tap the cornucopia of information on the Web, find the resources you want, and—just as important—evaluate the material you've found.

Each of the chapters contains at least one detailed activity or example in which you work with a Web browser to access information on the World Wide Web. These activities demonstrate concepts and techniques. As you read the activities and follow along, you'll receive step-by-step instructions for working with the World Wide Web. Remember, though, that these activities and examples reflect the Web at the time of writing. Because some things change frequently, they may not appear to you on your screen as they do in this book. The Web and the Internet are constantly changing, but don't let that hold you back. Be persistent and use your skills to work in this important environment. Change is one of the things that make the Internet and the World Wide Web exciting, vigorous, and useful.

At the end of each chapter, we provide a chapter summary and a list of terms. The terms are defined in the chapter and also appear in the glossary at the back of the book.

The World Wide Web as an Information Resource

You can think of the *World Wide Web* as a large collection of information that's accessible through the Internet. The *Internet* is a collection of tens of thousands of computer networks that exchange information according to some agreed-upon rules or protocols. Because of this uniformity, a computer connected to one of the Internet's networks can transport text and images and display them on a computer connected to another part of the Internet.

Whether you've worked on the Web before or not, you'll be pleased with how easy it is to use. It's also enticing. The World Wide Web gives a uniform means of accessing all the different types of information on the Internet. Since you only need to know one way to get information, you can concentrate on what you want, not on how to obtain it. The Internet is commonly used throughout the world, so there is easy and relatively quick access to information on a global scale. That alone is remarkable, but it gets better. The information on the Web is often in a multimedia format called a *Web page*, which may combine text, images, audio, or video. This format lets us take advantage of modern computers' multimedia capabilities. A Web page can also contain links to other resources or information on the World Wide Web. This is why it's called a web: One page contains links to another, and that one contains links to another, and so on. Since the information can be anywhere in the world, the term *World Wide Web* is most appropriate.

Tim Berners-Lee, credited with the concept of the Web, made the following statement in the document "About The World Wide Web": "The World Wide Web (known as 'WWW,' 'Web' or 'W3') is the universe of network-accessible information, the embodiment of human knowledge." (By the way, you can find that document on the Web by using the URL **http://www.w3.org/www**. We'll say more a little later about how to use URLs.) Berners-Lee has made a strong statement, but it's certainly true. There's a wide range of materials available on such subjects as art, science, humanities, politics, law, business, education, and government information. In each of these areas, you can find scientific and technical papers, financial data, stock market reports, government reports, advertisements, and publicity and news about movies and other forms of entertainment. Through the Web, you can find information about many types of products, information about health and environmental issues, government documents, and tips and advice on recreational activities such as camping, cooking, gardening, and travel. You can tour museums, plan a trip, make reservations, visit gardens throughout the world, and so on. Just a little bit of exploring will show you the wide range and types of information available.

To access the Web, you start a program on your computer called a *Web browser*. The browser makes the connections to a specific Web site, retrieves information from the site, and displays it in a window on your screen. The information in the window is often in multimedia format; it may have text, images, video, or audio. From there, you can go to other locations on the Internet to search for, browse, and retrieve information. You use a mouse to move a hand or pointer to an icon, menu item, region of a map or image, button, or underlined portion of the window, and click the mouse button (the left one if your mouse has more than one button). These items are called *hyperlinks*, or *links* for short. If you've clicked on a link in the document, the browser follows that link; the current document is replaced or another window pops up. Some Web pages, including those you'll use for searching and researching, have a place for you to type in a word or phrase, fill out a form, or check off options.

Items that are accessible through the Web give hypertext access to the Internet. In order for this to work, there are standard ways of specifying the links and creating documents that can be displayed as part of the Web. Information is exchanged according to a specific set of rules, or *Hypertext Transfer Protocol (HTTP)*; each link has a particular format, or a *Uniform Resource Locator (URL)*; and Web pages are written using a language called *Hypertext Markup Language (HTML)*, which the browser can interpret.

The browser window also has text and icons in the borders, outside the portion of the window containing the Web page. Clicking on text or icons in the upper border of a window pops up a menu or a dialog box from which you can choose an action. Figure 1.1 shows these and other portions of a browser window.

Throughout this book, we'll use version 6 of Microsoft Internet Explorer as the browser. If you're using a different browser—Mozilla, Opera, or the AOL browser—you'll see lots of similarities. While your view might be slightly different, we've tried not to rely on any special features of the browser. That way, the explanations and activities will be meaningful regardless of the browser you're using.

Figure 1.1 shows the home page for the Library of Congress. When a site has several Web pages available, as the Library of Congress's Web site does, the one that acts as the first or introductory page is called the *home page*. The term *home page* is used in other ways as well. Lots of people have Web pages that tell something about themselves; a page like that is called a personal home page. The first page you see when you start your browser is the home page for the browser.

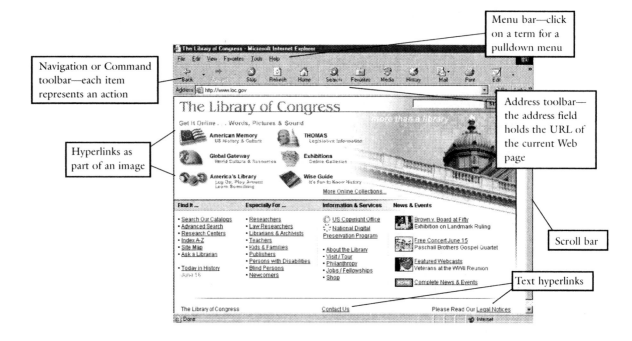

Figure 1.1—Home Page for the Library of Congress

Hypertext and Hypermedia

When you use the Web, you work in a hypertext or hypermedia environment. That means you move from item to item and back again without having to follow a predefined path. You follow hyperlinks according to your needs. Sometimes the items you select are words in other sentences or paragraphs; this way, the links to other Internet resources are presented in context. The links can also be represented by icons or images, or they may be regions in a map or graphic. Working with hyperlinks is fundamental to using the World Wide Web effectively, so we'll go into a little bit of detail on this topic.

The term *hypertext* is used to describe text that contains links to other text. When the hypertext and links are from a variety of media (text, video, sound), as is the case in the Web, we use the term *hypermedia*. On a screen or page, certain items will be boldfaced, underlined, or colored differently. Each one represents a link to another part of the current document or other Internet resource. Selecting one of these links allows you to follow or jump to the information the link represents. You can also return to a previous link. There's a definite starting point, but the path you take after that is your choice. You are not constrained by having to go in some sort of straight line; you can think of being able to move up, down, right, or left from any link.

As an example, we'll look at an excerpt from a hypertext glossary. The definitions and explanations in the glossary are connected through hypertext. The excerpt here comes from a glossary of Internet terms that accompanies this book. This glossary is available on the Web in hypertext form. To see it, use the URL **http://webliminal.com/search/glossary.htm**. Here's the excerpt:

> **Web Page** The information available and displayed by a **Web browser** as the result of opening a local file or opening a location (**URL**). The contents and format of the Web page are specified using **HTML**.

If you used your mouse to select one of the underlined words or phrases and you clicked on it, you'd be taken to another part of the glossary. For example, choosing (**URL**) takes you to a definition of URL (Uniform Resource Locator). From there, you could browse the glossary by following other links, or you could return to the entry for Web Page. You could always follow the links back to the place you started. The information in the glossary wouldn't change, but the way you accessed it and the order in which you did so would change.

Before we discuss other concepts related to the World Wide Web, let's do an activity that shows what we might see when we start a Web browser and search for some information. We'll use Microsoft Internet Explorer for all the activities in this book. Except for some of the details we give in Appendix C, we won't focus on the features of the Web browser you use. We hope that the explanations and activities will be meaningful to you regardless of your browser.

About the Activities

This is the first of many activities in this book. Each activity is divided into two parts: "Overview" and "Details." In the first part, "Overview," we discuss what we'll be doing and enumerate the steps we'll follow. The section "Details" goes through the steps, shows the results we got when we tried the activity, and provides some discussion. Your results might be different from what's shown here, but that's part of the dynamic nature of the Web; things are always changing. Don't let those changes confuse you. Follow the steps, use what's here as a guide, and pay attention to what you see. As you work through this and other activities, ✦ Do It! indicates something for you to do. These activities demonstrate fundamental skills that don't change, even though the number of results obtained or the actual screens may look very different.

ACTIVITY

1.1 USING A SEARCH ENGINE

OVERVIEW

We are assuming the browser program is properly set up on your computer and that you have a way of connecting to the Internet. In this activity, we'll search for information on the World Wide Web. We'll use a *search engine,* a program or service designed to search for information available through the Web, to help us find resources about a specific topic. A search engine is a collection of software programs that collect information from the Web, index it, and put it in a database so it can be searched. A search engine also contains tools for searching the database.

We type keywords or a phrase into a search form on a Web page, possibly set some options, and then click on a search button on the Web page. In what is usually a short time, we will see matching entries from the database—usually 10 per page. Each of the results contains a hyperlink to the entry, as well as a brief excerpt from the resource. All the results are ranked according to relevance or how closely they match the query.

Most of the search engines have indexed millions of Web pages, so it's likely that you'll get more results than you can check. The key to successful searching is to make your search expression as precise as possible. We'll discuss ways of doing that in much more detail in Chapter 5.

The topic for this sample search is Chinese art, specifically painting. Why that topic? Well, it's always nice to look at, try to understand, and learn about art, and we'll be able to use the topic to demonstrate some ways to use a search engine and move around the Web from page to page. We'll also go over using the online help from the search engine to make our search more precise.

When you try this activity, you're likely to see some differences in the results, because new resources are always being added to the search engine's database. Concentrate on the steps to take. You'll use the same techniques for other topics. We'll be using Internet Explorer for this activity.

The search engine we'll use for this activity is Google. It's very popular, has a large database of Web pages, and gets high ratings in the popular and computer press. We'll go directly to the Web page for Google by typing in its URL, and then we'll read its online help to get some tips on searching and using it. We'll use the search expression *"Chinese art" painting* since that describes the topic both generally (Chinese art) and specifically (painting). Then we'll look at some of the results by following some of the hyperlinks. Here are the steps we'll follow:

1. Start the browser.

2. Go to the home page for Google.

3. Read the online help.

4. Type in the search expression and start the search.

5. Follow one of the hyperlinks returned by Google.

6. End the session.

While you're going through the steps in this activity, practice using the **Back** and **Forward** buttons. If you click on **Forward** as many times as you click on **Back**, you won't lose your place.

DETAILS

1   Start the browser.

✦ Do It!   Double-click on the Internet Explorer icon. Look for an icon that looks like the following:

Internet
Explorer

2   Go to the home page for Google.

✦ Do It!   Click on the address field, type **http://www.google.com**, and press **Enter**.

When you start your Web browser, your home page will appear on the screen. We're going to access Google by typing its URL in the address field, as shown in Figure 2.6.

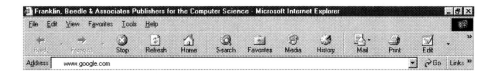

Figure 1.2—Going to Google by Typing Its URL

Soon after you press **Enter**, the search page for Google ought to appear in the browser window, as shown in Figure 1.3. We've labeled some of the items on the page for future reference.

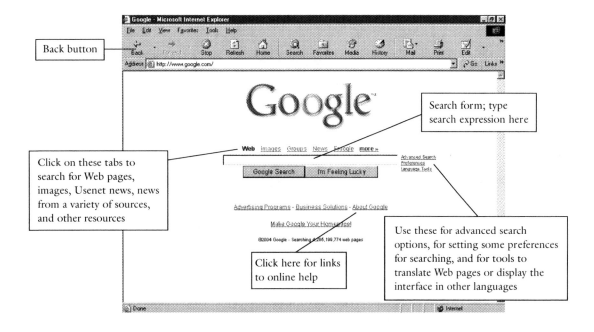

Figure 1.3—Home Page for Google

3   Read the online help.

Remember—it's a very good idea to read the online help before you start using a search tool. The help usually includes a description of the tool's features and what syntax to use for searching. The goal is to obtain more relevant and useful results.

Google's home page shown in Figure 1.3 doesn't have a hyperlink labeled **Help** or something similar. It would make accessing the online help easier, but we proceed undaunted! Checking some of the hyperlinks, we find that **About Google** is the one we need.

✦ Do It!   Click on the hyperlink labeled **About Google**.

You'll retrieve a Web page that has hyperlinks to help topics and answers some questions about Google itself. We're going to take a look at two of the online help pages about searching.

✦ Do It!   Click on the hyperlink labeled **Help and How to Search**.

This retrieves a Web page with links to help topics. Take a look at two of them.

✦ Do It!   Click on the hyperlink labeled **Basics of Search**.

After reading through that page, click on **Back** in the toolbar and then click on the hyperlink labeled **Advanced Search Tips**.

Be sure to read both of these Web pages to get the tips you need for making the best use of Google. Figure 1.4 shows a portion of the second Web page. You'll want to use the scroll bar to read through the tips on that page.

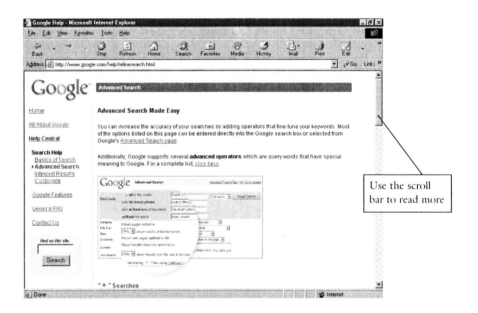

Figure 1.4—Google's Help "Advanced Search Tips"

Reading the text, we find several useful pieces of information:

✦ We ought to be specific when describing what we're searching for.

✦ By default, Google returns URLs for Web pages that contain *all* the words or phrases in the search expression. (Not all search engines use all the words so be sure to read the online help for any search engine before using it.) This gives more precise results than retrieving URLs for Web pages that contain *any* of the words.

✦ Google pays no attention to whether we use upper- or lower-case letters.

✦ We can require a match for phrases, not just individual words, by including a phrase in quotes.

We're interested in Chinese art, specifically painting, so we'll modify the search by using the phrase *Chinese art* and the term *painting*. After reading this online help, we see that a recommended way to get precise results is to use the search expression:

"Chinese art" painting

From what the online help says about the way Google treats upper- and lower-case letters, we also know the search expression **"chinese art" painting** would work just as well. Google also offers help on using other features and expressions for searching. When you have the time, read about using Boolean expressions and using other search features. Clicking on **Advanced Search** on Google's home page gives ready access to some of these.

4 Type in the search expression and start the search.

We'll go back to the home page for Google so that we can enter our search terms and start the search.

✦ Do It!   Click on **Back** in the toolbar until you get to the home page for Google.

✦ Do It!   Click on the search field, type the search terms **"Chinese art" painting**, and then click on the **Search** button.

The number of times to click on **Back** depends on where you are in the Google Web site. Typing the search terms is straightforward. If you want to replace or correct what you've typed, you can click on the search field pane to the right of the last word, backspace over the terms, and type new terms. You can also use the left and right arrow keys to add characters or to delete them from the search terms.

Figure 1.5 shows a portion of the previous page with the search expression typed in.

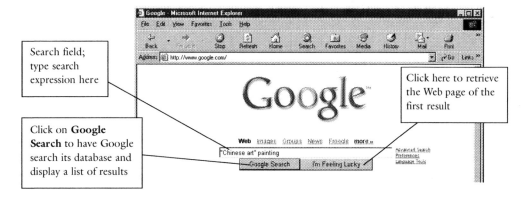

Figure 1.5—Google Search Form with Search Expression

After you click on **Search**, the search engine returns a list of hyperlinks to resources that have information containing one or more of the words in the search phrase. A portion of that page is shown in Figure 1.6. They are arranged in order so that those that may be most relevant are listed first. There are 10 on this page. We don't show it here, but if you move to the end of the page (use the down arrow keys, press **PgDn**, or use the vertical scroll bar), there's a link you can select to go to the next 10 items.

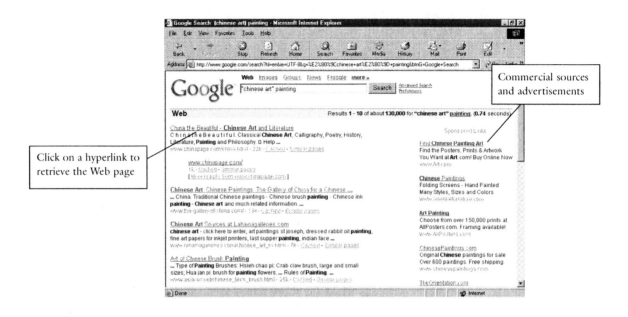

Click on a hyperlink to retrieve the Web page

Commercial sources and advertisements

Figure 1.6—Portion of First Page of Search Results

5 Follow one of the hyperlinks returned by Google.

Figure 1.6 shows the first few results of the search. There are more than 100,000 listed. This is a lot to consider, but the first few have a good chance of being ones we'd like to see. You can access the items listed by clicking on the hyperlinks. For each item, there's a brief description that you can use as a guide to help you decide whether to follow the link. For now, we'll follow the hyperlink for **China the Beautiful**, as it looks the most promising. (If that one isn't listed, pick another that you think is appropriate.) When you have time, follow some of the other hyperlinks to help determine which of the results are appropriate to your search..

✦ Do It!   Click on the hyperlink **China the Beautiful**.

Figure 1.7 shows the Web page "China the Beautiful." It has links to many topics related to Chinese art and Chinese literature. We see that there is a link **Painting**. We'll follow this one first; you're free to follow any you'd like. Before we follow any links, why don't we add this to our Favorites?

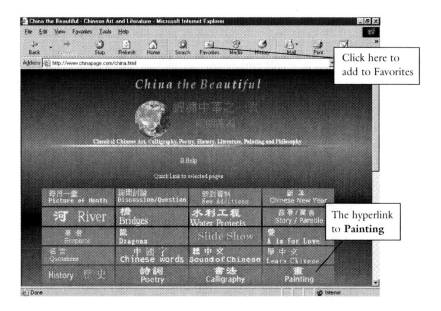

Figure 1.7—"China the Beautiful" Web Page

✦ Do It!   Click on **Favorites** on the menu bar, and then select **Add to Favorites**.

An alternate way to add this page to the favorites list is to use the keyboard shortcut
Ctrl+**D**. With this added to the favorites list, we'll be able to come back to this site any time
we'd like without having to go through the search. We'll show you how to manage your
favorites list in the next chapter.

Before moving on, take a look at the bottom of the Web page to see if it says who is
responsible for all these fine Web pages.

The information at the bottom of the page says that Dr. Ming L. Pei is the site's
Webmaster. That means he's responsible for maintaining the pages at this Web site. If we
click on his name, we can read more about him and see that he also created this Web site.

Now on to explore the other hyperlinks.

✦ Do It!   Click on the hyperlink **Painting**.

Clicking on the hyperlink **Painting** brings up a Web page that represents the start of a tour
(several linked Web pages) of Chinese painting, as shown in Figure 1.8. Feel free to follow
any of the links or take the tour to see images and, in some cases, to learn about the painters.
You can use the **Back** button in the toolbar to return to this Web page.

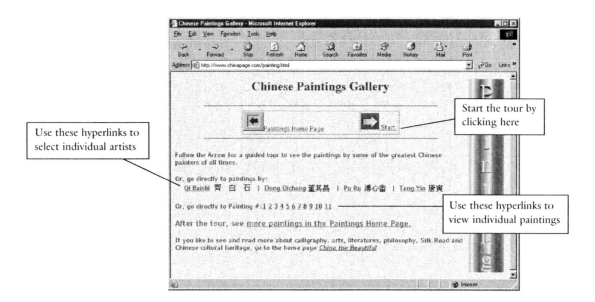

Figure 1.8—"Chinese Paintings Gallery" Web Page

Now let's take a look at some of the other resources on the Web page "China the Beautiful."

✦ Do It!   Click on the **Back** button to return to the "China the Beautiful" Web page.

This takes us back to the Web page shown in Figure 1.7. It contains several links to other resources related to Chinese art and culture, and we could easily spend an hour or more looking at the exhibits. Browse a little, but don't get lost or forget whatever else you need to do today.

There are still lots of links we may want to follow, and we can do that by using the **Back** button in the command toolbar to return to the Google page with the search results. There are still lots of items you may want to explore. Feel free to do so. Just remember, there may be other things going on in your life or work right now that need attention!

6   End the session.

You knew when we started that this had to end sometime. Now's the time. (You can, however, keep the Web browser open so that you're ready for the next activity.)

✦ Do It!   Click on **File** on the menu bar and select **Close** from the menu.

That's it!

END OF ACTIVITY 1.1

In this activity, we used a search engine to find hyperlinks to Web pages about Chinese art, specifically painting. After using the online help, we used search terms to make the search more precise. When you look at some of these Web pages, you may want to make the search even more specific. Perhaps you're interested in looking at the work and finding information about a specific painter, style of painting, or location. You can do that by modifying the search phrase or coming up with a new one.

Now we'll go over some key terms and concepts related to the Web and the way information is presented on it.

Key Terms and Concepts

In this section, we'll discuss some of the terms and concepts that are important to know about as you're working with the Internet and the Web. The topics we'll cover include:

✦ Client/Server

✦ HTTP (Hypertext Transfer Protocol)

✦ HTML (Hypertext Markup Language)

✦ URL (Uniform Resource Locator)

✦ Error Messages

✦ Selected Web-based Guides to the Internet and the World Wide Web

Client/Server

When you start a Web browser or follow a hyperlink, the browser sends a request to a site on the Internet. That site returns a file that the browser then has to display. This sort of interaction in which one system requests information and another provides it is called a *client/server* relationship. The browser is the client, and a computer at the site that provides the information is the server.

HTTP (Hypertext Transfer Protocol)

The documents or files are passed from a server to a client according to specific rules for exchanging information. These rules are called *protocols*. The protocol used on the Web is named HTTP, which stands for Hypertext Transfer Protocol, because the documents, pages, or other items passed from one computer to another are in hypertext or hypermedia form.

HTML (Hypertext Markup Language)

The rules for creating or writing a Web page are specified as HTML—Hypertext Markup Language. This language provides formal rules for marking text. The rules govern how text is displayed as part of a Web page. HTML would be used, for example, to mark text so that it appears in boldface or italics. In order for text or an icon to represent a hyperlink, it has to be marked as a link in HTML, and the URL has to be included. The URL doesn't appear, however, unless someone clicks on a hyperlink. Web pages are usually stored in files with names that end in **.html** or **.htm**.

In order for you to see or hear what's in the file, the browser has to be able to interpret the file's contents. Depending on the type of file, the browser may display text, graphics, or images. If the file is written using HTML, the browser interprets the file so that graphics and images are displayed along with the text. Depending on the HTML code in the file, the text is displayed in different sizes and styles, and hyperlinks are represented on the page.

URL (Uniform Resource Locator)

The hyperlinks are represented in a specific format called a URL, or Uniform Resource Locator. Each Web page has a URL as its address. For example, the URL for the Library of Congress's home page is **http://www.loc.gov**.

The URLs that point to Web pages all start with **http://** because they are all transmitted according to HTTP. You'll see something different for URLs that access information through other Internet services or protocols. *FTP*, or *File Transfer Protocol*, was one of the first protocols used on the Internet to exchange files. It's still in common use. For example, the URL for a collection of images from the European Space Agency is: **ftp://ftp.estec.esa.nl/pub/ photolib/images**.

You'll find it helpful to think of a URL as having the form:

```
how-to-get-there://where-to-go/what-to-get
```

When you cite a resource on the World Wide Web, you include the URL for it. You'll also want to include the URL when you're telling someone else about a resource, such as in an email message. It's much more effective to include URLs. Here's an example:

A good resource for information about African studies is *African Studies Internet Resources,* **http://www.columbia.edu/cu/libraries/indiv/area/Africa**, or the *World Wide Web Virtual Library* at **http://vlib.org**.

People reading this message can use their browsers to go directly to the items you mention.

We will now show you the different parts of a URL so that you have a better idea about the information a URL conveys:

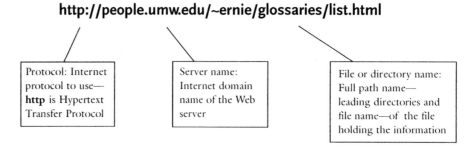

Most URLs have this format. By indicating which Internet protocol to use, they tell you how to retrieve the information. By naming both the Web server and the file or directory holding the information, they tell you where the site is located. If only a server name is present and not a file name, as in **http://www.loc.gov**, you still retrieve a file; by default, the server passes along a certain file, usually named **index.html**. Sometimes you'll see URLs written without **http://** in front. You can safely omit **http://** when you open a Web page or location by typing the URL into the browser's address box.

Error Messages

As amazing as some computer systems are, they generally need very precise instructions, so you have to be careful about spacing (generally there aren't blank spaces in a URL), the symbols used (a slash and a period are not interchangeable), and the case of the letters. Here's an example:

The URL for the online glossary that accompanies this book is **http://webliminal. com/search/glossary.htm**. Replacing search with SEARCH, as in the URL **http://**

webliminal.com/SEARCH/glossary.htm, will cause the server to report an error back to the browser. The information displayed will include:

```
404 - page not present on our server
The page you requested with URL
http://webliminal.com/SEARCH/glossary.htm isn't present
on our server. Please check the URL
```

The error message tells us that part of the URL was correct—the name of the Web server, **webliminal.com**—but that the Web server could not find the file on the server because there was something wrong with the rest of the URL.

A message such as this is called a *404 Error.* You may see this message if the URL is incorrect, if a Web page has been removed from a Web server, or if it is no longer available. If you click on a hyperlink and get a 404 message, you may have come upon what is sometimes called a *dead link.*

Here's another message you may see:

```
403 Forbidden
Your client does not have permission to get URL
/ernie/abc.html from this server.
```

That means the URL was correct and the file is on the server, but the file isn't available to the public.

If the URL contains the name of a Web server that your browser can't find, you'll see an error message such as this:

```
Host Name Lookup Problem
Check the spelling and try again.
```

Selected Web-based Guides to the Internet and the World Wide Web

Taking advantage of the resources on the World Wide Web, using a Web browser, and mastering the Internet aren't difficult, but they require a lot of knowledge. If you're not familiar with the Web or the Internet, you may want to look at some Web-based guides. We will now present a list of some of the good ones available on the Web, giving you the name of the resource and its URL. To access any of these guides, double-click on the address box (it should turn blue), type the URL, and press **Enter**.

- ✦ *Getting Started on the Web*
  http://www.microsoft.com/windows/ie/using/articles/default.asp

- ✦ *The HelpWeb: A Guide To Getting Started on the Internet*
  http://www.imaginarylandscape.com/helpweb/welcome.html

- ✦ *Internet and Web Essentials*
  http://webliminal.com/essentials

- ✦ *Learn the Net*
  http://www.learnthenet.com/english/index.html

There's a Web site to accompany the book you're reading. Here is the title of the site and its URL:

✦ *Searching and Researching on the Internet and the World Wide Web*
  http://webliminal.com/search-web.html

Information Sources Available on the Web

Because there's so much information available on the Web, it has to be organized so that you can find what you need. There must also be tools or programs to help you locate information. Throughout this book, we'll be discussing the major information sources on the Web.

Directories or Subject Catalogs

There are directories, arranged by subject, of a general collection of Internet and Web resources. Several of the directories contain reviews or descriptions of the entries. We discuss them in detail in Chapter 4. The Open Directory Project, **http://dmoz.org**, is a directory that is built by volunteers.

One way to access several of these is to go to the section "Internet Subject Directories," **http://www.digital-librarian.com/subject.html**.

Search Engines

Search engines provide keyword searching capability. These are covered in Chapter 5. The most popular one is Google, **http://www.google.com**, and it was discussed in this chapter.

A listing of search engines is available at "Search Engine Directory," **http://www.searchengineguide.com/searchengines.html**.

Meta-search Tools

A meta-search tool usually allows you to search several search engines or directories simultaneously. Many meta-search tools take your query, do the search, and then integrate the results. Some meta-search tools are good places to find lists of specialized databases.

Examples of meta-search tools are MetaCrawler, **http://www.metacrawler.com**, Ixquick, **http://ixquick.com**, and Vivisimo, **http://vivisimo.com**. A list of meta-search engines is available at "Meta-Search Engines," **http://www.lib.berkeley.edu/TeachingLib/Guides/Internet/MetaSearch.html**.

Virtual Libraries

Virtual libraries are directories or subject catalogs arranged by subject; these consist of Web resources that librarians or other information specialists have selected and evaluated. Several of the directories contain reviews or descriptions of the entries. We discuss them in Chapter 4.

Two excellent examples are *The Internet Public Library,* **http://www.ipl.org**, and *Librarians' Index to the Internet,* **http://lii.org**.

Specialized Databases

Specialized databases are self-contained indexes that are searchable and available on the Web. We discuss specialized databases in Chapter 6.

Take a look at *direct search*, **http://www.freepint.com/gary/direct.htm**, by Gary Price.

Library Catalogs Accessible on the World Wide Web

Libraries have often been at the forefront of making resources available through the Internet, and thousands of libraries allow Internet and Web access to their catalogs of holdings. We discuss searching library catalogs in Chapter 8.

Some resources for library catalogs accessible on the World Wide Web are *LibDex The Library Index*, **http://www.libdex.com**, and *Libweb*, **http://sunsite.berkeley.edu/libweb**.

FTP Archives

FTP stands for File Transfer Protocol. Dating back to the early 1970s, it's the original protocol used to share files among computers with access to the Internet. Before the appearance of the World Wide Web, FTP was the most popular and effective way of sharing information and resources. Naturally, people started collecting files and saving them in archives available to anyone with a connection to the Internet. There are thousands of FTP archives containing information in various formats, such as text, data, programs, images, and audio. We discuss using FTP and FTP archives in Chapter 10.

A list of FTP search tools is available at "ftp search engines," **http://www. ftpsearchengines.com/**.

Email Discussion Groups

Email discussion groups are sometimes called *interest groups*, *listservs*, or *mailing lists*. Internet users join, contribute to, and read messages to the entire group through email. Several thousand different groups exist. Individual groups may keep archives of the postings to the group, but most archives are arranged by date. In many cases, it's more appropriate to think of the group's members rather than the group's archives as good sources of information. We discuss email discussion groups and archives in more detail in Chapter 9.

Several services let you search for discussion groups. One is Catalyst, **http://www. lsoft.com/catalist.html**.

Usenet Newsgroups

Usenet newsgroups are collections of group discussions, questions, answers, and other information shared through the Internet. The messages are called articles and are grouped into categories called newsgroups. The newsgroups number in the thousands, with tens of thousands of articles posted daily. We discuss Usenet and searching archives of Usenet articles in more detail in Chapter 9.

You can browse or search an archive of Usenet articles dating back to 1981 at *Google Groups*, **http://groups.google.com**.

Browser Essentials

The Web browser is your primary tool for finding information and Web research. We're using Internet Explorer (IE) for the examples and activities in this book because IE is the most commonly available and widely used browser. Appendix C, "Browser Details," contains many of the details about using that browser. In this section, we'll discuss some of the capabilities and features of a Web browser, some ways to work with and improve a browser, and take a look at some browsers other than Internet Explorer.

Surveying a Browser's Features

Of course, a Web browser will allow you to look at Web pages or to connect to various sites to access information and explore resources. A Web browser will enable you to follow the hyperlinks on a Web page and to type in a URL for it to follow. A browser will have a number of other commands readily available through menus, icons, and buttons. And what about the times you need help? Your browser includes an easy way to find online help, as well as built-in links to other resources on the Web that can give you help or answers.

You'll definitely want a way to save links to sites you've visited on the Web so you can return to them during other sessions. Web browsers meet this need in two ways—with a *history list*, which keeps a record of the Web pages you've come across in recent sessions, and with a favorites list, which you use to note the Web pages you want to access in the future. The name of the site and its URL are kept in these lists. The browser contains tools to manage and arrange the bookmark or favorites list. For example, you can organize favorites into folders.

Web browsers include the means for you to search for information on a current Web page. You'll be able to save a Web page on your computer, print the page, and email its contents to others.

Some Web pages are designed using *frames*. This design allows for several independent Web pages—with their own scroll bars and URLs—to be displayed in one window. When a page is in a frame, the browser allows you to save, print, or email a particular frame. Take a look at *Searching and Researching - WebNet 98,* **http://webliminal.com/search/presentations/webnet98/frames.html**, as an example of a site that uses frames.

When you use the Web for searching and researching, you may need to fill out a form or transmit some information in a secure manner. Your browser can correctly display and handle this sort of Web page.

World Wide Web pages can contain text and images, as well as hyperlinks to digital audio, digital video, or other types of information. Your Web browser is probably equipped to handle many of these types of media. But whether you can access something also depends on the software and hardware on your computer. If you don't have the programs and the hardware (a sound card and speakers) to play a sound file, then your Web browser will be unable to handle sound files.

Web browsers let you add to the list of software they use to display or play different media, however. If you come across a file or hyperlink to something the Web browser isn't configured to handle, you can add *helper applications* or *plug-ins*. These programs allow you to work with certain types of files. You do this by setting preferences for your browser. In setting preferences, you can choose the font and colors used for displaying text, set your email address, and select other items.

Browsers also provide online help. Press F1 while you are using your browser for online help or click on **Help** in the *menu bar* and select an appropriate topic. For example, for help in customizing your browser when you are using Internet Explorer, press **F1**, click on **Contents**, and select **Customizing Your Browser**.

Just like other programs, a Web browser has to be started before you use it. You start it by clicking on the IE icon on your desktop, the same way you start other Windows programs. If you're already connected to the Internet through a network or modem connection, the browser will start and retrieve the Web page that is set as the browser's home page. If you are using a dial-up or phone connection to the Internet, you may have to wait while the modem contacts your Internet service provider. If the browser reports that it can't contact the site that supplies the home page, then check your network connection or try another site. When you're finished browsing the Web, you'll want to end the Web session by stopping the browser in the same way you stop or exit other Windows programs; click on the **X** in the upper right-hand corner of the browser, depress the **Alt** key and press **F4**, or click on **File** in the menu bar and select **Close.**

Exploring the Web Browser's Window

When you start a Web browser, a window opens on your screen. It's the Web browser's job to retrieve and display a file inside the window. What is in the window will change as you go from site to site, but each window has the same format. The items that help you work with the Web document in the window include the scroll bar, the menu bar, and the toolbar, which are the same every time you use the browser. The major components of a Web page displayed by Internet Explorer are labeled in Figure 1.9.

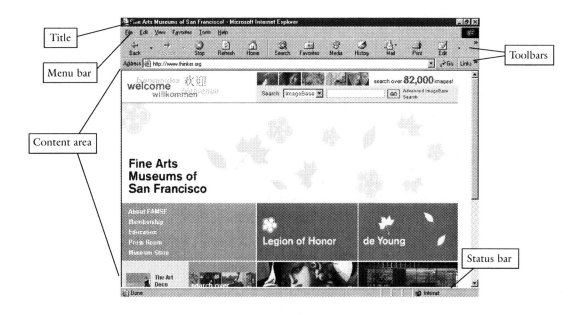

Figure 1.9—Internet Explorer Window with Components Labeled

Toolbars

Web browsers, like other Windows software, have one or more rows of icons or items called *toolbars* just below the menu bar. Each item works like a button. When you press it with the mouse, some operation or action takes place. In some cases, a dialog box pops up. For example, if you click on the item to print the current document, you can select a printer and specify whether you want to print the whole document or just a part of it. The icons give you a visual clue to the operation or action they represent. Their commands are all available through the items on the menu bar, but the icons give a direct path—a shortcut—to the commands.

Content Area or Document View

The *content area* is the portion of the window that holds the document, page, or other resource as your browser presents it. It can contain text or images. Sometimes the content area is divided into or consists of several independent portions called *frames*. Each frame has its own scroll bar, and you can move through one frame while staying in the same place in others.

The content area holds the Web page you're viewing, which likely contains hyperlinks in text or graphic format. Clicking on a hyperlink with the *left* mouse button allows you to follow the link. Clicking with the *right* mouse button (or holding down the mouse button without clicking if your mouse has only one button) brings up a menu that gives you options for working with a hyperlink. We discuss using the right mouse button in a later section.

Scroll Bar

If the document doesn't fit into the window, it will be displayed with vertical and/or horizontal *scroll bars*. The horizontal one is at the bottom of the window, and the vertical one is at the right of the window. These scroll bars and their associated arrows help you move through the document. The scroll bars work the same way as those in common Microsoft Windows applications.

Status Bar

When you are retrieving a document, opening a location, or following a hyperlink, the bar along the bottom of the window (the *status bar*) holds the URL that's being used. It also lets you know whether a site is being contacted, if it's responding, and how the transmission is progressing.

Using the Right Mouse Button

Most of what we've said about using the mouse relates to using the *left* or *primary* mouse button, but Internet Explorer takes advantage of the *right* or *secondary* mouse button as well. If your mouse has only one button, then holding it down is usually equivalent to pressing the right button on a mouse with two or more buttons.

Here are some of the ways to use the right mouse button:

◆ If the mouse pointer is on the **Back** or **Forward** icons, clicking the right mouse button brings up a list of sites; you can go backward or forward to any of these. Select one from the list and click on it.

◆ You can use the right mouse button to copy and paste information from a Web page, email, or other windowed source. Say that you're working with email or are in the content area of a Web page and are *not on a hyperlink*. Using the mouse, move the cursor or pointer to the beginning of the text you want to copy. Hold down the left mouse button, use the mouse to highlight the text, then click the right mouse button and select **Copy**. Now move the mouse pointer to where you want to paste the text—maybe you've copied a URL and want to put it in the address box. Press the right mouse button and select **Paste**. If you are pasting a URL into the address box or some other field in a form, be sure to click on the address box with the left mouse button first to highlight the text you want to replace.

✦ If the mouse pointer is in the content area but *not on a hyperlink,* clicking the right mouse button brings up a menu with several useful items, many of which appear as part of other menus or toolbars. These include items to go **Back** or **Forward** to a Web page and to **Reload** or **Stop** loading the current Web page. You can set the background image as wallpaper for your desktop, save the image in a file, add the current page to the book-mark or favorites list, create a desktop shortcut to the page, or send the Web page via email.

✦ If the mouse pointer is *on an image,* then you have the same choices as when it's in the content area and not on a hyperlink. In addition, you can view the image in a separate window, save the image in a file, or copy the URL for the image (in case you want to include it in a Web page you're constructing).

✦ If the mouse pointer is *on a hyperlink* (remember, when it's over a hyperlink, the pointer changes to a hand) and you click the right mouse button, then a menu appears with all the same items as when the pointer isn't on a hyperlink. In addition, the menu includes items to open the link in a new, separate window. You can also save the Web page repre-sented by the link to a file, or you can copy the link, which means copying the URL for later use with the paste operation.

Getting Around a Page and the World Wide Web

You've probably spent some time browsing the World Wide Web and some of the resources and information it has to offer. In this section, we'll go over how to move around within a page and how to go from one page or location to another. Knowing this, you'll be able to get around the Web effectively.

Moving Through a Page

When you start a Web browser, you see a portion of a page or document in the window. As you may remember, the starting page is called the *home page.* Many of these pages contain more information than is immediately displayed, so you need to know how to move through a docu-ment. You can do this by using the scroll bars, using the keyboard, or searching for a specific word or phrase.

Using the Scroll Bars
You can move around or through a document by using the vertical and horizontal scroll bars on the right and bottom of the window.

Using the Keyboard
Pressing the up or down arrow will move you up or down one line. Pressing the **PgUp** key moves up one window length, and pressing **PgDn** moves down one window length. Pressing **Ctrl**+**Home** takes you to the beginning of the document, and pressing **Ctrl**+**End** takes you to its end.

Finding Text or Searching a Page

You can search a document for a word, portion of a word, phrase, or any string of characters. To find a string, you first have to bring up the dialog box labeled **Find**, as shown in Figure 1.10. There are two ways to do this—either select **Edit** from the menu bar and choose **Find in Page...**, or press **Ctrl**+F on the keyboard.

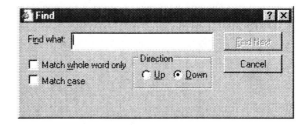

Figure 1.10—Find Box

Once the Find dialog box is up, type in a string of words or characters and either press **Enter** or click on the **Find Next** button. You can cancel a search by clicking on the **Cancel** button. You can search in one of two directions. **Down** searches from your current position to the end of the document. **Up** searches from the current position to the beginning of the document. Mark the **Match case** box if you want to match the capitalization in the string exactly.

Moving Between Pages

As you work with and browse the World Wide Web, you'll often go from one page to another. Much of the time, you do this by clicking on hyperlinks, but you can also go directly to a Web page, document, or location by typing its URL and then letting the browser retrieve it for you. To move between pages you've already visited during a session, you can use the **Back** or **Forward** arrow icons on the toolbar. Web browsers also let you save URLs or titles of the pages you've visited in one session so that you can access them easily during that or any other session. This information is saved in the *history list* (a list of all sites visited during recent sessions) and in the *favorites list* (a list of hyperlinks to sites you have explicitly saved from one session to the next).

❖ T I P ! **When you can't wait— breaking a connection or stopping a page.**

Press the key labeled **Esc** or click on the **Stop** icon to stop a page from being loaded into your browser or to stop connecting to a site. While you are browsing, you can watch the status bar to see if the remote site holding the information has been contacted and if it's responding. Your Web browser will try for a certain amount of time (a minute or so) to contact the remote site. If you don't want to wait that long or you don't want to wait for the browser to display a complete page, press **Esc** or the **Stop** icon. This doesn't close the browser; it just interrupts the transmission or attempted connection.

Going Directly to a Web Page

To go directly to a Web page you click on the address box, wait until it changes color, type the URL, and press **Enter**. The browser attempts to make the connection, and if it can retrieve the page, it will bring the page up in the window.

If the browser can't retrieve the page, check your typing to make sure you have the URL right. There could be other problems as well. If the page is not available to the public, you'll see the message "403 Forbidden" in the window. If the page doesn't exist, you'll get the message "404 Not Found." It could also be that the site is out of service or too busy to handle your request.

Using Back and Forward

You can move to a previous Web page by clicking on either of the icons **Back** or **Forward**. You can also go back or forward by selecting either option from the **Go** menu in the menu bar. The keyboard shortcuts are **Alt**+**←** to move backward and **Alt**+**→** to go forward. You can also move in these directions by pressing the right mouse button (while the pointer is on a Web page) and then selecting **Back** or **Forward** from the menu that pops up on the screen.

Keeping Track—The History List

The Web browser keeps a record of the path you've taken to get to the current location. To see the path and select a site from it, click on **View** in the menu bar and select **Go to.** You can also view the history list by depressing the **Ctrl** key, pressing **H**, and then releasing both keys. The history list appears in a panel on the left of the Web browser's window. Items are arranged in folders by the domain name of the sites you've visited.

You can select and highlight any item by using the up or down arrow on the keyboard or by using the mouse. Once you've highlighted the location you want, double-click (or single-click, depending on what version of Windows—and what settings in Windows—you're using) on the highlighted item. If you click on the right mouse button, a menu pops up that allows you to go directly to the Web page or to add the highlighted item to the favorites list.

The number of days an item may be kept on the history list is set as follows by clicking on **Tools** in the menu bar, selecting **Internet Options**, and then entering a value in the History section of the panel with the title **General**.

Keeping Track—The Favorites List

The *favorites list* is a collection of hyperlinks to Web pages that you want to save from session to session. They could be Web pages or sites you especially like, ones you find useful, or ones you've looked at briefly but want to return to in the future (particularly good when you're starting to research a topic). Each item on the favorites list is a Web page title, and each entry is a hyperlink. The browser includes a program to let you manage and arrange the list.

To use the favorites list to go from the current Web page to another, click on **Favorites** in the tool bar, then select an item from the list that appears in the panel to the left in the browser window.

Dealing with Pop-Up Windows and Adding A Tool Bar to Your Browser

It is possible to include instructions in a Web page's source code that will open a new window when you access the page. Perhaps you can see the advantages of doing this from an instructional point of view—additional information or tips can be presented along with the primary information. Unfortunately, this technology is used most commonly to display advertisements when you retrieve or leave a Web page. Some reputable sites, such as the online version of the New York Times, **http://www.nytimes.com**, use this technique for advertisements.

Windows popping up that you don't control can become a real bother, and there are a number of software solutions called pop-up blockers that suppress these windows. You install them as an enhancement to your browser. One that we've used is built into a toolbar from Google.

The program from Google appears as a toolbar in the portion of the browser above the content window. You can block all of the pop-up windows, or you can selectively turn off the blocking feature to view pop-up windows from specific sites. You can also use it to access Google easily. The toolbar has been in use for some time, and you can usually install it easily without worrying about corrupting your browser or Windows environment. Here are the steps to take to download and install it.

1. Retrieve the Web page that has a link to the toolbar by typing the URL **http://toolbar.google.com** into the address box and pressing **Enter**.

2. You can read information about the toolbar by clicking on the link **help pages.** This takes you to the page with the URL **http://toolbar.google.com/help**. You'll want to read this to learn what you can do after the toolbar is installed.

3. When you are ready to install the toolbar, select your language, and click on the button labeled **Download Google Toolbar**, as indicated in Figure 1.11.

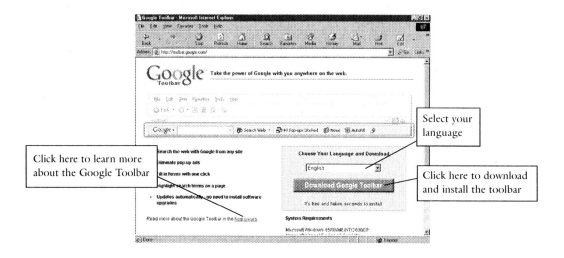

Figure 1.11—Download Page for Google Toolbar

When you click on that button, depending on your security settings a dialog box may pop up that warns you about downloading information from the Internet and asks you what you'd like to do with the downloaded file. Since this is coming from a trusted source (Google), it is all right to click on **Open**, as shown in Figure 1.12. If we weren't sure of the source of the file, then we might download it and check it with anti-virus software before opening and installing it.

24

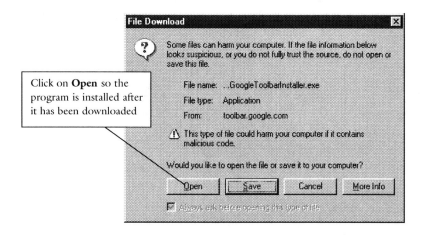

Click on **Open** so the program is installed after it has been downloaded

4. Once the program is downloaded and installation begins, you'll be asked to read and agree to the conditions of use from Google. The agreement is typical. It states how you can use the program and that the provider is not liable for much of anything. If, after reading it, you still want to install the toolbar, click on the button that accepts the agreement.

5. The next step points out that by using some of the features of the tool bar, you will be sending Google information about the sites you've visited. You can use the toolbar to block pop-ups either way. For the most privacy, select **Disable advanced features**.

6. Select the Google site that will be used for searches, choose to have all Explorer windows closed automatically, and click on **Next**.

7. The software is installed. Start Internet Explorer again and try using the toolbar. If the toolbar isn't visible, then click on **View** in the menu bar, select **Toolbars**, and click on **Google**.

There are other pop-up blockers available. The one from Google works well and has the advantage of also giving quick access to Google itself. Try it!

Other browsers—Mozilla, Opera

Internet Explorer is by far the most commonly used browser accounting for over 80 percent of browser usage, according to the statistics at "Browser Statistics," **http://www.w3schools.com/browsers/browsers_stats.asp**. It owes some of its popularity to the fact that it is distributed with virtually every new PC. Since the browser is written and maintained by Microsoft, it works well with Microsoft Windows. It does have some drawbacks, such as allowing for pop-up windows as noted above, and because it is so popular, it is a prime target for people who exploit security flaws through the spread of viruses, worms, and other types of harmful activities.

Mozilla and Opera are other popular browsers. They have all the features we expect to find in Internet Explorer, they are less likely to be vulnerable to security attacks, and they have features that make them more convenient to use. These features include the ability to block pop-up windows, faster downloading and rendering of Web pages, and the capability to open several browsing sessions within the current window. This latter feature is called *tab-browsing*. With tab-browsing, you can access Web sites in different panels or tabs of the current browser window. This makes it easier to deal with several sites at the same time. You don't have to move from window to window to work with more than one site. Figure 1.13 shows Mozilla with several Web sites available in different tabs. We started by looking at "Meeting the Challenge of Critically Evaluating Information on the Internet and the World Wide Web," **http://webliminal .com/khartman/educom98.html**, and then opened tabs to "The WWW Virtual Library," **http://vlib.org**, "The Internet Public Library," **http://www.ipl.org**, and "Hoover's Online— The Business Information Authority," **http://www.hoovers.com/free/**.

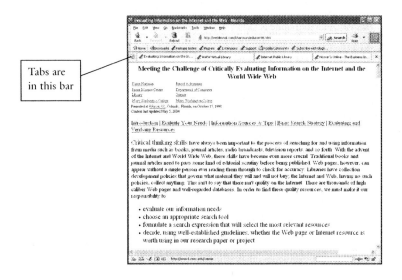

Figure 1.13—Mozilla Browser Window with Several Tabs Opened

You move from tab to tab by clicking on the titles. If you click on a link in a tab, then the link is followed in that same tab. If you right click on a hyperlink, a menu pops up that lets you open the link in a new tab or a new window. To open a new tab, depress the **Ctrl** key and press T.

Both of these browsers can be downloaded from the Internet at no charge and can be easily installed on your computer. (The software for the browsers is fairly large, so it is difficult sometimes to take the time to download them if you connect to the Internet using a dial-up modem connection.) Each of these is also available for other platforms including computers that use the Linux or Mac OS X operating systems, and they offer better management of bookmarks or favorites than IE does. Additionally, some people prefer using these browsers because Microsoft does not produce them. Each is compatible with the standards set forth by the World Wide Web consortium, but not all pages produced for Internet Explorer can be viewed with these browsers. Some Web page producers use features that are only implemented by Internet Explorer.

Here are some specifics about Mozilla and Opera.

Mozilla

Mozilla is an *open-source* project built on the software developed for Netscape, the first popular Web browser produced by a commercial organization. This means that the source code for the browser is available to anyone, and the software that supports the browser is written and maintained by a large community of volunteers. There is no charge for downloading or using the browser. At the time of this writing, Mozilla accounts for about 11 percent of browser use. To get the latest version of Mozilla, go to the Web page with the URL **http://mozilla.org/ download.html** and select the most recent stable version. Some experimental versions are also available. Mozilla.org has published several reasons for using Mozilla and this information is available at "Why Use Mozilla," **http://www.mozilla.org/why/**.

Opera

Opera was developed and is maintained by Opera Software ASA, Oslo, Norway. You can download a version at no charge from the Web page with URL **http://www.opera.com/download**. When you use that version, you'll see advertisements just below the menu bar. You can purchase a license at **https://secure.bmtmicro.com/servlets/Orders.CheckOut** for $39, at the time of this writing, that lets you use the browser without advertisements. Opera only accounts for about two percent of browser use. In addition to tab-browsing, Opera also lets you save your current session so that the next time you start Opera, all the Web pages you were using are present. Opera is also available for Linux, Mac OS X, and some PDA's and cell-phones. It also includes a notebook feature that lets you copy and paste portions of Web pages into one or more notebooks you create. Opera also publishes a list of reasons why you might want to use Opera; they are available on the page "Why Opera?," **http://www.opera.com/whyopera/**.

Summary

Millions of people around the world use the Internet for communication, research, business, information, and recreation. One of the most popular and effective ways to tap into its resources is through the World Wide Web. It is a vast collection of information that's connected like a web. There is no beginning or end; the information is accessible in a nonlinear fashion through connections called hyperlinks. You view the resources on the Web by using a program called a Web browser. You navigate through the Web by pointing to hyperlinks (underlined or boldfaced words or phrases, icons, or images) and clicking once with the mouse. To use the Web and the Internet effectively, you need to know how to find and use the services, tools, and programs that give you access to their resources.

It's possible to link information in almost any digital form on the World Wide Web. Text files, programs, charts, images, graphics files, digitized video, and sound files are all available. Not only can you find things from a variety of media, but you also get a great deal of information in many categories or topics.

When using the Web, you work in a hypertext or hypermedia environment. A Uniform Resource Locator, or URL, specifies items, services, and resources. Web browsers use these URLs to specify the type of Internet service or protocol needed and the location of the item. For example, the URL for the Web page "General Collections Library of Congress" is **http:// www.loc.gov/rr/coll-general.html**. The protocol or service in this case is HTTP, or Hypertext Transfer Protocol, and a Web browser using that URL would contact the Internet site **www.loc.gov** and access the file **coll-general.html** in the directory named **rr**.

The documents on the Web are called Web pages. These are written and constructed using a language called Hypertext Markup Language (HTML).

A number of different types of information sources are available on the World Wide Web. Those include:

+ Directories of a general collection of Internet and Web resources, arranged by subject

+ Search engines, which are tools that provide keyword searching capability

+ Meta-search tools, which allow you to access databases from one place

+ Virtual libraries, which are directories or subject catalogs consisting of selected Web resources

+ Specialized databases, which contain comprehensive collections of hyperlinks in a particular subject area, or which are self-contained, searchable indexes made available on the Web

+ Library catalogs

+ FTP archives, which are collections of files in various formats available on the Internet

+ Email discussion groups, of which several thousand groups exist to share opinions and experiences, ask and answer questions, or post information about a specific topic

+ Usenet newsgroups, which are collections of group discussions, questions, answers, and other information that have been shared through the Internet

A Web browser is used to access the information and resources on the World Wide Web. Whenever you start the browser or access a hyperlink, the browser—which is a computer program—sends a request to have a file transferred to it. The browser then interprets the information in the file so that it can be viewed in the browser's window, or in some cases viewed through another program. For example, if a hyperlink points to a text file, the file is then displayed in the window as ordinary text. If the hyperlink points to a document written in Hypertext Markup Language (HTML), then it's displayed by the browser. If the file is a sound file or an animation, then a program different from the browser may be started so the file can be heard or seen. Most of the facilities and capabilities are built into the browser, but in some cases your computer needs to be equipped with special equipment or programs. For instance, if a hyperlink points to a sound file, your computer needs to have a sound card, speakers, and the software to play the sounds.

It is possible to improve the operation of the IE browser by installing software that acts to block pop-up windows and provides a toolbar for the easier use of Google.

Some people prefer to use other browsers such as Mozilla and Opera because they provide a user interface that is easier to deal with than IE as well as offering other features. Although a large majority of people use IE, you may want to join the minority that use Mozilla or Opera.

Selected Terms Introduced in This Chapter

client/server

content area

favorites

File Transfer

  Protocol (FTP)

frame

history list

home page

hyperlink

hypermedia

hypertext

Hypertext Markup

  Language

   (HTML)

Hypertext Transfer

  Protocol

   (HTTP)

Internet

menu bar

open-source

scroll bar

status bar

tab-browsing

toolbar

Uniform Resource

  Locator

   (URL)

Web browser

Web page

World Wide Web

Review Questions

Multiple Choice

1. The computer network comprising thousands of networks that exchange information is known as the
   a. Wide Area Network.
   b. Client-Server Network.
   c. Internet.
   d. Arpanet.

2. You may get an error message accessing a site if
   a. there is a space in the address.
   b. you use the wrong case letters.
   c. you use a comma (,) instead of a dot (.).
   d. a and c.
   e. all of the above

3. A computer that provides information to your browser is called a
   a. server.
   b. client.
   c. backup.
   d. bookmark.

4. Text that provides links to other text is called
   a. multimedia.
   b. http.
   c. hypertext.
   d. a browser.

5. Each Web page has an address known as a(n)
   a. server.
   b. URL.
   c. WWW.
   d. hypertext.

6. Web pages are written using a language called
   a. http.
   b. hurl.
   c. hplm.
   d. html.

7. Which of the following can work as a hyperlink?
   a. underlined words
   b. an image
   c. a button
   d. a and b
   e. all of the above

True or False

8. T F All URLs start with **http://**.

9. T F A search engine allows you to search the Web by keyword.

10. T F A favorite or bookmark is a way to save a link to a site
           on the Web you'd like to visit again.

11. T F To navigate using a hyperlink, you click on the link
           with your left mouse button.

12. T F Usenet newsgroup archives cannot be searched for
           information contained in them.

13. T F You can copy text on a web page by using your left mouse button.

14. T F A Web page may include multimedia, such as audio or video formats.

Completion

15. A subject listing of Web resources is known as a(n) _____.

16. To access a Web site, you type its URL into your browser's _____.

17. A directory of Web pages selected and evaluated by an information professional or
    librarian is called a(n) _____.

18. Before the World Wide Web, a protocol used to share information through the
    Internet was _____.

19. A software program that allows you to access information on the World Wide Web is
    known as a(n) _____.

20. _____ is an open-source alternative to Internet Explorer.

Exercises and Projects

1. Let's go back to Google, as we did in the chapter. Did you save the site as a Favorite
   or Bookmark? If so, click on Favorites and then on Google. If not, type the URL
   http://www.google.com into your address bar and press **Enter**.

a. Before doing a search, look at the bottom of the page. How many web pages does Google search?

b. Let's look for information about NASCAR. Type **NASCAR** into the search box. What happens if you click the button that says "I'm Feeling Lucky?" What is the URL of the site that you arrive at?

c. Click your Back button to return to Google. **NASCAR** should still be showing in the search box. Click on the **Google Search** button. How many web pages are found for that topic?

2. This chapter talked about other kinds of search tools available on the Web. Try using the meta-search engine Vivisimo. It's available by typing in http://vivisimo.com in your address bar. You may want to set this site as a Favorite, as well. We'll put a different twist on our NASCAR search this time. Try putting in the words **NASCAR ballet** into Vivisimo's search box. Click the **Search** button. We'll try to find out what company created this dance.

a. How many results does Vivisimo return? Click on the first result. Does it tell you what dance company created this ballet? What is the name of the company? If that result doesn't give you the information, click your Back button to go back to your results list. Sometimes you need to click on more than one search result to find what you want to know! Click on some of the links till you find the answer.

b. Notice that Vivisimo clusters its results into **Categories**. What are the first five categories you find on the left hand side of your screen? Click on the first category. Does this help you to narrow down your search? How?

3. Do you know the meaning of the words *mendacious* and *singultus*? What would you do if someone called you mendacious? If you were diagnosed with singultus? Let's look them up before deciding what to do! Go to the Open Directory Project that was mentioned in the chapter at **http://dmoz.org**. Notice that besides the search box, there is also a directory of information that you can browse. Click on **Reference**. How many dictionaries does this directory include? Click on **Dictionaries**.

a. Scroll down the page. Click on **Merriam-Webster Online**. Look up the word *mendacious*. Type the word in the search box, then click the **Go** button or press **Enter**. What is the meaning of the word?

b. Notice that you can type in a new search from this screen. Try a search for the word singultus. Do you find a definition?

c. Go back to the list of dictionaries by clicking on your **Back** button till you return to the Open Directory Dictionaries page. Click on **OneLook Dictionaries**. Can you find the word *singultus* in here? What meaning is given for the word?

4. There are some other very different dictionaries listed here at the Open Directory Project. (We were particularly taken by the **Skeptic's Dictionary**.) Click on the words **By Subject**. Click on **Computers**. Click on **Computer Dictionary Info**.

a. Look up the word **Fortran** here. What is the definition of the word?

b. Go back to the **Open Directory Dictionaries** listing. Click on the category **Rhyming.** Choose one of the dictionaries listed and click on it. Type the word **flower** into the search box and search for it. What do you see? List three words that rhyme with it.

5. Since we're looking up words, here's a really different kind of thesaurus! Type **www. plumbdesign.com/thesaurus** into your location or address field. Type the word *labyrinth* in the search box and press **Look it up**. What words are related to it? Click on one of the words that appears. What happens? How do you like this site?

6. Now we can look at one of the virtual libraries mentioned in the chapter. Type the URL **http://www.ipl.org** into your address field and press **Enter**. This site is the home of the Internet Public Library.
   a. What collections are available here?
   b. Click on **Ready Reference**. Genealogy has become a very popular topic on the Web, so scroll down the page and click on **Genealogy**. Try clicking on the **Beginner's Guide to Family History Research**. What are the first two chapters listed? How many other resources are listed on the **Genealogy** page?
   c. Go back to the main page of the Internet Public Library. Look through the site by clicking on some other links. Do you find it easy to use? Why or why not?

7. Now try another well-known virtual library, the Librarians' Index to the Internet. Type **http://lii.org** into your address field and press **Enter.**
   a. Notice that here Genealogy information is found under the topic **People**. Click on **Genealogy**. How many resources are listed?
   b. Click your **Back** button to return to the main page of the LII site. Note that you can search the site using the search box at the top of the page. Try typing in a search for film history. How many results do you find?
   c. Again, browse through the Librarians' Index site to see what is available. Do you find it easy to use? What features do you like or dislike?

8. The World Wide Web is just the latest invention in a long history of communication breakthroughs. Let's go back to Google and look back in time at the beginnings of communication. Go to **http://www.google.com**. In the search box, type in **cuneiform writing**. Press **Google Search**.
   a. Look at the first three sites that appear in the results list. What are they? Give the titles and URLs of the first three sites.
   b. What is cuneiform writing? When and where was it invented? Do you get this information at one of those first three sites listed?
   c. Just for fun, there's a site that's called **Write Like a Babylonian** at **www.upennmuseum.com/cuneiform.cgi**. Take a look and see what your name looks like in cuneiform! You can go back to the museum's main pages, and find even more fun cuneiform information and projects at **http://www.museum. upenn.edu**.

MANAGING AND USING INFORMATION FROM THE INTERNET AND THE WORLD WIDE WEB

2

O nce you become adept at searching for and finding relevant information on the Internet, you may find yourself wanting to know more about how to manage and use the information you find. Some examples of ways to use Internet information are saving and printing Web pages and frames, emailing Web pages to other people, capturing images and using them in other documents, downloading data into spreadsheets, and so forth. Many of the procedures and tips shown in this chapter concern browser functions, while others require an understanding of the different types of files (for example, text, image, and data files) that are on the Internet and how to manipulate them using other software.

Because this chapter focuses on taking information from the Internet and either sharing it with or distributing it to others, copyright and intellectual property issues will also be discussed.

The sections in this chapter are as follows:

- ✦ Common Types of Files on the Internet and the Web
- ✦ Considering Copyright Guidelines Before Sharing and Copying Information
- ✦ Capturing and Using Text, Images, and Data from the Web and the Internet
- ✦ Using Favorites to Keep Track of Resources
- ✦ Procedures and Steps for Managing Internet and Web Information

Common Types of Files on the Internet and the Web

Web pages can contain text, images, video, audio, and other types of information. These can be part of the Web page, or the Web page can have hyperlinks to the information. Although information can appear as text, it is sometimes stored in a compressed format (to save space) or in some other format. In many cases, your browser can display the information, if it's an image or a video for example, or it can convert the information to sound, if it's an audio file (and if your computer is equipped with a sound card and speakers or earphones). In other cases, you need to get the appropriate software so that your computer can deal with the file.

Sometimes you can tell a file's type by its name. The letters following the dot (.) at the end of a file name are called the *file extension portion* of the file name. Files whose names end with **.txt** or **.text**, for example, usually contain only plain, printable characters.

Table 2.1 covers some of the more common file formats. For more information about working with different file formats, check the help in the menu bar of Internet Explorer, or use your browser to access the following two excellent resources:

◆ *Almost Every File Format in the World*,
   http://www.ace.net.nz/tech/TechFileFormat.html

◆ *Various File Formats and How to Deal With Them*,
   http://www.stack.com/file/extension/

FILE	EXTENSION	FORMAT	
Text files	**.txt** **.asc**	**Plain text files**	Plain text files contain printable characters, like the ones you see on this page, but without special fonts or typefaces, such as italic or bold. They're also called ASCII (rhymes with "pass key") files. ASCII stands for American Standard Code for Information Interchange, and it is the standard code used to represent characters in digital format in a computer. All browsers can display these files. The files often appear as if they were typed on a typewriter or computer terminal.
PostScript files	**.ps**		The PostScript file format was invented by Adobe Systems. The files contain text but usually not in a readable format. The files also contain commands that a printer or display device interprets; the commands pertain to the formatting of different fonts, font sizes, and images in the file.
	.pdf	**Portable Document Format**	Adobe Systems also invented PDF. These files contain instructions that allow them to be displayed with different fonts, typefaces, colors, and images. You can view these files

on your computer if you have Acrobat
Reader, which is free from the Adobe
Acrobat Web site, **http://adobe.com/
prodindex/acrobat**.

Word-processing files	.wpd .doc .rtf		Files produced by word-processing software contain text along with commands that format the text. Most of these files are in a format that other word-processing software can deal with, usually after being converted from one form to another. They can't be displayed as plain text files, however. Files produced by Microsoft Word usually have names ending with .doc, and files produced by WordPerfect have names ending with .wpd. RTF stands for Rich Text Format, a format that can be interpreted by several different word-processing programs.
Data files, Spreadsheet files	.wks .xls .wk1		Files produced by spreadsheet programs are in a special nontext format that's interpreted and used by the software. Two major types of files are produced by Microsoft Excel and Lotus 1-2-3. Excel spreadsheet file names end with .xls, and Lotus 1-2-3 file names end with .wks or .wk1. If you see file extensions like this on files you want to use, you'll need a spreadsheet program to display them. The newer versions of Excel and Lotus 1-2-3 can deal with data with any of the file extensions listed.
Image files	.gif .jpg .jpeg .tif .tiff	**Graphic Interchange Format** **Joint Photographic Expert Group** **Tagged Image File Format**	Graphic images are stored in a variety of file formats. Most browsers can display images, whether they are part of a Web page or on their own, if they are stored in GIF or JPEG format. Another format, TIFF, can store high-quality images. If your browser cannot display files in TIFF, you'll have to get some other software to display them. These two shareware programs can display images in various formats and can convert them from one format to another: Lview Pro, **http://www.lview.com** Paint Shop Pro, **http://www.jasc.com/products/paintshoppro/**

Audio files	.au	Next/Sun format	These files contain information in an audio or sound format. With a sound card and speakers, you can play such files on your computer. The browser contains the software to deal with all these types. Next/Sun and WAV files tend to be very large and thus may take a long time to retrieve.
	.wav	A standard format for computers using MS Windows	
	.ra .ram	RealAudio format	The RealAudio uses a different technology, called streaming technology, by which sound becomes available as it is being transferred to your computer through the Internet. Real Player, a free player for RealAudio files, is available using the URL **http://www.real.com**.
	.mp3	MP3 or MPEG-1	MP3 is a format and a method for compressing audio files. The compression scheme results in files that are less than a tenth of the original size with virtually no loss of sound quality.
Multimedia files	.mpg .mpeg	Moving Picture Expert Group	With these types of files, you can view video and hear accompanying sound. It's similar to viewing a movie or television show. There are several popular formats, including MPEG, QuickTime (created by Apple Computer, Inc.), QuickTime RealVideo (created by RealNetworks, Inc.), and Shockwave (created by Macromedia, Inc.).
	.mov .qt		A QuickTime player is available at no cost at **http://www.apple.com/ quicktime/**.
	.rm .ram	RealVideo	RealPlayer, a free player for RealVideo files, is available at **http://www.real.com/**.
	.dcr .dir .dxr	Shockwave	A free player for Macromedia Shockwave files is available at **http:// www.macromedia.com/ shockwave/download/**.
Compressed files	.zip .gz	Most common types of compressed format files	A file is compressed to save space on a server or to be transferred over the Internet more quickly. There are many types of compressed files, but the most common are those ending with .zip. If you retrieve a file in compressed format, you'll need software

to uncompress the file. Two popular shareware programs work with these types of files:

PKZIP, **http://www.pkware.com**

WinZip, **http://www.winzip.com**

See "A Note About Compressed Files" in the section that follows this table.

Table 2.1—File Types and Their Extensions

A Note About Compressed Files

You'll likely find yourself in a situation where you'll have to deal with ***compressed files***. Many sites on the Web make compressed files available to the public. You may want to retrieve, copy, or ***download*** a copy of one of these compressed files to your computer. Often the files are packages or collections of related files. The files, or packages, are processed by a compression program, which reduces the total number of bytes necessary to represent the information that is in the package. Reducing the size of the file means it takes less time to download the file. Before you can use a compressed file, you must uncompress it using a compression program such as PKZIP or WinZip.

Any single file or collection of files can be compressed and transmitted. In the course of writing this book, we used this technology to transfer chapters back and forth between the publisher, editors, and ourselves. Since each chapter has so many images, the files were quite large. To solve this size problem, we put each chapter and the images into a single package and then compressed it using either PKZIP or WinZip. We then attached the files to email messages or sent them using FTP. The people on either end would then uncompress the files.

To get your own copy of either utility, follow these directions:

+ ***To get a copy of PKZIP:***

Go to the home page for PKWARE, **http://www.pkware.com**. Spend a little time reading about PKZIP, the way it works, and file compression in general. Click on the hyperlink that takes you through the steps of downloading the software. Store the software in a new folder. Once it has finished downloading, there will be a new application (program) in the folder. Click on it and follow the instructions. It will install itself in a directory or folder. Once it's installed, go to that directory using Windows Explorer. Read the file named **Readme**, which contains information about the files you've installed. The program's name is PKZIP; click on it when you need to use it.

+ ***To get a copy of WinZip:***

Go to the home page for WinZip, **http://www.winzip.com**. Spend a little time reading about WinZip, how it works, and about the topic of file compression. Click on the hyperlink that takes you through the steps of downloading the software. Store the software in a new folder. Once it's finished downloading, there will be a new application (program) in the folder. Click on it, and it will lead you through the steps of installing the program in a folder on your computer. The name of the program is WinZip; click on it when you need it.

Considering Copyright Guidelines
Before Sharing and Copying Information

Much of what you find on the Web and Internet can be saved in a file on your computer, which makes it easy to share and distribute information to others. Exchanging information was one of the main reasons the Internet began, and it is a desirable activity, but there is a drawback. Free access to information makes it difficult to control unauthorized distribution of anything that's available. Anyone with a Web browser can make an exact digital copy of information. This sometimes is illegal.

Only the owners of the information can grant the right to copy or duplicate materials. This is called the *copyright*. Some documents on the Internet contain a statement asserting the copyright and giving permission for distributing the document in an electronic form, provided it isn't sold or made part of some commercial product. For example, here's a quote from **http://ibiblio.org/expo/vatican.exhibit/exhibit/About.html** describing limitations on the use of the materials in the exhibit "Rome Reborn" offered by the Library of Congress:

> The text and images in the Online Exhibit ROME REBORN: THE VATICAN LIBRARY AND RENAISSANCE CULTURE are for the personal use of students, scholars, and the public. Any commercial use or publication of them is strictly prohibited.

Regardless of whether a Web page is accompanied by a statement asserting copyright, it is still protected by the copyright laws of the United States, the Universal Copyright Convention, or the Berne Union. Most copyright conventions or statutes include a provision that makes it possible for individuals to copy portions of a document for short-term use. This is known as *fair use*. If information is obtainable on the Internet and there is no charge to access the information, it often can be shared in an electronic form. That certainly doesn't mean you can copy images or documents and make them available on the Internet, make copies and share them in a printed form, or distribute them to several people using email attachments. Quite naturally, many people who create or provide material available on the Internet expect to get credit and/or be paid for their work.

Remember that anything available in electronic form on the Internet or World Wide Web is a copyrighted work, and you need to treat it in the same way as a book, journal article, artwork, play, or a piece of recorded music. Just because something is available on the Web doesn't mean that you may copy it. You are allowed to copy the material for personal use, but in almost every case, you cannot use it for commercial purposes without written permission from the copyright holder.

Two good resources for information about copyright and intellectual property issues are:
The Copyright Website, **http://www.benedict.com,** by Benedict O'Mahoney
The Intellectual Property Law Server, **http://www.intelproplaw.com,** by George A. Wowk

Capturing and Using Text, Images, and Data from the Web and the Internet

There are several browser options for retrieving material from the Web. The following section will provide brief step-by-step instructions on how to work with information that you find. After this section is a hands-on activity covering how to save and insert images into a word-processing document.

The following are the examples that will be shown:

◆ Printing an Entire Web Page

◆ Saving the Text of a Web Page

◆ Printing Part of a Web Page

◆ Saving Part of a Web Page

◆ Capturing and Downloading Statistical Tables into a Spreadsheet or Word Processing Document

◆ Capturing Images

Printing an Entire Web Page

You've found a Web page that has information you need. You can print it out if you wish. Before you print a Web page in its entirety, you might want to make sure how many pages it has. You can do this by accessing Print Preview, which is located in the File menu, as shown in Figure 2.1. Without finding this out, you may print out more pages than you actually need.

1. After determining that you want the entire Web page printed, simply click on **File** in the menu bar and select **Print**.

2. When the Print menu pops up, click on **OK**.

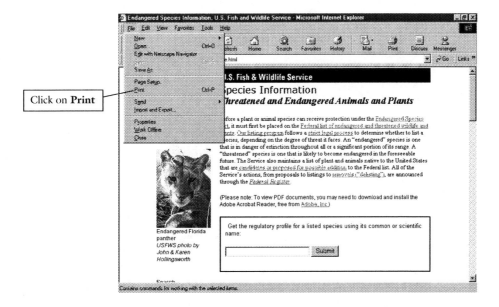

Figure 2.1—How to Print an Entire Web Page

Saving the Text of a Web Page

You have found a valuable resource on the Web, and you'd like to read the information later, but you're not connected to a printer. You could save the page as a favorite, as we describe later in the chapter, or download the page to a diskette in the A: drive or to a drive on your computer. Remember that when you download a Web page you'll be obtaining the text only and not any images that may be in the page. Images must be captured separately.

1. While viewing the desired Web page, click on **File**.

2. Choose **Save As** from the pull-down menu.

3. Click on the down arrow next to the Save in field and choose the appropriate drive and/or folder to place the Web page in. In Figure 2.2, we chose the A: drive.

4. If saving to the A: drive, put a diskette in the drive before saving.

5. You can rename the file if you want by typing in a name in the **File name** field.

6. Choose **Text file (*.txt)** from the Save as type pull-down menu.

7. Click on **Save**.

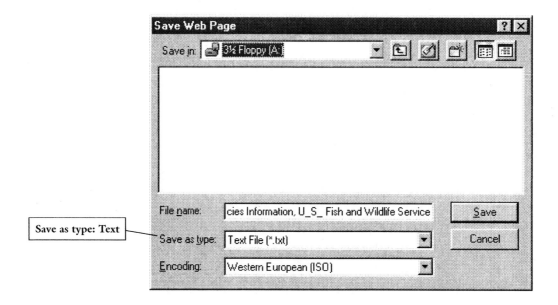

Figure 2.2—Saving a Web Page to the A: Drive

Printing Part of a Web Page

You have found useful information that exists on a couple of pages of a much larger Web site. You can print one section of a Web site if you'd like. There are two ways to do this.

Option #1

1. While you are viewing the Web page, click on **File**.

2. Select **Print Preview**.

3. Note the page numbers in the upper right corner of each page.

4. Click on the right-pointing arrow until you come to the page(s) you want to print.

5. When you come to the page(s) you want to print, click on **Print**, as shown in Figure 2.3.

6. After the Print menu appears, click on the radio button next to **Pages** and type the page number(s) you need to print.

7. Click on **OK**.

8. When you're finished with Print Preview, click on **Close**.

Indicate which pages you want printed here

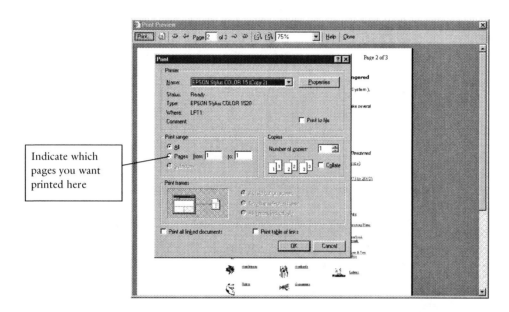

Figure 2.3—Using Print Preview to Print Part of a Web Page

Option #2

1. Use the left mouse button to highlight the section of text that you want to print.

2. Click on **File** and then select **Print**.

3. On the Print menu, click on the radio button next to **Selection**, as shown in Figure 2.4.

4. Click on **OK**.

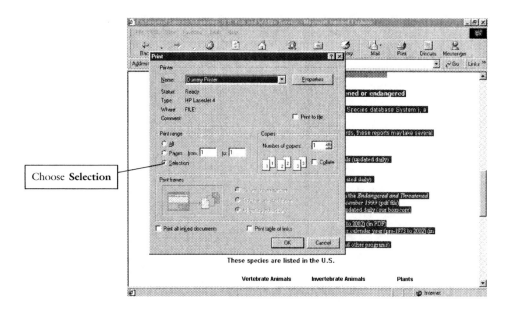

Choose **Selection**

Figure 2.4—Printing Part of a Web Page Using the Selection Option

Saving Part of a Web Page

Here are a few of examples of when you would save part of a Web page instead of printing part of a Web page:

✦ You aren't attached to a printer and you want to have the information you found accessible at a later time, but you don't want the entire page saved.

✦ You want to save less than one page, for example, a paragraph or a table.

✦ You want to have the information in electronic form.

Remember, if you download the text from a Web page and plan to use the information you located in a paper or presentation, you must cite the information properly.

The following are the simple steps to save parts of Web pages:

1. Highlight the part of the Web page you want to save by holding down the left mouse button and dragging the cursor across the text you want. When you have reached the last line, release the mouse button.

2. Click on **Edit** in the menu bar and select **Copy,** or right-click the mouse and choose **Copy,** or press **Ctrl**+C.

3. Open the word-processing program you intend to use and create a new document.

4. Click on **Edit** in the menu bar and select **Paste,** or right-click the mouse and choose **Paste**, or press **Ctrl**+V.

Note: If you are using a computer that doesn't have word-processing software installed, you can use Notepad, which is available in Windows. Notepad is located in the Accessories folder under Programs. You could copy the part of the Web page you wanted to Notepad and then save the file (click on **File** and select **Save As**) to a diskette in the A: drive or to your computer.

Capturing and Downloading Statistical Tables into a Spreadsheet or Word-processing Document

Statistical tables abound on the Internet, especially in government Web sites. Since government data is in the public domain and free to use as you want, you won't have to ask permission to use it, but you will need to cite it properly so that people know where you got the data. In this example, we'll show how to download a statistical table into a spreadsheet program. Using a spreadsheet allows you to perform calculations with the numbers that are in the columns and rows. We'll be using Microsoft Excel, but other spreadsheet programs follow similar procedures.

Some statistical tables are not in a worksheet format, but in a ***delimited format***. This means that the data fields are separated by commas, tabs, semicolons, or some other delimiter. Excel makes it easy for you to download a file that is delimited. Many other statistical tables are in text format. If the data is in text format, you can still download it in a spreadsheet program, but you'll need to change the column sizes to accommodate the data.

Figure 2.5 shows a list of statistical information you can download from the 2004 edition of the *Economic Report of the President*. The URL is **http://www.gpoaccess.gov/eop/tables04.html**.

1. To download an individual file from the list, place your cursor on the document you want, click the right mouse button, and choose **Save Target As**. In this example, we'll click on the first one listed, as shown in Figure 2.5.

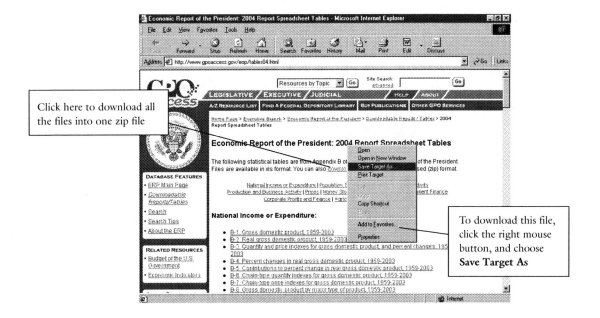

Figure 2.5—*Economic Report of the President* Statistical Tables

2. A dialog box will pop up on the screen, as shown in Figure 2.6. You'll need to decide where to save the file. You can choose a folder from the pull-down menu next to Save in. In this example, we will choose to put the file on a diskette in the A: drive. Note that the file is named **b2.xls**. Click on **Save**.

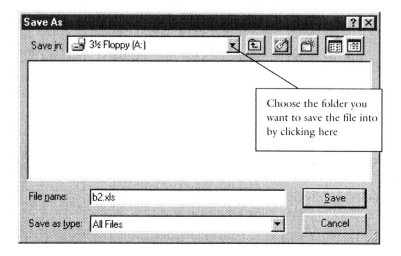

Figure 2.6—Saving a Spreadsheet File

Now you need to open the Microsoft Excel spreadsheet program. Click on **Start** and then choose **Programs**. Choose **Microsoft Excel** from the menu. When Excel is open, click on **File** and choose **Open** from the menu. You'll want to look in the A: drive for the file we downloaded. You'll need to choose **All Files** from the pull-down menu next to Files of type.

3. You should see the file named **b2.xls** on the list of files in the A: drive. Click on it, as shown in Figure 2.7.

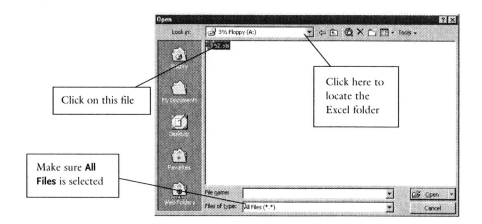

Figure 2.7—Opening a File in Excel

The file is automatically placed into a spreadsheet. Since this file was already in worksheet format (**.xls**), it downloaded easily into the Excel program, as shown in Figure 2.8.

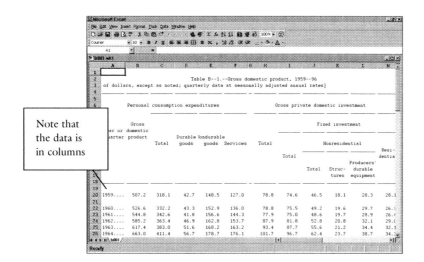

Figure 2.8—The File **b_01a.xls** as an Excel Spreadsheet

Sometimes you want to capture statistical data to insert in a word-processing document. To do this, follow these steps:

1. Copy and paste the statistical table like you would copy a portion of any Web page. If the tabular configuration is distorted, you might want to try changing the font to Courier or some other nonproportional font so that the columns don't appear crooked.

2. Save the file as a text file, just as you would save a Web page.

Capturing Images

Another useful skill to learn is how to save images and insert them into documents such as word-processing documents or PowerPoint presentations. Activity 2.1 will take you through the steps of this process.

ACTIVITY

2.1 CAPTURING AND DOWNLOADING IMAGES INTO A WORD-PROCESSING DOCUMENT

OVERVIEW

This activity will take you step-by-step through the process of saving an image and inserting it into a word-processing document. First, we'll go to Karen Hartman's home page and save an image that is on the page. After the image is saved, you'll insert the image into a word-processing document. We'll follow these steps:

1. Go to Karen Hartman's home page.

2. Find the image of Nuweiba and save it.

3. Create a word-processing document.

4. Insert the image into the document.

DETAILS

Before we begin, make sure your browser is opened and ready to go.

1 Go to Karen Hartman's home page.

✦ Do It!   Type **http://webliminal.com/khartman** in the address box and press **Enter**.

✦ Do It!   Click on the **Personal** hyperlink at the top of the page.

2 Find the image of Nuweiba and save it.

✦ Do It!   Scroll down until you see the image of a resort with mountains in the background.

The image that we will be saving appears in Figure 2.9. Whenever you want to save an image and use it for your own purposes, you should try to notify the person responsible for putting the image on the Web to ask for permission to use the image. Sometimes this is impossible, and if you aren't using the image for commercial reasons, it probably falls within the realm of "fair use" to use the image, especially for educational reasons. In any case, it's still a courtesy to try to obtain permission. On this Web page, there is a place to email the author and ask if it's okay to use her image. Let's go ahead and save the image.

Place your mouse on the image and right-click. A menu will appear, as shown in Figure 2.9.

✦ Do It!   Choose **Save Picture As**.

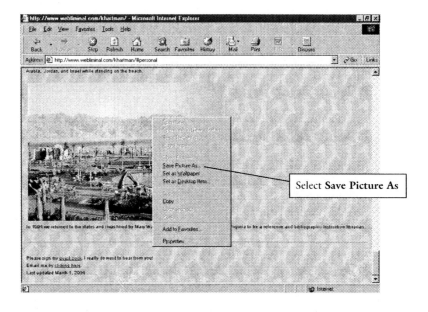

Figure 2.9—Saving an Image You Find on the World Wide Web

Now you'll need to decide where you want to put the image. You should save it to the drive that's most convenient for you. For the purposes of this activity, we will save to a diskette in the A: drive. Figure 2.10 shows the Save As window.

✦ Do It!   Click on the arrow next to the field labeled **Save in**. Choose **3½ Floppy (A:)**, as shown in Figure 2.10.

✦ Do It!   Click on **Save**, as shown in Figure 2.10.

Note that the image is a JPEG file.

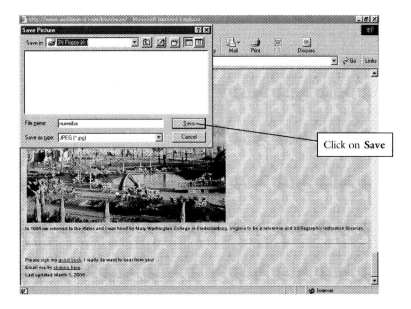

Figure 2.10—Saving an Image to the A: Drive

3   Create a word-processing document.

✦ Do It!   Open Microsoft Word.

✦ Do It!   Click on **File** and then select **New**.

✦ Do It!   Click on the **Blank Document** icon.

4   Insert the image into the document.

Place the cursor at the spot you'd like the picture to be inserted. Click on **Insert** in the menu bar, as shown in Figure 2.11.

After selecting **Picture** from the pull-down menu that appears, click on **From File**, also shown in Figure 2.11.

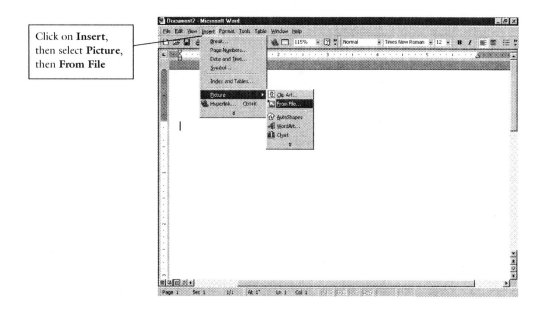

Click on **Insert**, then select **Picture**, then **From File**

Figure 2.11—Using Word to Insert a Picture in a Document

From the Insert Picture dialog box that pops up, you'll need to choose the drive and folder that holds the image you want to insert. In this example, we saved the image to the diskette in the A: drive. To make it easier to find an image, choose **All Pictures** from the pull-down menu next to the Files of type field, as shown in Figure 2.12.

✦ Do It!   Highlight the name of the image, **nuweiba**, and click on **Insert**.

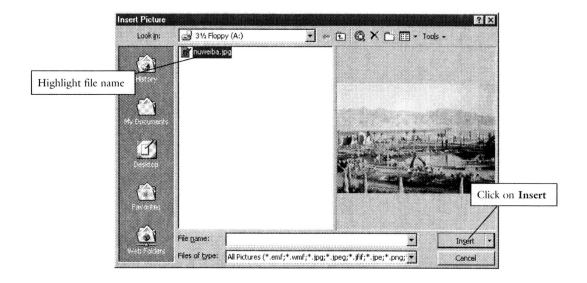

Highlight file name

Click on **Insert**

Figure 2.12—Steps for Inserting a Picture into a Word Document

Figure 2.13 shows the picture inserted into the Word document. You can resize the image by clicking on it and dragging a border arrow in any direction you want.

Figure 2.13—The Picture Inserted into a Word Document

If this were an actual research project, you would cite the title of the image, the author of the Web page, and the Web page's URL.

END OF ACTIVITY 2.1

Activity 2.1 illustrated how easy it is to copy an image and use it for your own purposes. The way the Web works makes it simple to take material and use it as your own. You should always be mindful of being courteous when using others' work and citing it properly.

Using Favorites to Keep Track of Resources

You can save links to interesting and useful Web pages by adding hyperlinks to your favorites list. Each item in the favorites list is a Web page title, and each entry is a hyperlink. Whenever you're using the browser, you can call up your favorites and follow any of the links. The browser gives you the tools to add, delete, and rename the favorites. You can also arrange them into folders, list them in various ways, keep different files, and otherwise manage the collection. There are a number of shareware and freeware programs available on the Web for managing favorites. We'll take a look at finding and installing programs from shareware and freeware sources in Chapter 10.

Add a Favorite

Adding a favorite means placing a Web page on the favorites list. Some ways to add a favorite using either browser are:

✦ Use the keyboard shortcut:

Ctrl + ↓

✦ Use the right mouse button:

Click the right mouse button when the mouse pointer is on a Web page, frame, or hyperlink, and select **Add to Favorites.**

✦ Use the menu bar:

Click on **Favorites** in the menu bar and select **Add to Favorites.**

✦ Drag and drop:

Move the mouse pointer to the Explorer icon in the address box, just to the left of the URL of the current Web page, and hold down the left mouse button. Without letting go of the mouse button, drag the icon to **Favorites** on the menu bar. That displays the favorites list. Still holding on to the left mouse button, move the icon to a folder (if you want to add it to an existing folder) or to a spot on the list and let go of the button.

Display the Favorites List in a Separate Window

To display the favorites list in a separate window, click on **Favorites** in the menu bar and select **Organize Favorites.**

Jump to an Item in the Favorites List

Jumping to an item means going directly to the Web page represented by the item. First display the list, then move the mouse to and click on the favorite you want to use. If the favorites are arranged in folders or categories, select a category and then a favorite.

Delete an Item from the Favorites List

To remove an entry, display the favorites list in a separate window and click on the item to delete. Once you select an item in this way, you can delete it by pressing the **Delete** key.

Using Favorites for Offline Browsing

Internet Explorer allows you to save favorites for viewing when you're not connected to the Internet. This is referred to as *offline browsing.* Some reasons why offline browsing may be useful are:

✦ You want to show a Web page in a presentation that you will be giving at a later time and you will not have an Internet connection. You can save the page using the favorites function while you're online, and then bring up the page in an offline mode later on to show your audience.

✦ You may want to view Web pages later, when you're not connected to the Internet. This is particularly useful for people that have expensive or unreliable Internet connections.

Example: How to save a favorite for offline browsing

1. Go to a Web page that you want to save.

2. Click on **Favorites** in the menu bar, and then select **Add to Favorites**.

3. The Add Favorite box will appear. Click on the radio button next to Make available offline, as shown in Figure 2.14.

4. Now click on **Customize**.

5. Then click on **Next.**

6. The Offline Favorite Wizard will now ask you if you want to save links from the page. If you select *yes*, then you will be asked to indicate how many levels deep from the page you want to go. If your Internet access speed is slow and you don't have much hard disk space, it's a good idea to answer *no* to this question.

7. Click **Next** on the next two dialog boxes.

8. In the box that asks if this site needs a password, choose **no** and click on **Finish**.

9. In the next box, click on **OK**.

10. When you are no longer connected to the Internet, open Internet Explorer.

11. Select **File** in the menu bar and click on **Work Offline**.

12. Select **Favorites** and find the Web page that you saved. Click on it. Note that you can't link to other hyperlinks on the page because no levels were downloaded. If you'd like to have those hyperlinks available as well, then choose the number of levels that you'd like to download in the Offline Favorite Wizard.

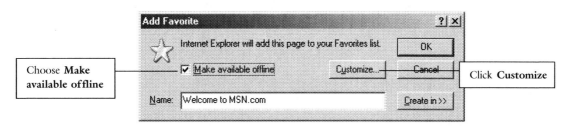

Figure 2.14—Making a Favorite Available Offline

Procedures and Steps for Managing Internet and Web Information

The following chart is a helpful reference to procedures outlined in this chapter and to some others that weren't discussed.

PROCEDURE	STEPS
Saving the text of a Web page	1. Click on **File**. 2. Choose **Save As**. 3. Choose the drive and folder in which to place the Web page. 4. Select **Text File** (*.txt) from the pull-down menu. 5. Click on **Save**.
Copying a portion of a Web page	1. Highlight the portion of the Web page you want by holding down the left mouse button and dragging the cursor down the screen. 2. Choose **Edit**, then **Copy**. 3. Open a word-processor or Notepad, which is located under Accessories in Windows. 4. Choose **Edit**, then **Paste**. 5. The portion of the Web page you highlighted will be placed in the document.
Saving items on a Web page into a file (without viewing them first)	1. Move the mouse pointer to the hyperlink and click the right mouse button. 2. Select **Save Target As** from the menu that appears. 3. A Save As dialog box will pop up. You'll need to select the drive where you want the link to be copied to. 4. Click on **Save**. Whenever you save a file from the Internet, there's a possibility that the file will contain a computer virus or other software that may damage or erase files. A good source for information about computer viruses is "virus — PC Webopedia," **http://www.pcwebopedia.com/TERM/V/virus.htm**.
Printing a Web page	1. Click on **File** in the menu bar. 2. Choose **Print**. 3. Click **OK**.

Printing parts of a Web page	1. Highlight the portion of the Web page you want to print by holding down the left mouse button and dragging the cursor down the screen. 2. Click on **File** in the menu bar. 3. Select **Print**. 4. In the box labeled Print range, choose the **Selection** option. 5. Click **OK**. OR 1. Click on **File** in the menu bar. 2. Select **Print Preview**. 3. Click on **Next Page** until you find the page(s) you want to print. 4. Click on **Print**. 5. Select the page number(s) you want printed. 6. Click **OK**.
Emailing a Web page (this means sending the source)	1. Click on **File** in the menu bar. 2. Select **Send**. 3. You can choose **Page by email** or **Link by email**. 4. Type the email address of the person you are sending the message to in the line next to To. 5. Click on **Send**.
Printing a page that is wider than 8½ inches	1. Click on **File** in the menu bar. 2. Select **Print**. 3. Click on **Properties** in the Print menu. 4. Choose **Landscape**. 5. Click **OK**.
Printing pages with dark backgrounds	1. Click on **Tools** in the menu bar. 2. Select **Internet Options** from the menu. 3. Click on **Colors**. 4. Deselect **Use Windows Colors** by clicking the radio button next to it. 5. Select the background color you want; usually white is a good choice. 6. Click **OK**.
Saving a frame	1. Click on the frame you want to save. 2. Click on **File**. 3. Choose **Save As**. 4. Select **Text File (*.txt)** from the pull-down menu. 5. Create a new file name if you want. 6. Click on **Save**.

Printing a frame	1. Click on the frame you want to print. 2. Click on **File** in the menu bar. 3. Choose **Print**. 4. Click **OK** on the print menu.
Using your browser to view local files	1. Choose **File** from the menu bar. 2. Select **Open**. 3. You can type in the file name or click on **Browse** and search until you find the one you want to view. 4. Click on **Open**.
Capturing images	1. Right-click on the image. 2. Choose **Save Picture As** from the pop-up menu. 3. Click on **Save** to save the image in the drive and folder listed, or select another location.
Inserting images into documents (Word documents, Web pages, or PowerPoint presentations)	1. Open the document in which you want to insert the image. 2. Make sure your cursor is located where you want the image to be located. 3. Click on **Insert** in the menu bar. 4. Choose **Picture**. 5. Choose **From File**. 6. Locate the drive and folder name that holds the image. (If the image is on a diskette, insert the diskette in the A: drive.) 7. After locating the image file, highlight it and click on **Insert**.
Downloading statistical tables into a spreadsheet	1. If the table is already in a worksheet format, either follow the directions from the Web page or click on **File** and select **Save As**. 2. Choose a folder in which to place the file. You can choose the Excel folder if you like. 3. Open the Microsoft Excel program by clicking on **Start** and then **Programs**. Choose **Microsoft Excel** from the menu. 4. When Excel is open, click on **File** and choose **Open** from the menu. 5. Choose **All Files** from the pull-down menu next to **Files of type**. 6. Click on the file you downloaded. If the file is delimited or in fixed-width format, you'll have to indicate which format. If it

is delimited, you'll need to determine which delimiter the file uses: commas, tabs, semicolons, or some other delimiter. Click on **Next** until the spreadsheet is ready to load. If the file is already in a spreadsheet format, it will automatically load into the spreadsheet.

Downloading statistical tables	1. Highlight the table by holding down the left mouse button and dragging the cursor down the screen. 2. Choose **Edit**, then **Copy**. 3. Open a word-processing document or Notepad, which is located under Accessories in Windows. 4. Choose **Edit**, then **Paste**. 5. If the tabular configuration is distorted, change the font to Courier or some other nonproportional font. OR 1. If the table is an entire Web page, click on **File**, choose **Save As**, and place the file in a folder. 2. Select **Plain Text** (*.txt) from the pull-down menu and name it something new. 3. Click on **Save**. 4. Open a word-processing program or Notepad, open the saved text file, and save it using the menu provided. 5. If the tabular configuration is distorted, change the font to Courier or some other nonproportional font.

Table 2.2—Procedures and Steps in Internet Explorer

Summary

Web pages may contain text, images, video, audio, and other types of information. These can be part of the Web page, or they can be accessed through hyperlinks. Information available on the Web is in a myriad of file formats. This chapter covered the common types of files that are found on the Internet and how to work with them. You can usually tell a file's type by its name. The letters following the dot (.) at the end of a file name are called the file extension portion of the file name. You may find yourself in a situation where you'll have to deal with compressed files. Before you can use a compressed file, you must uncompress it, using a compression program such as PKZIP or WinZip.

Using information from the Internet requires a familiarity with intellectual property issues. Much of what you find on the Internet and World Wide Web can be downloaded and distributed to others easily. Only the owners of the information can grant the right to copy or duplicate materials. This is called the copyright. In almost every case, you are required to obtain written permission from the copyright holder before distributing information on the Internet. Most copyright laws include a provision that makes it possible for individuals to copy portions of a document for short-term use. This is known as fair use.

Basic browser skills were outlined in this chapter. These include downloading, capturing, copying, emailing, and printing information from the Internet. Details on using favorites to keep track of resources and save them for offline browsing were also given.

Selected Terms Used in This Chapter

compressed file
copyright
delimited format
download
fair use
offline browsing

Review Questions

Multiple Choice

1. You may be able to tell a file's type by the
   a. file protocol.
   b. file extension.
   c. plug-in.
   d. PostScript.

2. A file may be compressed in order to
   a. be transferred more quickly.
   b. comply with copyright laws.
   c. save space on a server.
   d. a and c
   e. b and c

3. Image files can be saved
   a. only on your a: drive.
   b. only on your c: drive.
   c. where they are most convenient.
   d. only as part of an entire Web page.

4. Which of these extensions would tell you that a file was in a compressed format?
   a. .xls
   b. .zip
   c. .ram
   d. a and b
   e. b and c

5. The following extensions are all used in the names of files except
   a. pif.
   b. gif.
   c. jpg.
   d. rtf.

6. You may be able to print a portion of a large Web page by
   a. scrolling down to the part of the page you want to print.
   b. using the Print Preview option.
   c. highlighting the desired text and using Print/Selection.
   d. a and c
   e. b and c

True or False

7. T F An image that you download cannot be resized.

8. T F You can save both the text and all images on a Web page by clicking File/Save As.

9. T F You must ask for permission from the copyright holder before using any material from a Web page for commercial purposes.

10. T F You may copy a portion of a Web document for short-term, personal use.

11. T F If a Web page doesn't have a copyright statement, it is not protected by copyright laws.

12. T F To save an image from a Web page, you click on it with your left mouse button.

13. T F Multimedia files, such as movies, can be transferred over the Internet.

Completion

14. Before you save or print a frame, you must _____ the frame you want to work with.

15. You can email a Web page to a friend by using the _____ pull-down menu.

16. To add a downloaded image into a Word document, you click on _____ in the menu bar.

17. When data in statistical tables are separated by a comma, tab, etc. instead of being in a worksheet, they are in a(n) _____ format.

18. When you copy or transfer a file from a computer, you _____ the file.

19. If you wanted to send a word-processing file to a friend and didn't know what word-processing program they used, you might save the file in _____, since it can be read by many word processing programs.

20. The letters following the dot (.) in a file name are called the _____.

Exercises and Projects

In these exercises we'll be practicing the ways that information from the Web can be saved on your computer and used effectively. Remember that when you are using information from the Web, you need to keep copyright information in mind and ask permission from an author when it is appropriate. We'll be using some government sites, where information is in the public domain.

1. Before transferring files from the Web, it's a good idea to become informed about computer viruses. There are many good sites for facts about protecting your computer from viruses. Go to PC Webopaedia, mentioned in the chapter, at **http:// webopedia.internet.com/TERM/v/virus.html** and read through the information. It might be a good idea to save some of the information in the article for future reference, don't you think? Highlight the first three paragraphs of the article, click **Edit**, then **Copy**. Open Notepad, as described in the chapter, click **Edit**, then **Paste**. Print the document by clicking **File**, then **Print**. Remember that if you use the information in a paper you'll need to cite the page properly.

2. The Library of Congress's copyright information is available at **http://lcweb.loc .gov/copyright**. Access their site and click on the hyperlink **Frequently Asked Questions**.
    a. What does copyright protect? Must a work be registered in order to be protected?
    b. How long does copyright protection last?

3. Suppose you wanted to know about the services available through the U.S. Department of State. Go to their Web site at **http://www.state.gov/**. Perhaps you're interested in obtaining a passport. Click on the link **Passports for US Citizens.**
    a. Save the page for future reference as a text file on your desktop by following the instructions given in the chapter.
    b. Choose one of the hyperlinks on the page and save the information in that link by clicking on it with your right mouse button. Choose **Save Link** (or **Target**) **As** and save that file on your desktop as well.
    c. Double-click on one of the saved files and print it.

4. There is also an abundance of information available from the federal government on starting a small business. Access the Small Business Administration Web site at **http:// www.sba.gov** and look at what is included at the site. Click on **Starting Your Business**, then on **Business Plan Basics**.
    a. Print the page.
    b. Save the page on your desktop as a text file.
    c. Click on the link to **Writing the Plan**. Let's just highlight and print a portion of it. Scroll down to the section entitled **Financial Data** and highlight it using your left mouse button. Click on **File**, then **Print**. Click the button beside **Selection**, and click **OK**.

5. There's a wide variety of images available on the Web. One site that provides a wealth of images, icons, and backgrounds is The Hassle Free Clipart site at **http://www. hasslefreeclipart.com/** Access the site. Click on **Terms of Usage.**

   a. What are the terms of use of the site?
   b. Use your **Back** button to go back to the main site. Choose a category (There are some really cute holiday images under Cartoon Clip Art!), then click on one of the image thumbnails. Save the image to your desktop by clicking with your right mouse button and choosing **Save As.** Double click on the image file to open the image. Print the image.

6. Another good source for images is through AltaVista. Go to their site at **http:// www.altavista.com** and click on **Images.** Notice the options you have for searching.

   a. What are the options? Look for a picture of a sunset. You'll have a wide variety to choose from!
   b. How many images were found? Select one, and click on the link beneath it that says **More Info.** What information do you find on this page? Click with your right mouse button and save the image to your desktop.
   c. Insert the image into this assignment.

7. Now you have at least two images saved. Open Word and select a new document. Click on **Insert** in your menu bar, then choose **Picture/From File.**

   a. Select one of the images you saved in the previous exercises and add it to the document.
   b. Resize the image by clicking on it and dragging a border arrow.
   c. Print the document.

8. In the exercises for chapter one, we looked at cuneiform writing. Another early form of written communication was on papyrus scrolls. There are several websites that talk about papyrus scrolls and how they were created. One is available at **http://www. class.uh.edu/english/faculty/houston/2320web/scott/chapter1.html**. Another can be found at **http://www.geocities.com/TAREK-RAGAB/papyrushistory. html**. Or you can do a search for other pages that give the history of papyrus. Using your left mouse button, highlight a few sentences of text that describe the use of papyrus scrolls. Following the instructions in the chapter, copy and paste the text into this assignment. Be sure to include the URL of the page where you found it!

USING THE WEB
FOR RESEARCH

3

The Internet and the World Wide Web have revolutionized the way we do research. Instead of spending hours combing library indexes and catalogs, making endless telephone calls, or traveling to far-off places, with a few clicks of the mouse you can find an enormous amount of information on virtually any subject. You can find all types of information on the World Wide Web: government statistics, fast-breaking news stories, up-to-the-minute weather reports, sales catalogs and business information, radio programs, movies, music, and virtual art galleries and museums.

Searching the Web for this information can be a challenging and possibly frustrating task. The Web will not always have everything you're looking for, and sometimes the information you want is on the Web, but may be difficult to find. Keep in mind that even though the Web has more than a billion pages, most published literature is not Web-based, but rather exists in books and periodicals that are in paper form. Librarians can help you determine the best sources to consult for the subject you are researching. Once you've decided the Web is the place to look, how do you proceed? Several major search tools are available; which one do you start with?

In addition to introducing you to researching using the Web, this chapter also gives an overview of the current content issues that Internet users should understand. These issues include pornography, free speech, censorship, and filtering.

The sections in this chapter are as follows:

  ✦ The First Step: Evaluating Your Information Needs

  ✦ Browsing the World Wide Web: Using Directories

  ✦ Finding Information Gems in Virtual Libraries

  ✦ Searching the World Wide Web: Using Search Engines

✦ Using Several Search Engines Simultaneously: Meta-search Tools

✦ Content Issues: Pornography, Free Speech, Censorship, Filtering, and Filtering

In the course of this chapter, we'll provide you with an introduction to research skills on the World Wide Web so that you can start going out and finding whatever interests you. You will learn the difference between *browsing* and *keyword searching* the Web, and you will see examples that focus on each method. You'll discover when it is better to use a *directory* or *subject catalog* (topical lists of selected Web resources, hierarchically arranged) and when it makes sense to start with a *search engine* (a tool that provides keyword searching ability of Web resources). We will also cover the advantages of using virtual libraries, which are directories that contain only carefully selected resources. We will discuss employing several search engines simultaneously by using *meta-search tools*.

If you know different tactics for finding information on the Web, your searches will be more successful. We'll provide activities in this chapter that will give you practice in browsing and keyword searching. Once you learn how to use the Web to its fullest potential, you will be amazed at what you can locate in a short period of time.

Let's start researching!

The First Step: Evaluating Your Information Needs

Before you get online and start your search for information, think about what types of material you're looking for. Are you interested in finding facts to support an argument, authoritative opinions, statistics, research reports, descriptions of events, images, or movie reviews? Do you need current information or facts about an event that occurred 20 years ago? When is the Web a smart place to start? Keep in mind that a lot of information is on the Web, but much of it is part of proprietary or commercial services that are subscription-based. Your local library may subscribe to a database that will be useful for the subject you are searching for.

Types of Information Most Likely Found on the Internet and the World Wide Web

✦ **Current information.** Many major newspapers, broadcasting networks, and popular magazines have Web sites that provide news updates throughout the day. Current financial and weather information also is easily accessible.

✦ **Government information.** Most federal, state, and local government agencies provide statistics and other information freely and in a timely manner. Most foreign governments provide official information as well.

✦ **Popular culture.** It's easy to find information on the latest movie or best-selling book.

✦ **Full-text versions of books and other materials that are not under copyright restriction.** Works such as Shakespeare's plays, the Bible, *Canterbury Tales,* and hundreds of other full-text literary resources are available. Several of them have been made into searchable databases, which have enhanced scholarly research in the humanities.

✦ **Business and company information.** Not only do many companies provide their Web pages and annual reports, but several Internet-based databases also provide in-depth financial and other information about companies.

✦ **Consumer information.** The Internet is a virtual gold mine of information for people interested in buying a particular item and want opinions from other people about it. With access to everything from automobile reviews on the Web to Usenet newsgroups, consumers can find out about almost any item before they buy it.

✦ **Medical information.** In addition to the hospitals, pharmaceutical companies, and nonprofit organizations that publish excellent sources of medical information, the National Library of Medicine freely provides the MEDLINE database to the public.

✦ **Entertainment.** The Web is the first place many people go to find games, audio files, and video clips.

✦ **Software.** The Web hosts software archives in which you can search for and download software to your computer without cost.

✦ **Unique archival sites.** The Library of Congress, for example, archives Americana in its American Memory collection.

Some Reasons Why the World Wide Web Won't Have Everything You Are Looking For

✦ Publishing companies and authors who make money by creating and providing information usually choose to use the traditional publishing marketplace rather than make their information available for free via the Internet.

✦ Scholars most often choose to publish their research in reputable scholarly journals and university presses rather than on the Web. More academic journals are becoming Web-based, but a subscription to the online version often costs as much as the paper form. (However, many journal publishers' Web sites will provide a free article or two from an issue and include only abstracts of the other articles.)

✦ Several organizations and institutions would like to publish valuable information on the Web, but don't because of a lack of staff or funding.

✦ The Web tends to include information that is in demand to a large portion of the public. The Web can't be relied on consistently for historical information, which is often not in high demand. For example, if you need today's weather data for Minneapolis, the Web will certainly have it. But if you want Minneapolis climatic data for November of 1976, you might not find it on the Web.

By evaluating your goals before starting a research project, you may find that you don't need to get online at all. You may find out that your library has an excellent CD-ROM database that provides exactly what you need. Perhaps your library will have a better source in paper form. Don't be shy about asking a reference librarian to help you determine whether the Internet or some other resource will have the most appropriate material to choose from on the topic you are researching.

Choosing the Best Search Tool to Start With

Once you've decided that the Web is likely to have the information you're seeking, you'll need to choose an appropriate search tool. Table 3.1 shows the major types of search tools available on the World Wide Web and their major characteristics.

Directories and Virtual Libraries	✦ These contain topic lists of selected resources, usually hierarchically arranged. ✦ Most resources in these tools have been evaluated carefully. ✦ They can be browsed or searched by keyword. ✦ They contain links to specialized databases.
Search engines	✦ These attempt to index as much of the Web as possible. ✦ Most are full-text databases. ✦ Many require knowledge of search techniques to guarantee good results. ✦ They are most often used for multifaceted or obscure subjects. ✦ They search very large databases that are created by computer programs and are updated regularly.
Meta-search tools	✦ Some allow you to search several search engines simultaneously. ✦ Some supply lists of databases that can be searched directly from their pages. ✦ They provide a good way to keep up with new search engines. ✦ They may not fully exploit the features of individual search engines, so keep your search simple.

Table 3.1—Major Search Tools and Their Characteristics

A Checklist to Help You Choose the Right Tool

Directories and virtual libraries are most useful for finding the following:

✦ An overview of a topic

✦ Evaluated resources

✦ Facts such as population statistics or country information

✦ A specialized database for specific or very recent information

Search engines and meta-search tools should be consulted when looking for the following:

✦ Obscure information

✦ Multifaceted topics

✦ A large amount of information on a particular topic from different perspectives

Search engines and meta-search tools should not be used to find the following:

✦ News that happened yesterday or even last week. You'd be better off going to a specialized database that is updated daily or weekly.

✦ Information in a particular form, such as journal or newspaper articles. You'd be better off searching a specialized database that focuses on the format, and these are usually proprietary.

✦ Someone's telephone number or email address. Certain services focus specifically on this type of information.

✦ Maps. There are special databases for maps, too.

Browsing the World Wide Web: Using Directories

There are two basic ways to find information on the World Wide Web: You can browse directories by subject, or you can search by keyword in search engines. In this section, we'll focus on browsing directories; we'll cover keyword searching in search engines later in the chapter. While search engine databases are created by computer programs, directories are created and maintained by people. Directories don't cover the entire Web. In fact, directories are very small collections of resources, compared with the huge databases that search engines employ.

Browsing directories can be a very effective way to find the resources you need, especially if you need general information on a subject, such as recycling. If you are at the beginning of your research, or if you are searching for an overview of the topic at hand, it may also be helpful to use a directory. Many of the major search tools contain a directory and a search engine. You can try using both methods in one service. The directory part of the search engine is usually a subset of the entire database, and the sites listed in a directory are often evaluated, summarized, and given ratings. Some directories provide rudimentary search interfaces as well. Here are the most well-known directories on the World Wide Web:

✦ Galaxy
http://www.galaxy.com

✦ LookSmart
http://www.looksmart.com

✦ Open Directory Project
http://dmoz.org

✦ Yahoo! Directory
http://dir.yahoo.com

Directories, or subject catalogs, are topical lists of selected Web resources that are arranged in a hierarchical way. By *hierarchical,* we mean that the ***subject categories*** are arranged from broadest to most specific. For example, the following is a ***hierarchy:***

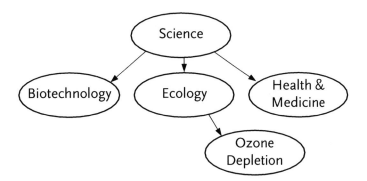

In this example, *Ecology* is a subcategory of *Science,* and *Ozone Depletion* is a subcategory of *Ecology.*

In a hypertext environment, such as the World Wide Web, browsing from one subject to a more detailed part of that subject is quite simple. We click on **Science**, which is the ***top-level category*** or heading, and the computer screen fills with a list of subject categories that are narrower than *Science.* This might include, for example, *Biotechnology,* or *Health & Medicine,* or, in our case, *Ecology.*

When we click on **Ecology**, the screen fills with even more subject categories, and we choose the subject we want, which is *Ozone Depletion.* In this case, the hierarchy ends here. After we choose **Ozone Depletion**, the screen fills in with a list of Web pages that we can now choose by clicking on their titles. This process is referred to as a ***structured browse***.

Some hierarchies have several levels, whereas others have only two. It depends on the directory you are using and the subject you are researching. The major directories do not use the same subject categories. In one directory, the term may be *Environment;* in another, the term may be *Ecology.*

To illustrate the process of browsing in a detailed way, let's try an activity

✦ T I P ! Remember that the Web is always changing and that your results may differ from those shown here. Don't let this confuse you. The activities demonstrate fundamental skills. These skills don't change, even though what you see when you do this activity may look different.

that will take you through a sample research problem in a different directory. We'll show you how easy it is to move from a broad subject category to a more specific one. We'll illustrate why browsing for information using directories can be a very satisfying way to do research on the Web. In this activity, as in all the activities in the book, we'll give you a numbered list of each of the steps to follow and include the results you would have seen at the time this book was written.

 ACTIVITY

3.1   USING A DIRECTORY TO BROWSE FOR INFORMATION

OVERVIEW

In this activity, we'll access the Open Directory Project, **http://dmoz.org**, to locate resources on opera. The Open Directory Project depends on volunteer editors who add and review resources and maintain subject categories. These editors may create new subcategories and move Web pages and sites from one category to another.

We'll follow these steps:

1. Go to the home page for the Open Directory Project.

2. Browse the Open Directory.

3. Add a Web page to your list of favorites.

Don't forget to practice using the **Back** and **Forward** buttons to avoid losing your place.

DETAILS

1   Go to the home page for the Open Directory Project.

We are assuming that your browser is already open.

✧ Do It!   Point to the address box and click the (left) mouse button.

The URL of the current Web page will change color. Now you can type in the URL for the Open Directory Project.

✧ Do It!   Type **http://dmoz.org** in the address box and press **Enter**.

2   Browse the Open Directory.

Take a look at the list of subjects listed on the Open Directory home page, as shown in Figure 3.1.

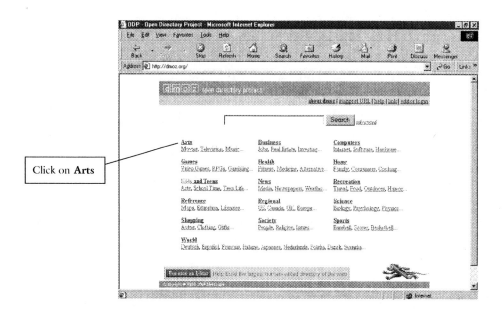

Figure 3.1—The Open Directory Project

To access resources in the Open Directory, you need to click on a top-level category. This will bring to your screen all kinds of resources available in that subject area. Since the types of resources we're looking for focus on opera, we need to find a subject category that would be related to this. A logical choice is **Arts**, since opera is a part of the art of music. Follow these steps:

✦ Do It!   Click on **Arts**, as shown in Figure 3.1.

After the screen fills, you'll see more detailed subject categories, or *subcategories*, appear on your screen. These are links to resources that have been placed in the general Arts category. See Figure 3.2.

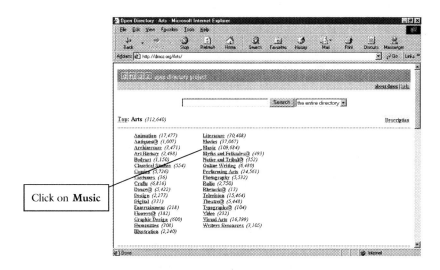

Figure 3.2—Subcategories Listed Under Arts in the Open Directory Project

To retrieve opera Web sites, you'll need to click on a more specific subject category. The most logical one is **Music**.

✦ Do It!   Click on **Music**, as shown in Figure 3.2.

After the screen fills, note that the second subcategory listed (at the top of the page) is called **Styles**, as shown in Figure 3.3. There are many other subcategories listed as well, but it seems like **Styles** might be the most appropriate hyperlink to choose.

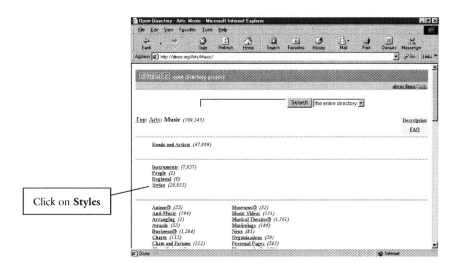

Figure 3.3—Subcategories of Music in the Open Directory Project

✦ Do It!　Click on **Styles**, as shown in Figure 3.3.

Figure 3.3 shows some of the music styles Web sites listed in the Open Directory. Note that opera is on the list.

✦ Do It!　Click on **Opera**, as shown in Figure 3.4.

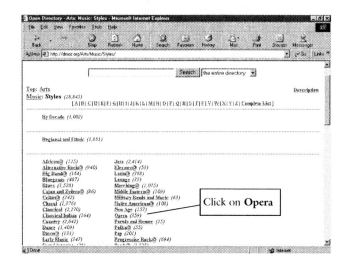

Figure 3.4—List of Resources in the Styles Subcategory

From this list of resources, find one that looks interesting, and click on the hyperlink.

3　Add a Web page to your list of favorites.

After you've found a Web page or Web site that looks useful, you may want to return to it again someday. To make sure you don't lose it, you can put it in your favorites list.

✦ Do It!　With the Web page or Web site on your screen, click on **Favorites** in the location toolbar and select **Add Favorite**.

The title of the URL is automatically added to your favorites list. You can access the Web page at a later date by clicking on the title in your list.

✦ T I P !　Several times throughout this book we'll be asking you to save the URL locations of valuable Web pages to your favorites list. You'll need to know how to delete these hyperlinks, especially if you're using a public computer. Follow these steps:

✦ Click on **Favorites** (located in Standard Buttons toolbar).

✦ Your favorites will appear on the left of your screen. Place your mouse over the favorite you want to delete and **click with the right button on your mouse**.

✦ From the menu that appears, choose **Delete**.

See Chapter 2 for more information about favorites.

END OF ACTIVITY 3.1

In this activity, we looked for an opera resource by browsing a directory. In the Open Directory Project, we started out by clicking on the top-level category **Arts**, then we selected the subcategory **Music**, then **Styles**, and finally, **Opera**, to take us to our desired location. There, we found a list of several relevant resources. Each directory on the World Wide Web will approach a subject differently. For example, in Yahoo!, **http://dir.yahoo.com**, resources on opera would be found using a different subject hierarchy. In Yahoo!, the hierarchy looks like this:

Arts & Humanities – Performing Arts – Opera

Or this:

Entertainment – Music – Genres – Classical - Opera

Browsing Versus Searching a Directory

It may be helpful to think of browsing a directory on the Web like going through subjects in a card catalog. You may find exactly what you are looking for by browsing through many pages or cards filled with information, but then again, you may not. You may miss some related information because your subject may appear in many different categories. For example, opera resources appear in a subcategory of the Music category in the Open Directory Project, but there are also opera resources in a subcategory of the Performing Arts section. You have to be careful about the direction in which you are going when you do a structured browse. Many directories have simple keyword-searching ability for just this reason. Keyword searching was created to help people find information without having to know ahead of time the category in which the information lies. Keyword searching helps us find Web information more quickly, just as computerized library catalogs help us find books more quickly.

If you don't want to take the time to browse categories in a directory, you may want to search the directory by keyword. Or you can do both. It is a good idea to use different tactics when looking for something on the Web. Keep in mind, however, that when you search most directories by keyword, you will find Web pages that have the word or words that you are searching for in their titles, annotations, or URLs, not in the Web pages themselves. In the next section, which focuses on virtual libraries, we'll explain how to search a directory using keywords.

Finding Information Gems in Virtual Libraries

Virtual libraries are directories that contain collections of resources that librarians or other information specialists have carefully chosen and organized in a logical way. The resources you find in a virtual library have been selected and placed there because of their excellence and usefulness. The Web pages included are usually evaluated by someone knowledgeable in that field. Typically, virtual libraries provide an organizational hierarchy with subject categories to facilitate browsing. Most include query interfaces in order to perform simple searches. Virtual libraries are great places to begin your research.

Here are several of the best-known virtual libraries on the Web:

✦ Academic Info: Your Gateway to Quality Educational Resources
   http://www.academicinfo.net

✦ Infomine
   http://infomine.ucr.edu

◆ Internet Public Library
   http://www.ipl.org

◆ Librarians' Index to the Internet
   http://lii.org

◆ Library Spot
   http://libraryspot.com

◆ Resource Discovery Network
   http://www.rdn.ac.uk

The main difference between virtual libraries and the directories we discussed earlier in the chapter is that virtual libraries are much smaller because the resources included are selected very carefully. The people who organize virtual libraries are usually on the lookout for three major types of information: subject guides, reference works, and specialized databases.

Subject Guides

A *subject guide* is a Web resource devoted to including hyperlinks to most, if not all, Web pages on a particular subject. For example, a resource devoted to listing Web pages on environmental ethics is a subject guide (see Figure 3.5).

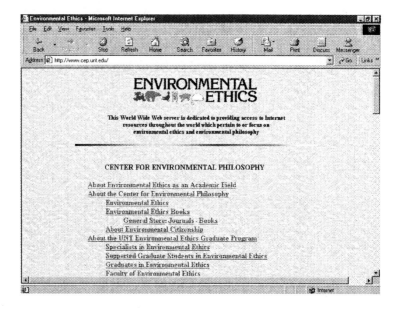

Figure 3.5—Subject Guide on Environmental Ethics (**http://www.cep.unt.edu**)

Reference Works

Another common type of resource collected by virtual libraries is a reference work. A *reference work* is a full-text document with self-contained information. In other words, it doesn't necessarily contain hyperlinks to other resources.

A reference work on the World Wide Web is very similar to its print counterpart. A dictionary on the Web would look very much like a dictionary on a reference shelf. The only difference is that it would allow you to move around the document using hyperlinks instead of turning pages and looking in the index for related topics. There are encyclopedias, handbooks, dictionaries, directories, and many other types of reference works on the World Wide Web. Virtual libraries are interested in including these types of works in their directories. Figure 3.6 pictures a reference work—the U.S. Postal Service's "Zip Code Lookup and Address Information."

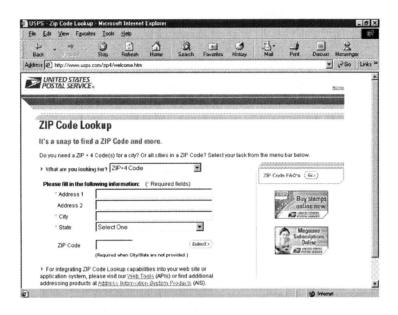

Figure 3.6—U.S. Postal Service's "Zip Code Lookup and Address Information"

(**http://www.usps.gov/ncsc/lookups/lookups.html**)

Specialized Databases

Virtual libraries can be useful for finding *specialized databases* as well. A specialized database is an index that catalogs certain material, such as patent information, medical journal article citations, company financial data, court decisions, and so forth. Specialized databases can usually be searched by keyword. We'll discuss them in detail in Chapter 5. Figure 3.7 shows a specialized database that covers medical literature—PubMed, a database of Medline citations provided by the National Library of Medicine.

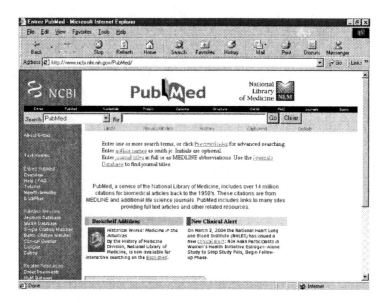

Figure 3.7—PubMed (**http://www.ncbi.nlm.nih.gov/PubMed/**)

Now that you know what types of information are collected in virtual libraries, we'll show you how to find these information gems. Let's do an activity to illustrate how useful virtual libraries can be for your research.

ACTIVITY

3.2   FINDING RESOURCES IN A VIRTUAL LIBRARY

OVERVIEW

Let's say you want to know the population of Egypt. We will find the answer by using the Internet Public Library (IPL), a virtual library maintained by librarians at the University of Michigan.

The IPL is organized much like a traditional library. It has a reference section, a youth section, and many others. If you can't find what you're looking for, you can submit the question to a real librarian who will email the answer back to you. You can browse the IPL or search its contents. Browsing is sometimes the easiest way to find information, however, because the search tool doesn't search the contents of the resources; only the titles of the resources and annotations attached to them are searched.

In this activity, we'll first browse the IPL by subject. Because we're trying to find an answer to a reference question, we'll open the Reference Collection. Then we'll go to the Geography section, as the population of Egypt would likely be found in a geographic resource. We'll also open a reference work and look for the statistic we want. After this, we'll show how to perform a keyword search in order to demonstrate the difference between searching and browsing in the IPL.

We'll follow these steps:

1.   Go to the home page for the Internet Public Library.

2.   Browse the IPL's directory

3. Open the *Information Please Almanac.*

4. Find the population of Egypt.

5. Search the IPL.

6. Browse the results of the search.

You'll see how quickly we can find not only the population of Egypt, but also other current information about that country. Let's get started!

DETAILS

1 Go to the home page for the Internet Public Library. (We're assuming your Web browser is already started.)

✦ Do It! Use the mouse to point to the address bar and click the (left) mouse button.

The URL of the current Web page will change color. Now you can type in the URL for the Internet Public Library.

✦ Do It! Type **http://www.ipl.org** in the address box and press **Enter**.

2 Browse the IPL's directory.

✦ Do It! Click on **Almanacs** under the Ready Reference heading, as shown in Figure 3.8.

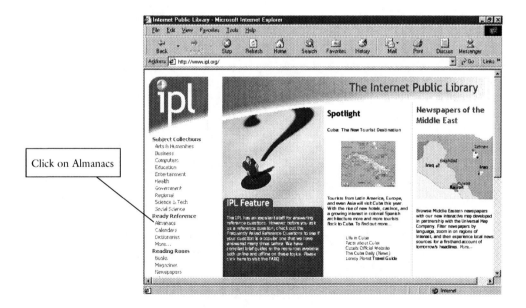

Figure 3.8—The Internet Public Library

Scroll down the list of almanacs to find the most appropriate source that would contain the answer to this question. By reading the annotations attached to the reference sources, we determine that the *Information Please Almanac* would be a good choice because almanacs typically provide facts and statistics for the world's nations.

3 Open the *Information Please Almanac.*

✦ Do It!   Click on **Information Please Almanac** as shown in Figure 3.9.

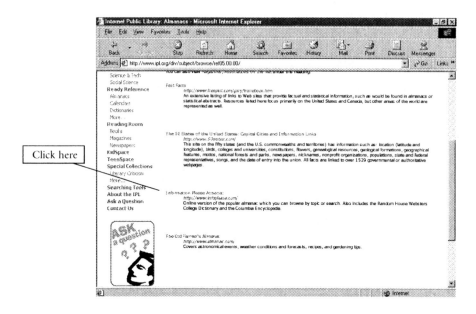

Figure 3.9—Almanacs Listed in the Internet Public Library

Figure 3.10 shows the home page for the **Information Please Almanac.**

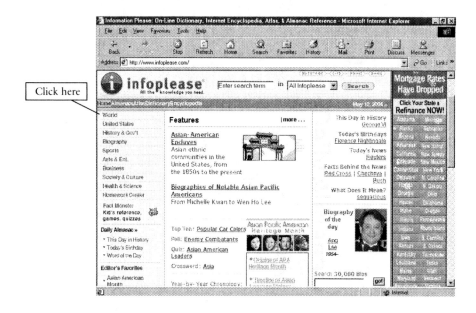

Figure 3.10—The Information Please Almanac

4 Find the population of Egypt.

✦ Do It!   Click on **World**, as shown in Figure 3.10.

✦ Do It!   Choose **World Statistics** from the list of links.

✦ Do It!   Now click on **Population Statistics.**

✦ Do It!   Finally, click on **Area and Population of Countries.**

This should take you to the information you need, as shown in Figure 3.11.

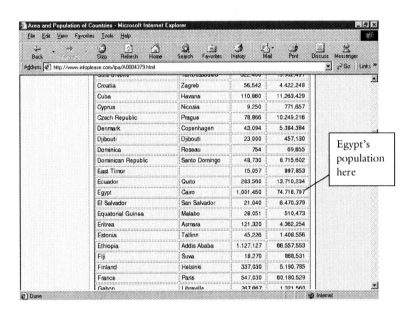

Figure 3.11—Demographic Information for Egypt from the Information Please Almanac

5   Search the IPL.

Now we'll show you how to search the Internet Public Library. Return to IPL's Almanacs page by clicking the **Back** icon until you are at this page. You will see a search form at the top of the page. We're going to type in the word **Egypt**.

✦ Do It!   Type in the word **egypt** (this search tool is not case-sensitive) in the form provided. Make sure that the pull-down menu next to the search button is set to "All of the IPL." Click **Search**.

The search tool responds with some Web pages, but none of them is from the *Information Please Almanac*.

✦ Do It!   Now try typing in **population**, as shown in Figure 3.12. Make sure the pull-down menu next to the Search button is set to **This Collection** and click **Search**.

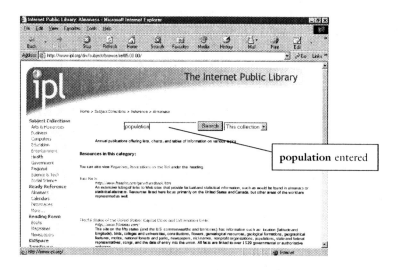

Figure 3.12—Searching the Reference Collection

6 Browse the results of the search.

To see the entire list of resources, you'll need to click on **View Results in Subject Collections**. As you move down the list, you'll notice several other resources that might help answer the question about Egypt's population. Note the *Information Please Almanac* isn't on this list because the word *population* doesn't appear in the title or the annotation.

END OF ACTIVITY 3.2

You can see from the preceding example that sometimes it is better to browse than to search a directory or virtual library. The search tool in the Internet Public Library doesn't find words that are in the body of the Web pages. The words indexed are in the Web pages' titles, their URLs, and their annotations. Because the word *Egypt* didn't appear in the title, URL, or annotation of the *Information Please Almanac,* the search tool didn't locate it. We also pointed out that searching for the word *population* didn't bring up the *Information Please Almanac.*

Directories can be useful if you have a broad subject and aren't sure how to narrow down the search. They are also helpful if you want to get a general idea about existing resources that will help you focus your topic. By browsing a directory in the first activity, we quickly found Web pages that focused on opera music. Virtual libraries are especially useful as starting points for research and evaluated information on a particular topic or as places to go for answers to quick reference questions, as we discovered in Activity 3.2.

But if you want to zero in quickly on Web pages that are specifically related to your topic, or if your topic is multifaceted or extremely detailed, or if you are sure about the keywords you are going to use, a search engine is what you need. In the following sections, we'll explore search engines and give a brief overview of the most common keyword search features.

Searching the World Wide Web: Using Search Engines

Search engines are tools that use computer programs called *spiders* or *robots* that go out on the Internet and locate hyperlinks that are available to the public. These spiders or robots load these resources in a database, which you can then search by using a search engine. These programs were created because the number of Internet documents increases so rapidly that people are unable to keep up with indexing them manually. Each of the major search engines attempts to do the same thing—namely, index as much of the entire Web as possible—so they handle a huge amount of data.

There are advantages to computer-generated databases. They are frequently updated, give access to very large collections, and provide the most comprehensive search results. If you are looking for a specific concept or phrase, a search engine is the best place to start. And you would be smart to look in more than one, because each engine gives different results.

Here are the major search engines:

◆ AlltheWeb
   http://www.alltheweb.com

◆ AltaVista
   http:// altavista.com

◆ Google
   http://www.google.com

◆ Lycos
   http://www.lycos.com

◆ MSN
   http://msn.com

◆ Teoma
   http://teoma.com

◆ Yahoo!
   http://www.yahoo.com

✦ F Y I   **Finding search engines and other databases on the World Wide Web.**

If you want to look for other search tools on the World Wide Web, or want to keep up to date with the new ones that have been added, there are two excellent places to go:

   ◆ Proteus Internet Search
      http://www.thrall. org/proteus.html

   ◆ Search Engine Watch
      http://www. searchenginewatch.com

Search Engine Similarities

All of the major search engines are similar in that you enter keywords, phrases, or proper names in a *search form*. After you click on **Search, Submit, Seek,** or some other command button, the database returns a collection of hyperlinks to your screen.

The database usually lists them according to their *relevance* to the keyword(s) you typed in, from most to least relevant. Search engines determine relevance in different ways. Generally, they base this determination on how many times the search terms appear in the document. Other search tools (Google, for example) rank results by the number of other Web pages that link to them, or by the most popular sites that others have chosen in the past (for example, Teoma).

All search engines have online help to acquaint you with their search options. Two common search options that most search engines support are *Boolean searching* and *phrase searching*. We will briefly discuss these two options below. Then, in Chapter 4, "Search Strategies for Search Engines," we will cover these and other search options, which are available on many (but not all) search engines, including *relevancy ranking, field searching, truncation searching,* and *proximity searching.*

Boolean Operators

The Boolean operators are AND, OR, and NOT.

✦ The use of AND placed between keywords in your *search expression* will narrow the search results.

For example, *hiking AND camping* would narrow your search so that you would receive only those sites that have both the words *hiking* and *camping* in them.

hiking AND camping

Placing an OR between keywords broadens your search results. For example, *hiking OR camping* would retrieve those sites that have either the word *hiking* or the word *camping* in them.

hiking OR camping

✦ The NOT operator will also narrow the search.

For example, *hiking NOT camping* would narrow your search so you would get all hiking that did not include camping.

hiking NOT camping

✦ If nothing is typed between two words, the following different relationships are possible:

✦ The two words are connected by AND

✦ The two words are connected by OR

✦ The two words will be searched as a phrase

These are what we refer to as *default settings*. The search engine's help pages should explain the relationship. In order to override the default settings, you'd have to type the desired Boolean operator between the words.

Phrase Searching

Searching by phrase guarantees that the words you type in will appear adjacent to each other, in the order you typed them.

Let's say you are searching for information on global warming. If you typed in the two words *global warming* separated by a space, the system you're using may assume that you are in effect saying *global AND warming,* or in some cases (depending on the search engine), *global OR warming*. In the last case, your search results would not be very precise because the words *global* and *warming* could appear separately from each other throughout the document.

global AND warming   global OR warming

Most search engines support phrase searching, requiring the use of double quotation marks around the phrase. We would type **global warming** in our example. There are some search tools that default to phrase searching when words are typed with no Boolean operator between them. To determine how the search tool handles phrases, always check the tool's help section.

Search Engine Differences

The major search engines differ in the following ways:

◆ Size of the index

◆ Search options (many search engines support the same options but require you to use different *syntax* in order to initiate them)

◆ Update frequency

◆ Ranking of the search results

◆ Special features such as the ability to search for news, newsgroups, images, and so forth

It is important to know these differences because in order to do an exhaustive search of the World Wide Web, you must be familiar with the different search tools. You cannot rely on a single search engine to satisfy every query.

At this point, it may be helpful to do a couple of activities to illustrate how search engines work. The first activity will focus on Boolean searching, and the second will demonstrate phrase searching.

ACTIVITY

3.3   USING BOOLEAN SEARCH OPERATORS

OVERVIEW

Let's try to find Web pages on aid to Sudanese refugees. We'll use the search engine AlltheWeb. To start, we will type in the keywords we want the Web pages to include. We'll examine the results and then check the help page to find out how AlltheWeb handles advanced search options. Then we'll do the search again using Boolean operators. We'll note how our search results were narrowed in size and how the contents of the pages were more relevant.

1.   Go to the home page for AlltheWeb.

2.   Type in keywords and start the search.

3.   Examine the search results.

4.   Consult search help.

5.   Create a Boolean search expression.

6.   Examine the results.

Ready? Let's start the engine!

DETAILS

1   Go to the home page for AlltheWeb. (We're assuming your Web browser is already started.)

◆ Do It!   Use the mouse to point to the address box and click the (left) mouse button.

The URL of the current Web page will change color. Now you can type in the URL for AlltheWeb.

✦ Do It!   Type **http://alltheweb.com** in the address box and press **Enter**.

2   Type in keywords and start the search.

✦ Do It!   Type the keywords **sudanese refugees aid** in the search form next to **Search**.

✦ Do It!   Now click on the **Search** button. Figure 3.13 shows the keywords typed in.

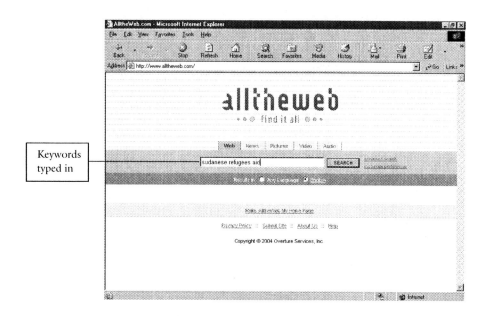

Figure 3.13—AlltheWeb Home Page with Keywords Typed In

3   Examine the search results.

Notice the large number of hyperlinks retrieved by AlltheWeb. They are listed according to their relevance to the search query, from most relevant to least relevant, as shown in Figure 3.14. After scrolling down through some of the Web pages retrieved by this search, we start to think of other possibilities. What if there are some useful Web pages that use the word *relief* instead of *aid*? How would we construct a search so we would get Web pages that included the words *Sudanese* and *refugees* and *relief* or *aid*? We're identifying the need to use Boolean operators, and we need to know whether AlltheWeb supports Boolean searching. We could most easily find out whether AlltheWeb supports Boolean searching by accessing its online help.

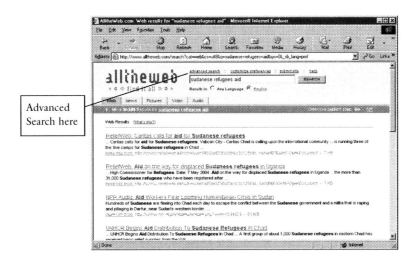

Advanced
Search here

Figure 3.14—Search Results in AlltheWeb

4 Consult search help.

First, access the Advanced Search mode.

✦ Do It!   Click on **Advanced Search**.

✦ Do It!   Click on **see examples**, next to the Boolean search box.

We discover that AlltheWeb does support Boolean searching. We can use AND, OR, and NOT (the Boolean operators need not be capitalized). Although it isn't specifically stated in the search help, we know that if there are ANDs and ORs in one search statement, then parentheses must be used around the terms connected by OR to guarantee good search results.

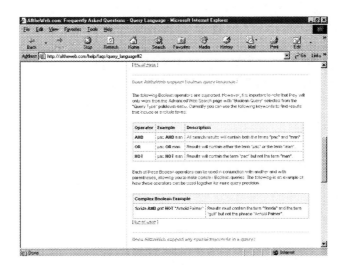

Figure 3.15—AlltheWeb Search Help

Click on **Back,** to return to the advanced search page.

You should now be back on the AlltheWeb advanced search page.

5   Create a Boolean search expression.

✦ Do It!   Make sure that the radio button next to **Boolean** is checked.

✦ Do It!   Type **sudanese AND refugees AND (relief OR aid)** as shown in Figure 3.16. Remember to capitalize the ANDs and the OR.

This search expression will retrieve hyperlinks to those sites that have the words *Sudanese* AND *refugees* (must have both words) AND *relief* OR *aid* (must have either word).

✦ Do It!   Click on **Search.**

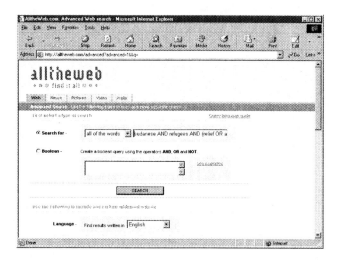

Figure 3.16—Boolean Searching in AlltheWeb

6   Examine the results.

Note that the results may include either or both of the words *relief* and *aid* and must include both the words Sudanese and refugees. This search modification gave us more results than the first search did. Using the OR connector always expands search results.

That's all there is to it!

END OF ACTIVITY 3.3

In the last activity, we illustrated the importance of looking at a search engine's online help pages. This caused us to type in the search expression that gave us the most precise and relevant results. In the following activity, we'll use another search engine to show the phrase-searching feature. We will search for the symptoms of post-traumatic stress disorder by using the search engine Google, **http://www.google.com**.

3.4   USING PHRASE SEARCHING TO FIND INFORMATION

OVERVIEW

In this activity, we will access Google and look at the online help before we begin searching. We will type in the phrase *post-traumatic stress disorder,* start the search, and then narrow the results to those that have the term *symptoms* included. We'll use the syntax that is particular to Google, and we will examine the results. We'll have you bookmark the best site we find so that you can start building your own reference library. We'll follow these steps:

1. Go to the home page for Google.

2. Read the help pages in Google.

3. Use the search form provided and type in a search expression.

4. Narrow the results by adding another term.

5. Examine the results and click on a hyperlink that appears to have the information you need.

6. Add the Web page to your favorites list.

Once you see how easy it is to find an answer to a reference question on the World Wide Web, you will see how useful the Web can be in providing useful, reliable information. After adding the Web page that provides the answer to your favorites list, you'll be able to flip to the information whenever you need it in just a few seconds. Let's go find it!

DETAILS

1   Go to the home page for Google. (We assume your browser is already open.)

✦ Do It!   Use the mouse to point to the address field and click the (left) mouse button.

The URL of the current Web page will change color. Now you can type in the URL for Google.

✦ Do It!   Type **http://www.google.com** in the address box and press Enter.

2   Read the help pages in Google.

✦ Do It!   Click on **Advanced Search**, as shown in Figure 3.17.

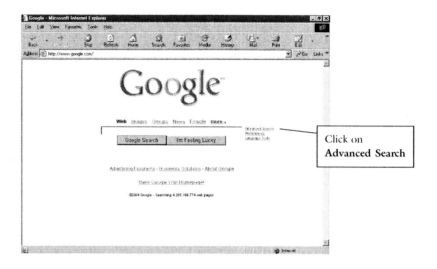

Figure 3.17—Google Home Page

✦ Do It!   After the window fills, click on **Advanced Search Tips**.

Your screen should look like the one in Figure 3.18.

Notice that in Google, you can place quotation marks before the first word and after the last word in the phrase you are searching for. This will ensure that the words in the phrase appear together. Note that you should also put a + before the phrase if any of the words in the phrase are very common words that may not be indexed by Google, for example, *of*, *about*, *to*, and others.

Figure 3.18—Phrase Searches from Google Search Help

3   Use the search form provided and type in a search expression.

✦ Do It!   Scroll up to the top of the page and click on the **Google icon**.

✦ Do It! Type the search expression **"post-traumatic stress disorder"** in the search form provided and click on **Google Search**, as shown in Figure 3.19.

Figure 3.19—Phrase Searching in Google

4 Search the results by adding another term.

Google provides the feature of being able to search only the results of your original search. This makes it easy for you to narrow your results. For example, in this activity, an appropriate word to add to our search expression might be *symptoms*. Let's try combining this word with the search results.

✦ Do It! Scroll down to the bottom of the first page of search results. You'll see a search form with the original search inserted. There is also a link under the form **Google** entitled **Search within results**. You'll need to click on this link.

✦ Do It! Click on **Search within results**, as shown in Figure 3.20.

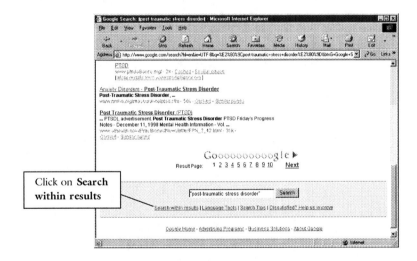

Figure 3.20—How to Search Within Results in Google

Figure 3.21 shows the Search within results form.

✦ Do It! Type **symptoms** in the search form provided.

✦ Do It! Click on **Search within results**.

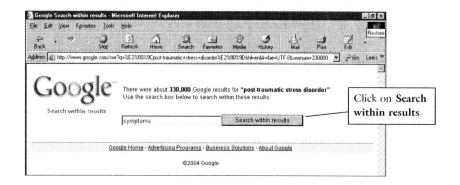

Figure 3.21—Google's Search Within Results Form

5 Examine the results and click on a hyperlink that appears to have the information you need.

Your screen should look similar to the one pictured in Figure 3.22. At a quick glance, it appears that there are several relevant Web pages listed. The one that appeals to us the most is a page provided by the **National Center for Post-Traumatic Stress Disorder** entitled **What is Post-Traumatic Stress Disorder?**. If this title appears in your results, go ahead and open it. If not, you can open another page that appears relevant to the search expression.

✦ Do It! Click on a relevant Web page (in our case, **What is Post-Traumatic Stress Disorder**), as shown in Figure 3.22.

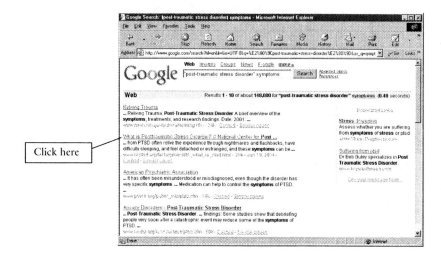

Figure 3.22—Results of Modified Search in Google

A portion of this Web page is shown in Figure 3.23. If you scroll down the page a bit, there is a discussion about the symptoms of post-traumatic stress disorder.

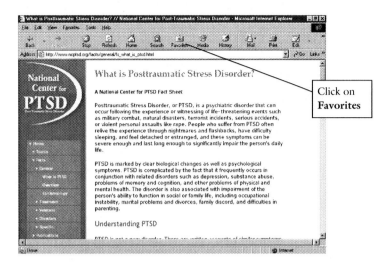

Figure 3.23—Post-traumatic Stress Disorder Information

6　Add the Web page to your Favorites list.

After finding this informative Web page, you may want to locate it again quickly, so let's put it in your favorites list.

✦ Do It!　Point your mouse to **Favorites** in the location toolbar and click, as shown in Figure 3.23. Select **Add to Favorites** from the pull-down menu. Automatically, the title of the URL is added to your list. You can access this Web site later by clicking on the title in your list.

END OF ACTIVITY 3.4

In this activity, we focused on the phrase-searching feature. Most search engines support this feature. You can see how important it is. Imagine if we were only able to search for post-traumatic stress disorder without specifying that the words appear next to each other in that order. We might get pages that had the word *post-traumatic* in the first paragraph and *stress* in the last paragraph, with no relationship between the words. In Chapter 4, we'll discuss this and other search features in more detail.

In the next section, we'll talk about using meta-search tools. These resources allow you to use several search engine databases simultaneously.

Using Several Search Engines Simultaneously: Meta-search Tools

We have mentioned the importance of looking in more than one search engine when trying to find relevant Web pages. Each search engine varies in size, indexing structure, update frequency, and search options. It can be confusing and time-consuming to do your search in several databases, especially if you have to keep track of all of their differences.

To solve some of these problems, database providers have come up with meta-search tools. If meta-search tools allow you to use several search engines simultaneously, they are often called *parallel search tools* or *unified search interfaces*. Instead of building their own databases, meta-search tools use the major search engines and directories that already exist on the Internet and provide the user with search forms or interfaces for submitting queries to these search tools. Simply by submitting a query, the meta-search tool collects the most relevant sites in each database and sends them to the screen. Here are the most popular meta-search tools:

- ✦ Proteus Internet Search
  http://www.thrall.org/proteus.html

- ✦ Dogpile
  http://www.dogpile.com

- ✦ Ixquick
  http://ixquick.com

- ✦ MetaCrawler
  http://www.metacrawler.com

- ✦ ProFusion
  http://profusion.com

- ✦ Search.com
  http://www.search.com

- ✦ Vivisimo
  http://vivisimo.com

Proteus Internet Search is a service that provides access to several major search engines and some specialized databases. It can be referred to as an *all-in-one search tool* because it allows you to search one database at a time. With Proteus, a search expression may be used in a particular search tool and reused in another one. See an example of a Proteus Internet Search in Figure 3.24.

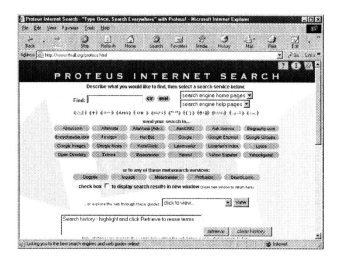

Figure 3.24—Proteus Internet Search Home Page

Proteus also includes direct links to the search tools' help pages. This way, you can see which search features you'll need to include in the search expression. Below the search form are Boolean and implied Boolean operators, quotes for phrases, parentheses, and other possible syntax. Unlike Proteus, most of the meta-search tools listed won't allow you to use each individual search engine's capabilities to their fullest because you will be using a search interface to search several databases at once. For this reason, simple searches work best.

It can be interesting to do a search in one of these meta-search tools and to notice what different hyperlinks the various search engines return to you. What is most relevant in one database is not considered as relevant in another. The following example will illustrate how a meta-search tool performs a search in several databases at once. We'll discover how and when these tools can be useful.

ACTIVITY

3.5 USING A META-SEARCH TOOL TO FIND INFORMATION

OVERVIEW

We'll be using ixquick, a meta-search tool that not only includes many major Web search indexes and directories, but also indexes news, MP3, and image databases. Some of the search tools ixquick searches are AltaVista, Lycos, the Open Directory Project, and Yahoo!

In this activity, we'll try to find information on the 2000 U.S. Presidential election results in Florida. We want to keep the search simple because we will be searching several databases at once, and meta-search engines have difficulty performing complicated searches in more than one database at a time. We will be typing in the words *florida presidential election 2000*. We will take the following steps:

1. Go to the home page for ixquick.

2. Type the search expression in the search form.

3. Follow some of the hyperlinks returned by the databases.

Let's find out how to use ixquick!

DETAILS

1 Go to the home page for ixquick.

✦ Do It! Use the mouse to point to the address box and click the (left) mouse button.

The URL of the current Web page will change color. Now you can type in the URL for ixquick.

✦ Do It! Type **http://ixquick.com** in the address box and press **Enter**. Your window should look like the one pictured in Figure 3.25.

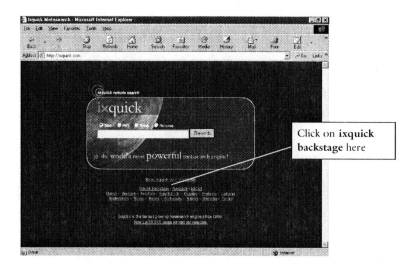

Figure 3.25—ixquick Home Page

2 Access the help pages and type a search expression in the search form.

Before typing a search expression, it's always a good idea to check the help pages of the tool you're using. The only hyperlink on ixquick's home page that might lead us to help is ixquick backstage, located below the search form.

✦ Do It!   Click on **ixquick backstage**, as shown in Figure 3.25.

✦ Do It!   Click on **Hints and Help** in the left frame, then click on **How to Improve Your Search.**

By reading the help information, we find that you care able to use quotes, parentheses and other search features. However, because not all search tools support each feature, the search will be forwarded only to those databases that support the features used in your search expression.

✦ Do It!   Click on the **ixquick** icon to return to the home page.

✦ Do It!   Type the following keywords in the search form: **florida presidential election 2000**.

✦ Do It!   Click on **Search**.

Your window should look similar to the one in Figure 3.26.

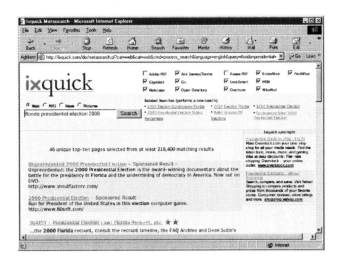

Figure 3.26—ixquick Search Results

3 Follow some of the hyperlinks returned by the databases.

After you submit your search expression to ixquick, the search engine selects unique Web pages that appeared in the top pages of the search engines and directories it searched. In this example, there were 42 unique top-ten Web pages selected from over 200,000 results, as shown in Figure 3.26. You may notice that your search brought back results from different databases. After looking at the results, we decide that there are several promising ones on the list. If this were an actual research project, you'd probably want to add the most useful pages to your list of favorites.

END OF ACTIVITY 3.5

In this activity, we used ixquick. Meta-search tools such as this one can save you time because you can use several search engines or directory databases at once. A major drawback of using a meta-search tool is that you can't use the individual databases to their fullest capabilities because the tool has to search more than one database at a time using a search query mechanism that will satisfy all of them.

Content Issues: Pornography, Free Speech, Censorship, and Filtering

Because any individual or organization can publish information on the Internet easily without editorial and other content control, you can expect to come across material that mirrors the wide range of preferences and interests of people throughout the world. A small portion of the material found may be offensive to some people or inappropriate for children. Sexually explicit or pornographic material may exist as text, pictures, or chat and can be accessed deliberately or sometimes unintentionally. However, seldom does one encounter explicit material in a casual way—usually there is an introductory page that warns the user that the material linked to it is for adult viewing only. Most pornographic sites also require a fee for access. The focus of the debate about this so-called "cyberporn" has been whether the material should be readily available to children and whether it's appropriate to pass laws that restrict the content of the Internet.

Free Speech vs. Censorship

The debate regarding civil liberties, free speech, and sexually explicit material led to the United States Congress approving and the President of the United States signing legislation called the *Communications Decency Act of 1996*. On June 27, 1997, in Reno vs. the American Civil Liberties Union, the U.S. Supreme Court ruled that this act abridged the freedom of speech that is protected by the First Amendment. The court stated, "The interest in encouraging freedom of expression in a democratic society outweighs any theoretical but unproven benefit of censorship." You can read this opinion by going to **http://supct.law.cornell.edu/supct/html/96-511.ZO.html**. This opinion held that the Internet should not be viewed as a broadcast medium like television or radio but as a medium in which individuals are guaranteed free speech.

Filtering and Blocking Devices

Parents and others concerned about what children may be viewing on the Web can install computer programs that restrict access to certain material. These programs are referred to as *filters* or *blocking devices*. These programs control access to information in a number of possible ways.

While filters may be helpful, keep in mind that they may screen some sites with useful material. For example, when using filters, Web pages for gay teens, safe sex information, or information about drug legalization or other controversial issues may not appear in the results list because certain words have been filtered out and therefore made inaccessible. Certain medical topics such as breast cancer may also be avoided because the words that describe these medical conditions and body parts may be on the filter list. It is for this reason that the American Library Association has stated in "Access to Electronic Information, Services, and Networks: An Interpretation of the Library Bill of Rights," **http://www.ala.org/alaorg/oif/electacc.html**, that by using filters, a library would be restricting access to information when it's a library's role to provide access to information and let users choose what they want to read, hear, or see. Opponents of this view say that libraries don't generally collect pornography in book or magazine form, so why should they allow this material to be accessed on the Internet? In the future, filtering or blocking software may be developed that could be turned on or off, so that individuals could choose whether they want restrictions placed on their searches.

Summary

The World Wide Web is an immense collection of valuable information generated by such organizations as universities, corporations, hospitals, associations, and government agencies. Most countries and several languages are represented on the Web. In addition to this, hundreds of thousands of individuals, such as scholars, students, doctors, librarians, teachers, and virtually anyone who wants to contribute to this vast accumulation of resources, are adding their home pages to the Web every day, all over the world.

Finding information on the World Wide Web is becoming easier all the time. There are two basic ways to accomplish it: You can either browse or search directories, or you can search by keyword in search engines. Browsing directories can be a very effective way to find the resources you need, especially if you're sure of the general information you're seeking. Directories index neither all of the pages in the World Wide Web nor all of the words that appear in the Web pages they catalog, however, so if you need specific information, a search engine is the tool you'll want to use. Search engine databases aim to cover as much of the Web as possible, and most of them index every word in each Web page.

A directory would be more likely used if we were looking for general information; for example, resources on the AIDS virus. Directories depend on human beings to create and maintain their collections, with virtual libraries being the most dependent on people. Virtual libraries are the best directories to go to for subject guides, reference works, and specialized databases. Virtual libraries are similar to traditional libraries, in that the information specialists who manage them select and catalog the Web pages that are included in their directories, much as librarians select and catalog materials that are included in their libraries.

The information found on the World Wide Web is diverse, and some of it may be offensive to some people or inappropriate for children. There are software programs that have been designed to block or filter Web sites that have certain words in them. There was a movement to force the government to control the content on the Web and the Internet. The U.S. Supreme Court ruled in 1997 that the Communications Decency Act of 1996 was unconstitutional in that it abridged the freedom of speech upheld by the First Amendment.

Selected Terms Introduced in This Chapter

all-in-one search tool	meta-search tool	spider
blocking device	parallel search tool	structured browse
Boolean searching	phrase searching	subcategory
browsing	reference work	subject catalog
Communications	relevance	subject category
Decency Act of 1996	robot	subject guide
directory	search engine	syntax
filter	search expression	top-level category
hierarchy	search form	unified search interface
keyword searching	specialized database	virtual library

Review Questions

Multiple Choice

1. A directory

   a. is a subject listing of Web resources.
   b. may be searchable by keyword.
   c. is also called a search engine.
   d. a and b
   e. a and c

2. Doing a structured browse means to

   a. use phrase searching.
   b. create a search expression.
   c. move from broad to specific subjects in a directory.
   d. move to a top-level directory category.

3. A searchable index that catalogs a specific type of material (such as medical articles or court decisions) is known as a

   a. subject guide.
   b. specialized database.
   c. reference source.
   d. multi-search tool.

4. Search engines use _____ to gather information from the Web.

   a. computer programs
   b. information professionals
   c. a and b
   d. none of the above

5. Search engine results are usually arranged

   a. alphabetically.
   b. by subject.
   c. hierarchically.
   d. by relevance or popularity.

6. A meta-search tool is one that

   a. allows you to search a specialized database.
   b. may use several search engines and directories at once.
   c. may give access to many search engine search forms from one page.
   d. a and c
   e. b and c

True or False

7.   T   F   A meta-search tool lets you search different search engines at one time.

8.   T   F   To find information on a very specialized topic, it's best to browse a directory.

9.   T   F   Spiders and robots are software programs associated with search engines.

10.   T   F   Many virtual libraries can be searched by keyword.

11.   T   F   Virtual libraries are usually larger than directories since they try to include all resources on a topic.

12.   T   F   A hierarchical directory is one where the subjects are arranged from broadest to most specific.

13.   T   F   One advantage of a search engine is that your results have been screened by real people.

Completion

14.   The two basic ways to find information on the Web are to _____ a directory or to use _____.

15.   Encyclopedias, dictionaries, and other full-text resources on the Web are known as _____.

16.   If we type the words **lakes and pollution** into a search engine, we are performing a(n) _____ search.

17.   If we type **"genetically engineered crops"** into a search engine, we are engaging in _____ searching.

18.   _____ refers to how closely a database entry matches a search request.

19.   The three major types of information included in virtual libraries are _____, _____, and _____.

20.   To find general or background information on a subject, a _____ might be the best place to start your search on the Web.

Exercises and Projects

1.   Using the Open Directory Project, **http://dmoz.org**, as we did in the chapter, find a list of resources available on children's nutrition by browsing the directory. Give the title, URL, and a brief description of each of the three most relevant sites you find. (You may find some interesting recipes here as well!)

2. Using Galaxy's directory, at **http://www.galaxy.com**, look for information about depression. Choose four sites to visit and compare the range of information you find at each one. Would you, too, recommend these sites? Give the title and URL of the site you think is the best, and explain why you like it.

3. Suppose you collect comic books as a hobby and are interested in finding Web sites about them.
   a. Try browsing through LookSmart's directory at **http://www.looksmart.com**. How do you like the way this directory is set up? What categories did you browse to find your topic? Is this directory searchable by keyword?
   b. Look for the same subject at Yahoo! Notice that you need to scroll to the bottom of the page to find Yahoo!'s directory. Is their directory searchable by keyword? **http://www.yahoo.com**. In what category was your topic found here?
   c. Did you prefer one directory over another for this topic? Why?

4. Now let's look at virtual libraries.
   a. Go to the Librarians' Index to the Internet at **http://lii.org** and browse the categories to find resources about dance. Under what category did you find the topic? What other sub-topics are listed under Dance? Click on **General Resources**. How many are listed?
   b. Go to the Internet Public Library at **http://www.ipl.org** and look for the same topic. Can you find a section on Dance? What category is it under? Try doing a search for dance at this site. How many resources do you find listed?

5. Go back to the Librarians' Index at **http://lii.org** and, using the Search feature, look for sites about the following topics. How many do you find? Go to one site for each topic and describe what is available there.
   a. Motorcycles
   b. RSS
   c. Cosmology

6. Go to Google at **http://www.google.com** and search for information about Nilo Cruz, the Pulitzer Prize winning playwright. How many results did you obtain? What play of his won the Pulitzer Prize? Give the URL of a site that includes this information.

7. Using All the Web at **http://alltheweb.com**, look for Dadaism. Find a page that gives a definition of the term. Give both the definition and the URL of the site where you found it.

8. Here's a little exercise on the importance of phrase searching:
   a. Go to Google at **http://www.google.com**. Type the words **bats in your belfry** into the search box. How many results did you find? Look at the first page of results. Are they relevant to your search for that phrase? Now go back and add quotation marks around the phrase. How many results did you obtain this time?

b. Now suppose you are looking for historical information about the medieval Norsemen and their battles. Go to Alta Vista at **http://www.altavista.com**. You are looking for a place called the Kirk of Skulls. Type the words **Kirk of Skulls** in at AltaVista. How many results do you find? Now add the quotation marks around the phrase. How many results did you find? Did you find your answer? Where is the site located?

9. Our look at how communication has changed over the years has brought us to the era of illuminated manuscripts. Go to Google at **http://www.google.com** and look for information about them. Will you use a phrase search? How many results do you obtain? Click on some of the results and give the title and URL of a site that gives good information about the history and making of these manuscripts.

A RESEARCHER'S TOOLKIT: DIRECTORIES AND VIRTUAL LIBRARIES

4

In Chapter 3, "Using the World Wide Web for Research," we introduced different ways to investigate topics using the World Wide Web. One of the ways to find information is to browse directories. Directories can help you find the best resources on a particular topic. For example, they would help with the questions "What are the best sites on the topic of legal research?" and "What are the most useful American literature resources on the Web?"

Virtual libraries are the most selective of all directories. They are therefore the best places to find sites that collect Internet resources that have been evaluated and are judged most useful by information specialists. For example, if you wanted the best Web sites that focus on the Middle East and North Africa, a virtual library would be a good start. In the last chapter, we covered a virtual library—the Internet Public Library. In this chapter, we'll look at another one and show how to use it.

In Chapter 3, we also browsed the Open Directory Project for information on opera. In this chapter, we'll cover directories in more detail by discussing features that are common to all directories and by showing how they can differ from one another. We also will walk you through several activities to show you how best to use directories on the World Wide Web.

As a follow-up to this discussion, we will provide a convenient Researcher's Toolkit: Web sites that will help you find practical information as well as the most important academic research sites that will get you started on a myriad of scholarly topics.

The sections in this chapter are as follows:

- ✦ Characteristics of Directories
- ✦ Browsing and Searching Directories
- ✦ Virtual Libraries: Directories with a Difference
- ✦ A Researcher's Toolkit

Major Directories on the World Wide Web

✦ Galaxy
   http://www.galaxy.com

✦ LookSmart
   http://www.looksmart.com

✦ Open Directory Project
   http://dmoz.org

✦ Yahoo! Directory
   http://dir.yahoo.com

Characteristics of Directories

Directories are topical lists of Internet resources arranged in a hierarchical way. Although they are organized by subject, directories can also be searched by keyword. They differ from search engines in one major way—the human element involved in collecting and maintaining the information. Directories are created and maintained by people, whereas search engines rely on spiders or robots to crawl the Internet for links. There are a number of differences between directories. One way to determine directories' particular characteristics is to ask the following questions about each of them:

✦ Who selects the included Web resources—directory administrators or people in the Internet community?

✦ Who categorizes the Web pages and sites—the people who submit them or directory administrators?

✦ How are the results displayed—alphabetically, by relevance, or by type of Web page?

✦ Are the resources rated? Are they annotated? Are they reviewed?

Each directory differs from others mainly in the level of quality control involved in its management. For example, some directory managers have very little control over their collections, relying on Web page submitters to provide annotations and decisions about where their resource should be placed in the directory's hierarchy. Other directory managers are much more selective not only about which resources they include, but also about where in the subject hierarchy the pages will be located.

Some directory editors write detailed *annotations* of the pages. These annotations can be evaluative, descriptive, or both. Annotations are Web page descriptions that either the Web page submitter or the directory editor attaches to the Web pages.

Of all the directories, virtual libraries rely most on human beings in selecting and controlling the resources included in their collections. Virtual libraries are organized in a way that tames the Internet's chaotic nature and thus attempts to create a more traditional "library-like" setting in which to do research.

The human element involved in creating and maintaining directories creates both advantages and disadvantages for the user. Some of the inherent strengths of directories can be weaknesses, and vice versa. We'll examine some of these strengths and weaknesses here.

Strengths

The major advantages of using directories are as follows:

✦ Directories contain fewer resources than search engine databases.

✦ Many directories rate, annotate, or categorize chosen resources.

✦ Directories increase the probability of retrieving relevant results.

Because directories rely on people to select, maintain, and update their resource lists, they contain fewer resources than search engine databases. This can be a plus, especially when you are looking for information on a general topic. It's a lot easier and less time-consuming to go through a list of 50 or so Web pages than to sort through the thousands of pages that a search engine may present. In addition, many directories rate, annotate, analyze, evaluate, and categorize the resources included, which helps you find resources of the highest quality.

Although we'll discuss the evaluation of Internet resources in detail later in the book, now is a good time to mention quality control and filtering. With thousands of new resources appearing on the Web each day, it is important that people work to determine which sites and Web pages have the highest quality.

Weaknesses

There are three major disadvantages inherent in World Wide Web directories. They are as follows:

✦ Arbitrary hierarchical arrangements

✦ Infrequent updates

✦ Subjectivity of rating and annotating resources

One of the major disadvantages of using some directories is that the hierarchical arrangements may be arbitrary. For example, let's say we are looking for information on ozone depletion. We want to start by finding a few sites. We decide to use the Yahoo! Directory, one of the best-known directories on the Web.

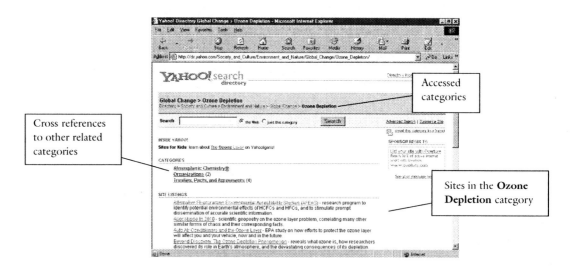

Figure 4.1—Ozone Depletion in the Yahoo! Directory

Note in Figure 4.1 that **Ozone Depletion** is located under the subcategory or subheading **Global Change**, which is located under the category **Environment and Nature**, which is placed under the top-level category **Society and Culture**. The people who organized this directory chose this hierarchy. Another directory might place **Ozone Depletion** under the top-level category **Science**. The ability to search Yahoo! and most other directories by keyword solves this problem of arbitrary hierarchical arrangements.

Another drawback is that selecting and categorizing Web pages take a lot of time, so directories tend to be less up-to-date than search engine databases, which are periodically updated by computer programs that automatically gather new Web pages.

The third disadvantage inherent in some directories is also an advantage—the resources are chosen by people who subjectively decide which ones are best. What seems to be a good resource to one person may not to the next. This is why it is important for the directory management to have well-stated criteria for selecting resources.

Browsing and Searching Directories

There are two ways to find information in directories. You can browse by subject or search by keyword. These will be discussed in the following section.

Browsing

Browsing a directory is not difficult. You simply click on a subject category that you think will contain the subject you are seeking. This will take you to another level in the hierarchy, where you will choose another subject from the list of subjects that appear on your computer screen. You then examine the choices that are returned to you and select the one most closely related to your research topic. You continue this process until your window fills with a list of resources that you can then examine to find the information you need.

Sometimes this process has two levels; other times it has several. It depends on the directory and how detailed the subject is. For example, if we were to browse the Open Directory Project for resources about economics, we would start by clicking on the top-level category **Science**. Next, we would click on **Social Sciences**, and from the resulting list of subcategories, we would choose **Economics**.

These are specialized topics within economics

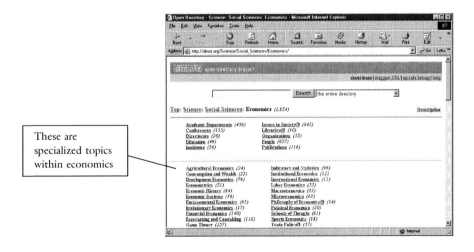

Figure 4.2—Subcategories Under Economics in the Open Directory Project

Now let's try to find economics resources in Yahoo!'s directory. The top-level category we need to click on is **Social Sciences**. Figure 4.3 shows that **Economics** is a subcategory of **Social Sciences**. Several subcategories under **Economics** cover specific aspects of the subject.

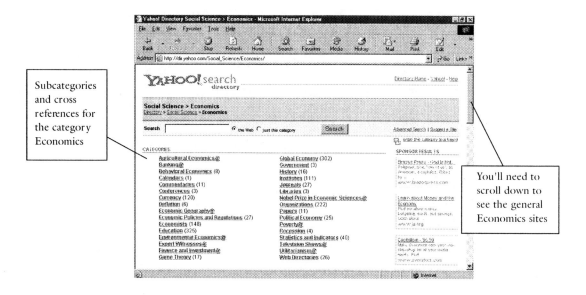

Figure 4.3—Economics Resources in Yahoo!'s Directory

Searching

By now, you can probably see the advantage of being able to search a directory. It may be difficult to determine where in a directory's hierarchy a particular subject will be found. Searching a directory is not the same as searching the Web using a search engine. The primary difference is that when you search a directory, you have access to only those resources that are included in the directory, not the entire Web. Also, in some directories (such as Yahoo!'s), you do not search the full text of Web pages; you search only the words in the URLs (Uniform Resource Locators), the titles of the Web pages, and annotations (if they exist).

❖TIP! If you don't find any resources on the topic you are looking for while browsing, you can use the **Back** button of your browser to return to another level. There you can try a different subject heading that may lead you to successful results.

ACTIVITY

4.1   A MAJOR DIRECTORY AND HOW TO USE IT

OVERVIEW

The Yahoo! Directory, **http://dir.yahoo.com**, is one of the most comprehensive directories on the World Wide Web. Yahoo! relies on Web page submitters to annotate and categorize the resources that are included, so some sites have a brief descriptive note, and some do not. Yahoo! strives to be extensive; consequently, there is minimal filtering of resources. You can browse Yahoo!'s directory or search it by keyword. If you instruct Yahoo! to do so, its search engine will perform your search for you in its Web database.

In the following activity, we'll browse for information in Yahoo!'s directory and then we'll search for the same information using the search query interface that Yahoo! provides. We'll be looking for some general information on the Human Genome Project. We don't know much about it and want to find a general information page. We'll follow these steps:

1. Go to the Yahoo! Directory.

2. Browse the directory for information on the Human Genome Project.

3. Add the Web page to your list of favorites.

4. Search Yahoo! for information on the Human Genome Project.

5. Access the Web pages that the search engine retrieved.

✦ T I P !   Remember that the Web is always changing and that your results may differ from those shown here. Don't let this confuse you. The activities demonstrate fundamental skills. These skills don't change, even though the number of results obtained or the actual screens may look very different.

DETAILS

1   Go to the Yahoo! Directory.

✦ Do It!   Type **http://dir.yahoo.com**, and press enter.

2   Browse the directory for information on the Human Genome Project.

✦ Do It!   Click on **Science**, which is one of the top-level categories on Yahoo!'s list, as shown in Figure 4.4. Because the Human Genome Project is related to scientific research, this would be the most logical category to start with.

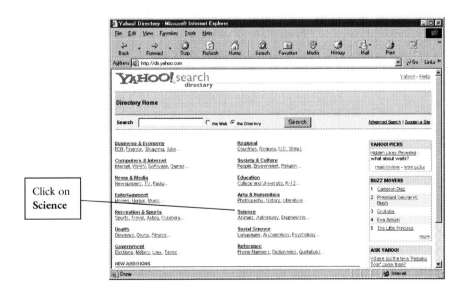

Figure 4.4—Top-level Category List in Yahoo!

✦ Do It!   Click on **Biology** from the list of subcategories.

✦ Do It!   Now click on **Genetics** from the list of subcategories that appear under **Biology**.

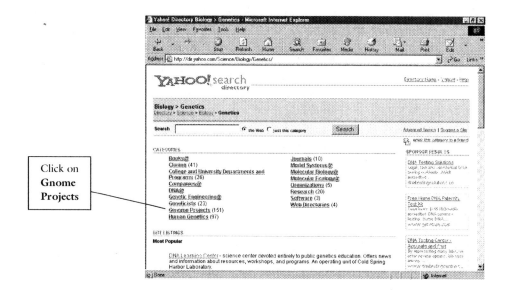

Figure 4.5—Subcategories of Genetics in Yahoo!

Figure 4.5 shows the resources listed under **Genetics**. One of the hyperlinks listed, **Genetic Engineering@**, is a cross-reference to another category. Whenever you see a hyperlink with the @ sign after it, you'll know that this will link you to resources in another category. In this case, clicking on **Genetic Engineering@** would take you to resources that are located in the following hierarchy: **Science > Biology > Biotechnology**. Because we are looking for Human Genome Project information, the **Genome Projects** link may be the best choice.

✦ Do It!   From this list, click on the category **Genome Projects**, as shown in Figure 4.5.

✦ Do It!   After the page is displayed, click on **Human Genome**.

Note that in Figure 4.6 that there are several genome project resources listed, and one of them is titled **Human Genome Project Information**. This may be the best place to start. If you can't locate this Web page, click on another that looks promising.

✦ Do It!   Click on **Human Genome Project Information** as shown in Figure 4.6.

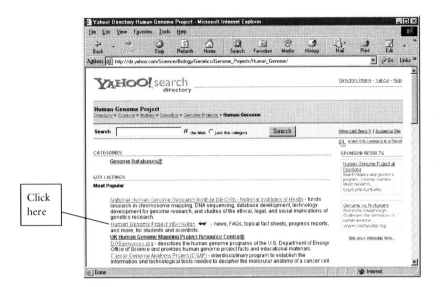

Figure 4.6—Results of Browsing Yahoo! for Resources

3 Add the Web page to your list of favorites.

Now that you've found this informative site, you don't want to lose track of it. It's a good idea to place a hyperlink to it in your favorites list.

✦ Do It! Click on **Favorites** in the location toolbar. Point your mouse to **Add to Favorites** and click. Then click on **OK** in the dialog box. Automatically, the title of the URL is added to your favorites list. You can access this Web site at a later date by clicking on the title in your list.

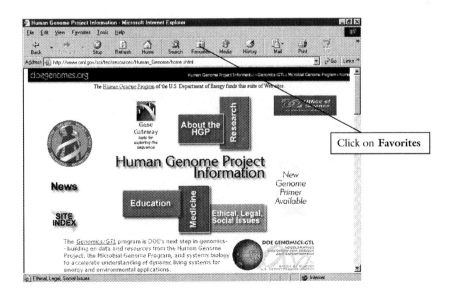

Figure 4.7—Human Genome Project Information, **http://www.ornl.gov/ sci/techresources/Human_Genome/home.shtml**

4   Search Yahoo! for information on the Human Genome Project.

Keyword searching in the Yahoo! Directory is simple. You can save time by doing a keyword search. You should keep your search terms broad, however, because Yahoo! doesn't search the words in the bodies of Web pages.

✦ Do It!   Click on the **Back** icon to return to Yahoo!

✦ Do It!   To discover what the search options are for Yahoo!'s directory, click on **help** in the upper right corner. Click on the following hierarchy:

Help> Yahoo! Search Help> Search Basics > Search Tips

We find out that Yahoo! allows phrase searching by placing quotation marks around the words that are to be searched as a phrase. We also learn that Yahoo! is case insensitive, so we don't need to capitalize the beginning letters of the words in the phrase.

✦ Do It!   Return to Yahoo!'s directory by typing **http://dir.yahoo.com** in the address bar.

✦ Do It!   After making sure that the radio button next to **the Directory** is checked, type in the form next to the **Search** button the search expression **"human genome project"** and click **Search**, as shown in Figure 4.8.

This search will retrieve Web sites that have the phrase *human genome project* in their titles, URLs, or annotations. The results are listed in order of relevance to the search topic.

Figure 4.8—Searching Yahoo!'s Directory by Keyword Phrase

5   Access the Web pages that the search engine retrieved.

The sites that Yahoo! retrieved for us may be all we need, but let's say that after we read the short descriptions, we want to see what a larger part of the World Wide Web has on this topic.

✦ Do It!   Click on the **Web** link at the top of the screen, as shown in Figure 4.9.

Click on **Web** here

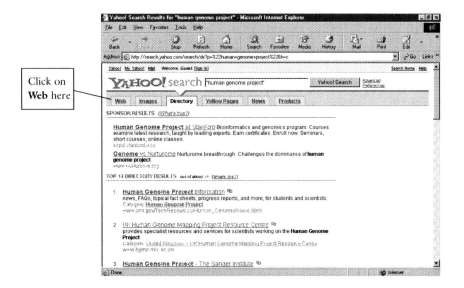

Figure 4.9—Search Results in Yahoo!'s Directory

Automatically, the Yahoo! search engine searches its huge database for the phrase *human genome project*. The results are listed by relevance and usefulness, as shown in Figure 4.10.

Note that there are over 400,000 Web sites on the topic in the search engine database

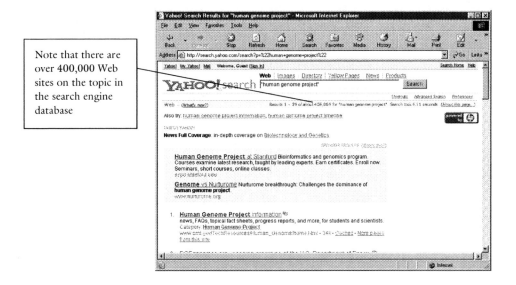

Figure 4.10—Results of the Search Request in Yahoo!

As you can see, the search engine found hundreds of thousands of Web pages on this topic. Yahoo!'s search engine uses a database that attempts to cover as much of the Web as possible, whereas Yahoo!'s directory covers only a small portion of it. Yahoo!'s search engine also indexes most every word in every page on the Web, whereas Yahoo!'s directory's search capability is limited to URL titles, category or Web site titles, and descriptions. Because the pages are listed by relevance to the topic (using an algorithm that takes into account how others have found the sites useful in the past), we can be quite sure that the first 10 or 20 resources listed will be highly relevant to your search request.

END OF ACTIVITY 4.1

In Activity 4.1, we saw the difference between browsing the Yahoo! Directory's subject categories for a topic and performing a keyword search. A keyword search in Yahoo!'s directory looks for words that are in the URLs, the subject categories, and the titles of the Web pages.

Virtual Libraries: Directories with a Difference

Virtual libraries are directories with resources that information professionals, including librarians, have organized in a logical way. In Chapter 3, we looked closely at a virtual library—the Internet Public Library. Virtual libraries are often referred to as ***annotated directories*** or ***academic directories***. It is helpful to think of these specialized directories as being similar to libraries because people who are committed to finding the very best resources on the Internet carefully select and maintain the resources in a virtual library. These people usually rate or analyze the resources and arrange them so they will be found easily.

The Major Virtual Libraries

- ✦ Academic Info: Your Gateway to Quality Educational Resources
  http://www.academicinfo.net
- ✦ Digital Librarian: A Librarian's Choice of the Best of the Web
  http://www.digital-librarian.com
- ✦ Infomine
  http://infomine.ucr.edu
- ✦ Internet Public Library
  http://www.ipl.org
- ✦ Librarians' Index to the Internet
  http://lii.org
- ✦ Library Spot
  http://libraryspot.com
- ✦ Resource Discovery Network
  http://www.rdn.ac.uk

As we discussed in Chapter 3, there are three major types of resources that virtual libraries are most apt to contain: ***subject guides, reference works,*** and ***specialized databases***.

Subject guides are Web resources that include hyperlinks to sites on that particular subject. Reference works are full-text documents, such as dictionaries, encyclopedias, almanacs, and so forth. Specialized databases are searchable indexes that catalog certain types of material, such as journal article citations, financial data, and so forth.

It may be helpful to do an activity in a virtual library to show you how to obtain a reference work. We will be using The Librarians' Index to the Internet for this activity.

ACTIVITY

4.2 USING A VIRTUAL LIBRARY

OVERVIEW

In this activity, we will use The Librarians' Index to the Internet (LII). The LII is a virtual library that contains thousands of annotated and evaluated resources in most subject areas. It can be searched as well as browsed. The LII was initiated and is still maintained by librarians from California who choose the sites and write the annotations. The Librarians' Index to the Internet is organized a lot like the Yahoo! Directory, so you should feel familiar with it quickly.

We're going to use the LII to find Kelley Blue Book, the "Blue Book" for automobiles. After this, we will locate a subject guide on the Middle East. A virtual library is the best place to go to find resources such as these because the librarians make every attempt to include reference works that will answer their patrons' questions. We'll follow these steps:

1. Go to the Librarians' Index to the Internet.

2. Browse the library's directory for the Blue Book for automobiles.

3. Search the library's directory for the Blue Book.

4. Search the library for a subject guide on the Middle East.

DETAILS

1 Go to the Librarians' Index to the Internet.

✦ Do It! Type **http://lii.org** and press ⌷Enter⌷.

See the "Librarians' Index to the Internet home page" in Figure 4.11.

2 Browse the library's directory for the Kelley Blue Book for automobiles.

You'll need to scroll down the page a bit to notice that there is a subcategory called **Cars** under the top-level category **Sports, Recreation, & Entertainment**.

✦ Do It! Click on **Cars**.

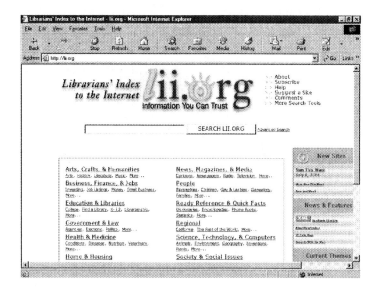

Figure 4.11—Home Page of the Librarians' Index to the Internet

Figure 4.12 shows a list of subcategories in the **Automobiles** category. (Note that while the subcategory on LII's title page was called **Cars**, on the actual directory page, it's entitled **Automobiles**.) Because we know that the Kelley Blue Book is a reference book that provides automobile prices, we'll choose the **Prices** subcategory.

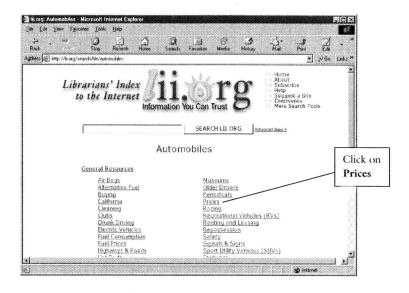

Figure 4.12—The Automobile Category in the Librarians' Index to the Internet

✦ Do It!   Click on **Prices**, as shown in Figure 4.12.

Figure 4.13 shows a partial list of the resources that are in the **Prices** category, including the **Kelley Blue Book**.

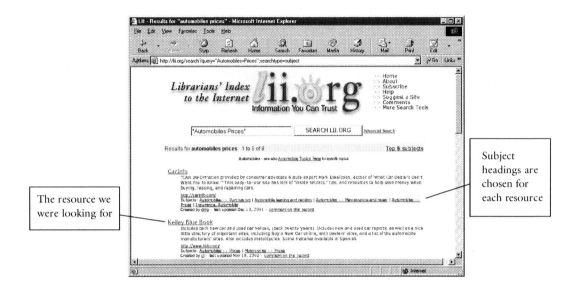

Figure 4.13—List of Car Price Resources in the Librarians' Index to the Internet

Browsing the LII for this resource worked out quite well. Now we're going to show you how easy it would be to search for this resource using keywords.

3   Search the library's directory for the Blue Book.

To determine the best way to search with any tool, it's always a good idea to read the help section.

✦ Do It!   Go to the top of the home page and click on **Help**, as shown in Figure 4.14.

Figure 4.14—Accessing Help in the LII

The search tips note that phrases should be surrounded by quotation marks.

Figure 4.15—Basic Search Help in LII

✦ Do It!   Type **"blue book"** in the search form provided on the Help page and click on **SEARCH LII.ORG**, as shown in Figure 4.15.

Figure 4.16 shows partial results of the result of this search.

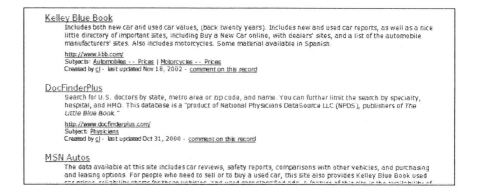

Figure 4.16—Partial Results of Search for *"blue book"* in the Librarians' Index to the Internet

Now we're going to locate a subject guide on the Middle East.

4   Search the library for a subject guide on the Middle East.

We want to find a subject guide on the Middle East. It would help to search the subject headings.

✦ Do It!   Click on **Advanced Search** at the top of the window next to the search form.

✦ Do It!   Select **Subject** from the pull-down menu, as shown in Figure 4.17.

✦ Do It!   Type **"middle east"** in the search form, as shown in Figure 4.17.

✦ Do It!   Click on **SEARCH LII.ORG**.

Figure 4.17—Searching for a Subject Guide on the Middle East in LII

Several Web sites are provided by this search. Scroll down until you see the sites that are shown in Figure 4.18.

✦ Do It!   Click on **Middle East Institute**, as shown in Figure 4.18. (You may need to Click on View: **Next 14** at the bottom of the first page of results.)

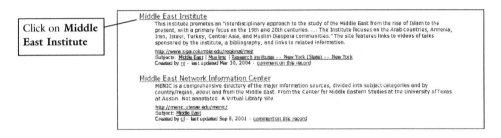

Figure 4.18—Some Subject Guides for Middle East Studies

Figure 4.19 shows the home page for The Middle East Institute at Columbia University. Note that this Web site is a gateway to Middle East research projects, including Internet research, library programs, reference sites, and so forth.

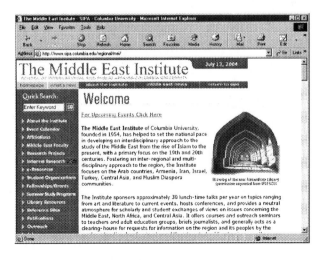

Figure 4.19—The Middle East Institute – A Subject Guide on the Middle East

END OF ACTIVITY 4.2

This activity showed how selective virtual libraries are. Virtual libraries are the places to go if you are looking for a reference source like a dictionary, handbook, encyclopedia, subject guide, or specialized database. The Librarians' Index to the Internet is a good resource to have on your favorites list.

A Researcher's Toolkit

The following list of Web sites are organized in two categories. The first part focuses on Web sites that contain practical information that you can consult on a daily basis, such as maps, stock information, weather, dictionaries, and so forth.

The second section covers some of the best academic research sites that will assist you in preparing for school projects, papers, and presentations.

All of the sites listed in the Toolkit were found by browsing and searching the directories and virtual libraries discussed in this chapter.

Practical Information Web Sites

Dictionaries, Handbooks, and Almanacs

✦ Bartleby.com, **http://www.bartleby.com/**
Bartleby.com is a mega-site consisting of full-text classic fiction and non-fiction, reference works such as *The Columbia Encyclopedia, The American Heritage Dictionary, Roget's Thesaurus, Barlett's Familiar Quotations, Strunk's Elements of Style, Gray's Anatomy,* and more. A one-stop-shop for students and researchers, *Bartleby.com* is a fundamental resource to add to your favorites list.

✦ Information Please: On-line Dictionary, Internet Encyclopedia, Atlas & Almanac Reference, **http://www.infoplease.com**
Look here for most of the content found in the print *Information Please* almanac: U.S. and international statistics,biographical information, and sports, entertainment, and weather data.

✦ How Many? A Dictionary of Units of Measurement, **http://www.unc.edu/~rowlett/units**
This dictionary describes the relationship between various English and metric units. Look here for measurement information covering most everything from solar flare intensity to paper sheet sizes to wind chill charts.

✦ Whatis.com The IT-Specific Encyclopedia, **http://whatis.techtarget.com/**
Whatis.com serves as both a dictionary and an encyclopedia of thousands of computing and information technology terms. This well-designed and useful site is a benefit to users at all levels. It is updated and expanded regularly.

✦ Zip Code Lookup and Address Information, **http://www.usps.com/zip4**
This specialized database will assist you in finding a zip code by address or company name. It will also find all the zip codes of a city or town, and all the cities and towns that use a particular zip code.

Maps

✦ MapQuest, **http://www.mapquest.com**

MapQuest provides maps and driving directions for individual addresses, airports, and businesses (both by name and by type) in the United States. It also provides similar sites for European countries and the United Kingdom.

✦ Perry-Castañeda Library Map Collection, **http://www.lib.utexas.edu/maps**

This collection is a must-see for everyone who is interested in locating a map. The Perry-Castenada Library of the University of Texas has scanned over 4,000 non-copyrighted maps from its own collection, making them available to the public on the Web. While most of the maps in the collection are provided by the U.S. Central Intelligence Agency, there are also maps from obscure agencies and institutions.

Money & Stocks

✦ Oanda, **http://www.oanda.com**

This site contains a currency converter for 164 currencies. Updated daily.

✦ PCQuote, **http://www.pcquote.com**

Look here for securities quotations, stock market information, financial news, and other investment tools.

Telephone and Email Directories

✦ Anywho, **http://www.anywho.com**

This site contains publicly accessible local telephone records for individuals and businesses. It also provides addresses, a maps, and driving directions. The user can also find an address by typing in the telephone number if they know it (reverse lookup).

✦ Infospace, **http://www.infospace.com**

In addition to the services provided by *Anywho*, this site also provides email addresses.

News

✦ Google News, **http://news.google.com**

Google News covers 4,500 news sources and arranges headlines by relevance, with articles from several newspapers and other sources grouped under each story. The database is updated every 10 to 15 minutes. International in scope, *Google News* uses mathematical algorithms to determine which stories will be listed on its main page.

✦ Newslink, **http://newslink.org/**

This site provides links to U.S. and foreign newspapers, college newspapers, radio stations, and magazines. Can also search for radio stations and newspapers by city and state.

Weather

✦ National Weather Service, **http://www.nws.noaa.gov**

   This U.S. National Oceanic and Atmospheric Administration site provides up-to-date weather forecasts for all 50 states. You can search the area of interest by zip code or by clicking on a map. Also included are research articles that may be searched by subject.

✦ The Weather Channel, **http://www.weather.com**

   This resource provides weather forecasts, traveler's tips, vacation ideas, gardening information, and more.

Academic Research Web Sites

Reference Sites

✦ AltaVista's Babelfish, **http://world.altavista.com**

   Babelfish allows you to translate a section of text or a Web page from English to several languages, and from some other languages to English. The translations aren't always perfect, but the site can be a time saver.

✦ Biography.com, **http://www.biography.com**

   Providing biographical information for over 25,000 people, this A&E network site also includes video clips and educational materials to support classroom discussions.

✦ Online! A Reference Guide to Using Internet Resources,
   http://www.bedfordstmartins.com/online/citex.html
   This site covers details on how to cite electronic sources in the major styles, including APA, Chicago Manual of Style, MLA, and CBE (Council of Biology Editors). Based on a book by Andrew Harnack and Eugene Kleppinger.

✦ Guide to Grammar and Writing, **http://webster.commnet.edu/grammar/index.htm**

   This site covers virtually everything you'll ever want to know about grammar and writing, including writer's block and how to overcome it, paragraph development, parts of speech, tense consistency, and much, much more.

✦ Online Writing Lab, **http://owl.english.purdue.edu/**

   This site provides information for students and teachers on writing; including grammar, punctuation, and research skills. English-as-a-second-language resources are included as well.

✦ Plagiarism, **http://www.web-miner.com/plagiarism**

   Contains material for faculty and students about plagiarism. There are links to plagiarism detection sites, term paper writing sites, and more. Provided by a librarian at the University of Illinois at Urbana-Champaign.

✦ Refdesk.com, **http://www.refdesk.com/**

   You'll find hundreds of links to current news, electronic reference works, statistical information, directories, dictionaries, encyclopedias, and more. The site can also be searched by keyword.

Area/Country Studies

✦ CIA World Factbook, **http://www.odci.gov/cia/publications/factbook/index.html**

This is the online version of the CIA's *World Factbook*. Published annually, it contains information on all the countries of the world, including a map of the country, brief historical information, geography overview, population data, description of current government, economic statistics, communications and transportation infrastructure, military conflicts, and more.

✦ Country Studies - Area Handbook Series,
http://lcweb2.loc.gov/frd/cs/cshome.html

This series consists of online versions of books published in paper form by the Federal Research Division of the Library of Congress under the Country Studies/Area Handbook Program sponsored by the U.S. Department of the Army. The series presents the history, culture, government, economics, sociology, and geography of lesser-known countries of the world—Canada, France, and the United Kingdom, for example, are not included.

Business

✦ Country Commercial Guides, **http://www.state.gov/e/eb/rls/rpts/ccg/**

These are annual in-depth studies of countries' commercial environments. Prepared by U.S. embassies in countries that have a U.S. consular presence, the *Guides* are intended for U.S. business people who may want to invest in a country, but political science and international business students can also benefit from the information found here.

✦ EDGAR—SEC Filings & Forms, **http://www.sec.gov/edgar.shtml**

This site provides U.S. Securities and Exchange Commission (SEC) financial statements that are required from all public U.S. companies with less than $10 million in assets and 500 shareholders. Available free from the SEC, EDGAR is a well-designed and reliable resource, with over 1 million documents in its collection.

✦ Hoover's Online, **http://www.hoovers.com**

This is a useful site for the busy student or librarian who needs company information. You can find a brief overview of a company, including street address, telephone and fax numbers, location map, hyperlink to the company's home page, top competitors, company type (whether private or public), key people in the company, links to news, and links to industry information. If the company you have looked up is private, you may get very brief financial information with links to business reports prepared by Dun & Bradstreet and other firms that you will have to pay for.

✦ Industry Research Desk, **http://www.virtualpet.com/industry/**

This is an excellent starting point for the person researching an industry. The author brings together hyperlinks for industry data, industry home pages, the North American Industry Classification System (NAICS), and office tools such as package costs and tracking devices, and more.

+ Researching Companies Online,
  http://home.sprintmail.com/~debflanagan/index.html

  Undoubtedly one of the most-cited business tutorials on the World Wide Web, Debbie Flanagan's *Researching Companies Online* is the best place to start a business-related research project. All of the links provided in the tutorial are free and open to the public without subscription.

Education

+ ERIC—The Educational Resources Information Center, **http://eric.ed.gov**

  This is the world's largest source of education information, containing more than 1 million abstracts of education journal articles, documents, and other resources.

+ Lesson Plans Library, **http://school.discovery.com/lessonplans/**

  Use this site to find lesson plans written by teachers for teachers. You can browse by subject and grade level.

+ New York Times Learning Network, **http://www.nytimes.com/learning/**

  The New York Times Learning Network is a free service for teachers, parents, and students in elementary and secondary schools. Updated each weekday, it contains summaries of news stories from the current day's New York Times.

+ PBS Teacher Source, **http://www.pbs.org/teachersource/**

  One of the best features of the Public Broadcasting System's (PBS) *TeacherSource* is the collection of over 2,500 lesson plans and activities for classroom teachers.

Humanities

+ American Memory: Historical Collections for the National Digital Library,
  http://lcweb2.loc.gov/ammem/amhome.html

  The American Memory Historical Collections consist of digitized documents, photographs, recorded sound, moving pictures, and text from the Library of Congress' Americana collections. Examples of content found here are music from the Civil War, slave narratives, and World War II interviews.

+ A Biography of America, **http://www.learner.org/biographyofamerica**

  Created to be a companion Web site to the video series and telecourse of the same name, *A Biography of America* provides a text transcript of each of the 26 videos, maps, timelines, and Webliographies that enhance the content of the series. In-depth articles that complement the series' content are also included.

+ EHistory, **http://www.ehistory.com/**

  Maintained by Ohio State University's Department of History, eHistory is a portal to history divided by the following broad topics: Ancient, Middle Ages, Civil War, World War II, Vietnam War, Middle East, and World. For each section, there are articles and primary source documents, biographies, maps, timelines, and more.

+ Luminarium, **http://www.luminarium.org/lumina.htm**

This site is devoted to medieval English literature, the Renaissance period, and the early 17th century and is an excellent starting point for students and other interested researchers.

✦ Stanford Encyclopedia of Philosophy, **http://plato.stanford.edu/contents.html**

Each entry in this encyclopedia is written, maintained, and updated by a qualified expert or group of experts in that particular field. Arranged in a simple alphabetical layout, each entry consists of a typical encyclopedic overview of the topic, plus a bibliography of print and Internet resources at the end of the article. The Encyclopedia may also be searched.

✦ Internet Sacred Text Archive, **http://www.sacred-texts.com/index.htm**

This site seeks to promote religious tolerance and scholarship by providing electronic texts about religion, mythology, legend, and folklore. Most documents have been translated into English.

Law

✦ Country Reports on Human Rights Practices, **http://www.state.gov/g/drl/rls/hrrpt/**

These reports review a country's record from the previous year on internationally recognized individual, civil, political, and worker rights, as set forth in the Universal Declaration of Human Rights. Press freedom, religious freedom, democratic trends, treatment of women and children, prison conditions, trafficking in persons, worker's conditions, and arbitrary arrest, detention, or exile, are just some of the subjects covered in these reports.

✦ Foreign Governments: Constitutions, Laws, and Treaties, **http://www.lib.umich.edu/libhome/Documents.center/forcons.html**

Part of the incomparable *University of Michigan Documents Center* at http://www.lib.umich.edu/libhome/Documents.center, this directory focuses on the laws, treaties, and constitutions of foreign countries. It's also one of the best places to start if you've got an international law question.

✦ Copyright Crash Course, **http://www.utsystem.edu/OGC/IntellectualProperty/cprtindx.htm**

This site focuses on a wide range of copyright issues written in language that the layperson can understand. While the primary audience of the site is college and university faculty, the content may be applied to anyone who is considering reproducing or distributing someone else's work and wants to know the legal limits of doing so.

✦ FindLaw, **http://www.findlaw.com/toc.html**

A major portal to legal resources, *FindLaw* serves several audiences, including legal professionals, students, businesses, and the public. Essentially a directory to a myriad of legal subject areas, its main value lies in its collection of full-text legal opinions.

Medicine & Health

✦ AEGIS: AIDS Education Global Information System, **http://www.aegis.com**

A comprehensive site that covers AIDS treatment, prevention, news services, legal information, and more. It also provides a bulletin board for people to communicate to each other about HIV/AIDS. Founded by the Sisters of St. Elizabeth of Hungary, it is now a non-profit organization in the state of California.

✦ HealthWeb, **http://www.healthweb.org**

Maintained by health science librarians throughout the United States (National Network of Libraries of Medicine), this virtual library contains links to medical information in most areas.

✦ MEDLINEplus, **http://medlineplus.gov**

This site, provided by the National Institutes of Health and the National Library of Medicine, contains carefully selected Web resources on 650 health topics. It also provides a medical dictionary, drug information, interactive health tutorials, and links to pre-formulated searches of the MEDLINE/Pubmed database.

✦ PubMed, **http://www.ncbi.nlm.nih.gov/PubMed/**

This service provides a search interface to the National Library of Medicine's MEDLINE database, which includes over 14 million article citations from more than 4800 biomedical journals, with coverage back to the 1950s.

Political Science

✦ Council on Foreign Relations, **http://www.cfr.org**

This site, provided by the publisher of *Foreign Affairs,* contains up-to-date information about U.S. foreign policy.

✦ Foreign Relations of the United States, **http://www.state.gov/r/pa/ho/frus/**

This site provides the official documentary historical record of major U.S. foreign policy decisions. Information comes from the Dept. of State, Presidential libraries, the National Security Council, the Central Intelligence Agency, the U.S. Agency for International Development, and other sources. Coverage on the Web site goes back to the Truman administration.

✦ Political Science Resources on the Web, **http://www.lib.umich.edu/govdocs/poliscinew.html**

Provided by the University of Michigan Library, this is a directory to political science resources, arranged by broad subject areas such as reference tools, international relations, think tanks, dissertations, political theory, and more.

Science & Technology

✦ Chemistry.org, **http://www.chemcenter.org/portal/Chemistry**

This portal site from the American Chemical Society contains recent articles, grants information, and career development resources. Educational information is provided for teachers and students from the K–12 level all the way to graduate school.

✦ Physics Internet Resources, **http://www.aps.org/resources/**

This is the place to go if you need anything related to physics. It contains homework help, links to journals, Web sites in all areas of physics, exhibitions and special events, and much more.

✦ Programmer's Heaven, **http://www.programmersheaven.com**

A Programmers Heaven - Where Programmers Go! is a portal to tutorials, articles, source code, shareware, news, and other information about a variety of popular programming languages, operating systems, and applications.

Social Sciences

✦ American Psychological Association, **http://www.apa.org**

Geared toward psychology students, faculty, and professionals, this site provides information on psychology careers, conferences, ethics, selected articles from APA journals, links to information on AIDS, parenting, depression, aging, and more.

✦ Bureau of Labor Statistics, **http://stats.bls.gov**

The *Bureau of Labor Statistics* is a mega-site filled with some of the most useful economic, career, and other workplace-related information available on the Web. For example, you can find the last six months of various U.S. economic data, including the unemployment rate, consumer price index, average hourly earnings, and so forth, with links to historical information on all of these segments. The Employment Projections section develops information about trends in the labor market for ten years into the future. Several publications that are used in career guidance are provided here, including the *Occupational Outlook Handbook* and the *Monthly Labor Review.*

✦ Economic Growth Resources, **http://www.bris.ac.uk/Depts/Economics/Growth/**

As its title indicates, this site is a collection of economic growth and development resources. Examples include: information about people who are experts in the field of economic growth, a list of the premier journals in the economic development field, a bibliography of select survey articles in the field of development and economic growth, a collection of growth data sets that can be downloaded, and news about upcoming conferences.

✦ Social Sciences Virtual Library, **http://www.clas.ufl.edu/users/gthursby/socsci/**

This site contains links to social sciences Web sites, electronic journals, directories, and scholarly societies. It covers anthropology, economics, women's studies, psychology, and more.

Statistics

✦ Statistical Abstract of the United States, **http://www.census.gov/statab/www/**

This is the official source of social and economic data for the United States. Some examples of data included are national health expenditures, crime rates, households that have televisions, computers, Internet access, and much more. Statistics dealing with industry and trade, business, natural resources, transportation, agriculture, and some international statistics are also provided.

✦ Statistical Resources on the Web, **http://www.lib.umich.edu/govdocs/stats.html**

Perhaps the most useful site for statistics from a wide variety of sources. Resources are arranged in broad categories such as business and industry, foreign governments, housing, labor, politics, and so forth. An index is also provided in the left frame that allows you to find a specific type of statistic; for example, child abuse, food stamps, life expectancy, ozone, crime, and more.

Summary

Directories are topical lists of Internet resources arranged hierarchically to facilitate browsing by subject. Most directories have a search capability, which can help you avoid occasionally becoming lost in arbitrary subject categories. Directories depend on the work of individuals who collect, categorize, maintain, and, in many cases, evaluate Web sites to make it easier for people to find what they are looking for. Directories vary in how they are organized, which sites get to be evaluated, and, if they are, what criteria are used.

Because directories rely on people for their selections and maintenance, they are necessarily much smaller than the databases that search-engine spiders or robots create. This difference can be an asset in some cases and a detriment in others. When you are looking for a "few good sites" to start with, a directory can save you time, especially if your subject is broad and you're at the beginning of your research. Search engines are not meant to give you a few sites. They exist to bring everything to your screen that is on the World Wide Web and that fits your search expression. Search engines are best for finding very specific information or for researching multifaceted topics.

Virtual libraries are directories maintained by librarians or other information specialists who select material for the directory based on its excellence and value to the Internet public, much as librarians in a traditional library do. Virtual libraries are the best places to find subject guides. These guides are usually maintained by people who are knowledgeable about the subjects covered.

It is a good idea to know how to use the different directories we covered in this chapter and to explore others. Keep one or two on your favorites list so you can find them quickly.

Selected Terms Introduced in This Chapter

annotated directory
annotation
reference work
specialized database
subject guide

Review Questions

Multiple Choice

1. The following are advantages of using directories *except:*

   a. They may rate and annotate a site.
   b. They contain more resources than search engine databases.
   c. They increase the probability of finding relevant results.
   d. They rely on people to select their resources.

2. A virtual library may also be called

   a. an annotated directory.
   b. a subject directory.
   c. a cyber-directory.
   d. a specialized database.

3. If you wanted to use Boolean searching to search in a directory for scholarships available in the field of physics, you could phrase your search

   a. physics or scholarships
   b. scholarships for physics
   c. physics and scholarships
   d. A directory cannot be searched.

4. To browse a directory for the topic of electronic books, you would start with the category

   a. computers.
   b. literature.
   c. technology.
   d. any of the above

5. If you were looking for a specialized database on a subject, you would start your search with a

   a. reference work.
   b. virtual library.
   c. hyperlink.
   d. subdirectory.

6. A disadvantage of using a directory is

   a. resources are selected by a spider or robot.
   b. the ratings of sites are subjective.
   c. they decrease the probability of finding relevant results.
   d. they include more sites than a search engine.

True or False

7. T F One weakness of using directories to look for information is that they are updated infrequently.

8. T F A directory would be a good first choice to find information about a broad subject.

9. T F When you perform a keyword search in the Librarians' Index to the Internet, you are searching the entire Web.

10. T F One strength of directories is that they all use the same subject headings.

11. T F Some sites, like HotBot, may serve both as a directory and as a Web search engine.

12. T F Descriptions of Web sites in a directory are always written by the editors of the directory.

13. T F Directories list the most popular Web pages first since they are the best on a subject.

Completion

14. A _____ is a topical list of Internet resources arranged hierarchically.

15. A list of search results is often called a(n) _____.

16. A Web page description that evaluates, rates, or otherwise describes a Web site is called a(n) _____.

17. In Yahoo! a(n) _____ is a category or heading with the search phrase in the category heading.

18. In Yahoo! a(n) _____ is a site with the search phrase in its title, page, or annotation.

19. Selective directories organized by information professionals are known as

    _____.

20. A Web resource that includes hyperlinks to sites on that particular topic is called a(n)

    _____.

Exercises and Projects

1. It's helpful to learn more about a directory before deciding whether it fits your needs. A good way to start is to look at that small print at the site's home page. See if you can find selection criteria for sites to be included at the following directories and describe how the criteria differ.
    a. Yahoo! **http://www.yahoo.com**.
    b. Galaxy, **http://galaxy.com**
    c. Open Directory Project, **http://dmoz.org**
    d. Librarians' Index to the Internet, **http://lii.org**.

2. Let's compare two resources for the same topic:

   a. Using the Open Directory Project at **http://dmoz.org**, browse through the categories to find information on the subject of immigration. In what category did you find it? Now search the directory for the topic. How many results did you find? How do they compare to your results from browsing? Which method worked better for the topic?

   b. Now go to the Internet Public Library's Reference Center at **http://www.ipl.org/ref**. Browse this virtual library for the topic of immigration. How many sites are included here? Can you find a subject guide?

   c. For this topic, did you find the Open Directory Project or the Internet Public Library more helpful? Why?

3. See if you can find Moroccan recipes by browsing the Looksmart directory at **http://www.looksmart.com**. Write down the categories and subcategories you chose as you browsed. Print a recipe for couscous.

4. One of the remarkable aspects of the Web is the availability of the full texts of literary works. Find the full text of Shakespeare's *A Midsummer Night's Dream* by using Yahoo! at **http://www.yahoo.com**. Did you search or browse at Yahoo!? Give the URL of a site where the work is located.

5. Now find a work that's not in English. Go to the Open Directory at **http://dmoz.com**. Find the full text of St. Augustine's *Confessions* in Latin by performing a keyword search at the directory. Describe how the search results are presented. Give the URL of a site where the Latin text of the *Confessions* is located.

6. Go to the Librarians' Index to the Internet at **http://lii.org**. See if you can find information about Internet filtering in public libraries. How did you find it? How many Web sites did you find? Go to one of them and describe what Internet filtering is. Give the URL of the site you used.

7. Aromatherapy is a fast-growing aspect of alternative medicine.

   a. Does the Librarians' Index to the Internet, **http://lii.org**, list any resources about the topic?

   b. Go to Galaxy at **http://www.galaxy.com** and look for aromatherapy. How many resources did you find at this directory? What categories did you browse to find them? Go to one of the sites listed, find out what aromatherapy is, and give a definition and the URL of the page you visited.

8. Go to Galaxy at **http://www.galaxy.com** and browse through the topics to find information about another step in the history of communication. Browse to see what you can find about Johannes Gutenberg and the invention of the printing press. What categories did you browse? How many results were listed? Give the URL of one of the sites that gives the information.

SEARCH STRATEGIES FOR SEARCH ENGINES

In Chapter 3, "Using the World Wide Web for Research," we introduced keyword searching in search engine databases. In this chapter, we'll cover searching these databases in detail. Why is it so important to learn how to search these databases? Search engines are the most powerful search tools on the World Wide Web, with the most popular being those that access the largest databases. And while most of the major search engines index hundreds of millions of documents, none of their databases are exactly alike. Some are better for certain kinds of information than others. Maybe you've tried a few search engines and have found that some engines retrieve too many documents that aren't at all what you wanted. Perhaps at other times they don't retrieve enough information. This chapter should clear up some questions you may have about why some searches work well and others don't.

This chapter will include the following sections:

- ✦ Search Engine Databases
- ✦ Search Features Common to Most Search Engines
- ✦ Output Features Common to Most Search Engines
- ✦ A Basic Search Strategy: The 10 Steps

The Major Search Engine Databases on the World Wide Web

✦ All the Web, **http://alltheweb.com**

✦ AltaVista, **http://altavista.com**

✦ Google, **http://www.google.com**

✦ Lycos, **http://www.lycos.com**

✦ MSN, **http://msn.com**

✦ Teoma, **http://teoma.com**

✦ Yahoo, **http://www.yahoo.com**

Search Engine Databases

When to Use Search Engine Databases

Search engines are the best tools to use when you are looking for very specific information or when your research topic has many facets. We saw in Chapter 3 that directories are helpful when you are looking for general and single-faceted topics. Usually when you need information on a very detailed or multifaceted subject, a search engine will give you not only more information, but also the most precise and up-to-date information possible. In one database, the best Web page for your research purposes may be fiftieth on the list; in another database, that document may be first. In order to retrieve the most relevant and useful documents, you should become familiar with the many search engines and their features.

Knowing how search engine databases are constructed can help you select the most appropriate tool for your research needs, retrieve the most relevant information, and understand why results vary from one database to another.

Search Engine Similarities and Differences

All of the major search engines are similar in that you enter keywords in a *search form*. After clicking on **Search**, **Submit**, **Find**, or some other command button, the database returns a collection of hyperlinks, which are usually listed according to their *relevance* to the keyword(s) you typed in, from most relevant to least relevant. Even though most of the major search engine databases attempt to index as much of the Web as possible, each one has a different way of determining which pages will be listed first. Some databases list results by term relevancy, employing algorithms that measure how closely a Web document matches the search expression used. Others list them by using link analysis, which takes into account the context of the Web pages in relation to the search expression, how many quality Web pages link to the pages, or how "popular" they are.

The major search engines differ in several ways:

✦ Size of index

✦ Search features supported (many search engines support the same features but require different syntax to initiate them)

✦ How frequently the database is updated

✦ Ranking algorithms

It is important to know these differences because to do an exhaustive search of the World Wide Web, you must be familiar with a few different search tools. No single search engine can be relied upon to satisfy every query.

How Search Engines Work

In search engines, a computer program called a *spider* or *robot* gathers new documents from the World Wide Web. The program retrieves hyperlinks that are attached to these documents, loads them into a database, and indexes them using a formula that differs from database to database. Then, when you consult the search engine, it searches the database looking for documents that contain the *keywords* you used in the *search expression.* No search engine actually indexes the entire Web. There is information that is inaccessible to search engines, commonly referred to as the "*invisible Web*" or the "*hidden Internet.*" Much of this content can be located in special databases, which we will discuss in Chapter 6. Although robots have many different ways of collecting information from Web pages, the major search engines all claim to index most of the text of each Web document in their databases. This is called *full-text indexing.* In some search engines, the robot skips over words that appear often, such as prepositions and articles. These common words are called *stop words*.

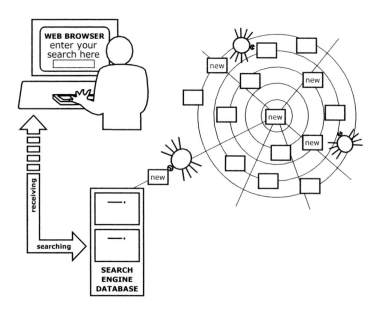

How a Spider Works—Searching the Internet for New Documents

Spiders automatically do this gathering of documents at intervals that differ from service to service. You need to keep in mind that it may be that some portions of a search engine's database may not have been updated in a few weeks. People can also submit their Web pages to be included in the database. This often results in a robot visiting the page and collecting information for the search engine's database.

Some robot programs are intuitive; they know which words are important to the meaning of the entire Web page, and some of them can find synonyms to the words and add them to the index. Some full-text databases use robots that enable them to search on concepts as well as on the search query words. Some Web page authors include *meta-tags* as part of the

HTML code in their pages. Meta-tags may contain keywords that describe the content and purpose of a Web page, but may not appear on the page. They appear only in the HTML source file. You can view the HTML source code by looking at the page source. Click on **View,** and then select **Source**. Meta-tags allow Web pages that don't contain a lot of text to come up in a keyword search. The two most important meta-tags are the *description* and *keywords* tags. Some search engines will use the description section as the short summary that appears next to the URL in the results list.

Becoming proficient in search techniques is crucial in a full-text environment. The chance of retrieving irrelevant material is high when you can type in a word and conceivably retrieve every document that has that word in it. The following two sections define search features and can be referred to when formulating search expressions.

Search Features Common to Most Search Engines

It's important to understand the different search features before you begin using a search engine for research. The reason for this is that each search engine has its own way of interpreting and manipulating search expressions. In addition, many search engines have *default settings* that you may need to override if you want to obtain the most precise results. Because a search can bring up so many Web pages, it is very easy to have a lot of hits with few that are relevant to your query. This is called *low precision/high recall*. You may be satisfied with having very precise search results with a small set returned. This is defined as *high precision/low recall*. Ideally, using the search expression you enter, the search engine would retrieve all of the relevant documents you need. This would be described as *high precision/high recall*.

Search engines support many search features, though not all engines support each one. If they do support certain features, they may use different *syntax* in expressing the feature. Before you use any of these search features, you need to check the search engines' help pages to see how the feature is expressed or if it is supported at all. We will now list the most common search features and explain how each feature is used.

Boolean Operators

We discussed Boolean operators briefly in Chapter 3. Knowing how to apply Boolean operators in search expressions is extremely important. The diagrams show the different operators and how they are used.

hiking AND camping

Use an AND between search terms when you need to narrow your search. The AND indicates that only those Web pages having both words in them will be retrieved. Some search engines automatically assume an AND relationship between two words if you don't type AND between them. This would be a default setting of the search engine.

hiking OR camping

An OR between search terms will make your resulting set larger. When you use OR, Web pages that have either term will be retrieved. Some databases automatically place an OR between two words if there is nothing typed between them. This would be a default setting of the search tool.

hiking NOT camping

The NOT operator is used when a term needs to be excluded. In this example, Web pages with *hiking* would be retrieved but not those with the word *camping*. Some search engines require an AND in front of the NOT. In that case, the expression would be *hiking AND NOT camping*.

hiking AND (camping OR swimming)

This example shows **nested Boolean logic**. Use this technique when you need to include ANDs and ORs in one search statement. For example, say that there is a term that must appear in your results. You want to search for this term along with a concept that you can describe with synonyms. To do this, you will need to tell the search engine to find records with two or more synonyms and then to combine this result with the first term. In the example above, the parentheses indicate that *camping OR swimming* will be processed first, and that this result will be combined with *hiking*. If the parentheses were not there, the search engine would perform the search from left to right. All pages with both the words *hiking* and *camping* would be found first, and then all pages with the word *swimming* would be included. This would give you an unacceptable result, so you must be careful when using ANDs and ORs together in a search expression.

Implied Boolean Operators

Implied Boolean operators, or pseudo-Boolean operators, are shortcuts to typing AND and NOT. In most search engines that support this feature, you type + (plus sign) before a word or phrase that must appear in the document and – (minus sign) before a word or phrase that must not appear in the document.

Phrase Searching

A *phrase* is a string of words that must appear next to each other. *Global warming* is a phrase, as is *chronic fatigue syndrome*. Use phrase-searching capability when the words you are searching for must appear next to each other and must appear in the order in which you type them. Most search engines require double quotation marks to differentiate a phrase from words searched by themselves. The two phrases mentioned above would be expressed like this: "global warming" and "chronic fatigue syndrome." In some search tools, a phrase is assumed when more than one word is typed together without a connector between them. You should read the help pages of the database you are using to find out how **phrase searching** is performed.

Proximity Searching

Proximity operators are words such as *near* or *within*. For example, you are trying to find information on the effects of chlorofluorocarbons on global warming. You might want to retrieve results that have the word *chlorofluorocarbons* very close to the phrase *global warming*. By placing the word NEAR or WITHIN between the two segments of the search expression, you would achieve more relevant results than if the words appeared in the same document but were perhaps pages apart. (Some search tools that use this operator use a W/# words between the two segments, such as: *Hillary W/2 Clinton*.) This is called *proximity searching*.

Truncation

Truncation looks for multiple forms of a word. Some search engines refer to truncation as *stemming*. For example, to research postmodern art, you might want to retrieve all the records that had the root word *postmodern*, such as *postmodernist* and *postmodernism*. Most search engines support truncation by allowing you to place an asterisk (*) at the end of the root word. You will need to see the help pages in the search engine you are using to find out which symbol is used. For example, in this case, we would type **postmodern***. Some search engines automatically truncate words. In those databases, you can type **postmodern** and to be sure to retrieve all the endings. In these cases, truncation is a default setting of the search engines. If you don't want your search expression to be truncated, you need to override the default feature. You can find out how to do this by reading the search engine's help pages.

Wildcards

Using *wildcards* allows you to search for words that have most of the letters in common. For example, to search for both *woman* and *women,* instead of typing **woman OR women**, we place a wildcard character (most often an asterisk) to replace the fourth letter, like this: **wom*n**. In addition to searching for both the American and British spellings of certain words, wildcards are also useful when searching for those words that are commonly misspelled. For example, take the word *genealogy*. By placing the wildcard character where the commonly mistaken letters are placed, like this: **gen*logy**, you can be sure to get documents with the word spelled correctly. Of course, you'll also get pages where the word is misspelled!

Field Searching

Web pages can be broken down into many parts. These parts, or *fields,* include titles, URLs, text, summaries or annotations (if present), and so forth. (See Figure 5.1.) *Field searching* is the ability to limit your search to certain fields. This ability to search by field can increase the relevance of the retrieved records. In AltaVista, for example, you can search for a picture of the Statue of Liberty by typing the following in the search form: **image: "Statute of Liberty"** You can also limit your search to a specific domain, such as educational institutions (.edu), commercial sites (.com), and so forth. In addition, a search can be limited to a particular host, such as a company or institution Web site.

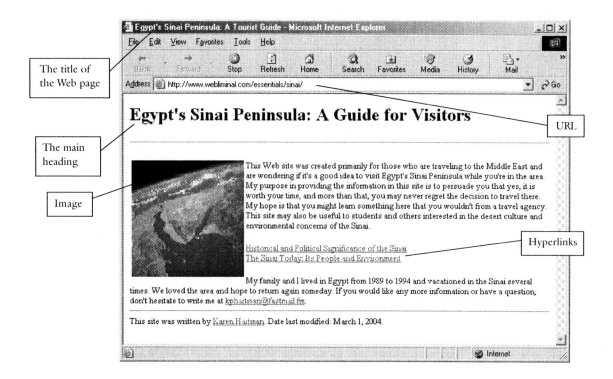

Figure 5.1—The Parts of a Web Page

Language Searching

The ability to limit results to a specific language can be useful. Several search engines support this feature, including AltaVista, All the Web, and Google. Some search engines also provide a translation service.

Case Sensitivity

Case sensitivity is an important feature, especially if you are looking for proper names. Some search engines recognize capitalization, but some do not. If a search engine recognizes capitals, it can lead to a much more precise search, especially if you're looking for proper names such as *Sting* or *The Who*. If the search engine you were using didn't recognize capitals, just think of the results you'd get by entering *sting* in the search query box.

Searching within Search Results

Some search engines allow you to search only the results of an earlier search, which can be extremely helpful. Google and AltaVista are two services that provide this feature.

Limiting by Date

Some search engines allow you to search the Web for pages that were added or modified between certain dates. In **limiting by date,** you can narrow your search to only the pages that were entered in the past month, the past year, or a particular year.

Output Features Common to Most Search Engines

The way a search engine displays results can help you decide which search engine to use. The following features are common to many engines, but as we saw earlier with the search features, the engines all have different ways of determining and showing these features.

Results Ranking

Many search engines measure each Web page's relevance to your search query and arrange the search results from the most relevant to the least relevant. This is called *relevancy ranking*. Each search engine has its own algorithm for determining relevance, but it usually involves counting how many times the words in your query appear in the Web pages. In some search engines, a document is considered more relevant if the words appear in certain fields, such as the title or summary field. In other search engines, relevance is determined by the number of times the keyword appears in a Web page divided by the total number of words in the page. This gives a percentage, and the page with the largest percentage appears first on the list. Some search engines, such as Google and Teoma, determine relevancy by how many Web pages link to it or how many people have accessed particular pages in response to similar questions in the past.

Annotations or Summaries

Some search engines include short descriptive paragraphs of each Web page they return to you. These annotations, or summaries, can help you decide whether you should open a Web page, especially if there is no title for the Web page or if the title doesn't describe the page in detail.

Results Per Page

In some search engines, the *results per page* option allows you to choose how many results you want listed per page. This can be a time saver because it sometimes takes a while to go from page to page as you look through results.

Meta-tag Support

Some search engines acknowledge keywords that a Web page author has placed in the meta-tag field in the HTML source document. This means that a document may be retrieved by a key-word search, even though the search expression may not appear in the document.

A Basic Search Strategy: The 10 Steps

The following list provides a guideline for you to follow in formulating search requests, viewing search results, and modifying search results. These procedures can be followed for virtually any search request, from the simplest to the most complicated. For some search requests, you may not want or need to go through a formal search strategy. If you want to save time in the long run, however, it's a good idea to follow a strategy, especially when you're new to a particular search engine. A basic search strategy can help you get used to each search engine's features and how they are expressed in the search query. Following the 10 steps will also ensure good results if your search is multifaceted and you want to get the most relevant results.

The 10 steps are as follows:

1. Identify the important concepts of your search.

2. Choose the keywords that describe these concepts.

3. Determine whether there are synonyms, related terms, or other variations of the keywords that should be included.

4. Determine which search features may apply, including truncation, proximity operators, Boolean operators, and so forth.

5. Choose a search engine.

6. Read the search instructions on the search engine's home page. Look for sections entitled "Help," "Advanced Search," "Frequently Asked Questions," and so forth.

7. Create a search expression using syntax that is appropriate for the search engine.

8. Evaluate the results. Were the results relevant to your query?

9. Modify your search if needed. Go back to Steps 2 through 4 and revise your query accordingly.

10. Try the same search in a different search engine, following Steps 5 through 9 above.

Search Tips

If you feel that your search has yielded too few Web pages (low recall), there are several things to consider:

+ Perhaps the search expression was too specific; go back and remove some terms that are connected by ANDs.

+ Perhaps there are more terms to use. Think of more synonyms to OR together. Try truncating more words if possible.

+ Check spelling and syntax (a forgotten quotation mark or a missing parentheses).

+ Read the instructions on the help pages again.

If your search has given you too many results and many are unrelated to your topic (high recall/ low precision), consider the following:

+ Narrow your search to specific fields, if possible.

+ Use more specific terms; for example, instead of *cancer*, use the specific type of cancer in which you're interested.

+ Add additional terms with AND or NOT.

+ Remove some synonyms if possible.

In order to explain these concepts in the most practical way, we'll do some activities in a few different databases.

ACTIVITY

5.1   SEARCH STRATEGIES IN ALTAVISTA

OVERVIEW

In this activity, we are going to search for resources on a multifaceted topic. We want to find World Wide Web documents that focus on how self-esteem relates to young girls' likelihood of developing eating disorders.

There has been a lot of research in the past 10 years about how changes in modern life have hurt teenage girls' development, and we'd like to see what research has been published on the Web.

Following most of the steps of the basic search strategy, we need to examine the facets of our search, choose the appropriate keywords, and determine which search features apply. Then, we'll go to AltaVista and read the search instructions. Let's see how this search engine handles this multifaceted topic.

◆ T I P !   Remember that the Web is always changing and that your results may differ from those shown here. Don't let this confuse you. The activities demonstrate fundamental skills. These skills don't change, even though the number of results obtained or the actual screens may look very different.

We'll follow these steps:

1. Identify the important concepts of your search.

2. Choose the keywords that describe these concepts.

3. Determine whether there are synonyms, related terms, or other variations of the keywords that should be included.

4. Determine which search features may apply, including truncation, proximity operators, Boolean operators, and so forth.

5. Choose a search engine.

6. Read the search instructions on the search engine's home page. Look for sections entitled "Help," "Advanced Search," "Frequently Asked Questions," and so forth.

7. Create a search expression using syntax that is appropriate for the search engine.

8. Evaluate the results. Were the results relevant to your query?

9. Modify your search if needed. Go back and revise your query accordingly.

10. Try the same search in a different search engine, following Steps 5 through 9 above.

DETAILS

1   Identify the important concepts of your search.

The most important concepts of this search are the development of eating disorders in adolescent girls and the way this is related to their lack of self-esteem.

2   Choose the keywords that describe these concepts.

The main terms or keywords include the following: *teenage girls*, *self-esteem*, and *eating disorders*.

3   Determine whether there are synonyms, related terms, or other variations of the key-words that should be included.

For teenage: adolescent, adolescence
For eating disorders: anorexia nervosa, bulimia
For self-esteem: none

4   Determine which search features may apply, including truncation, proximity operators, Boolean operators, and so forth.

When developing a search expression, keep in mind that you place OR between synonyms and AND between the different concepts, or facets, of the search topic. If you write down all the synonyms you choose, it may help with the construction of the final search phraseology. Table 5.1 shows the three major concepts, or facets, of the search topic with their synonyms connected with the appropriate Boolean operators. Keep in mind there can be different ways to express the same idea. Before you get online, take a few minutes to determine whether you've included the major keywords and the appropriate search features. It can save you a lot of time in the long run.

Concept 1	Concept 2	Concept 3
global warming (phrase)	climate change (phrase)	infectious disease* (phrase)
ozone depletion (phrase)		
greenhouse effect (phrase)		(* denotes the word will be truncated)

AND (between Concept 1 and Concept 2); AND (between Concept 2 and Concept 3); OR (between global warming and ozone depletion); OR (between ozone depletion and greenhouse effect)

Table 5.1—Formulation of the Search Strategy

5   Choose a search engine.

For this search, we would like to start with a search engine that supports nested Boolean searching. We have a complex search, with phrases that will be OR'd together and AND'd with other phrases. AltaVista, **http://altavista.com**, is a full-text database that supports nested Boolean searching in its Advanced Search mode, and has special features that are appealing

✦ Do It!   Click on the address box, type **http://altavista.com**, and press ⌐Enter⌐.

Your screen should look like the one in Figure 5.2.

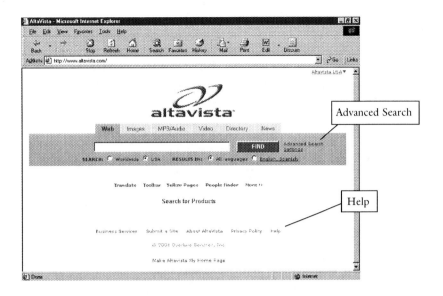

Figure 5.2—AltaVista Home page

6 Read the search instructions on the search engine's home page. Look for sections entitled "Help," "Advanced Search," "Frequently Asked Questions," and so forth.

✦ Do It!   Click on **Help**.

The information provided in the search help section tells us that it is necessary to use quotation marks around phrases. Words are treated as phrases if they have no Boolean connectors (AND, OR, or NOT) between them. We learn from AltaVista's Advanced Search mode help page that it supports a full range of search features, including full Boolean searching (AND, OR, and NOT must be in upper case), field searching, limiting a search by date, and many others.

Because we want to do a full Boolean search, we need to access the **Advanced Search** mode.

✦ Do It!   Click on **Advanced Search**, as shown in Figure 5.2.

7 Create a search expression using syntax that is appropriate for the search engine.

Now that you've read the search help, it's time to formulate the search expression. It will help to write it out before you type it in the search form. Here is a possible way to express this search:

("teenage girls" OR "adolescent girls") AND ("eating disorders" OR "anorexia nervosa" OR bulimia) AND "self-esteem"

AltaVista's help section didn't give us guidance on using ORs with ANDs in a single search expression, but from our experience, we know that when you have both of these connectors in one Boolean search expression, it's best to place the OR'd phrases within parentheses.

137

Keep in mind that you can always modify your search later. Let's try entering it in AltaVista's search form.

✦ Do It! Type the following search expression in the search form provided:

("teenage girls" OR "adolescent girls") AND ("eating disorders" or "anorexia nervosa" OR bulimia) AND "self-esteem"

✦ Do It! Click on **FIND**.

8 Evaluate the results. Are the results relevant to your query?

Look at the results of the search query, as shown in Figure 5.3. Your results may differ.

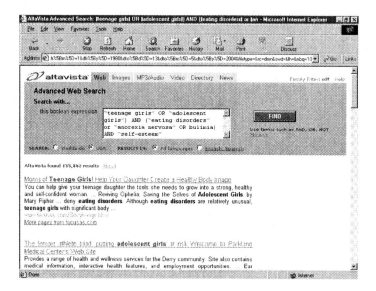

Figure 5.3—AltaVista Search Results

9 Modify your search if needed. Go back and revise your query accordingly.

Since we found relevant results, we don't need to modify our search. To retrieve different results in the first few pages, you could change the keywords entered in the sort box, as the terms entered here impact which Web pages are listed first.

10 Try the same search in a different search engine, following Steps 5 through 9 above.

See Activity 5.2 for this step.

END OF ACTIVITY 5.1

As we saw in this activity, AltaVista's Advanced Search handles multifaceted search queries very well. There are pros and cons to using any of the search engines. Sometimes it comes down to which service you are more comfortable with using. In the following two activities, we'll be searching for the same topic in two very different databases: Google and Vivisimo. Google is a single search engine database, whereas Vivisimo is a meta-search tool that allows you to search several search engines simultaneously. In performing searches in each of these indexes, we will follow the steps laid out in the basic search strategy.

ACTIVITY

5.2   SEARCH STRATEGIES IN GOOGLE

OVERVIEW

We'll be searching for the same information that we did in Activity 5.1—how self-esteem relates to teenage girls' likelihood of developing eating disorders. In Activity 5.1, we have already done Steps 1 through 4 of the basic search strategy, so we'll now do the following steps, which correspond to Steps 5 through 10 of the strategy:

1. Choose a search engine.

2. Read the search instructions on the search engine's home page. Look for sections entitled "Help," "Advanced Search," "Frequently Asked Questions," and so forth.

3. Create a search expression using syntax that is appropriate for the search engine.

4. Evaluate the results. Were the results relevant to your query?

5. Modify your search if needed. Go back and revise your query accordingly.

6. Try the same search in a different search engine.

DETAILS

1   Choose a search engine.

We'll be searching Google, another popular search engine. Google doesn't support full Boolean searching as AltaVista's Advanced Search does, but with its unique and effective link analysis page ranking method, most searches result in highly relevant hits. Let's go to Google and see how it handles our topic.

✦ Do It!   Click on the address box, type **http://google.com**, and press **Enter**.

View the Google home page, as shown in Figure 5.4.

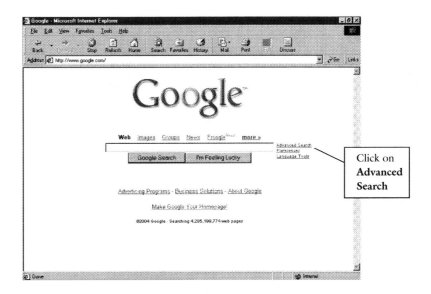

Figure 5.4—Google's Home Page

2 Read the search instructions on the search engine's home page. Look for sections entitled "Help," "Advanced Search," "Frequently Asked Questions," and so forth.

We don't see a link for Help or Frequently Asked Questions, so we'll try the Advanced Search link.

✦ Do It!   Click on **Advanced Search**, as shown in Figure 5.4.

Google's Advanced Search window appears. We may end up using the Advanced Search mode, but at this point we're not sure.

✦ Do It!   To find out more, click on **Advanced Search Tips**.

This page describes the special attributes of the Advanced Search mode. There are a few other links that we'll try as well: **Basics of Search** and **General FAQ**. After reading through these searching help tips, we determine:

✦ Google supports phrase searching by requiring quotes to be placed around words that must be together.

✦ Google supports the OR Boolean operator but doesn't support nested Boolean searching, as AltaVista does.

✦ The AND operator is implied between terms (no need to type AND).

✦ Google allows you to search within the current search results.

After reading through the information provided, we decide to use Google's Advanced Search mode for our search because the main search mode doesn't support the mixing of ANDs and ORs in a nested Boolean operation. The Advanced Search mode will not allow us to OR several phrases together either, but it will allow us to OR several terms and combine these terms with a phrase. Because Google allows searching within results, we can always add that final feature in later.

3 Create a search expression using syntax that is appropriate for the search engine.

✦ Do It!   Return to the Advanced Search page by clicking **Advanced Search page** on the Advanced Search Help page or by clicking **Google** in the upper left corner and selecting **Advanced Search** from the home page.

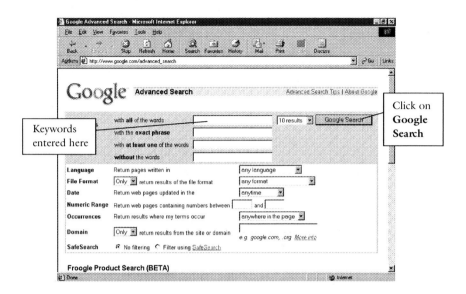

Figure 5.5—Google's Advanced Search

✦ Do It!   Type **girls** in the search form next to **with all the words**. This will guarantee that every Web page has this word included in the text. Then type **eating disorders** in the search form next to "with the exact phrase." Note that it is not necessary to place quotation marks around the phrase when using this field-based search form. Finally, type **teenage adolescent** in the form next to "with at least one of the words." Doing so means that either one of the words must be in the documents. This is equivalent to an "or" search.

✦ Do It!   Click on **Google Search** to begin.

4   Evaluate the results. Were the results relevant to your query?

This search retrieved over 70,000 documents. The first 10 to 20 appear to be relevant from scanning the titles. Because we left out one important facet of our search, the term *self-esteem*, we would like to find documents that focus on this issue from among the results.

5   Modify your search if needed. Go back and revise your query accordingly.

Google allows you to search only the results of a previous search. Let's say that of the documents that the search retrieved, we want to know which ones have the phrase *self-esteem* in them. All that is required is to type **"self-esteem"** in the search form provided and to indicate that only these results should be searched. Let's do that now. First, we need to find the search form for searching within results. This form is located at the bottom of the search results pages in Google.

✦ Do It!   Scroll down to the bottom of the page. Figure 5.6 shows the form that we're looking for.

✦ Do It!   Click on **Search within Results,** as shown in Figure 5.6.

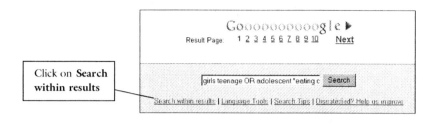

Figure 5.6—Bottom of Search Results Page in Google

The **Search within results** form will then appear, as shown in Figure 5.7.

✦ Do It!   In the search form provided, type **"self-esteem"** as shown in Figure 5.7.

✦ Do It!   Click on the button labeled **Search within results**.

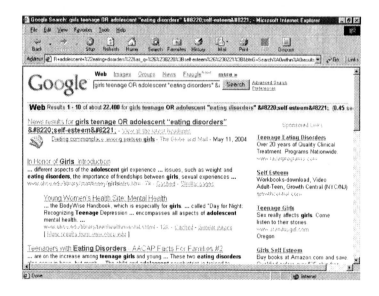

Figure 5.7—Searching Within Results in Google

Figure 5.8 shows the results of this modification. Remember that you may have different results because the Web is always changing.

Figure 5.8—Results of Modifying the Original Search in Google

6   Try the same search in a different search engine.

Next we're going to try the same search in Vivisimo in Activity 5.3.

END OF ACTIVITY 5.2

Google proved to be an effective search engine. We learned how to search within existing results, which is one of Google's many useful features.

ACTIVITY

5.3 SEARCH STRATEGIES IN VIVISIMO

OVERVIEW

In this activity, we'll look for information on the same topic in Vivisimo. As stated before, Vivisimo is a meta-search tool. Also known as parallel-search tools or unified search interfaces, meta-search tools don't create their own indexes. They merely provide a search interface so that you can use several search engines and directories at the same time with one search expression. Meta-search tools can be very useful for single-word subjects, but unreliable for multiterm, multifaceted searches, such as the one we have been using in this chapter. Let's see how Vivisimo handles our topic. We will be following Steps 5 through 10 of the basic search strategy, as we did in Activity 5.2.

1. Choose a search engine.

2. Read the search instructions on the search engine's home page. Look for sections entitled "Help," "Advanced Search," "Frequently Asked Questions," and so forth.

3. Create a search expression using syntax that is appropriate for the search engine.

4. Evaluate the results. Were the results relevant to your query?

5. Modify your search if needed. Go back and revise your query accordingly.

DETAILS

1 Choose a search engine.

Let's go to Vivisimo.

✦ Do It! Click on the address box, type in the URL for Vivisimo, **http://vivisimo.com**, and press **Enter**.

Your screen should look like the picture in Figure 5.9.

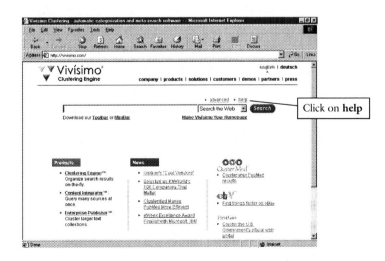

Figure 5.9—Vivisimo's Home Page

2 Read the search instructions on the search engine's home page. Look for sections entitled "Help," "Advanced Search," "Frequently Asked Questions," and so forth.

In order to find out how to use Vivisimo, read its documentation.

✦ Do It!   Click on **Help!**, as shown in Figure 5.9.

✦ Do It!   To find out about Vivisimo's search options, click on **Search Syntax**, as shown in Figure 5.10.

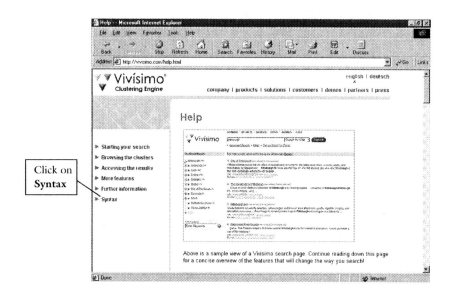

Figure 5.10—Vivisimo Help

After reading the Vivisimo Syntax page, we determine that

✦ Vivisimo translates queries into the corresponding syntax of the search engines that are searched.

✦ While most search features are supported, it may be best to keep our search simple so that the search engine can pull from as many sources as possible.

✦ Vivisimo supports implied Boolean operators and phrase searching with quotation marks around the phrase.

✦ The Advanced Search mode may be the best form for us to use, as it supports more detailed features.

3 Create a search expression using syntax that is appropriate for the search engine.

✦ Do It!   Click on the Vivisimo icon in the upper left corner.

✦ Do It!   Click on the **Advanced Search** link at the bottom of the window.

Your window should look like the one in Figure 5.11.

✦ Do It!   Type the following in the search form provided:

+"teenage girls" +"eating disorders" +"self-esteem"

✦ Do It!   Click on **Search**.

This will initiate your search request. See Figure 5.11. By using this search expression, you are telling Vivisimo to find all the Web pages in which each of these three phrases occur. The + in front of each phrase indicates that the phrase *must* appear somewhere in the Web pages.

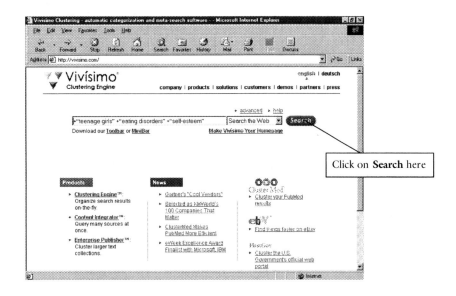

Figure 5.11—Submission of Vivisimo Search Query

4   Evaluate the results. Were the results relevant to your query?

A portion of the search results are shown in Figure 5.12. Note that Vivisimo places the results in folders on the left side of the window.

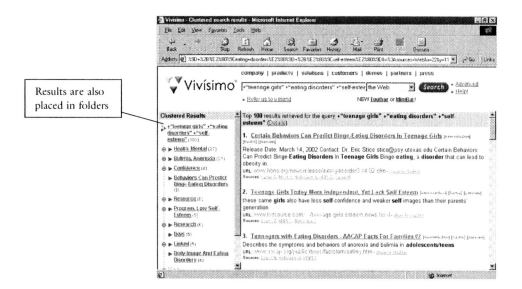

Results are also placed in folders

Figure 5.12—Vivisimo Results

5   Modify your search if needed. Go back and revise your query accordingly.

This search seemed to provide many relevant hits, and Vivisimo's feature of placing the documents in search folders in a frame is helpful as well. Note that Vivisimo allows searching within results to locate a specific term in the title or annotations. We typed **self-esteem** in the form on the lower left of the window and clicked on **Go**. This gave us a smaller set of documents that included this term prominently in the document's record. Give it a try if you wish.

6   Try the same search in a different search engine.

If you like, you could try the same search in a different search engine on your own.

END OF ACTIVITY 5.3

In Activities 5.1, 5.2, and 5.3, we searched for information on the same topic in three different search engines. Each one had its own particular syntax and individual search and output features. We saw the importance of reading each search engine's documentation before initializing the search. All of the search engines gave relevant results, but none of them gave the same results.

Summary

Search engines are information retrieval systems that allow us to search the vast collection of resources on the Internet and the World Wide Web. A search engine consists of three components: a computer program called a spider or robot that retrieves hyperlinks attached to documents, a database that indexes these documents, and software that allows users to enter keywords in search forms to obtain ranked results.

Each search engine database is unique and accesses its database differently. Even though many search engine databases claim to cover as much of the Web as possible, the same search performed in more than one database never returns the exact same results. If you want to do a thorough search, you should become familiar with a few of the different search engines. Toward this end, it is important to understand the major search features, such as Boolean logic, phrase searching, truncation, and others before you get online. It is also necessary to read each search engine's documentation before you enter the search request in the search form. You may want to check the documentation often, since search engines are constantly changing their search and output features.

It can help to try your search in a meta-search tool if you're not overly concerned about obtaining precise and comprehensive results. That way, you can gather hits from several databases at once.

In this chapter, we introduced the basic search strategy, a 10-step procedure that can help you formulate search requests, submit them to search engines, and modify the results retrieved. We have focused on the major search engines on the World Wide Web, but there are several hundred smaller search engines on the Web that search smaller databases. We'll discuss these in some detail in Chapter 6, "Specialized Databases." Our intent in this chapter was to give you a foundation in searching any database, no matter whether it is large or small, fee-based or not. All of the steps in the basic search strategy apply to any database.

Selected Terms Introduced in This Chapter

case sensitivity	high precision/ low recall	meta-tag
concept searching		nested Boolean logic
default setting	implied Boolean operator	proximity searching
duplicate detection		relevancy ranking
field	invisible Web	results per page
field searching	keyword indexing	stop word
full-text indexing	limiting by date	syntax
hidden Internet	low precision/high recall	truncation
high precision/ high recall		wildcard

Review Questions

Multiple Choice

1. A results list, or hit list, that has many results with few that are relevant to your query would be described as
   a. high precision/low recall.
   b. high precision/high recall.
   c. low precision/low recall.
   d. low precision/high recall.

2. The configuration a search engine automatically uses for a search unless it you override it is called the
    a. syntax.
    b. nested Boolean logic.
    c. default setting.
    d. field searching.

3. A search engine that indexes all the words of each Web document in its database is doing
    a. abstracting.
    b. full-text indexing.
    c. citation indexing.
    d. subject indexing.

4. The following is an example of truncation:
    a. psyche near soul.
    b. +internet.
    c. -unix.
    d. colleg*.

5. The expression *mining and (coal or iron)* shows the concept of
    a. phrase searching.
    b. implied Boolean operators.
    c. nested Boolean logic.
    d. proximity searching.

6. If a search returns too many results and they are not relevant to your topic, you could
    a. narrow your search by using more specific terms.
    b. add additional terms to your search with **OR**.
    c. a and b
    d. none of the above

True or False

7. T F Typing a **+** or **–** before a word in a search is making use of implied Boolean operators.
8. T F Truncation is also known as stemming.
9. T F It's best to use a meta-search tool to search for a complex, multiterm topic.
10. T F Some search engines allow you to limit a search to a part of the page, such as the title.
11. T F The first step in planning a search is to choose a search engine.
12. T F All search engines allow you to limit your results by date.
13. T F The subject folders in Vivisimo can help you screen your results.

Completion

14. Common words that a search engine skips over, such as *of* or *the*, are known as
_____.

15. In a search expression, the words *near* or *within* are known as
_____.

16. Typing a search expression with one character that stands in for a group of characters, such as m*n, is making use of a(n) _____.

17. The _____ is that part of the Internet that is in special databases and isn't easily searchable with search engines.

18. A keyword that does not appear on a Web page but is included in the source code of the page and may be indexed by a search engine is called a(n) _____.

19. _____ means that a search engine recognizes capital and lowercase letters.

20. A part of a Web page, such as a title or URL or annotation, is known as a(n)
_____.

Exercises and Projects

1. Using the advanced search mode in AltaVista, **http://altavista.com**, and in All the Web, **http://alltheweb.com**, look for relevant resources on the following topics:
   a. The life expectancy of a Sun Conure.
   b. Mary Kingsley's travels in Africa.
   c. Maria Mitchell's contributions to astronomy

   Write down the titles of the first three Web pages retrieved by each search engine. Were any of these the same in the two search engines? Write down the search expression you used in each database.

2. Sometimes it is helpful to look for specific types of Web sites about a topic. Go to Google at **http://www.google.com** and look for Web pages about the inventor Nikola Tesla. Can you tell how many results are found? Now go to Google's advanced search page and do the same search, limiting your results to domains that end with **.edu**. How many results do you find now? Change your search to look for results with the **.gov** domain which were updated in the last year. How many results do you find?

3. Find the most recent annual report and a mission statement for Pfizer. What would be the best strategy to use to find this information?

   a. Go to Teoma at **http://www.teoma.com**. What search expression(s) did you use at Teoma to find the annual report and mission statement? Give the URL's of the page(s) where they are found.

   b. Try the same search in Google at **http://www.google.com**. Which search engine gave you more relevant results?

4. Look for information on how genetically altered corn is affecting Monarch butterflies.

   a. First, write down your search strategy. What keywords will you use? What other words might be used instead of "genetically altered?" What search expression will you start with?

   b. Try your search at MSN, **http://www.msn.com**. How many results did you find? Go to the first three sites listed. How relevant are they to your search? Give the URLs of the sites you visited. Do you need to modify your search expression?

5. Virtual Humans have become a topic of interest. Besides being the stuff of speculative fiction, they are becoming the stuff of reality!

   a. Go to Google at **http://www.google.com** and search for virtual humans. How many results do you find? Look at some of the first ten sites in your results list. What is a virtual human? Give the URL of the site where you found your answer.

   b. Now search for pages that show Peter Plantec's contribution to the field of virtual humans. What was your search expression? How many results did you find? Who is Peter Plantec? Give the URL of the page where you found the answer.

6. Using the advanced search mode in Alta Vista, **http://altavista.com**, look for information on how mad cow disease (also known as Bovine Spongiform Encephalopathy) causes Creutzfeldt-Jakob disease in humans.

   a. Write down your search expression and the total number of results. Do you need to modify your search expression?

   b. Were your results relevant to your request? Write down three of the most relevant titles and their URLs.

7. Go to MSN at **http://www.msn.com**, to find comparison studies of the drugs venlafaxine XR and fluoxetine. What search expression did you use? Go to the first three Web sites listed. What are the brand names of these drugs? Give the titles and URLs of the three sites you visited. Which was most relevant?

8. Just as the Web is constantly changing, search engines do as well. Go to Lycos at **http://www.lycos.com** and do a search for comparisons and reviews of search engines. Scan through the search results and go to the most promising sites. Give the titles and URLs of the sites you visited. Which was the best? Why? You may want to put one of these sites in your list of favorites or bookmarks. (A good site for keeping up with the rapid pace of change in search engines is Search Engine Watch at **http://www.searchenginewatch.com**. You can even subscribe to a free email newsletter at the site to stay up to date!)

9. From cuneiform writing to the printing press, written communication kept changing and becoming more pervasive. By the 19th Century, a new invention made a big difference. Try a search for the history of the fountain pen.

a. Who invented it? When did the invention take place?

b. Tell what search engine you used, what search expression you used, and give the URL of the site where you found your answer.

SPECIALIZED
DATABASES

Much of what is available on the World Wide Web that is not accessible from the major search engines is to be found in *specialized databases*. Some folks describe this group of resources as the *invisible Web* or the *hidden Internet.* Databases containing public information or material not proprietary in nature commonly appear on the Web. These databases, many of which are maintained by government agencies and nonprofit organizations, can quickly provide you with a wealth of information that formerly was difficult or time-consuming to obtain.

Specialized databases are indexes that can be searched, much like the search engines explored in Chapter 5. The main difference is that specialized databases are collections on particular subjects, such as medical journal article abstracts and citations, company financial data, United States Supreme Court decisions, phone number and email addresses, maps, census data, patents, and so forth. You can find information in specialized databases that you often would not locate by using a global search engine. If you know there is a specialized database on the subject you are researching, using that database can save you time and give you reliable, up-to-date information.

We covered subject guides in Chapter 3. The difference between a subject guide and a specialized database is that subject guides are collections of URLs in a particular area (many times these URLs are hyperlinks), whereas a specialized database contains the actual data or information you are seeking.

This chapter will include the following sections:

- ♦ Overview of Specialized Databases
- ♦ Information in Specialized Databases is Often Not Accessible Via Search Engines
- ♦ How to Find Specialized Databases
- ♦ Using Specialized Databases

Overview of Specialized Databases

Bibliographic and Full-text Databases

In this chapter, we'll show you two major types of databases: bibliographic and full-text. A *bibliographic database* includes citations that describe and identify titles, dates, authors, and other parts of written works. It doesn't contain the full text of the articles themselves. An example of a bibliographic database is MEDLINE, which we'll cover in Activity 6.1. A *full-text database*, on the other hand, includes the entire text of the indexed works. A full-text database can contain financial, scientific, or other types of data. An example of a full-text database is *FindLaw: Supreme Court Opinions,* which we'll explore in Activity 6.3. The major difference between a bibliographic and a full-text database is that a bibliographic database describes an entity, whether it be an article, a book, a work of art, or any other product, whereas a full-text database includes a description *and* the work itself.

Proprietary Databases

There are hundreds of *proprietary* or *commercial databases* on the World Wide Web, but these are available only if you or your organization has purchased access to them. For example, FirstSearch, **http://www.ref.oclc.org**; DIALOG, **http://www.dialogselect.com;** STN, **http://www.cas.org/stn.html;** and Lexis-Nexis, **http://www.lexisnexis.com**, all provide proprietary databases.

Proprietary databases have certain value-added features that databases in the public domain do not have. Here are some examples of that enhanced content:

✦ Proprietary databases are likely to include extra information that helps researchers. For example, most of the databases in FirstSearch (the Online Computer Library Center's [OCLC] proprietary database system) have links to library holdings. This means that if you find an article or book in a database provided by FirstSearch, such as MEDLINE, you can immediately find out which libraries own the material. Even though MEDLINE is available free to the public from the National Library of Medicine, you might prefer to use the FirstSearch version if you want to know who has the listed journal articles.

✦ Proprietary databases also allow you to download information easily. For instance, some of these databases include financial information that is commonly free to the public, but they charge for the use of their databases because they have made it much easier for the user to download the information to a spreadsheet program.

✦ Proprietary databases often index material that others do not. The information is distinguished by its uniqueness, its historical value, or its competitive value (for example, private company financial information).

✦ Proprietary database systems are more responsive to their users. Because they charge money, they are more apt to provide training and other user support, such as the distribution of newsletters that update their services.

There are also databases on the Web that are free to the public but charge for the full text of the articles, for example, High Beam Research, **http://www.highbeam.com/library/index.asp?**. Many newspaper archives work the same way. You can search the archive, but if you want a copy of the newspaper article, there is a fee involved.

Accessing Fee-based Databases

Ask a reference librarian at your local library about accessing proprietary databases. The library may have databases on CD-ROM or may have purchased access to databases via the Internet. If it is an academic library, use from your home computer may require that you are a current student at the institution, but most college libraries will allow visitors to search the databases from the library. Many public libraries provide access to databases from home for members with a library card.

The specialized databases covered in this chapter are all free and open to anyone.

Information in Specialized Databases Is Often Not Accessible Via Search Engines

The major search engines discussed in earlier chapters build their databases by collecting URLs that exist on the World Wide Web. The Web pages that are attached to the URLs are then indexed. When you type a word or words in a search engine's search form, you retrieve a list of URLs that already exist in the search engine's database. To put it simply, a search engine typically cannot search a specialized database because of the following reasons:

✦ A database usually cannot search another database without some very special programming. The search engine you are using may come across a specialized database but then may be stopped from going any further because the special database has a search form that requests information from the user. For example, you wouldn't look in AltaVista to see what books are in your library, you'd look at your library's Web-based catalog.

✦ Many specialized databases contain information that is retrieved dynamically every time a request is made, and the URLs that are generated are different each time. A search engine usually cannot build its database with URLs that may work today and not tomorrow. (Although we have seen that a search engine occasionally picks up information from a dynamic Web site and indexes the unstable URL. If you retrieved that page from your results list, your keywords would not appear.)

✦ Most search engines are unable to index content from specially formatted files. For example, the content in Adobe PDF (portable document format) files is inaccessible to many search engines because the text is formatted in such a way as to be unable to be indexed.

Google, **http://www.google.com**, has made great progress with its attempts to reach the Invisible Web. It now indexes PDF files and has been able to include some dynamically generated Web pages in its search results. Look for other Web search engines to start to improve their ability to reach more content on the Internet as well.

How to Find Specialized Databases

By some accounts, there are more than 8,000 specialized databases on the World Wide Web. How do you find them? Sometimes you'll stumble across specialized databases while doing a keyword search in a search engine. Occasionally, a Web page will have a hyperlink to a database, or a friend or colleague will tell you about a particular site. There are more precise ways to find them, but even these are not always foolproof.

◆ You can go to a search engine and type in the kind of database you're searching for along with the word **database**. For example, each of these search expressions typed in Google's search form provided excellent databases in the areas requested:

> **medical database**
>
> **flags database**
>
> **"zip codes" database**

◆ Virtual libraries, meta-search tools that include lists of databases, and directories are often the best sources to use when looking for specialized databases. Following is a list of some of the most popular ones:

TOOL	URL AND DESCRIPTION
Beaucoup	**http://www.beaucoup.com** Beaucoup lists more than 2,500 specialized databases and directories and also serves as a meta-search tool.
Digital Librarian: a Librarian's Choice of the Best of the Web	**http://www.digital-librarian.com** The Digital Librarian is maintained by Cortland, NY, librarian Margaret Vail Anderson.
Direct Search	**http://www.freepint.com/gary/direct.htm** Direct Search is a collection of links to specialized databases compiled by Gary Price.
Internet Public Library (IPL) Reference Center	**http://www.ipl.org/** The IPL is a virtual library that provides a good starting point for finding reference works, subject guides, and specialized databases.
LibrarySpot	**http://libraryspot.com/** LibrarySpot collects links to quality reference resources and provides links to more than 2,500 libraries around the world.
Librarians' Index to the Internet	**http://lii.org** A virtual library that is both searchable and browsable, this is an excellent source for specialized databases.
Open Directory Project and Yahoo!	**http://dmoz.org** and **http://di.yahoo.com**, two of the most comprehensive directories on the Web, are also good places to find subject guides and specialized databases.
The Scout Report	**http://scout.cs.wisc.edu/** The Scout Report is a good way to keep up with new search tools, especially specialized databases. You can view its weekly report and its archive of previous Scout Reports on the Web. You can also have the report delivered to you via email by subscribing through a listserv. Send an email message to **listserv@cs.wisc.edu**. Type **subscribe SCOUT-REPORT** in the body of the message.

Table 6.1—Some Tools That List Specialized Databases

Using Specialized Databases

Just like search engines, specialized databases support different search features. Most of these databases support many of the same search features covered in Chapter 5, such as Boolean searching and phrase searching. Many databases have search instruction pages, just as the major search engines do.

In this chapter, we'll be doing several activities that will familiarize you with some of the most useful types of databases on the World Wide Web. We've chosen databases that cover the following topic areas: medicine, business, law, and finding people, businesses, and maps. We selected these areas because the Web is an excellent medium for research in these fields. Much of the useful information needed for research in these areas is in the public domain. We'll search first for medical information. While you move through the activities, you may want to review the search features and the basic search strategies introduced in Chapter 5.

In the first activity, we'll look for a specialized database to help us find journal articles on a medical topic. In the example, we'll use the Librarians' Index to the Internet to help us find a hyperlink to MEDLINE, which is a bibliographic database devoted to medical journal literature. There are several ways to find hyperlinks to MEDLINE providers on the Web. Keep in mind that we are showing you only *one* way to do it.

Remember that the Web is always changing and that your results may differ from those shown here. Don't let this confuse you. The activities demonstrate fundamental skills. These skills don't change, even though the number of results obtained or the actual screens may look very different.

ACTIVITY

6.1   SEARCHING MEDLINE

OVERVIEW

We are doing research on Creutzfeldt-Jakob disease. This is the human disease that has been linked to eating beef from cows with bovine spongiform encephalopathy (BSE), commonly referred to as *mad cow disease*. We need to find recent articles from medical journals that would update our general knowledge of Creutzfeldt-Jakob disease, focusing on the connections between it and BSE.

We know that the National Library of Medicine publishes a database called MEDLINE, and we've heard that it may be available on the Web for free.

✦ F Y I   Searching for
Medical Information

The World Wide Web can be a useful source for health and medical information. Medical centers and physicians create home pages that discuss specific aspects of health care, and you can find these pages by doing searches in the major search engines. Medical reference books are also appearing on the Web. For example, the entire *Merck Manual of Diagnosis and Therapy*, **http://www.merck.com/mrkshared/mmanual/home.jsp/**, a well-known medical diagnostic handbook, is online. You can also find citations to medical journal articles on the Web.

How can we find it? Let's try the Librarians' Index to the Internet. After we find it, we'll access MEDLINE, search it, and view the results. We will take the following steps:

1. Go to the home page for the Librarians' Index to the Internet.

2. Starting with the list of health and medicine resources, locate and select MEDLINE.

3. Look at basic search help.

4. Type in search terms and retrieve results.

5. Choose a citation from the list of results.

6. Display the full record of the selected citation.

DETAILS

1 Go to the home page for the Librarians' Index to the Internet.

✦ Do It! Click on the address box, type **http://lii.org**, and then press **Enter**.

✦ Do It! Click on **Health & Medicine** from the Librarians' Index to the Internet home page, as shown in Figure 6.1.

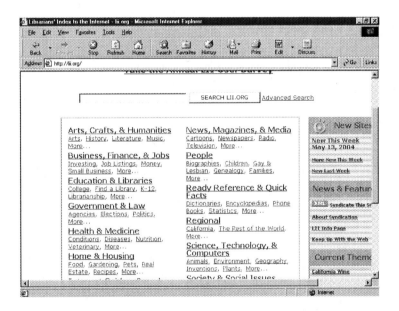

Figure 6.1—Home Page for the Librarians' Index to the Internet

2 Starting with the list of health and medicine resources, locate and select MEDLINE.

You will see a listing of several health and medical categories from which to choose, as shown in Figure 6.2.

✦ Do It! Click on **MEDLINE**.

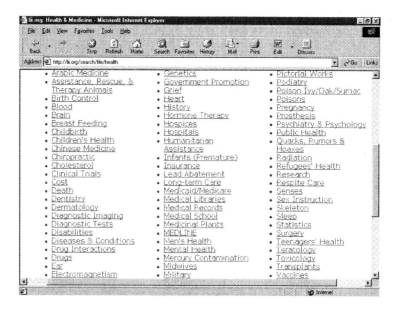

Figure 6.2—Health and Medicine Categories—Librarians' Index to the Internet

The MEDLINE category has several resources listed. The first one on the list is the database we want.

✦ Do It!   Click on the hyperlink titled **Entrez PubMed**, as shown in Figure 6.3.

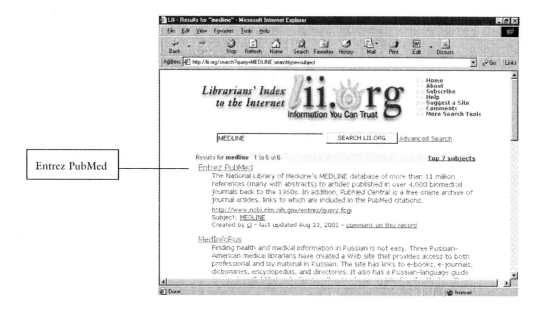

Figure 6.3—MEDLINE Databases

3 Look at basic search help.

The Overview section tells us that PubMed is a project developed by the National Library of Medicine (NLM), which is located at the National Institutes of Health (NIHMEDLINE is the premier database covering the fields of medicine, nursing, dentistry, veterinary medicine, and other health-related sciences). The MEDLINE file contains bibliographic citations and abstracts from about 4,600 current biomedical journals published in the United States and 70 foreign countries. The file contains approximately 11 million records dating back to 1966. Most records are from English-language sources or have English-language abstracts.

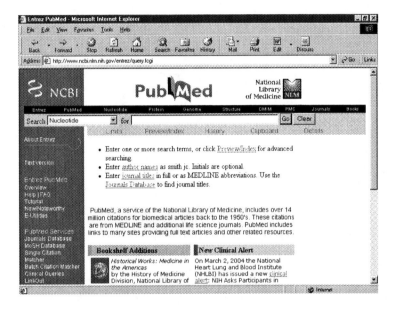

Figure 6.4—NLM's MEDLINE Home Page

Now that we know a bit more about what PubMed consists of, let's find out how to search it effectively by reading the help section.

For search help, we need to access the help section. Help is located below the Overview hyperlink on PubMed's main page.

✦ Do It!   Click on **Help**.

By reading the search help information, we discover the following:

✦ Boolean searching using operators other than AND is supported in the advanced search mode only.

✦ Boolean search operators (AND, OR, and NOT) must be capitalized.

✦ Phrase searching is supported by placing quotation marks around the phrase.

✦ PubMed is not case-sensitive.

✦ The Preview/Index search mode allows you to easily limit your search to particular fields, such as individual journal titles, article types (for example, review articles and clinical trials), certain years, languages, and many other specifications.

4 Type in search terms and retrieve results.

Now we're ready to do our search.

✦ Do It!   From the help window, click the **Back** button.

Since our search has two facets, Creutzfeldt-Jakob disease and bovine spongiform encephalopathy, we'll need to use the Boolean operator AND. We also want to limit our search to those articles that are in the English language. We learned from the help section that to limit results to those in certain fields, it's best to use the Preview/Index mode.

✦ T I P !   If you want to find a company's home page but don't know the URL, you can often guess it by typing the company's name with **http://www.** at the beginning and **.com** at the end. For example, if you were looking for the home page for Sears, Roebuck, and Company, you could try typing **http://www.sears.com**. This is the correct URL for Sears, Roebuck, and Company. You could also use a search engine to look for the company's name, limiting the results to URLs that include **sears.com**.

✦ Do It!   Click on **Preview/Index**, which is located in the center of the screen.

Now you should be at a screen that looks like the one pictured in Figure 6.5. Remember that PubMed is not case-sensitive so there is no need to capitalize proper nouns. Also note that we'll need to search for both of the concepts as phrases by placing quotation marks around each one.

✦ Do It!   Type **"creutzfeldt-jakob disease" AND "bovine spongiform encephalopathy"** in the search form.

To narrow the search to those articles that are written in English, access the pull-down menu, select **Language** from the fields provided, and type **english** in the search form.

✦ Do It!   Click on **Preview/Index**, as shown in Figure 6.5.

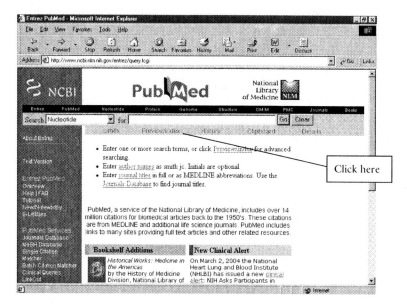

Figure 6.5— Search Expression Entered in PubMed's Preview/Index Mode

A query information page is shown in Figure 6.6. Note that the search has been given a number (#1) and gave 700 results. Your screen may show a different number. We could add more terms to the query by clicking on the pull-down menu arrow under **Add Term(s) to Query or View Index:,** but for right now, we're ready to view the current results.

✦ Do It!   Click on the number of results, as shown in Figure 6.6.

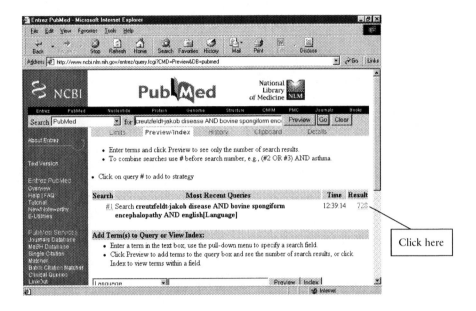

Figure 6.6—Query Information Page in PubMed

5   Choose a citation from the list of results.

Figure 6.7 shows a portion of the results of this query. If you want to see a full record, you can click on the author hyperlink. If you'd like to see more than one record at a time, click on the boxes next to the citations you wish to see.

In this example, we'll click on the citation that represents an article written by Lezmi S, etal.

✦ Do It!   Click on the hyperlink **Lezmi S**, et al., as shown in Figure 6.7.

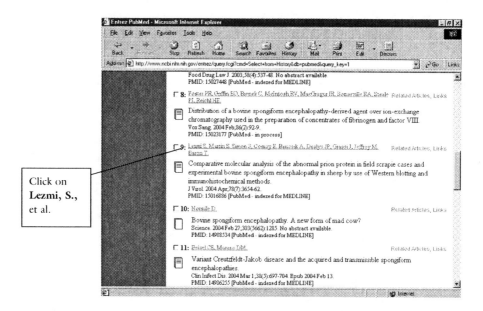

Figure 6.7—Results of the MEDLINE Search

6   Display the full record of the selected citation.

✦ Do It!   Look at the portion of the record that appears in Figure 6.8.

✦ Do It!   Scroll through the complete record.

Note the detailed information that the abstract provides.

Let's say you wanted a copy of this article, which appears in the *Journal of Virology*. You could go about this in several ways:

✦ Find out if your local public or academic library carries this journal. If so, copy the article there.

✦ Call your local hospital and find out if it owns the journal and if the public is allowed to photocopy articles from its library.

✦ Initiate an interlibrary loan request from your library if the journal is not available from the previously mentioned sources.

✦ If your library has an agreement with Lonesome Doc, NLM's document delivery program, you can use that service to request documents.

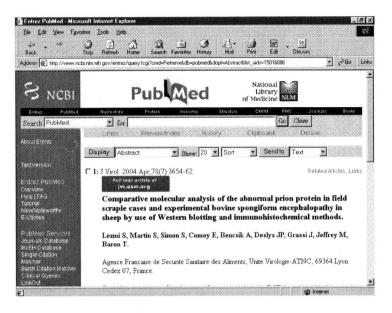

Figure 6.8—MEDLINE Record with Abstract

END OF ACTIVITY 6.1

PubMed's MEDLINE database can provide you with the most up-to-date medical research information available anywhere. This example barely scratches the surface of the searching possibilities in this database. Whether you're researching an illness or gathering information for a biology paper, MEDLINE is an invaluable resource.

Searching for Company and Industry Information

The World Wide Web has become a useful place to conduct business research. Most companies use their home pages as marketing or communications tools. These home pages may include annual reports, press releases, and biographies of the people in top-level management. Home pages may also include information about companies' products and services, including catalogs.

If you want to do industry research, you can use business-related subject guides. These contain hyperlinks to businesses within the particular industry that interests you. You can easily find subject guides in virtual libraries and major directories.

You can also find business directories on the Web by using one of the virtual libraries or meta-search tools listed at the beginning of the chapter. Keep in mind that companies that provide the most financial information on the Web are usually publicly traded. Public companies are required to provide very detailed information about themselves to the U.S. government, whereas privately held companies are not. If a private company is listed in a nonproprietary (open-to-the-public) database, some financial information will be available, but not nearly as much as if it were a public company.

ACTIVITY

6.2   FINDING COMPANY INFORMATION

OVERVIEW

In this activity, we'll find information about a specific company. The company we'll be searching for is The Gap. Suppose you need to find a home page, address, annual financial information, and recent newspaper articles about this company. There are several company directories on the Web that would provide a starting place for this type of research. Virtual libraries and meta-search tools list databases by subject. In this activity, we'll use LibrarySpot, **http://libraryspot.com**, which is a virtual library. After we find a company directory that gives general information, we'll search it. We'll locate general information about the company and financial information that can be accessed from the page.

Let's get started!

We'll follow these steps:

1. Go to LibrarySpot and find a company directory.

2. Search Hoover's Online to find the company's address, home page, and other basic information.

3. Find financial information and news about the company.

DETAILS

1   Go to LibrarySpot and find a company directory.

✦ Do It!   Click on the address box, type **http://libraryspot.com**, and press **Enter**.

Along the left side of the LibrarySpot's home page is a list of subject categories.

✦ Do It!   Click on **Business**, located under **Reference Desk**, as shown in Figure 6.9.

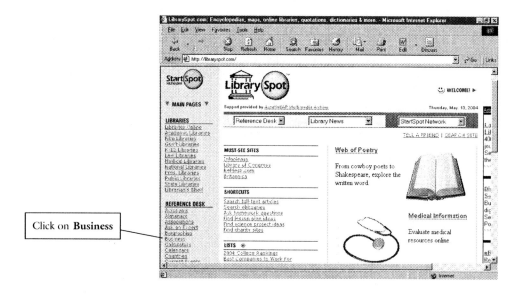

Click on **Business**

Figure 6.9—LibrarySpot's Home Page

Figure 6.10 shows a partial view of the current page.

Let's access Hoover's Online.

✦ Do It! Click on **Hoover's Online**, as shown in Figure 6.10.

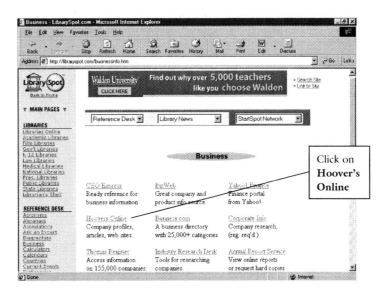

Figure 6.10—Business Resources Listed in LibrarySpot's Directory

2 Search Hoover's Online to find the company's address, home page, and other basic information.

Figure 6.11 shows Hoover's home page.

✦ Do It! Type **gap** in the search form (make sure that the radio button next to Company Name is checked).

✦ Do It! Click on **Search** as shown in Figure 6.11.

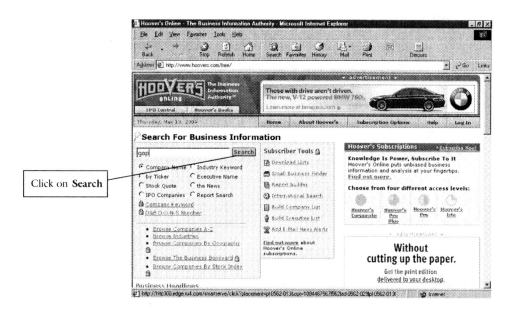

Figure 6.11—Hoover's Online Home Page with Company Name Entered

Your window will fill with companies that have the word *gap* in them, as shown in Figure 6.12. The hyperlink we need is **The Gap, Inc**.

Note that there are five hyperlinks associated with the company listings: **Fact Sheet, News, People,** and **Financials**. To read an overview of the company, **Fact Sheet** is the best place to start.

✦ Do It!   Click on **Fact Sheet**, as shown in Figure 6.12.

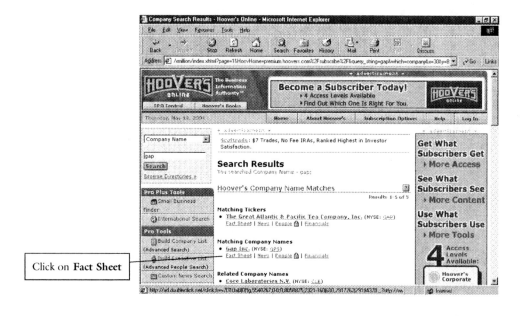

Figure 6.12—Results of Searching for The Gap in Hoover's Online

Figure 6.13 shows the entry for The Gap, Inc. Note the information provided by Hoover's Fact Sheet. It provides The Gap's corporate address, a map, phone and fax numbers, and a link to The Gap's home page. There are also links to financial information, news reports, and industry data. Information marked with a key is proprietary and requires a subscription fee to access.

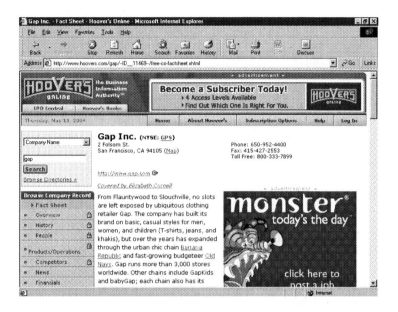

Figure 6.13—Fact Sheet for The Gap in Hoover's

3 Find financial information and news for the company.

The United States Security and Exchange Commission (SEC) requires public companies to make an annual financial disclosure, called a 10-K report. The 10-K not only gives recent financial information about the company, it also lists the top people in the company, their salaries, and stock ownership information. To obtain The Gap's 10-K, you could locate an EDGAR database that contains this information by going to a virtual library and searching for it. You can also view some of this financial data (both annual and quarterly information) from Hoovers.

✦ Do It!   Click on the **Back** icon until you are at the search results page.

✦ Do It!   Click on **Financials**.

✦ Do It!   Next to **Financial Filings**, note a link to **SEC**. Click on this link.

✦ Do It!   Look down the list for a 10-K report. To read the report, click on **Filing**, as shown in Figure 6.14.

✦ Do It!   To read recent news articles about The Gap, click on the **News** link located on the left side of the window.

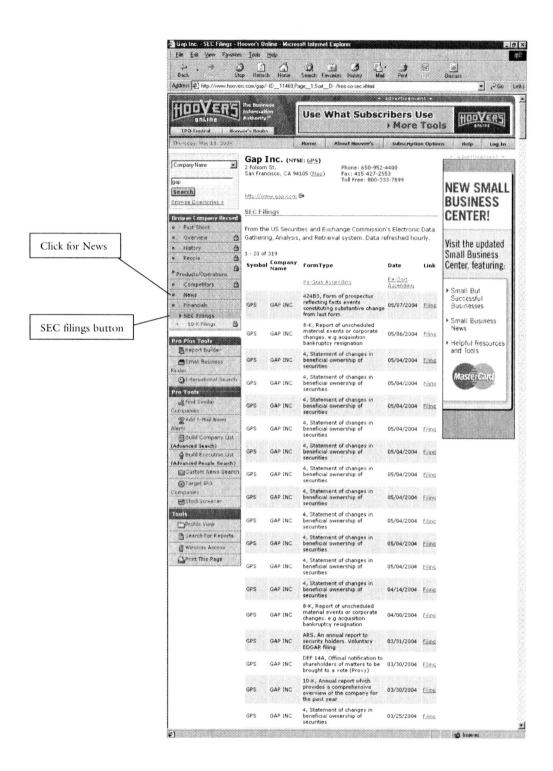

Figure 6.14—SEC Filings listed in Hoovers.com

END OF ACTIVITY 6.2

The purpose of this activity was to provide an overview of what's involved with researching a company. Using special databases for information like this can be more effective than searching with global search engines, since you can more precisely pinpoint the information you need.

Searching for Legal Information

Legal information is plentiful on the World Wide Web. The U.S. federal government has put much of its legal documentation online. For example, the *United States Code* (the text of current public laws enacted by Congress), the *Federal Register* (the daily report of new laws passed by government agencies), and the *United States Code of Federal Regulations* (the *Federal Register* codified by subject) are all on the Web in searchable form. A growing number of states also publish their statutes or laws on the Web in collections similar to the ones the federal government provides.

In addition to statutes or laws, court opinions from all jurisdictions are appearing on the World Wide Web. In this activity, we'll show how easy it is to get a full-text copy of a U.S. Supreme Court opinion.

ACTIVITY

6.3   SEARCHING FOR UNITED STATES SUPREME COURT OPINIONS

OVERVIEW

In this activity, we'll show how to obtain a copy of the Supreme Court opinion from the famous 1954 case Brown v. Board of Education. To find the database that indexes U.S. Supreme Court opinions, we'll use Yahoo! This activity will follow these steps:

1.   Go to the home page for the Yahoo! Directory.

2.   Browse Yahoo!'s directory for databases on U.S. Supreme Court decisions.

3.   Select **FindLaw: Supreme Court Opinions**.

4.   Search FindLaw for Brown v. Board of Education.

5.   Display the full text of the court opinion.

DETAILS

1   Go to the home page for the Yahoo! Directory.

✦ Do It!   Click on the address box, type **http://dir.yahoo.com**, and press **Enter**.

2   Browse Yahoo!'s directory for databases on U.S. Supreme Court decisions.

✦ Do It!   From Yahoo!'s top-level subject categories or headings, click on **U.S. Government**, a subheading of **Government**.

✦ Do It!   From the list of subject categories that appear, click on **Judicial Branch**.

✦ Do It!   From this list of subject headings, click on **Supreme Court**.

✦ Do It!   Click on **Court Decisions**.

Your screen should look like the one in Figure 6.15.

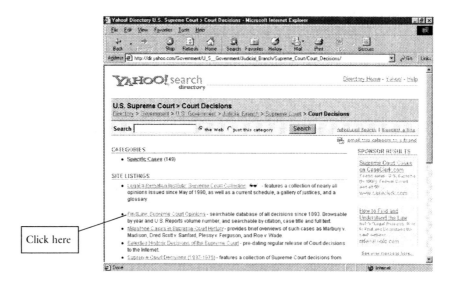

Figure 6.15—Results of Browsing for a Supreme Court Decisions Database

3   Select **FindLaw: Supreme Court Opinions**.

✦ Do It!   Click on **FindLaw: Supreme Court Opinions**, as shown in Figure 6.15.

Note that there are a few other databases that index full-text versions of U.S. Supreme Court decisions, but at the time of this writing, FindLaw appears to be the one that indexes the most opinions.

Your screen should look like the one pictured in Figure 6.16. Note that FindLaw has a search help link (**options** next to the **Search** button). If you wanted to search FindLaw by keyword, you'd be wise to look at the help pages. Because FindLaw has a **Party Name Search** category, we won't need to do a keyword search in the entire database.

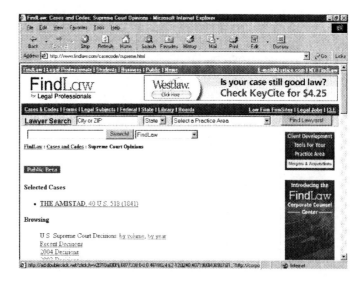

Figure 6.16—The *FindLaw: Supreme Court Opinions* Site

4   Search FindLaw for Brown v. Board of Education.

✦ Do It!   Scroll down the page until you come to **Party Name Search**.

✦ Do It!   In the box under **Party Name Search**, type the following: **Brown v. Board of Education**

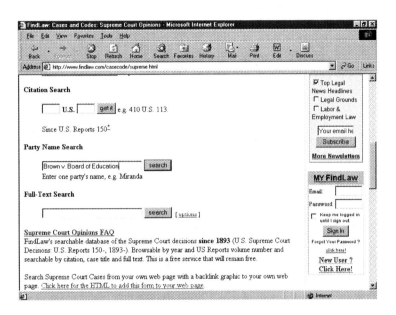

Figure 6.17—Party Names Entered

✦ Do It!   Click on **Search**.

Your screen should look like the one in Figure 6.17.

FindLaw has returned a few citations that match our search request. We are interested in the 1954 case.

5   Display the full text of the court opinion.

✦ Do It!   As shown in Figure 6.18, click on **BROWN v. BOARD OF EDUCATION 347 U.S. 483 (1954)**.

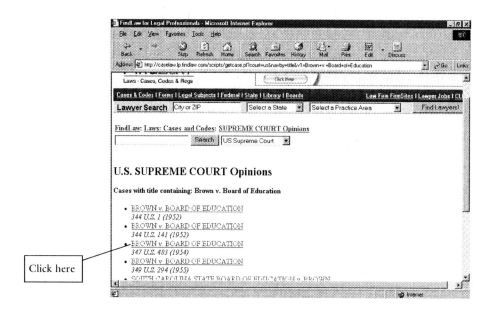

Figure 6.18—Results of Search for Brown v. Board of Education

The full text of the court opinion partially appears in Figure 6.19.

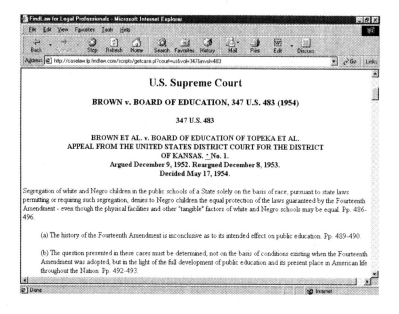

Figure 6.19—Full-text Opinion of Brown v. Board of Education

Moving from a court opinion to a related court opinion is very simple in a hypertext environment. Throughout the court opinion, you'll find links to related cases, as Figure 6.20 illustrates. Click on the hyperlink, and you'll be taken to the full text of these related cases.

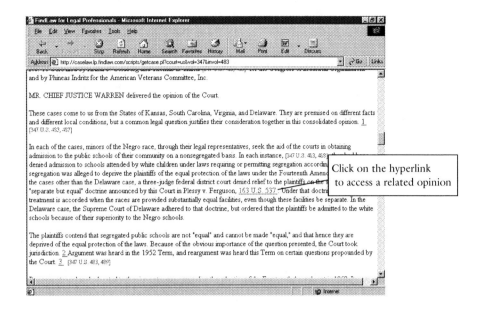

Figure 6.20—Hyperlinks to Related Court Opinions

END OF ACTIVITY 6.3

In addition to providing the full text of U.S. Supreme Court opinions, FindLaw, **http:// findlaw.com**, provides links to cited Supreme Court cases. It has links to state law resources, as well as law school information. The *United States Code* and the *Code of Federal Regulations* are also available, as well as the full text of the U.S. Constitution. You can see the advantage of linking all of these resources in one database, as it is easy to read related material in a hypertext environment.

Searching for Telephone Numbers, Email Addresses, and Maps for Individuals and Businesses

There are several services for finding information about people or businesses, and their Web sites are relatively easy to locate. You can find them listed in directories and virtual libraries, such as The Open Directory Project, **http://dmoz.org**, and the Librarians' Index to the Internet, **http://lii.org**. Because these services are used to look up addresses and phone numbers, they're often called *white page services,* for individual information; and *yellow page services,* for business listings. Each of the services are similar in that they search their databases using the information you enter into fields in a form. Each field holds a specific type of information that matches entries in the database. For example, typing **El Paso** in the field labeled **Last Name** isn't likely to help you find information about an address in El Paso. The database will instead be searched for people whose last name is El Paso. This type of searching, which is based on the entries or values of specific predefined categories, is called *field searching*.

Advantages and Disadvantages of Using These Services

White and yellow page services give you fast access to very large databases of email addresses, phone numbers, street addresses, and other information. Some services also provide maps, driving directions, and information about businesses in a specific area. Here are several good reasons to use these services:

✦ You met people at a conference, business meeting, or another situation, and you want to get in touch with them again.

✦ You wonder which of your old or current friends have email and what their addresses might be.

✦ You're applying for a job or interviewing at a company, so you want the company address, a map of the surrounding area, information about the community in which it's located, and directions by car.

The main disadvantage is that many times, you can't find the information you'd like for an individual. The overwhelming majority of entries in these databases are related to businesses. Listings for individuals usually only appear when people register in these directories. Individual listings also come from addresses people use when they post an article on Usenet or from membership or mailing lists that are often related to computers. It is impossible to find a directory of everyone with access to the Internet—there's no central control of registry service for Internet users, and no single agency could keep pace with the increasing numbers of people using the Internet and World Wide Web. Sometimes you can only find information for folks who use computers and the Internet, or the information that you find may be out-of-date or inaccurate. On the other hand, these services may be the only means of finding someone's email address quickly. The surest way, if you can do it, is to ask people directly for their email addresses!

Now we'll show you how to use one of the white page services to find an email address, street address, and phone number.

ACTIVITY

6.4   FINDING AN INDIVIDUAL'S EMAIL ADDRESS,
MAILING ADDRESS, AND PHONE NUMBER

OVERVIEW

In this activity, we'll use InfoSpace to search for an individual's email address, specifically that of Ernest Ackermann. We'll also follow a link that would give us his street address and phone number if they were available. Here are the steps we'll take:

1.   Go to the home page for InfoSpace.

2.   Fill in the form for an email search.

3.   Activate the search and note the results.

DETAILS

1   Go to the home page for InfoSpace.

✦ Do It!   Click on the address box, type **http://infospace.com**, and press **Enter**.

A portion of the home page for InfoSpace appears in Figure 6.21. Before we do our search, click on the hyperlink **Privacy Policy** (at the bottom of the page) to learn more about the site's policy for dealing with information it provides or you supply to it. This also addresses issues about commercial use of the database information, privacy, and the accuracy of the information users provide. Note that you'll have the opportunity to provide information about yourself.

Remember that anyone on the Web can access this information, so don't include information that you wouldn't feel comfortable or safe sharing with any stranger browsing through this database.

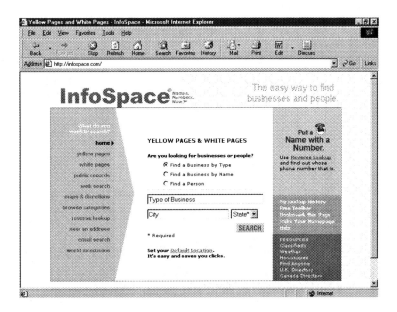

Figure 6.21—Home Page for InfoSpace

2   Fill in the form for an email search.

✦ Do It!   Click on **Email Search**.

✦ Do It!   Type **Ackermann, Ernest** into the field labeled **LastName*, FirstName**. Note that **Ackermann** ends with *two* n's.

✦ Do It!   Choose **United States** from the pull-down menu labeled **Any Country.**

175

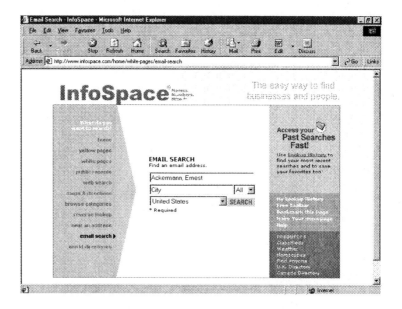

Figure 6.22—Email Search at InfoSpace

Filling in more fields makes your search more specific and will restrict the results retrieved. If we knew the state that Ackermann lives in, we could choose its two-letter abbreviation in the state field.

3 Activate the search and note the results.

✦ Do It!   Click on the button labeled **Search**.

Clicking on **Search** sends the request to InfoSpace for processing. Figure 6.23 shows the results of our search.

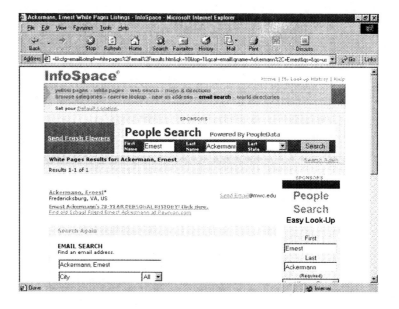

Figure 6.23—Results of Search for Email Address

Figure 6.23 shows only one entry with the name Ernest Ackermann. Is this the person we're looking for? You can click on **Send Email@mwc.edu** to send email to this person. Wait a minute, this doesn't give us an email address for Ernest Ackermann! InfoSpace does that to discourage people using this service from developing mailing lists and also to protect the privacy of the person listed. When you click on **Send Email@mwc.edu** you'll be presented with a form to use to send the message. It will be sent, and if this Ernest Ackermann feels like replying, he will.

Before following one of these links, you ought to know that our search criteria may not yield any results or may give too many results. If we don't get any results, we might want to make the search more general by not filling in so many fields. If we get too many results, then we need to make the search more specific, usually by providing more information in the fields.

✦ Do It!   Click on the link **Ernest Ackermann**.

Clicking on this link brings up a Web page, shown in Figure 6.24. Here we can see his address and phone number as well as other information.

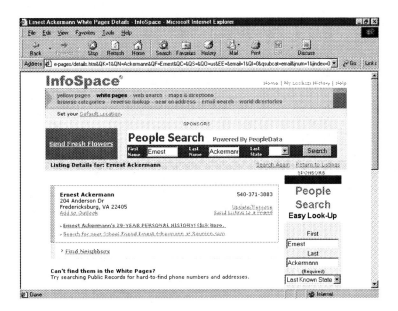

Figure 6.24—InfoSpace Details for **Ernest Ackermann**

As we see in Figure 6.24 we can view Ackermann's mailing address and phone number. You can use other hyperlinks on this page to view a map that includes the address above, obtain driving directions from another location to this address, or see the information in this database about other people with addresses close to Ackermann's.

END OF ACTIVITY 6.4

In Activity 6.4, we looked for an individual's email and street address using InfoSpace, one of many search services. Other services may be somewhat different, but they will be similar enough that you'll be able to use them without difficulty.

Privacy and Ethics Issues

In the last activity, you saw how easy it is to find an individual's mailing address and phone number. Some white page services make it even easier to get this information, and they freely give out email addresses. Services such as these make it possible to search a centralized collection of millions of records in seconds. This capability raises a number of questions related to privacy and the ethical use of the information in such records.

An example of such a question is this: Where does the information in these databases originate? Most of the services obtain their information from public sources, such as published phone books and registration lists for online services. All services encourage individuals to register with them. If you register, you must provide information about yourself. In return, you gain access to some features not available to the general public.

What control does an individual have over the information in these databases? As much of it comes from public sources, accuracy and issues of whether a listing appears at all sometimes need to be addressed at the source of the information. You can request that you not be listed in such services. Most of the online white page services make it relatively easy for you to do that. The problem is that you have to send an email request or fill out a form for *each* service. There's no way to ask that information about you be hidden or removed from every service.

Can users perform so-called reverse searches? For example, can they type in a phone number and find the name and address of the person with that number? This feature is available in several services. Using this capability would help someone identify a person based on the phone number.

Questions related to ethical use of the information almost all deal with using the information for online junk mail—mass mailings related to commercial activity. Such unsolicited email (usually advertising something or soliciting money) is called *spam*. Phone listings in online databases could also be used to generate lists for commercial calls for telemarketing.

Most of the services on the Web include a policy statement saying that the information they provide isn't to be used for commercial purposes, but the services don't police the people searching their databases. In their statements, they only promise to respond to complaints from others. It's really up to individuals to protect their privacy and to demand ethical behavior on the Web and the Internet.

Before registering for one of these services, you need to read policies about how your personal information will be used. You can usually find such policies by clicking on hyperlinks labeled **Help**, **Privacy Policy**, **Acceptable Use Policy**, or **FAQ** from the service's Web page.

The questions raised by the use of this technology are typical of what we need to be aware of and concerned about as more information becomes readily available electronically. There are many advantages to using these tools, but we need to think about, and act on, the ramifications of making this type of information so easily accessible.

6.5 SEARCHING FOR A BUSINESS ADDRESS, A PHONE NUMBER, A MAP, AND DRIVING DIRECTIONS

OVERVIEW

In this activity, you will find information about a specific business. Suppose you have a job interview scheduled with Franklin, Beedle & Associates (the publisher of this book) in Wilsonville, Oregon. You'd like to know the address and phone number of the office, and it would help to have a map of the area. It would also be nice to know a little about the community. No problem! Again, we'll go to the InfoSpace Web site, access the yellow page services, and search for Franklin Beedle's address and phone number. Once you have that information, you'll use InfoSpace's hyperlinks to find the following things: a map showing the business's location, the names and types of businesses in the area, some background information about the city, and even driving directions!

You'll follow these steps:

1. Go to the home page for the InfoSpace Web site.

2. Access the yellow pages and search for the company name.

3. Locate a map and driving directions.

DETAILS

1 Go to the home page for the InfoSpace Web site.

✦ Do It! Click on the address box, type **http://infospace.com**, and press **Enter**.

A portion of the InfoSpace home page appears in Figure 6.25. It has links to different types of information. These include telephone directories and lists of email addresses for individuals, businesses, and the government at the city, county, state, and federal levels; as well as lists of Web pages, fax numbers, and toll-free phone numbers.

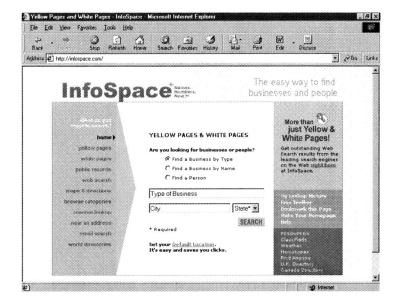

Figure 6.25—Portion of InfoSpace's Home Page

2   Access the yellow pages and search for the company name.

✦ Do It!   Click on the hyperlink **Yellow Pages**.

Figure 6.25 shows where to click. You should now have a search form that looks like the one in Figure 6.26.

✦ Do It!   Click on the radio button next to **Find a Business by Name**.

✦ Do It!   Click on **Business Name** in the search form and insert **Franklin, Beedle.** Insert **Wilsonville** in the field labeled **City.** Select **OR** from the list of states.

It isn't necessary to fill in all of the fields, but you have to provide the city or the state. The less information you give here, the more general the search will be and the more items it will return.

Your window should look like the one pictured in Figure 6.26.

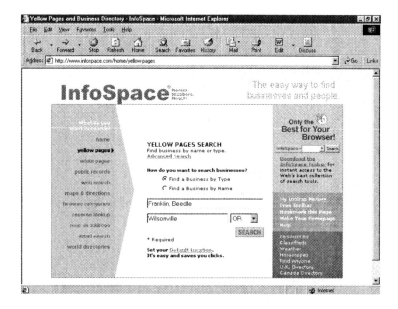

Figure 6.26—InfoSpace Search Form for Quick Business Search

3   Locate a map and driving directions.

✦ Do It!   Click on the button labeled **Search**.

The results of the search are shown in Figure 6.27.

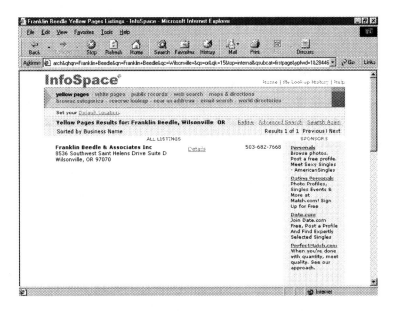

Figure 6.27—Search Results from InfoSpace

To save space here, we won't show what happens if you follow all the possible links available when you click on **Details.**

✦ Do It!   Click on the hyperlink labeled **Details**.

This brings up a page with a variety of services to give you information about where the business is located and its surrounding area. We won't show the page, but here are some things to look for.

> **A map.** You'll find a map of the town or city where the business is located. The Web page holding the map has controls, so you can zoom in or zoom out for more or less detail about the region. In some cases, you'll want to print the map to take with you on your travels.

> **Directions**. Use the form that's provided to give a starting address. The address you've selected is used as the destination address. Click on one more hyperlink to obtain detailed driving directions. You may want to print these or email them to someone else (or for yourself!).

> **Area resources**. You'll find a collection of hyperlinks you can use to find out about nearby airports, restaurants, entertainment, and more.

END OF ACTIVITY 6.5

In Activity 6.5, you used search forms provided by InfoSpace to obtain information about a business. You'd go through similar steps and have many of the same options (for example, seeing a map and getting driving directions) if you used InfoSpace to find the address of an individual or an institution.

Summary

Specialized databases are searchable collections on particular subjects. The U.S. government and nonprofit organizations maintain many of the free, nonproprietary databases on the Web, but commercial databases are also starting to appear with greater frequency. The difference between a specialized database and a subject guide is that a subject guide is a collection of URLs in a particular subject area, whereas a database contains the actual data or information you are seeking. Many databases provide hyperlinks that take you from one related field to another. Some databases have hyperlinks to other specialized databases or related URLs as well.

You can easily find specialized databases by accessing meta-search tools or virtual libraries, such as LibrarySpot. Specialized databases are also found in subject guides. These databases are like search engines, in that they all support different search features. Most databases have search instruction pages that you should read before you start searching. This chapter focused on databases in the fields of medicine, business, law, and people and business finders. We chose these topics because the World Wide Web has become an excellent medium for research in these fields.

Several services that let you search for email addresses, phone numbers, mailing addresses, and other information about individuals and businesses are available on the World Wide Web. They provide electronic access to the white and yellow pages of a phone book. However, you can also search for email addresses. Plus, instead of searching an individual phone book, you can search a very large collection of phone books.

Having rapid access to this type of information raises questions about privacy and the ethical use of this information. Most services have a hyperlink from their home page that takes you to policy statements regarding these issues. You need to be aware of your rights and responsibilities when you register with or use these services. Also, be sure not to give these services information that wouldn't be safe to share with a complete stranger. Putting information on these services is like tacking it up on thousands of bulletin boards throughout the world.

Selected Terms Introduced in This Chapter

bibliographic database
commercial database
field searching
full-text database
proprietary database

spam
specialized database
white page services
yellow page services

Review Questions

Multiple Choice

1. The best place to start a search for a specialized database on your subject is often
   a. a general search engine.
   b. a virtual library.
   c. a news archive.
   d. a commercial database.

2. Which statement is true of specialized databases?
   a. They all use the same search syntax.
   b. They are available on the Web for free.
   c. They are also called subject guides.
   d. They include information you often wouldn't find on a search engine.
   e. a and b

3. The following are characteristics of proprietary databases except
   a. they may be searched by a general Web search engine.
   b. they may include extra information unavailable elsewhere.
   c. they make it easy to download information.
   d. they may provide training to users.

4. A bibliographic database includes
   a. the full text of the works it indexes.
   b. virtual libraries.
   c. citations that identify the works it indexes.
   d. a and c

5. One problem with white pages services is
   a. They may infringe on people's privacy.
   b. They sometimes have inaccurate information.
   c. There is centralized control of all email addresses.
   d. a and b
   e. all of the above

6. The following is true of white pages services:
   a. You cannot have your name removed from a listing.
   b. They prohibit users from obtaining addresses for spam.
   c. They have privacy policies that you should read before using them.
   d. all of the above

True or False

8. T F The information in a specialized database can be easily found using a Web search engine.
9. T F A bibliographic database includes the full text of the works.
10. T F There is one central registry that holds all email addresses on the Internet.
11. T F Medline allows you to limit your search to find articles available only in English.
12. T F It is more difficult to find information online about publicly traded companies than those that are privately held.
13. T F In searching FindLaw, you can often find links to related court opinions.

Completion

14. Many specialized databases are maintained by _____ and _____.

15. A _____ includes the full text of the indexed works.

16. A database that includes citations that describe titles, dates, and authors, but does not include the works themselves is called a(n) _____.

17. A database that is available only if you or your organization has purchased access is known as a(n) _____.

18. Typing in a phone number to find the person's name and address is called a(n)

    _____.

19. _____ is the database published by the National Library of Medicine.

20. _____ is a specialized database that gives access to U. S Supreme Court decisions, the Constitution, and the U. S. Code.

Exercises and Projects

1. Do the following:
    a. Go to PubMed at **http://www.ncbi.nlm.nih.gov/PubMed** and do a search for *fibromyalgia*. How many results do you find?
    b. Following the instructions given at the site (click on **Limits** under the search box), limit the search to articles in English published during the last two years. How many articles are listed now?
    c. It can sometimes be frustrating just to see the title of the article. To avoid the frustration, click on **Limits** again and check the box to just find articles with abstracts of the content included. How many articles are there now? What happens when you click on the authors' names now?

2. Here is a specialized database on a completely different topic than those we studied in the chapter: the Internet Broadway Database at **http://www.ibdb.com/ default.asp**. Let's look for some information about the production of *The Lion King*. Type the title into the search box, choose the proper category, and click **Submit**.
    a. What date did the production open? What is the name of the theater?
    b. Who wrote the music for the show? Who choreographed all those dances in the production? Did he win any awards for it?
    c. Now look up the production of *Ragtime*. When did it open? When did it close? Who sang the role of Sarah on opening night?

3. Suppose you want to invest in the stock market and need information about a company or two you are considering in the food industry. Let's try a search for information about Mars, whom you know makes wonderful candy bars. You know you can search for the company at Hoover's Online, as we did in the chapter. Access their site at **http://hoovers.com** and look for Mars.
    a. What is the URL that is given for Mars? Is this a publicly traded company or a private one? What is the corporate address?
    b. Now try looking for Hershey Foods. What is the URL for the company?
    c. Is Hershey a publicly traded company? Go to their website. Where do you find their latest annual report?
    d. Does Hershey have a direct purchase plan for buying its stock? Where did you find this information?

4. Now look for another company in Hoover's database. Look for Apple Computer.
   a. What were their sales in the most recent year? How many employees do they have? What is the URL for the company's home page?
   b. Who is the president of the company? Who is their CFO (Chief Financial Officer)? What companies are listed as some of Apple's competitors?

5. Go to the Librarians' Index to the Internet at **http://lii.org** and find the Internet Movie Database. How did you find it?
   a. Access the site, and search for the actress Adrian Booth. What was her real name? What other name did she use? In what films did she appear with John Wayne?
   b. Now look for The Lord of the Rings movies. If you just type **Lord of the Rings** into the search box, how many results do you see? Click on the 2003 film, *Lord of the Rings: The Return of the King.* On the left side of the page, click on **Awards and Nominations**. How many Academy Awards did it receive?
   c. Now click on **Trivia.** Give a fun fact about the film

6. Another excellent government-produced database is Thomas, at **http://thomas.loc. gov**. Thomas is the U.S. Congress Web site.
   a. Access the site and search for bills currently in Congress about hate crimes legislation. How many results do you find?
   b. Is the Congressional Record searchable as well? What about bills that are still in committee?

7. Go to FindLaw at **http://www.findlaw.com**. Click on **Search FindLaw for the Public**. The search box will be located on the left side of the site. See if you can find the rules for common law marriage in Pennsylvania.
   a. What did you use as a search term? How many results did you have for your search?
   b. Copy and paste the information about rules for Pennsylvania into your assignment.

8. Using InfoSpace at **http://infospace.com**, as we did in the chapter, find the address for Cartier Inc. in New York. I think the store is on the corner of 52nd Street and 5th Avenue. (I don't want the store at Trump Tower!) Name three department stores that are close to it.

9. Go to Yahoo!'s People Search at **http://people.yahoo.com** and to Bigfoot at **http://search.bigfoot.com/directories/en/peoplesearch.do**. Look for their privacy policies and compare them. Is it easy to find their policies? Is one more strongly protective of privacy than another? Can you remove your name from either listing?

10. Go to WhoWhere at **http://whowhere.lycos.com**.
    a. Find the address and phone number of the Ordway Center in St. Paul Minnesota.
    b. Print a map that shows the location of the theater, and print driving directions from your location to the theater.
    c. Find the same information (address, phone number, map, driving directions) for the MacArthur Park restaurant in San Francisco.

11. Public libraries have made a huge contribution to written communication! Why not try to find the address of the oldest public library in the United States? A hint: It's in Wrentham, MA, and it was founded with a donation of books from Benjamin Franklin! Try going to Infospace to find the address.

SEARCHING FOR NEWS AND MULTIMEDIA

7

◆

The nature of the Web makes it a perfect medium for news. With the ability to update content throughout the day, to include color images, video and audio clips, and for readers to easily write editorials in reaction to stories, news on the Web is engaging, lively, and interactive. In the not-so-distant past, there were daily newspapers that came out in paper form once or twice a day. Now most newspapers have online versions that are updated around the clock. This is also true about magazines. *Time* and *Newsweek* may be available weekly on the newsstand, but the content changes daily on their Web sites. There are also e-zines, Web-based magazines that do not have print counterparts. Some news services include text transcripts of television and radio shows, as well as video and audio transcripts. In addition to major news organizations, thousands of individuals and institutions publish weblogs that may be updated several times a day. This chapter will help you systematically search for news by using the hundreds of news search tools that are available. How do you avoid being overwhelmed trying to keep up with news coverage? Staying current with news stories that interest you has been made easier by technology that provides tracking of news stories or news alerts. RSS, or Really Simple Syndication, makes it possible to have headlines from sources that you subscribe to brought to your own personal news aggregator.

Multimedia such as images, movies, and audio files are also abundantly available. With the proper software installed on your computer, you can listen to and view these files. This chapter will provide an overview on where to start looking for these files and the multimedia databases that index them.

This chapter includes the following sections:

◆ Searching for News

◆ Weblogs & E-Zines

◆ News Tracking and Alerts

◆ RSS and News Aggregation

◆ Searching for Multimedia

Searching for News

Before you start searching for news on a particular topic, it helps to think about what the nature of that news is. Is it an international story that is being covered on major news television channels and will be covered on the front page of major newspapers? Or is it a local story that will likely be of limited interest: for example, to a small community, city, state, or country? Another very important issue is the period of time in which the story took place. If it is a current major story from today to 30 days ago, you will most likely find what you need by using one of the major search engines' news services. If it took place before that, you'll need to search individual online newspapers' archives.

Search Engine News Sites

Search engines themselves aren't the best place to start when searching for news, especially recent news, because their databases get updated too infrequently—usually once every 10 days to two weeks. Most of the major search engines have developed their own separate news search tools. These are primarily used for big news and fast-breaking stories that have national and international interest. The better-known ones are listed below.

◆ Google News, **http://news.google.com**

> Google News covers 4,500 news sources and arranges headlines by relevance, with articles from several newspapers and other sources grouped under each story. The database is updated every 10 to 15 minutes. International in scope, Google News uses computer algorithms to determine which stories will be listed on its main page. By using its advanced search mode, you can limit your search to a specific source title, to a particular country or state, and by date. The news coverage goes back 30 days. Google News also has an alert feature, which we will explore later in the chapter.

◆ Yahoo! News, **http://news.yahoo.com**

> Yahoo! News covers over 7,000 sources in 35 languages. It relies extensively on wire services such as Reuters and Associated Press. Archives are kept from seven days to one month, depending on the source. Advanced searching allows searching for stories written in foreign languages and limiting results to a specific source or location (country or state). Yahoo! News also has a news alert service.

Newspaper Directories

If you are looking for information of a local nature, for example, stories from a small town newspaper, you can go to directories that list newspapers all across the United States and around the world. The following directories have links to thousands of newspapers.

◆ News Directory, **http://www.newsdirectory.com/**

◆ NewsLink, **http://newslink.org**

◆ NewsVoyager, **http://www.newspaperlinks.com/voyager.cfm**

News Archives

Several newspapers provide archives of their stories on their Web sites, but they often require a fee to obtain the articles. For example, *The New York Times* allows free searching for the past seven days of its articles, but if you want to search its archives back to 1851, you will have to pay for access.

- ✦ Documents in the News—Current Events Research
  http://www.lib.umich.edu/govdocs/docnews.html
- ✦ U.S. News Archives on the Web
  http://www.ibiblio.org/slanews/internet/archives.html
- ✦ NewsLibrary (fee-based)
  http://www.newslibrary.com/nlsite/
- ✦ New York Times Article Archive (back to 1851, fee-based)
  http://www.nytimes.com/ref/membercenter/nytarchive.html

Television and Radio News

The following are the mainstream television and radio news Web sites:

- ✦ ABC, **http://abcnews.go.com**
- ✦ BBC, **http://www.bbc.co.uk**
- ✦ CBS News, **http://www.cbsnews.com**
- ✦ CNN.com, **http://www.cnn.com**
- ✦ MSNBC, **http://www.msnbc.msn.com/**
- ✦ NPR, **http://news.npr.org**

Commercial News Databases

Your school, college, or public library may have access to commercial databases such as Lexis-Nexis or Factiva. These databases index thousands of newspapers and magazines and provide the full text of the articles. Most of the titles are archived here as well. It is important to know that these services usually index the paper versions of the publications, so the content may be different than the online versions. Both Lexis-Nexis and Factiva provide text transcripts of radio and television programs.

Weblogs and E-Zines

A *weblog*, or blog, is a frequently updated Web page that contains links to resources, personal commentaries, and opinions. In 1998, when weblogs first made their appearance on the Web, there were maybe a few dozen in existence. As of mid-2004, there were over 4.3 million weblogs and it is estimated that there will be 10 million by the end of 2004. One of the reasons why weblogs have become so popular is the simplicity of publishing them. There is no need for the author to know HTML, and there are free weblog automated publishing tools, such as *Blogger*, **http://www.blogger.com**, that make it easy for anyone to create a weblog. Weblogs are often defined as personal online journals, operated by individuals who compile lists of links and comment on these links to provide information that interests them, with new links on the top of the page, and older ones at the bottom. Recently, however, blogging culture has grown to include political campaigns, institutions such as libraries and museums, and virtually any entity that wants to create a community of interest around particular topics. Blogs are also a good way to uncover news that the regular media cannot or will not cover. It is important to keep in mind that because virtually anyone can publish a weblog, you must evaluate the information the blogger has provided. Make sure you can verify the author's credentials before relying on the information that he or she has published.

What Makes a Weblog Unique from a Web Site?

✦ Weblogs tend to be more dynamic than Web sites—it is expected that a blog will be updated each day and perhaps several times a day.

✦ Weblogs entries may be added from any browser that's connected to the Internet.

✦ Each entry is time- and date-stamped automatically by the blogging software.

✦ Weblog entries are automatically archived.

✦ Readers may comment on individual blog entries.

How to Find Topical Weblogs

To find weblogs on a particular topic, it's best to go to a directory such as The Open Directory Project or Yahoo! Directory. For example, if you wanted to find a list of news weblogs in the Open Directory Project, you would do the following:

1. Go to the Open Directory Project by typing **http://dmoz.org** in the address box.

2. Type **weblogs** the search form.

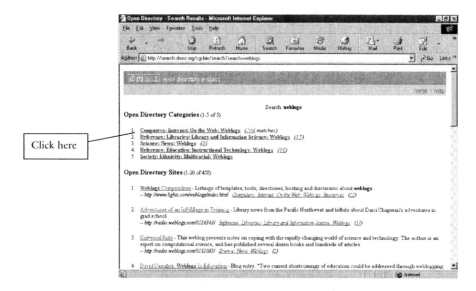

Figure 7.1—Finding Weblogs in the Open Directory Project

3. Figure 7.1 shows the results of this search. Listed are five different categories where weblogs may be found, plus a list of 444 sites.

4. If we click on the first category, **Computers: Internet: On the Web: Weblogs**, we will have the opportunity to select a weblog from subject categories, as shown in Figure 7.2. To find a list of weblogs that focus on the news, click on **News.**

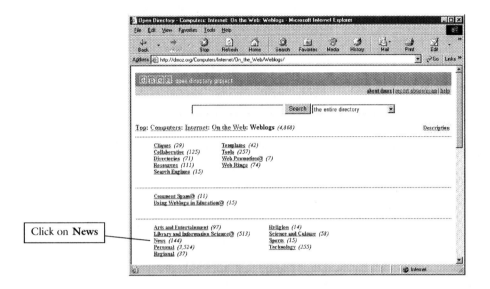

Click on **News**

Figure 7.2—Finding News Weblogs in the Open Directory Project

Many of the weblogs listed are written by journalists, as shown in Figure 7.3.

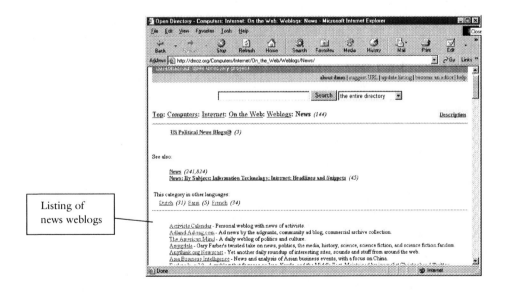

Listing of news weblogs

Figure 7.3—List of News Weblogs

Searching the Content of Weblogs

Search engines, including Google and Yahoo!, integrate weblog content in their search results. Ways to limit results to only weblogs in both Google and Yahoo! are shown here:

Google: Enter search terms followed by **~blog inurl:archives**:

"global warming" ~blog inurl:archives

Yahoo!: Add **blog inurl:archives** to your search keywords:

"global warming" blog inurl:archives

There are also specialized weblog search engines that allow you to search the content of blogs:

- Blog Search Engine, **http://www.blogsearchengine.com/**

  This site provides a search engine that allows searching content across blogs as well as a weblog directory that will help you find blogs on particular subjects.

- Daypop, **http://www.daypop.com**

  Daypop allows you to search over 59,000 news sites, weblogs, and online magazines—excellent for breaking news, major news sites are crawled every three hours, and blogs are crawled every 12 hours. Daypop also has lists of the 40 most popular weblogs and the most popular topics written about in weblogs and the news during that day.

- Waypath, **http://www.waypath.com**

  In addition to providing a search engine database that allows keyword searching across thousands of weblogs, *Waypath* also lets you find weblog posts that link to particular Web pages, Web sites, or other weblogs.

E-Zines or Online Magazines

These publications are periodicals that are published solely online. They cover most topics and can provide extremely useful information that will not be found in the more mainstream publications. These two resources will help you find them: **Ezine Directory, http://www.ezine-dir.com/**, and **John Labovitz's E-Zine List, http://www.e-zine-list.com/**.

News Tracking and Alerts

Tracking news stories can be done by continually searching in a news database for information on a particular story you're following. This can be time-consuming, and you can never be sure if you're finding everything that is available. News alerts are requests made to the database using keywords that describe the subject. When a new story is published on the issue, the search tool will email you the link to the article(s) immediately. The alert is kept until you cancel it. Google News is one service that has a very effective news alert program. Let's say that you want to track developments on a topic such as the development of a SARS vaccine.

1. Go to Google News at **http://news.google.com**.
2. Click on **News Alerts**, a link on the left side of the window.

3. In the box next to News Search, type **SARS vaccine**.

4. In the box next to How Often, choose **as it happens**. If this was a news story that had a lot of news coverage, you might want to choose **once a day**, so that you aren't overwhelmed with email messages throughout the day.

5. Insert your email address in the box titled **Your Email**.

Your alert setup should look much like the one in Figure 7.4.

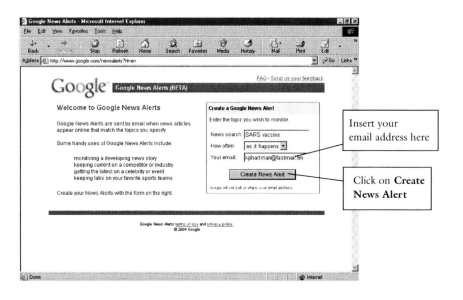

Figure 7.4—Google News Alert

6. Click on **Create News Alert**, as shown in Figure 7.4.

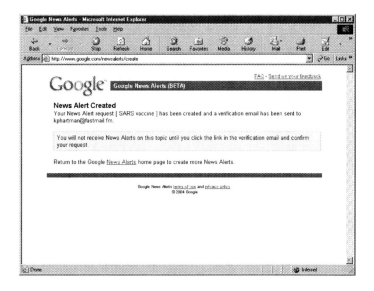

Figure 7.5—Google News Alert Created

The news alert will be initiated after you click on the link that is sent to you in a verification email message. The news alert will remain in effect until you cancel it.

News alerts can help you because you can avoid wasting time searching for and keeping up with news on a topic—the search tool does it for you. The following section covers news aggregators and RSS technology, which is another way to keep up with the news.

RSS and News Aggregation

You can set up news alerts, arrange for email updates from online newsletters and e-zines, or save frequently used weblogs and news Web sites to your favorites list; but if you want to monitor several sites on a regular basis, it makes sense to use news readers or aggregators. These use RSS technology. *RSS* stands for *Really Simple Syndication*, or *RDF Site Summary* or *Rich Site Summary*. Really Simple Syndication seems to be the term most people use to describe it. RSS is an *XML (Extensible Markup Language)*-based format for distributing and aggregating Web content. *Syndication* in this media can be described very much like syndication in the newspaper or radio business. A columnist may be syndicated, which means that his or her material is distributed to newspapers all over the world: for example, Dave Barry's weekly column, or the Dear Abby advice column. RSS allows someone to distribute his or her content on a large scale. A small newspaper or newsletter, with sought-after content, can compete with bigger news sources.

Newsreaders/Aggregators

Newsreaders or aggregators are software packages that use RSS to allow you to receive, within one page, news sources that you choose, including weblogs, e-zines, and newspapers such as the *New York Times*, broadcast news, and so forth. Headlines are updated regularly throughout the day, and if you want to read the entire article, you can easily click on the headline to go to it. It is important to note that not all news sources are RSS-enabled. If the source is available via a newsreader, the source will usually clearly indicate this by using an icon on its main page labeled **XML** or **RSS**. *News aggregators* may be Web-based services that are free and accessible from any computer that is connected to the Internet. If you choose a Web-based service, you may set up an account for free and will be assigned a user name and password to protect your privacy. There are also aggregators that require software that you may download to your computer—some of these packages are free and others are fee-based.

Finding News Aggregators

The following resources provide links to several news aggregators that are Web-based or available for downloading to your computer.

- Open Directory, **http://dmoz.org/Reference/Libraries/ Library_and_Information_Science/Technical_Services/Cataloguing/Metadata/ RDF/Applications/RSS/News_Readers**

- RSS Readers, **http://www.ourpla.net/cgi-bin/pikie.cgi?RssReaders**

- Weblogs Compendium, **http://www.lights.com/weblogs/rss.html**
  This service lists dozens of RSS readers, both free and fee-based, Web-based and downloadable.

- Yahoo! Directory, **http://dir.yahoo.com/Computers_and_Internet/Data_Formats/ XML__eXtensible_Markup_Language_/RSS/News_Aggregators/**

Finding RSS Feeds

These databases collect RSS-enabled news sources. Search these to find resources to add to your aggregator.

✦ Feedster, **http://www.feedster.com**

Feedster allows you to search the content of thousands of RSS feeds, including weblogs and news sources, and also provides a free customizable Web-based newsreader that you may sign up for.

✦ NewsisFree, **http://www.newsisfree.com**

In addition to providing a free Web-based newsreader, *Newsisfree* updates its more than 11500 new sources every fifteen minutes. It lists RSS feeds, or channels by topic and by headline.

ACTIVITY

7.1 SETTING UP A PERSONAL NEWSREADER, OR AGGREGATOR

OVERVIEW

In this activity, you'll learn how to find and establish your own personal Web-based news aggregator, and how to search for resources that are RSS-enabled that you can add to it. Although there are aggregators that you pay for, and there are those that you must download to your computer, the aggregator we will show is free and Web-based, so you won't need to download anything. Some aggregators that are downloaded have more features than the Web-based versions, and of course the ones you pay for would also have more features than the free tools.

In this activity, we will create a personal news aggregator that focuses on publications for research and information retrieval trends on the Web.

We will follow these steps:

1. Find a Web-based newsreader.

2. Log in and create an account.

3. Unsubscribe from unwanted RSS feeds, or channels.

4. Select resources and add to the newsreader.

DETAILS

1 Find a Web-based newsreader.

The Weblogs Compendium, **http://www.lights.com/weblogs/rss.html**, has an excellent list of **RSS newsreaders**, or aggregators, both free and commercial, Web-based and PC-dependent. We will go to this site and look for a free Web-based newsreader.

✦ Do It! Type **http://www.lights.com/weblogs/rss.html** in the address box.

Your window will look much like the one pictured in Figure 7.6.

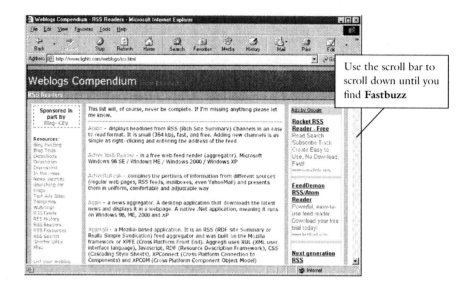

Figure 7.6—The Weblogs Compendium List of RSS Readers, or Aggregators

Scroll down the list until you find Fastbuzz News. Fastbuzz News is a free, Web-based service that is in beta testing.

✦ Do It!   Click on the **Fastbuzz News** hyperlink.

2   Login and create an account.

In order to use Fastbuzz News, you'll need to create an account. By creating an account, you will need to enter a username and password whenever you use the service. Because Fastbuzz is Web-based, you can access it from any computer that is connected to the Internet.

✦ Do It!   From the Fastbuzz News home page, click on **Sign up**, as shown in Figure 7.7.

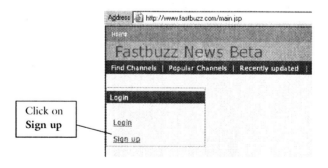

Figure 7.7—Fastbuzz News Sign Up

You will now be instructed to fill in a registration form. You'll need to insert your name and your email address. Your email address will serve as your username, and this is where your activation key will be sent. You can create your own password.

✦ Do It!   After filling out the registration form, click on **Sign up**, as shown in Figure 7.8.

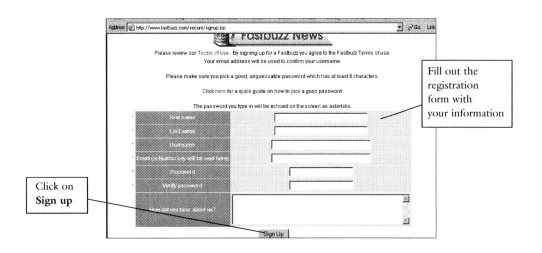

Figure 7.8—Fastbuzz News Registration Form

After submitting the form, Fastbuzz News will send you an email message with a link that you must click on to activate your account.

✦ Do It!   Access your email account, find the message from Fastbuzz News, and click on the activation hyperlink.

3   Unsubscribe from unwanted RSS feeds, or channels.

You will now have your own newsreader that can be personalized with resources that you choose. In Figure 7.9, you'll notice that there are several resources listed on the left side. These are the default channels or RSS feeds that Fastbuzz News has subscribed to. If you'd like to keep these resources, you may. But if you aren't interested in receiving them, you can easily unsubscribe from them. We will now show you how this is done.

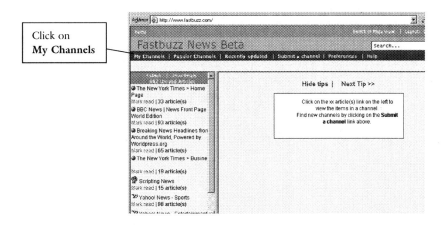

Figure 7.9—Fastbuzz News Aggregator

✦ Do It!   Click on **My Channels,** as shown in Figure 7.9.

Figure 7.10 lists the channels that the service currently subscribes to.

✦ Do It!   Click on **Unsubscribe Channels**, then click on the radio buttons next to the resources that you don't wish to receive.

✦ Do It!   Click on **Select.**

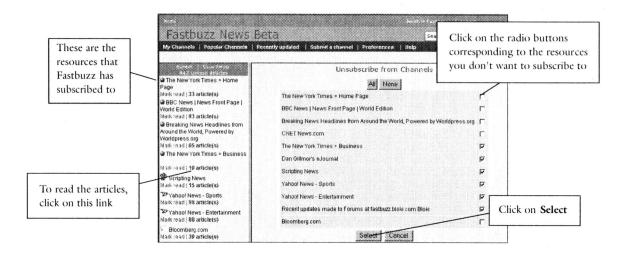

Figure 7.10—Unsubscribing from Channels in Fastbuzz News

Fastbuzz will send a confirmation message to your window, listing the resources that you have chosen.

✦ Do It!   Simply click on the **Unsubscribe** button, as shown in Figure 7.11.

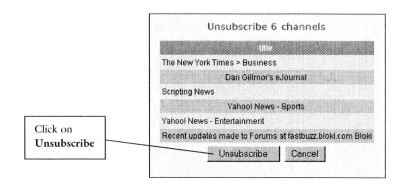

Figure 7.11—Deleting Channels in Fastbuzz

4   Select resources and add to your newsreader.

Now we will add some channels or news feeds to the newsreader. There are two ways to do this. Fastbuzz News, like most aggregators, has hundreds of RSS channels indexed at its site. Let's say you've heard about a resource that you'd like to subscribe to. The resource is the weekly update of the Librarians' Index to the Internet. You'd like to keep up with the new resources that are added to this directory every week. You can search for it at Fastbuzz, and if it's included in its database, you can add the resource easily.

✦ Do It! From Fastbuzz's main page, click on **Submit a Channel**.

Your window will look much like the one pictured in Figure 7.12.

✦ Do It! Under the section entitled **Search for channels to add**, type **librarians index to the internet**, and click on **Search.**

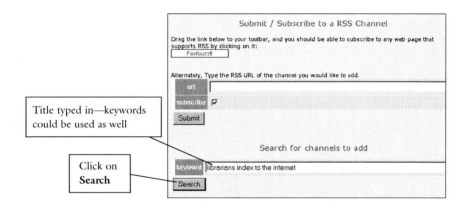

Title typed in—keywords could be used as well

Click on **Search**

Figure 7.12—Searching for Channels in Fastbuzz

Figure 7.13 shows the results of the search. Fastbuzz has returned two hits—but we aren't sure which one to choose. They are both the same title, and it looks like they may be the same RSS file. We will choose the second one.

✦ Do It! Click on **Subscribe**, as shown in Figure 7.13.

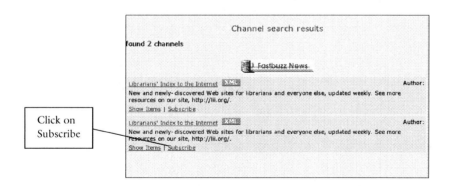

Click on Subscribe

Figure 7.13—Channel Search Results in Fastbuzz

Now we will show you another way to add a channel, or RSS feed, to your aggregator. We will use the same resource, Librarians' Index to the Internet, **http://lii.org**.

✦ Do It!   First of all, minimize Fastbuzz by clicking on the ▣ symbol in the upper right corner of your window.

✦ Do It!   Click on the Internet Explorer icon on the desktop to open a new browser session.

✦ Do It!   Go to the Librarians' Index to the Internet by typing **http://lii.org** in the address box.

You will note on the right side of the window, an icon with **XML** on it, with a hyperlink entitled **Syndicate this site** next to it, as shown in Figure 7.14. This is a link to the RSS feed.

Figure 7.14—Librarians' Index to the Internet

✦ Do It!   Click on the XML icon or the link **Syndicate this site**, as shown in Figure 7.14.

Your window will fill with the RSS file's source code. The URL that is located in the address box is what you'll need to add to the Fastbuzz aggregator.

✦ Do It!   Place your cursor on the URL and highlight it. Right click with your mouse and choose **Copy**.

Figure 7.15—RSS File for Librarians' Index to the Internet

Now, you'll need to return to Fastbuzz.

✦ Do It!   Click on the Fastbuzz icon that you minimized at the bottom of your window. Click the Back button, if necessary, to get back to the page labeled Submit/Subscribe to a RSS Channel.

✦ Do It!   Place your cursor in the form next to url, as shown in Figure 7.13. Right click with your mouse, and choose **Paste.**

✦ Do It!   Make sure the radio button next to subscribe is checked (click on it if needed), and click on **Submit**.

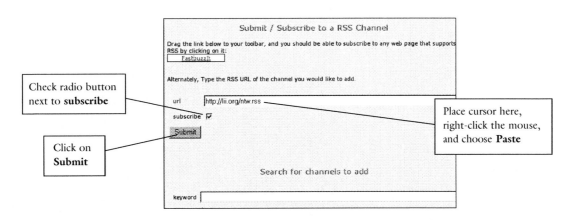

Figure 7.16—Submitting the RSS URL for LII to Fastbuzz

After you've added some resources that you want in your newsreader, you can access them at anytime, from anywhere there is a Web connection, and read new articles. You won't need to visit the individual sites, they will all be in your news aggregator. Figure 7.17 gives you an idea of how a typical aggregator works. The resources that you have subscribed to are listed on the left side. If you want to see a list of recent articles in a resource, simply click on the link underneath the title (# articles). In Figure 7.17 we clicked on this link under the Librarians' Index to the Internet. The list of articles appear in the window to the right. If we want to read any of the articles, we would click on the title of the article—or in this case, Web site—which will take us to the site that is being abstracted.

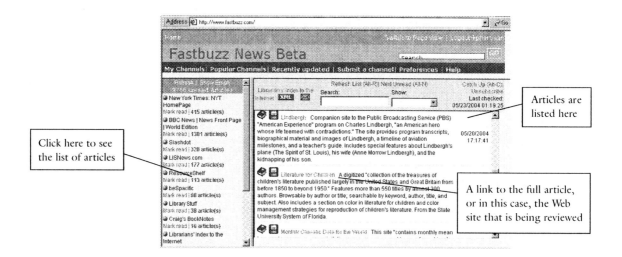

Figure 7.17—Accessing the Librarians' Index to the Internet Update Service on Fastbuzz

END OF ACTIVITY 7.1

This activity showed how simple it is to set up your own personal RSS reader and find resources to add to it. Now you can go to the Web-based aggregator by typing in the URL (in this case, **http://www.fastbuzz.com**), log in with your username and password, and scan headlines from the many resources that you have chosen, and go to the actual articles themselves without having to keep the items in your favorites list or receiving email alerts. You can check these items from wherever you happen to be—at a conference, on vacation, or wherever there is an Internet connection. It's an excellent way to keep up-to-date with news on just about any topic you choose.

Searching for Multimedia

Much of the Web (almost 70%, by some estimates) is non-textual. There are specific formats for multimedia files, such as graphical images, video, audio, Shockwave, and more. Searching for multimedia files can prove more challenging than searching for text files because when we search for text it is fairly straightforward—we type in keywords that we want to match to the text on the pages. When searching for multimedia such as images, video, or audio files, we depend on descriptive text that has been attached to the media in order to search for it. Sometimes the file names attached to images and other media may not correspond to the file's subject. We can search for these multimedia files by using general multipurpose search engines that provide multimedia searching services, or specialized databases that focus on a particular format. Advances in pattern recognition software for images and speech recognition software for audio files will continue to make searching for this content much easier.

Copyright Issues

Just as with text files, images, sounds, and any other electronic files, you need written permission granting you the right to use them, especially if you are publishing the files on a Web page or some other media. When you want to use a file for your own purposes, and there is no information on the Web site that provides guidelines for using the files included, look for the contact details of the person responsible for posting the file—usually the Webmaster or author of the Web page. Contact the person and ask if you can use the file; be sure to include the purpose. If the author of the file doesn't grant you the right to copy and use the file, doesn't reply to your letter or email, or if you can't locate the person who has provided the file, it's best not to use it for any purpose.

Software Requirements

In order to hear and see audio and video files on your computer, you will need to have a sound card and a video card installed. You will also need some plug-ins, or players. Some *plug-ins* may already be part of your computer's system, and some may not. If your computer already has a player installed, it will be activated when you access a file that requires it. If the required plug-in is not on your computer, a dialog box may pop up with an option to download it. Some plug-ins are free of charge, and others require purchase. The following are some of the more popular plug-ins that you'll need in order to use multimedia files.

- ✦ QuickTime, a player for video files, is available at no cost at
  http://www.apple.com/quicktime/download/

- ✦ Real Player, a free player for most multimedia formats,
  is available at **http://www.real.com.**

- ✦ Windows Media, a player for audio and video files,
  is freely available at **http://windowsmedia.com/download.**

Each of these players is an option for accessing files that you download to your computer, as well as for *streaming media* files. Before streaming media was available, audio and video clips had to be downloaded as files to your computer before you could view them. The files would then be opened using the plug-ins mentioned above. With streaming technology, you can view and hear the media clip as it is downloaded. The advantages to this are that you don't have to wait until the entire file is downloaded, nor is there any hard disk space required to hold the file.

Searching for Images

Most of the major search engines provide image databases. Two of the best ones are those from Google and AltaVista.

- ✦ Google Image Search, **http://images.google.com** (or click on Images from the Google home page at **http://www.google.com**)

  Google Image Search has over 800 million images in its database. Google's advanced search mode allows you to limit your search to particular image file types, including GIF, JPG, and PNG files. It also can limit your search to black and white images, or those that are small, medium, or large. Figure 7.18 shows the advanced search mode. In this example, we are searching for images of sand dunes in Namibia, a country in Southern Africa. We've specified that we want medium sized pictures, formatted as GIF files, and in full color.

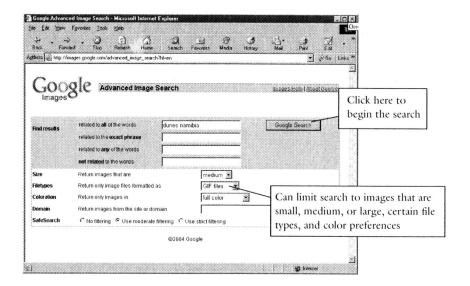

Figure 7.18—Google's Advanced Image Search

After clicking on **Google Search**, the results show the first four of 53 results, as shown in Figure 7.19. A thumbnail image is shown, with the file name, plus the Web site where the image can be found. Clicking on the image will bring us technical information about the image in the top frame, with the Web page where the image is located in the bottom frame, as shown in Figure 7.20.

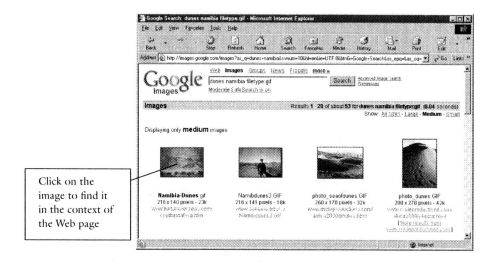

Figure 7.19—Search Results from Searching Google Images

Technical information about the image

The image will be found on this Web page

You'll need to scroll down the page in order to find it

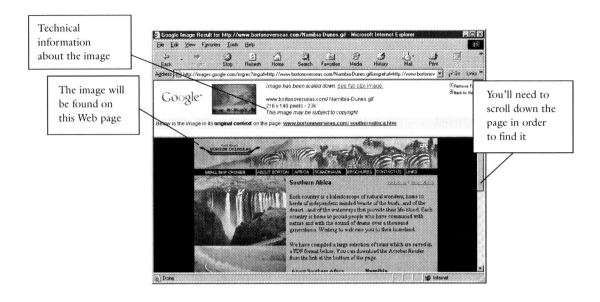

Figure 7.20—Seeing Image in Context of the Web Page in Google

✦ AltaVista Image Search, **http://www.altavista.com/image/default** (or click on **images** from the AltaVista home page).

AltaVista is similar to Google in that you can limit your search to images of a particular size, but it also provides a way to limit to certain types of image collections, such as, news, movies, Corbis.com (a commercial service), and more. Figure 7.21 shows the types of sources that are available. In this search, we are looking for photographs of Joni Mitchell from all available sources.

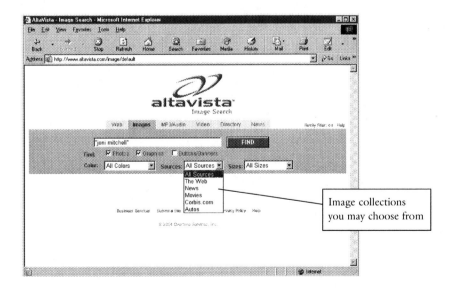

Image collections you may choose from

Figure 7.21—AltaVista Image Search

205

✦ Ditto.com, **http://ditto.com**

> Ditto.com provides a browsable directory of images by subject. It also allows you to search its database by keyword. A thumbnail image is provided, with a link to the source Web page where the image appears. Searchers are requested to contact the owners of the images to gain permission to use them.

Searching for Audio and Video Files

While many of the major search engines have audio and video search services, there are also several specialty search engines that focus on multimedia. Most of the video files will have sound attached, but some will not. You'll need to have the appropriate plug-ins installed on your computer in order to view and hear the files. We have listed a few of the most popular audio and video search tools below.

✦ AlltheWeb Video Search, **http://www.alltheweb.com**

> To search for video clips, you can simply click on the video tab and type the key-words that describe the type of video you're looking for in the search form and click the SEARCH button. In order to limit your search results to certain types of file formats, or to request that the files be streaming media or downloads, you can access the advanced search option by clicking on **Advanced Search.** Figure 7.22 shows the Advanced Search page. We have typed in the phrase "Rolling Stones" and are requesting all types of file formats, but have limited the results to streaming media files only.

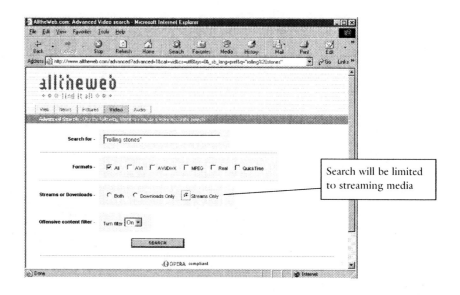

Figure 7.22—Video Searching in AlltheWeb

After clicking the **SEARCH** button, the results appear, with links to the videos, as shown in Figure 7.23. Click on a hyperlink and the video will begin to play in streaming mode. Depending on the speed of your connection, it should take a few seconds. If you have a dial-up connection, it may take a minute or two.

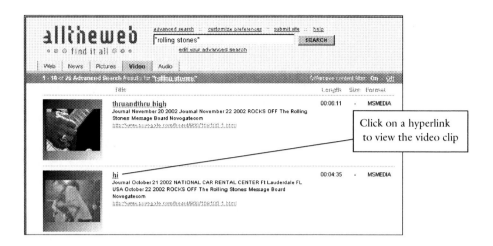

Click on a hyperlink to view the video clip

Figure 7.23—Results of Searching for Videos in Alltheweb

✦ Internet Moving Images Archive Movie Collection, **http://www.archive.org/movies**

The moving images collections of the Internet Archive are free and open to the public. They are for scholarship and research purposes only. Included are open source movies, the Prelinger Archives, and more.

✦ Singingfish, **http://www.singingfish.com/**

SingingFish is a search engine that allows you to locate streaming audio and video files from across the Web. Look here for music, movies, television, radio, and more. The search tool will locate MP3 files, QuickTime, RealAudio, and Microsoft Windows Media files. The Singingfish search engine uses advanced technologies especially designed for multimedia files that make locating files easier. It relies on metadata incorporated in the files to better understand their content. Clicking on the **Find** button gives you the advanced search form, which allows you to limit your search to video or audio only, file format type, length of file, and category (news, music, movies, radio, television, and so forth).

✦ SpeechBot, **http://speechbot.research.compaq.com**

SpeechBot indexes about 20 popular U.S. radio shows. The index goes back as far as July 1996 for some shows. SpeechBot uses speech recognition software to index the programs. In order to hear the programs, you must have RealAudio installed on your computer. You can download this software for free at **http://www.real.com/ freeplayer/?rppr=rnwk**. **SpeechBot's** home page is shown in Figure 7.24. Notice that you can limit your keyword search to specific topics, and dates, and there is a directory of radio shows, arranged by subject, that can be browsed as well.

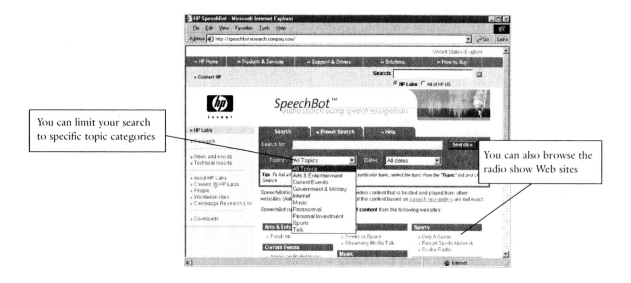

You can limit your search to specific topic categories

You can also browse the radio show Web sites

Figure 7.24—Searching in SearchBot

◆ Findsounds.com, **http://findsounds.com**

> Findsounds.com is a Web site that allows you to search for sound effects. You can find sounds from animals, insects, musical instruments, machines, nature, and so forth. The tool will allow you to search by text and by performing a "sounds like" search. You can find audio files in WAV, AIFF, and AU formats. Each search result will include a URL of an audio file and information about it, such as its resolution, and duration. It is simple to download and play the files, if your computer has the proper software installed.

Summary

The Web, for many people, has become the preferred medium for accessing news. With content updated throughout the day, the Web provides on-demand coverage of current stories and archives of those from the past. Television networks, radio stations, newspapers, and magazines provide content updates along with audio and video clips. Searching for news has been facilitated by specialized news databases that are provided by major search engines such as Google and Yahoo! Several resources list newspapers and television and radio programs by locality in order to find local stories.

In addition to major network news, individuals and institutions publish news via weblogs, Web pages that are frequently updated and focus on narrow audiences. With hundreds of thousands of news sources available, it becomes difficult to track new developments without continually checking each resource throughout the day or week. With the advent of XML technology, Web information can now be syndicated using RSS, or Really Simple Syndication. RSS makes it possible for you to set up a personal news aggregator, retrieving news feeds automatically to your desktop. In order to receive these feeds, or channels, you must have a newsreader configured. Newsreaders may be Web-based or downloaded to your computer. They may be free or require a fee. The major advantages of using RSS include the fact that you have control over which RSS feeds or channels you'd like to read, the news reader gives you a headline and description making it easy for you to scan the topics and decide which articles you'd like to read, and the hyperlinks provided will take you directly to the article you want.

Much of the Web (almost 70%, by some estimates) is non-textual. There are specific formats for multimedia files, such as graphical images, video, audio, Shockwave, and more. Searching for multimedia files can be more of a challenge than searching for text files because when a search for text is fairly straightforward—we type in keywords that we want to match the text on the pages. When searching for multimedia, we must depend on descriptive text that has been attached to the media in order to search for it. We can search for these multimedia files by using general multipurpose search engines that provide multimedia searching services, or specialized databases that focus on a particular format. Advances in pattern recognition software for image files and speech recognition software for audio files will continue to make searching for this content much easier.

Selected Terms Used in This Chapter

news aggregator
plug-in
RSS (Really Simple Syndication)
RSS newsreader
syndication
streaming media
weblog
XML (Extensible Markup Language)

Review Questions

Multiple Choice

1. At Google News you can limit a search by
   a. title of source.
   b. date of the article.
   c. Both a and b
   d. You can't limit a search

2. Blogs differ from websites because
   a. they are more dynamic.
   b. they are authoritative resources.
   c. the author must know HTML to write one.
   d. All of the above
   e. None of the above

3. The best way to find a weblog on a topic is to
   a. search through Google.
   b. search your school's web site.
   c. search a directory such as Yahoo! Directory.
   d. a and b
   e. none of the above

4. The term RSS stands for

   a. RDF Site Summary.
   b. Rich Site Summary.
   c. Really Simple Syndication.
   d. a and b
   e. all of the above

5. Newsreaders allow you to receive

   a. e-zines.
   b. newspapers.
   c. broadcast news.
   d. a and b
   e. all of the above

6. About what percentage of the Web is non-textual—that is, images, audio files, video, etc.?

   a. 7 %
   b. 30 %
   c. 50 %
   d. 70 %
   e. 90 %

7. An advantage of using RSS feeds is

   a. you can control what feeds you want to read.
   b. the hyperlinks included take you directly to the article.
   c. they are always authoritative information.
   d. a and b
   e. a and c

True / False

8. T F Local news stories are most easily found using one of the major search engines' news services.

9. T F Articles back to 1851 are available for free from the New York Times website.

10. T F It is important to verify the credentials of an author of a blog before using it as a source.

11. T F You may be able to access old news articles for free through your library's database subscriptions.

12. T F Search engines cannot search weblogs.

13. T F Searching for media files such as video is more difficult than searching for text files.

14. T F There are few image files in Google's database.

Fill in the Blanks

15. A frequently updated Web page that includes links to personal commentaries and opinions is known as a _____.

16. To limit a search in Google to only weblog content you would add the term _____ to your search expression.

17. A request made to a news database to be notified when a keyword appears in an article is called a _____.

18. You need to request permission to use a media file from the Web in order to abide by _____ laws.

19. In order to see and hear video and audio files on your computer, you need sound and video cards as well as some _____.

20. Periodicals that are only published online are known as _____.

Exercises and Projects

1. Suppose you are looking for news articles about the use of video games in education.
   a. Go to Google News at **http://news.google.com** and look for that subject. What search expression did you use? How many results did you find? Give the titles of the first three articles.
   b. Now go to Yahoo! News at **http://news.yahoo.com** and try the same search. Again, how did you formulate your search expression? How many results did you find here? Give the titles of the first three articles.
   c. Which news searching site did you prefer? Why?

2. Go to the Open Directory Project at **http://dmoz.org** and type **weblogs** in the search form as we did in the chapter.
   a. Search for weblogs on typewriters and see what you find. How many different categories were listed? How many sites were found?
   b. Choose one of the results and click on it. Describe what you find at the site.

3. Now go back to the main page of the Open Directory Project at **http://dmoz.org** and again type **weblogs** into the search form.
   a. Choose a topic you are interested in (motorcycles, dance, antique furniture, whatever you'd like!) and search for it. Again, tell how many categories are found. How many sites?
   b. Choose two blogs from the list and describe what you find at each of them

4. Search on Google just for content contained in weblogs on a topic. Travel is something that is often described in blogs. Try looking for information about travel in the country of Belize that is contained in a weblog. Go to **http://www.google.com** to get started.
   a. Remember that you want to limit the search to content in blogs. How do you formulate your search to accomplish that limit?
   b. How many results do you find?
   c. Go to three of the results, give the URLs, and describe what you find at each site.

5. Now let's try setting a news alert at Yahoo! Go to **http://news.yahoo.com** and go to Alerts.

   a. Set a news alert for computer viruses. Choose the option for Immediate Delivery. How many alerts did you receive in two days?

   b. Go to Google News at **http://news.google.com** and set a news alert for a topic of your choice. Choose As It Happens. What topic did you choose? How many alerts did you receive in two days?

   c. Remember to go in and cancel your alerts if you want to!

6. Activity 7.1 in the chapter had you set up your own RSS reader by going to Fastbuzz. Let's add a channel of content to our reader.

   a. Go to the RSS section at **http://news.yahoo.com**. Click on **Technology News XML** Following the instructions in the chapter, highlight and copy the URL that is given, go back to Fastbuzz and add the channel to your subscription.

   b. Check to make sure the channel is added. Now go to this new link listed on the left side of your page, and describe what news is listed.

7. Images are a popular item to search for on the Web. Let's compare a search at Google and at AltaVista's image search sites.

   a. Go to Google at **http://images.google.com** and search for images of the Washington Monument. How many do you find? Now do a search limiting the file type to JPG files. How many images do you find now?

   b. Go to AltaVista's image search at **http://www.altavista/image/default** and perform the same search for the Washington Monument. How many images do you find if you search through all available sources? How many do you find if you limit the search to the Corbis.com collection?

8. Now let's look for an audio file using Singingfish.

   a. Go to Singingfish at **http://www.singingfish.com** and search for Bach's Goldberg Variations. How many files do you find? Try limiting the search to those performed by Glenn Gould. Now how many do you find?

   b. What file types are listed? Choose one and see if you can hear it. Are you told that you need a plug-in?

   c. Go back to your search and choose another file. How does it compare to the first one you selected? Is it the same file type? A different one?

   d. Now search for a music selection of your own choice. What did you look for? How many files were listed?

SEARCHING
LIBRARY CATALOGS

In this chapter, we will discover the wealth of information to be found in library catalogs. Numerous types of libraries exist in the world, and every one has a catalog of its holdings. In addition to the large national libraries (such as the Library of Congress), academic libraries (such as the Harvard University Library), and public libraries (such as the New York Public Library), there are thousands of special libraries that are part of larger organizations, corporations, and government agencies. Most of the libraries in all of these categories, in the United States and in foreign countries, are rapidly making their catalogs accessible to the public through the Internet. Because of the World Wide Web's graphical interface and its hypertext environment, it is easy for people to access and use these catalogs.

This chapter will give you several ways to find library catalogs on the World Wide Web and provide you with pointers on how to use them most effectively.

It will include the following sections:

✦ Overview of the Development of Online Catalogs

✦ Characteristics of Online Library Catalogs

✦ Ways to Find Library Catalogs

Overview of the Development of Online Catalogs

For years, libraries kept track of their holdings by putting information about each item on cards. In recent years, libraries have been converting their card catalogs to *online catalogs*, commonly known as *OPACs (online public access catalogs)*. Each record in a library catalog contains information that is very useful to the librarian and the researcher. For instance, every record has a classification code, or call number, which is determined by whatever classification system the library has chosen to use. Most academic libraries use the *Library of Congress classification system*, whereas most public libraries use the *Dewey decimal classification system*. Because special libraries have collections that cover very specific subjects, some of them have invented their own classification systems to describe their materials in a better way.

With the advent of OPACs, libraries have improved their service by allowing users to search their collections much more quickly and thoroughly. When a library's OPAC is available through the Internet, people can search that library's holdings from wherever they are. For several years, libraries made their catalogs accessible via *Telnet*, a program that allows for remote login capability. Increasingly, libraries are converting their collections to *graphical user interface (GUI)* database systems. With these systems, one can use a mouse to point, click, and move through a library catalog in the World Wide Web's hypertext environment. This chapter will focus on Web-based catalogs.

Why Search a Remote Library Catalog?

There are many reasons why you might need to search a library catalog remotely. For example, you may be traveling to a college or university library in another part of the country or the world, and you may want to know ahead of time what the library's holdings are on the topic you are interested in. There may be instances where you don't want to travel to the library at all. Perhaps you want to search a larger library collection than the one you have access to in order to know what has been published on a particular topic. You can then have an idea of what you want to request through interlibrary loan at the library you're affiliated with. There may also be situations where you want to search a *special collection* that is part of a larger library or a *special library* that collects information on a narrow subject and catalogs its holdings in greater detail than a larger library. There are other reasons why you may need to search another library's catalog. This chapter will give you several ways to find library catalogs on the World Wide Web and provide you with pointers on how to use them most effectively.

Characteristics of Online Library Catalogs

♦ **Library online catalogs provide more than library holdings information for books and journals.**

By using online library catalogs, you can learn a good deal of information. You can determine whether a book is checked out and which books and articles have been placed on reserve. Library catalogs can tell you the different names periodicals have had in the past.

◆ **Each library catalog vendor offers different features.**

Each time you search another library's catalog, you'll see different search features because libraries don't all use the same software for their online catalogs. Each library chooses a *vendor*, or software company, to organize its records in that vendor's style. The catalogs' various search features are similar to those of search engines, which we discussed in Chapter 5.

◆ **Library catalogs are different from search engines.**

Unlike Internet search engines, library catalogs do not usually index each word in every work that the library holds. Instead, they index the records of the library's collection.

◆ **Each record in a library catalog can be searched by field.**

Each record in a library catalog has specific searchable fields. For example, subject headings, titles, authors, and so forth are fields. Some catalogs allow you to search by keyword. When you perform a keyword search, you search for words that appear anywhere in the records.

◆ **Full-text cataloging is possible.**

More and more academic libraries are cataloging the full-text version of journals to which they have access via proprietary databases. For example, Project Muse is a collection of full-text journals published by Johns Hopkins University. If an academic library has subscribed to Project Muse, it may create links from its OPAC to the full-text journals. If you were searching the library catalog remotely, you would probably not be allowed access to the full-text journals because you would not be an authorized user of the service.

◆ **Special library collections can be searched.**

You can use catalogs to search for materials in specialized libraries. You might want to search a special collection that is part of a larger library, or a special library with detailed information on a narrow subject. You may also wish to search for a *digital collection*. Many libraries have developed digital collections of such archival materials as photographs, records, manuscripts, and maps. You can find a few of these digital collections at the LIBCAT site, **http://www.metronet.lib.mn.us/lc/lc1.cfm**, which we will visit in Activity 8.2.

In any of these situations, if you find a useful holding in a remote library, you can obtain that resource through interlibrary loan from your local library. It is also becoming easier for you to email records to yourself when you do searches in Web-based catalogs. Despite this ease of use, you might be looking for ways to save time. Like search engines, library catalogs have faster response times in the early morning. It may also save time to search several libraries' catalogs at once. Some regions have set up multi-library consortia, which have catalogs that contain the holdings of all the libraries in the groups. You can find regional library consortia by looking in Libweb, **http://sunsite.berkeley.edu/libweb**.

Ways to Find Library Catalogs

The following sites are the most useful for finding library catalogs on the Web.

✦ Libweb at Berkeley, **http://sunsite.berkeley.edu/libweb**

Use Libweb to find all types of libraries. Some require you to use Telnet, and others allow you to use your Web browser. Be aware that the library catalogs for some of the libraries listed here are unavailable for remote use, especially those of foreign libraries. In some cases, the library's home page is all that is included.

✦ LIBCAT, **http://www.metronet.lib.mn.us/lc/lc1.cfm**

LIBCAT gives lots of information on searching library catalogs—Telnet and Web-based alike. Look here to find a list of special collections and the names of libraries in which they are located.

✦ LibDex, **http://www.libdex.com**

Use LibDex for finding Web-based library catalogs. You can also use it to search for libraries by vendor, which would locate only library catalogs using the type of catalog software with which you are familiar.

✦ UNESCO Libraries Portal
http://www.unesco.org/webworld/portal_bib/Libraries/

This service lists over 11,000 libraries in the academic, government, national, public, and institutional sectors.

We'll demonstrate how to find two different types of library catalogs and search them. In the first activity, we'll go to a national catalog, the Library of Congress. The second activity will take us to the University of Nebraska's library catalog.

Remember that the Web is always changing and that your results may differ from those shown here. Don't let this confuse you. The activities demonstrate fundamental skills. These skills don't change, even though the number of results obtained or the actual screens may look very different.

ACTIVITY

8.1   USING LIBWEB TO FIND A NATIONAL CATALOG

OVERVIEW

In this activity, we are going to search the national catalog of the United States—the Library of Congress. We will be searching for materials about the Cuban missile crisis. If you want to find out almost everything that's been published on a certain topic, it's a good idea to start either with a large university library or the Library of Congress. To help us connect to the OPAC, we will go to Libweb, a service available through the University of California at Berkeley. We'll follow these steps:

1.   Go to the home page for Libweb.

2.   Select **The Library of Congress**.

3.   Find the online catalog and select a mode of searching.

4.   Search for resources on the Cuban missile crisis.

5.   Print or email a catalog record.

DETAILS

1   Go to the home page for Libweb.

✦ Do It!   Point to the address box and click. Type **http://sunsite .berkeley.edu/libweb** and press **Enter**.

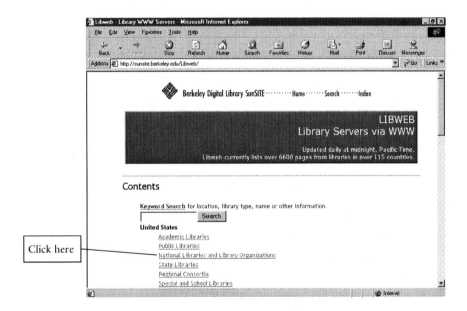

Figure 8.1—Using Libweb to Find National Library Catalogs

2   Select **the Library of Congress**.

✦ Do It!   Click on the hyperlink **National Libraries and Library Organizations**, as shown in Figure 8.1.

Your screen will fill with an alphabetical list of library names.

✦ Do It!   Scroll down until you see **Library of Congress**. Click on its hyperlink.

This will take you to **the Library of Congress Home Page**, as shown in Figure 8.2.

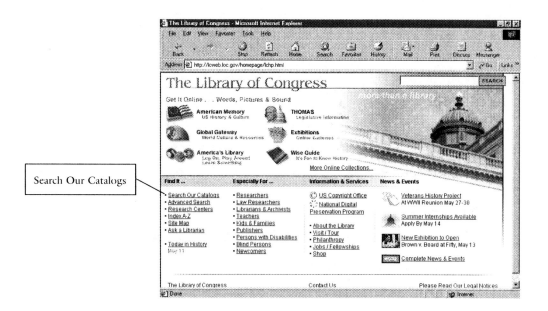

Search Our Catalogs

Figure 8.2—Home Page of the Library of Congress

3 Find the online catalog and select a mode of searching.

✦ Do It!   Click on **Search Our Catalogs**, as shown in Figure 8.2.

Your screen should look very much like the one in Figure 8.3.

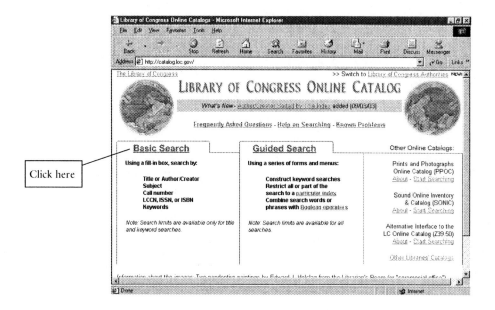

Click here

Figure 8.3—Information About the Library of Congress Catalog

✦ Do It!   Click on **Basic Search**.

Your screen will look like the one in Figure 8.4. Selecting an appropriate search method is an important step when searching by subject in library catalogs. If you know the *Library of Congress subject heading (LCSH)* for the subject you are researching, you can initiate a subject search using the proper subject heading. Often, however, you won't know what subject headings are used. In these cases, you can search by keyword. This is where electronic databases have expanded the user's ability to locate items in a library catalog. The keyword search looks for the words or phrases in the entire record. Once you have a record that is relevant to your search, you can view the subject headings that were assigned by the Library of Congress. Then you can view other materials in the same subject area that may not have the keywords that you searched in their records. In this case, we are looking for resources on the Cuban missile crisis. Because we don't know which subject heading(s) the Library of Congress may have assigned to materials covering this subject, we'll do a keyword search. This way the words *Cuban missile crisis* may appear in any part of the records: the title, subject headings, notes, and so forth.

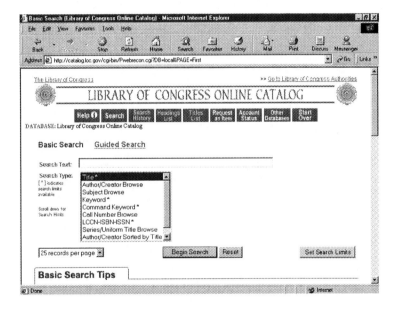

Figure 8.4—Basic Search in the Library of Congress Catalog

4   Search for resources on the Cuban missile crisis.

Figure 8.5 shows the search query screen. If you scroll down a bit on the page, you would learn that the Library of Congress Online Catalog supports phrase searching by placing quotation marks around the phrase. You would also find out that this catalog is not case-sensitive; there is no need to capitalize proper nouns.

✦ Do It!   Select **Keyword**, as shown in Figure 8.5.

✦ Do It!   Type **"cuban missile crisis"** in the search form, as shown in Figure 8.5.

✦ Do It!   Click on **Begin Search**.

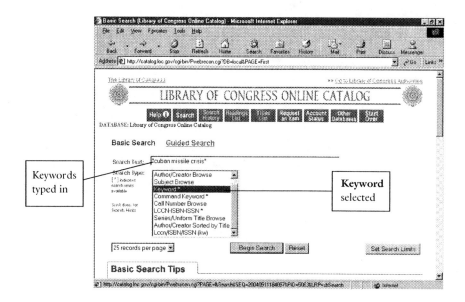

Figure 8.5—Search Form with Query Entered

The catalog has returned a list of records that include the words *Cuban missile crisis* in some part of the record. (See Figure 8.6.) To view more information about a resource, click on the title hyperlink, or the record number, as shown in Figure 8.6. If you'd like to view, print, or email several records at once, you can check the radio buttons next to the records that you wish to capture.

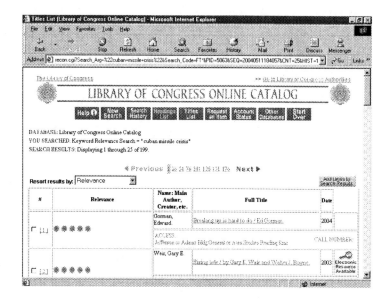

Figure 8.6—Results of the Keyword Search "cuban missile crisis"

✦ Do It!   Click on **Cuban Missile Crisis / William S. McConnell, book editor**. Figure 8.7 shows a portion of the record. To view the full record of this book, you'll need to click on the tab titled **Full Record**.

✦ Do It!   Click on **Full Record**, as shown in Figure 8.7.

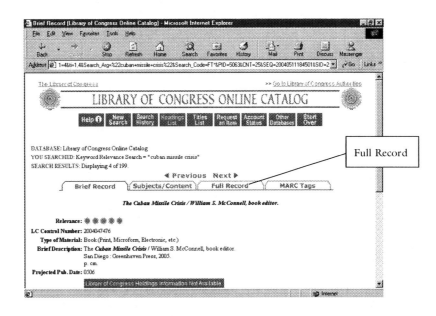

Figure 8.7—One Result of the Subject Search

Figure 8.8 shows the full record of this book. Note the subject headings that were assigned to it. If you wanted to see other materials in this subject area, you could click on one of the subject headings, and a list of materials in that subject would be listed.

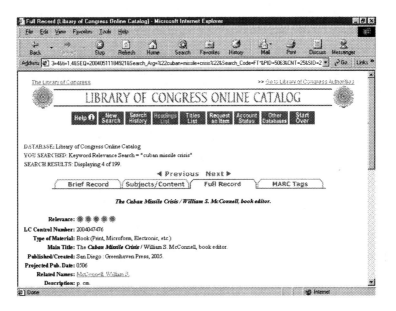

Figure 8.8—The Full Catalog Record

5   Print or email a catalog record.

If you would like to print or email this record, simply scroll down to the bottom of the Web page. Make sure the radio button next to **Text Format** is marked, and either click on **Print or Save Search Results** if you want to print or save, or type your email address in the search form and click on **Email Search Results**, as shown in Figure 8.9.

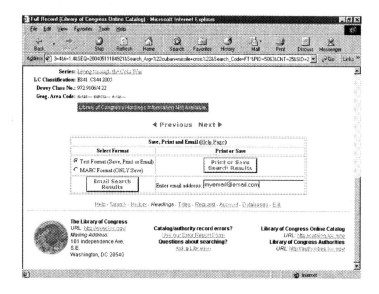

Figure 8.9—Printing, Emailing, or Saving Records in the Library of Congress Catalog

END OF ACTIVITY 8.1

This activity showed how easy it is to search a Web-based library catalog. Searching a large library such as the Library of Congress can be a very good way to start finding materials on your topic. After doing such a search, you can try to obtain the items by requesting an interlibrary loan through your own library. The interlibrary loan office will find the materials for you and let you check them out for a period of time. Because the Library of Congress doesn't loan out its materials, the interlibrary loan personnel at your library will try to find the materials at a library that does lend materials. The availability of non-book items, such as films, videos, and microform, will depend on the individual libraries that hold the items. Some lend non-book items and some do not.

ACTIVITY

8.2   USING LIBCAT TO FIND SPECIAL COLLECTIONS

OVERVIEW

If you are doing research on a particular subject and want to gather virtually everything ever written on that subject in any format, a special collection can help you immeasurably. Many academic and public libraries across the country (and the world) maintain special collections on a myriad of subjects. Usually, items in a special collection do not circulate, so visitors can always find what they want on the library shelves. In addition to books, special collections may contain original letters, documents, sound recordings, audiotapes, and so forth. Special collections may also catalog privately published books and individual articles from obscure journals that may not be in libraries near you.

In this activity, we want to find books and reports about the Taliban, the rebel faction that took control of Kabul, the capital of Afghanistan, in 1996 and imposed strict Islamic law in the country. We want to find out if there is a library somewhere in the United States with a special collection on Afghanistan. Since LIBCAT has a list of special collections that are included in libraries in the United States, we'll start there. We'll follow these steps:

1. Go to the home page for LIBCAT.

2. Search the list of special collections for Afghanistan.

3. Connect to the University of Nebraska's library catalog.

4. Search by the keyword **taliban**.

5. View the full record of a catalog entry.

DETAILS

1 Go to the home page for LIBCAT.

✦ Do It! Click on the address box, type **http://www.metronet.lib. mn.us/lc/lc1.cfm**, and press **Enter**.

2 Search the list of special collections for Afghanistan.

✦ Do It! Click on **Special Collections via Online Library Catalogs**, as shown in Figure 8.10.

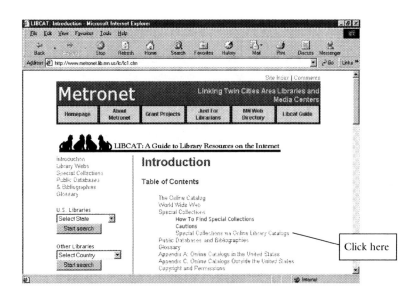

Figure 8.10—Introduction to LIBCAT

Your screen will fill with a list of special collections arranged in alphabetical order by the collection name. The libraries that house the special collections are listed next to the collection names.

✦ Do It!   Scroll down the list until you find **Afghanistan Collection**. Note that this special collection is located at the University of Nebraska, Omaha, as shown in Figure 8.11.

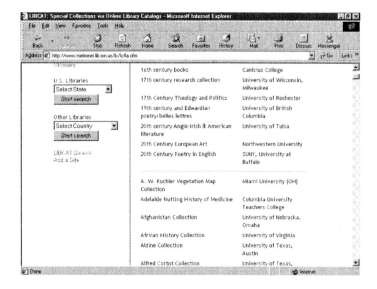

Figure 8.11—The Afghanistan Collection at the University of Nebraska, Omaha

3   Connect to the University of Nebraska's library catalog.

On the left side of the window, there is a pull-down menu entitled **U.S. Libraries**.

✦ Do It!   Select **Nebraska** from the pull-down menu, as shown in Figure 8.12

✦ Do It!   Click on **Start search**, as shown in Figure 8.12.

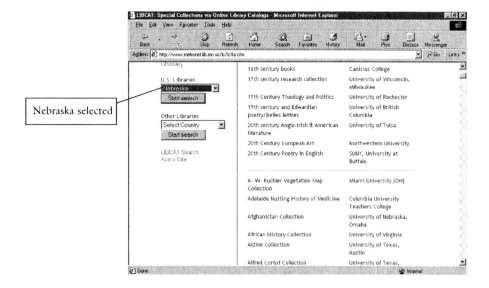

Figure 8.12—Choosing Library Catalogs by State in LIBCAT

You need to scroll down the list until you come to **University of Nebraska, Omaha**. You will see the URL for the University's library catalog listed.

✦ Do It!   Click on the URL for the University of Nebraska, Omaha's library catalog, **http:// revelation.unomaha.edu**, as shown in Figure 8.13.

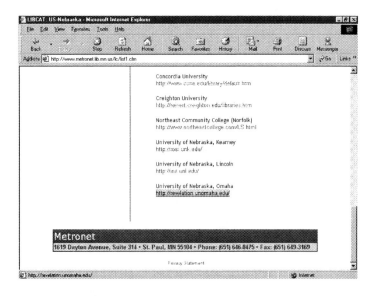

Figure 8.13—University of Nebraska on the LIBCAT List of Libraries

You should be viewing the Library information page for the University of Nebraska. You need to access the Library's catalog. There is a link to the catalog on this page.

✦ Do It!   Click on **Library Catalog**, as shown in Figure 8.14.

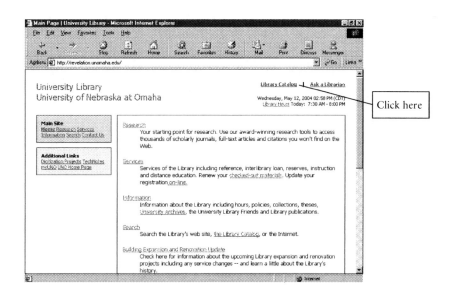

Figure 8.14—University of Nebraska's Library Home Page

Now you are at the catalog's main menu, as shown in Figure 8.15.

4 Search by the keyword **taliban**.

Because we are looking for information about the Taliban, this will be a subject search. But as in the last activity, we don't know which subject headings are appropriate for this topic. So we'll first look for the word in subjects, titles, and notes, which would constitute a word or keyword search. The catalog's Quick Search option is essentially a keyword search option, so we will type the keyword in to that search form.

✦ Do It!   Type the word **taliban** in the search form.

✦ Do It!   Click on **Search**.

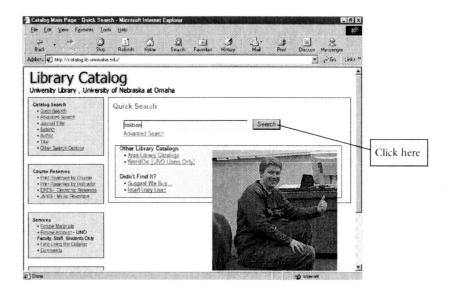

Figure 8.15—Search Request Entered in the Library Catalog

5 View the full record of a catalog entry.

Figure 8.16 shows the results of the search query. The catalog lists the title and numbers each resource retrieved. To view the full record of any resource, click on its title, which is a hyperlink.

✦ Do It!   Click on **Reaping the Whirlwind: Afghanistan, Al-Qa'ida, and the holy war**, as shown in Figure 8.16.

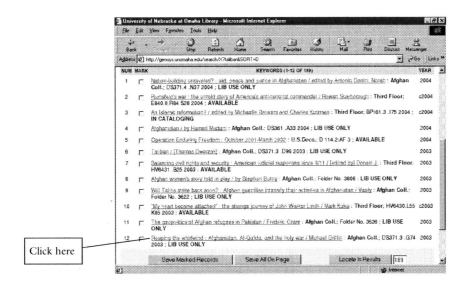

Figure 8.16—Results of Keyword Search

The full record of this report is shown in Figure 8.17.

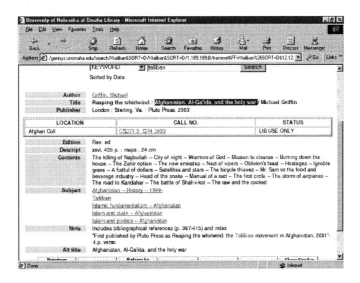

Figure 8.17—Full Description of the First Book Listed

END OF ACTIVITY 8.2

Searching for items in a special collection proved to be quite simple. If this had been an actual research project, you would have been wise to print the search results. Then, you could have taken the citations with you when you traveled to the University of Nebraska library. You might also have checked to see if there were any items in the circulating collection at the University of Nebraska that interested you. If so, you could have gone to your area library and submitted an interlibrary loan request for them.

Summary

Libraries around the world are making their library catalogs compatible with the World Wide Web. These graphical user interface (GUI) systems have made it easier for people to search library catalogs from remote sites. The Web makes it possible for a library to integrate text, graphics, and other media and to include hyperlinks to outside resources. There are some libraries that have yet to migrate to Web-based systems and still use Telnet programs to enable access. This chapter focused on Web-based systems.

There are many reasons why you may want to search a library catalog remotely. You may need to visit a library collection that might contain useful research information, and you want to be sure of what's there before you go. You may also want to do an exhaustive search of your subject to find bibliographic records that you could then request through interlibrary loan from your library. There are many types of libraries, and certain types are better for some topics than for others. This chapter covered some of the major library catalog-finding services on the World Wide Web.

Selected Terms Introduced in This Chapter

Dewey decimal classification system	online catalog
digital collection	online public access catalog (OPAC)
graphical user interface (GUI)	special collection
Library of Congress classification system	special library
Library of Congress subject heading (LCSH)	Telnet
	vendor

Review Questions

1. Call numbers in libraries are determined by
   a. the interface the catalog uses.
   b. the librarian.
   c. the library's classification system.
   d. the library's vendor.

2. Library catalogs may be available via
   a. Telnet.
   b. a graphical user interface.
   c. GUI.
   d. all of the above

3. The following are characteristics of library catalogs except:
   a. You can see whether a book is checked out.
   b. Each record can be searched by field (title, subject heading, and so forth).
   c. They each use the same search syntax.
   d. Full-text cataloging is possible.

4. A special collection may contain
    a. privately published books.
    b. original letters.
    c. audiotapes.
    d. all of the above

5. The following are true of special libraries except:
    a. They use the Library of Congress classification system.
    b. They are part of a business, agency, or association.
    c. They use more detailed cataloging procedures.
    d. Their collections may not be accessible to the public.

6. If you don't know the subject heading that applies to your topic, you can
    a. search by field.
    b. search by keyword.
    c. search via telnet.
    d. search by LCSH.

True or False

7. T F Most academic libraries use the Dewey decimal classification system.

8. T F A library's online catalog may also be called an OPAC.

9. T F Library catalogs index each word in the books or other works the library owns.

10. T F Library catalogs may be available through a GUI database system or through Telnet.

11. T F Special libraries often have more detailed cataloging procedures and records than public libraries.

12. T F An advantage of library catalogs is that they share the same search features.

13. T F LCSH means Library of Congress Subject Headings

Completion

14. A program that accesses library catalogs by logging in remotely is known as _____.

15. A group of archival materials such as photographs, maps, or manuscripts that are displayed on the Web is known as _____.

16. An independent library or collection affiliated with a business or association is called a(n) _____.

17. A(n) _____ is a software company that organizes a library's records to create the online catalog.

18. The classification system used by most public libraries is called the _____.

19. The classification system used by most academic libraries is known as the _____.

20. A subject collection (including documents, letters, and other materials) within a library is known as a(n) _____.

Exercises and Projects

1. Use Libweb at **http://sunsite.berkeley.edu/libweb** to find the British Library. Choose the option to **search the catalogues**. Remember to look for online help before performing your search! At the search form, choose to search the combined reference collections. Does the library have a copy of the book *The Gold Bug Variations* by Richard Powers? If so, print the catalog entry for the book.

2. Use LibDex, **http://www.libdex.com**, to find library catalogs organized by vendor. Search one academic library catalog that uses Innovative Interfaces and one that uses SIRSI. In each system, perform a search on an author or two with whom you are familiar. Were the search features the same or different in each system? Which system did you like the best? Why?

3. Try using LIBCAT, **http://www.metronet.lib.mn.us/lc/lc1.cfm**, to locate a special collection on the Wright Brothers. Where is it located? Access the library's catalog (you'll have to go back to LIBCAT's main page and choose the LIBCAT search) and search for manuscripts and archives about them. Print a description of some material that is available in the special collection.

4. Go to LibDex, **http://www.libdex.com**, to look for a special library in Australia that collects information on the Great Barrier Reef. Hint: the library is in Queensland. Find the catalog of The Great Barrier Reef Marine Park Authority library and perform a search on the keywords **coral reef fauna**. How many results did you obtain?

5. Choose one of the sites we've used to look for the Winterthur Museum Library's catalog. How did you find it? What is the name of its catalog? Look for titles about Henry Francis Du Pont. How many did you find? When you've finished your search, you may want to browse the site to find more information about Winterthur itself.

6. Access the National Library of Medicine's Library catalog by using Libweb, **http://sunsite.berkeley.edu/libweb**, and looking under the category **National Libraries and Library Organizations**.
    a. In its online catalog, LOCATOR*plus*, do a **keyword anywhere search** for multiple myeloma. How many entries did you find?
    b. Now go back and change your search to a subject search. How many subject headings did you find searching this way? How many entries? How do the results compare with the keyword search?
    c. Go to the Library's home page to see if it allows visitors to use the Library.

7. You are doing research on the Battle of Wounded Knee, which took place in South Dakota in 1890. It makes sense to look for information in that state. Go to LIBCAT at **http://www.metronet.lib.mn.us/lc/lc1.cfm**, and search for libraries in South Dakota. Note that there is a consortium in South Dakota that would give us access to the catalogs of many libraries. It is called the South Dakota Library Network. To access this catalog, click on the hyperlink, click on **Search the SDLN Catalog**, select the option to search all SDLN libraries, and enter the topic.

   a. What search expression did you use? How many results did you find? Do you need to limit your search?

   b. Click on the number to the left of a title in your results list that looks relevant to see the holdings for that record. Print the page.

   c. What are the advantages to using the catalog of a library network?

8. Go to Libweb at **http://sunsite.berkeley.edu/libweb** and look for the Ann Arbor, Michigan public library. Click on the link to its catalog. Perform an author search on Charles Baxter. How many items does the Library have in its collection by this author? Now go back to the list of Michigan's public libraries and select Albion Public Library. Perform the same search on Charles Baxter and see how many items this library has in its collection. Any idea why Ann Arbor has the number of items it does in its catalog by this author?

SEARCHING EMAIL DISCUSSION GROUPS & USENET NEWS

Email and Usenet news are two popular uses of the Internet. In fact, email is *the* most popular, and both show some of the unique features of communication on the Internet. With no difference in effort, one person can send a message to one or thousands of people, and one person can receive information on a topic or an answer to a question from anywhere on the Internet. People have been using email since the beginning of the Internet, and those with common interests have formed email *discussion groups*—also called *interest groups*, *mailing lists*, or *listservs*—based on specific topics. *Usenet*, which originated independently of the Internet, is a system for exchanging messages called *articles* arranged according to specific categories called *newsgroups*. The articles or messages are passed from one system to another, not as email between individuals. Group discussions take place as individuals compose and post messages, answer questions, and respond to other people's statements.

In this chapter, we'll concentrate on finding discussion groups and newsgroups that deal with specific topics and determining the resources available through the groups. We'll also cover ways of searching archives of Usenet articles. We will give a brief overview of how to access and use email discussion groups and Usenet newsgroups. There are some differences in the methods and tools you use to work with each. The last section of the chapter covers an important topic: proper etiquette or behavior in a discussion group or newsgroup.

The chapter will include the following sections:

- ✦ Email Discussion Groups
- ✦ Usenet Newsgroups
- ✦ Etiquette in a Discussion Group or a Usenet Newsgroup

Both email discussion groups and Usenet newsgroups allow for group communication. The primary difference is that you must first subscribe to or join an email discussion group, whereas anyone with a *newsreader*—such as the one included with Internet Explorer—can browse and interact with a newsgroup. You can interact with a newsgroup via the Web by accessing the services at "Google Groups," **http://groups.google.com**. Both email discussion groups and Usenet newsgroups give you valuable resources when searching for information on specific topics or seeking answers to questions. Here are a few reasons that these resources are so helpful:

✦ The group itself. The articles or messages posted to discussion groups and newsgroups are sometimes read by thousands or millions of people throughout the world. Replying to messages, giving help, and supplying accurate information when possible are part of Internet culture. Although it's unreasonable to expect group members to do your research for you, the group can be very helpful.

✦ The discussions—the messages or articles—are often archived and can be searched and retrieved.

✦ The collections of frequently asked questions (FAQs) and periodic postings on a specific topic are usually compiled and updated by volunteers.

Email Discussion Groups

Email discussion groups are made up of people anywhere on the Internet who agree to communicate about a certain topic using email. The group named "Blues-L," for example, supports discussions about blues music and its performers. Anyone can join or subscribe to the list. Discussions are usually on the main topic, but messages on other topics are usually tolerated or redirected to other groups. Each message sent to the group's address is routed, virtually immediately, through email to all group members. In this section we'll cover the details of working with discussion groups. We'll use the term *discussion group* or *list* to refer to any of these types of groups. Some of the topics we'll cover are:

✦ Essential Information About Discussion Groups

✦ Ways to Join, Contribute to, and Leave a List

✦ Ways to Find and Retrieve a Group's Archives

✦ Ways to Locate Discussion Groups About Specific Topics

✦ Sources of Information About Discussion Groups on the Internet

Essential Information About Discussion Groups

It's All Done by Email

Email is the medium for all communication in a discussion group. Using email, a person makes a request to join, or *subscribe* to, a group. That person then shares in the group discussions. Any message sent to the group is broadcast via email to all group members; these discussions are public. There is an exception, however; some groups are moderated, in which case a message sent to the group is first routed to the *moderator*. Some groups are very large, with thousands of subscribers. Some are very diverse, with members throughout the world. An active group generates several email messages per day.

You Decide How Much You Want to Participate

Being a member of a discussion group means that you can join in discussions, ask questions, help others with questions, make announcements related to the group, or just see what others are talking about. You'll find members with all levels of experience. You don't have to respond to every message; you can simply read or even ignore some of the discussions. It's usually a good idea just to read messages when you first join a group, so you can get an idea of the discussion's general tone and level. Some folks use the term *lurking* to describe this act of observing discussions. Lurking is just fine; it may be exactly what you want.

When Everything Goes Well, the Group or List Is Managed by Software

Most of the management of a list—tasks such as adding new members or subscribers and removing members who choose to leave (or *unsubscribe* from) a list—is handled automatically by software. A program runs on the computer that serves as the host system for the list. The software maintains the files associated with the list and responds to commands from the membership. These requests for service are handled by commands you send to an email address, called the *administrative address,* which passes the commands on to the software managing the list. Because a computer program satisfies these requests automatically, the requests need to be in a specific form that the software can understand.

Know the Difference Between the Group or List Address and the Administrative Address

When you're a member of a list, you need to know two addresses, and you need to know when to use them.

1. The address of the group, sometimes called the *list address* or *group address,* is what you'll use to communicate with the group. When you send email to this address, the mail is delivered to all group members.

2. The address you use to request services or to give commands to the software managing the list is sometimes called the *administrative address.* With this address, you can subscribe, unsubscribe, receive several messages in one email as a digest, retrieve a list of members, request archives, and so on. This is the same address you use to join the list.

It's easy to make a mistake and confuse the two addresses. If you send a request to the wrong address, a member of the list will usually remind you of the correct address. If you send a message that's passed on to the managing software but was meant for the members of the list, you'll usually get a reply back indicating that the message wasn't in the proper form.

Each Group Has a Name

The name of a discussion group is usually part of the group address. Here are some examples:

- ◆ One list for contemporary opera and music theater is called **c-opera**. The list address is **c-opera@listserv.unb.ca.**

- ◆ One list that's open to anyone who wants to discuss literary issues related to science fiction is named **sf-lit**. The list address is **sf-lit@loc.gov.**

◆ One of several lists used for practice working with a discussion group is called **test-listproc**. The list address is **test-listproc@listproc.umw.edu**.

Remember: Never Send a Message to Join (Subscribe) or Leave (Unsubscribe) a Discussion Group to the List Address

Use the administrative address for these. Below, we'll point out some ways of finding the names and administrative address for a list.

Getting Help and a List of All Commands

Send the simple message

help

to the administrative address. You'll receive by email a list of all the commands you can use with the list. This works for any type of software managing a list. Some lists also provide a reference card (via email) that explains all the commands. If the managing software is Listserv, send the command

info refcard

to the administrative address of any system that supports Listserv.

Ways to Join, Contribute to, and Leave a List

Several different types of software are used to manage mailing lists. The most common ones are Listproc, Listserv, and Majordomo. Most of the commands are the same for the different types of lists. We'll work with one type, Listproc, and use the list test-listproc. This list was set up for people to learn about using a discussion group, so feel free to practice with it.

Here is the information you'll need about this list:

List Name:	**test-listproc**
Administrative Address:	**listproc@listproc.umw.edu**
List Address:	**test-listproc@listproc.umw.edu**

To Join a Discussion Group or Mailing List, Send Email to the Group's Administrative Address

The body of the message should contain only **subscribe**, the list name, and your full name. Using the example, you would send email to **listproc@listproc.umw.edu** with the following message:

subscribe test-listproc *your-full-name*

For example: **subscribe test-listproc chris athana**

This email list is managed by software that only recognizes messages in plain text format. Be sure that you have your email program do that when you try to subscribe.

What Happens Next?

If you've used the proper address and the list still exists, you ought to receive a response from the software managing the list within a few minutes, hours, or maybe a day or two. The response will either say that you've succeeded in subscribing or ask you to confirm your request to join. To confirm, you usually just have to reply *OK* in the body of the message. If the address isn't correct, you'll probably have your mail returned as undeliverable or you'll get email saying that the list doesn't exist at the site. Look up the address once more and try again.

Let's assume you've succeeded in subscribing and that you've received email about the list. In most cases, you'll receive an email message welcoming you to the list. *Save the welcome message!* It usually contains important information about unsubscribing from the list and about other commands with which you can request services. It also tells you how to get more information. Once again, save that message! You'll probably need it in the future.

To Leave, or Unsubscribe from, a Discussion Group or Mailing List, Send Email to the Group's Administrative Address

The body of the message should contain only **unsubscribe** and the list name. Using the example, send email with the message

unsubscribe test-listproc

to **listproc@listproc.umw.edu**. Some lists allow you to unsubscribe from or send a message to the list only from the same address you used to join or subscribe to the list. That is a strict policy; some users access the Internet from a network of systems, and they may not always be using a system with the same address. If you have problems sending or posting a message to a list, try posting a message from the address you used to subscribe to the list.

To Post a Message, Question, or Reply to the Group, Send Email to the List Address

Using the example, send email to **test-listproc@listproc.umw.edu**.

One Other Address You May Need Is That of the List Owner or Moderator

You'll probably get that address with your "welcome to the group" email. Write to the owner or moderator when you have questions about the nature of the list, if you think something is wrong with the list, or if you want to volunteer to help the moderator. Send special requests or questions you can't resolve to the address of the list owner, administrator, or moderator.

Ways to Find and Retrieve a Group's Archives

Most discussion groups keep archives of the messages posted to the group. They sometimes contain useful information, so you'll want to know how to gain access to and retrieve files from the archives.

Searching the Archives by Topic

Many lists are archived, which means that collections of past messages are kept so that members can retrieve them. These are usually categorized only by date, so it may be difficult to search the archives for messages related to a specific subject. Some progress is being made in this area. The University of Buffalo, for example, provides a forms-based interface for searching the archives of the lists hosted there. Use the URL **http://listserv.acsu.buffalo.edu/archives** to try this service. Some lists also keep FAQ collections about the topics discussed on the list and other files useful to the group members. To get a list of the names of the files in a group's archives, send email containing the command

index *list-name*

to the list's administrative address. Substitute the name of a specific list for *list-name*. For example, to get the archives for the list test-listproc, send the message

index test-listproc

to **listproc@listproc.umw.edu**.

Retrieving a File from the Archives

You can retrieve any of the files in the list's archives by sending a command to the administrative address. You might see something in the archives you'd like to retrieve, or someone may tell you about a file in a list's archives. The precise commands you use may differ from one type of list to another. For specific instructions, send the command **help get** or **help send**.

You either use the command **get** or the command **send** to retrieve a file from an archive (depending on the type of software that manages the list). Include the list name and the file name. Table 9.1 lists the commands to use for each type of software, along with an example. Substitute the specific list name for *list-name* and the specific name of a file for *file-name*. Remember to send your commands to the administrative address for the list.

List Type:	**Listproc**
Command:	**get** *list-name file-name*
Example:	**get photo-1 photo-1.sep-25**

List Type:	**Listserv**
Command:	**get** *file-name file-type list-name*
Example:	**get aou101 txt birdchat**

Note: Listserv software requires you to specify the type of file. This file type appears in the list of files in the archive.

List Type:	**Majordomo**
Command:	**get** *list-name file-name*
Example:	**get f-costume topics**

Table 9.1—Retrieving a File

Ways to Locate Discussion Groups About Specific Topics

The number of discussion groups and the rate of increase make it almost impossible to keep current with the available groups. It's probably more important (and certainly more practical) for you to know how to find the names of lists that focus on a topic that interests you.

You're likely to hear about some lists from your correspondents on the Internet. You'll also see lists mentioned if you read Usenet news. To find lists by topic you can use one of the following services:

- ✦ CataList, **http://www.lsoft.com/lists/listref.html**, a catalog of listserv lists. CataList allows you to search or browse the database of the more than **60,000** lists that use Listserv.

- ✦ The lists section of Tile.Net, **http://tile.net/lists**. You can browse the collection or search for lists. In this case, the search brings back all the information you need to join a list, along with hyperlinks that make it easy to subscribe.

In the next activity, you will practice using one of these services. When you use such services, you will type in a keyword or phrase, and the software will search a database of list names, descriptions, and associated addresses. You'll obtain the information you need (list name, address for joining the list, address of the list, address of the list owner or moderator, and so forth) for the appropriate list.

Remember that the Web is always changing and that your results may differ from those shown here. Don't let this confuse you. The activities demonstrate fundamental skills. These skills don't change, even though the number of results obtained or the actual screens may look very different.

ACTIVITY

9.1   FINDING A DISCUSSION GROUP

OVERVIEW

One collection of discussion groups is CataList, an online catalog of listserv lists. The site gives useful information about the discussion groups in its database. We can search by typing one or more keywords into a form, or we can browse the list by group title or subject area. Instructions are readily available through hyperlinks on the home page.

We'll follow these steps:

1.   Access the home page for CataList.

2.   Search the database for discussion groups dealing with science fiction.

3.   Select an item to learn about a discussion group and how to subscribe.

DETAILS

1.   Access the home page for CataList.

✦ Do It!   Click on the address box, type **http://www.lsoft.com/lists/listref.html**, and press **Enter**.

Using this URL, we retrieve the home page for CataList. A portion of it appears in Figure 9.1. Like other Web or Internet services, CataList regularly improves or expands its service. The Web pages you see may be different from these, but they will be similar.

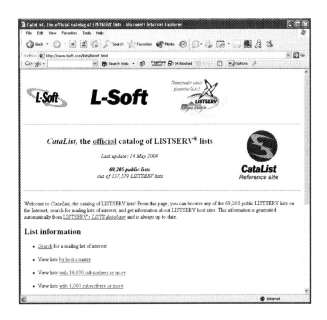

Figure 9.1—The CataList Home Page

2   Search the database for discussion groups dealing with science fiction.

The home page for CataList includes a link to search its database and links to browse the more popular lists.

✦ Do It!   Click on **Search** on the CataList home page.

This brings up a form, as shown in Figure 9.2. The search page includes instructions for searching, a form to use for searching, and some options for searching. We'll type the words **science fiction** in the search form and, while using the default settings, search the database.

Figure 9.2—Search page for CataList

✧ Do It!   Type **science fiction** in the form and click on **Start the search!**

This brings up a list of discussion groups that have **science fiction** in their title or name. Some listings include the number of subscribers in the list and an icon indicating that archives are available online. We're going to select the entry for SF-LIT.

3 Select an item to learn about a discussion group and how to subscribe.

✧ Do It!   Click on **SF-LIT**.

Figure 9.3 shows the page that appears.

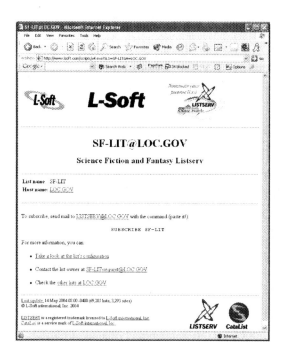

Figure 9.3—CataList Web Page About the Discussion Group SF-LIT

This page has the addresses and the instructions you need to subscribe to the discussion group. You can use CataList to find other lists that may interest you.

END OF ACTIVITY 9.1

Activity 9.1 showed how to use CataList to search for discussion groups based on their titles or descriptions of a topic. For each group found, we can retrieve information about the group and ways of subscribing.

Sources of Information About Discussion Groups on the Internet

For more information on discussion groups, you may want to consult the following Web resources.

✦ "Discussion Lists: Mailing List Manager Commands, by James Milles," contains information about working with discussion lists, interest groups, and mailing lists. The file is available by email and on the Web. To retrieve it through your Web browser, use the URL **http://learn.ouhk.edu.hk/~u123/unit2/mirror2/mailser.html**.

◆ "Internet Mailing Lists Guides and Resources" **http://www.ifla.org/I/training/ listserv/lists.htm**. The International Federation of Library Associations and Institutions maintains this comprehensive resource.

Usenet Newsgroups

Another popular means of exchanging information is Usenet news. Sometimes it's called *Netnews* or just *News*. Usenet was originally created for people to share information on Unix computer systems. Now it's available to everyone through the Internet. You use Usenet news for the same reasons you use a discussion group—to exchange or read information about specific topics. Here are some ways in which Usenet news differs from discussion groups:

◆ With Usenet, you have access to many groups. Some sites carry hundreds or thousands of groups; others carry fewer groups or different ones, depending on the policies and procedures of that site.

◆ Messages to a group aren't exchanged between individuals using email; instead, messages are passed from one computer system to another.

◆ You use software called a *newsreader* to read and manage the news (articles) available through Usenet, instead of using your email program or sending commands to a remote site.

Usenet is similar to a bulletin board system (BBS), except that most bulletin boards are managed by one person and are run on one computer. With Usenet, there is no single person, group, or computer system in charge. All the computers and people that are part of Usenet support and manage it. Usenet is a community with its own generally agreed-upon code of etiquette. Involving thousands of computers, hundreds of thousands of messages, and millions of people, Usenet is very large. Once you become comfortable with Usenet news, you'll find that it helps you find answers to different types of questions, get help on a variety of topics, and keep up with what's happening in the world and on the Internet.

In addition to the articles in each newsgroup, many newsgroups have FAQs available. Volunteers maintain these collections of commonly asked questions. Several search engines give the option of searching archives of articles or postings to Usenet news. Later in this chapter, we'll take a detailed look at using one of those—Google Groups.

We don't have space here to go into all of the details of using a newsreader and working with Usenet news. We will give enough information to get you started. Here's a list of the topics we'll cover in this section.

◆ Essential Information About Usenet News

◆ Organization of Usenet Articles

◆ FAQs

◆ Ways to Locate Newsgroups About Specific Topics

◆ Sources of Information About Usenet News on the Web

◆ Ways to Search Usenet Archives

Essential Information About Usenet News

It's not easy to define Usenet because it's so diverse. Instead, we'll try to describe how it works and how to work with it.

◆ Usenet is made up of computers and people that agree to exchange or pass on collections of files.

◆ Each file is called an article and belongs to one or more newsgroups. There are newsgroups on all sorts of topics. Some are specialized or technical groups, such as **comp.protocols.tcp-ip.domains** (topics related to Internet domain style names). Some deal with recreational activities, such as **rec.outdoors.fishing.saltwater** (topics dealing with saltwater fishing). One, **news.newusers.questions**, is dedicated to questions from new Usenet users.

◆ People at each site can read the articles, ignore them, save or print them, respond to them through email to their authors, or *post* their own articles. *Posting* means composing either an original article or a response to someone else's article and then passing it on to Usenet.

◆ There are thousands of computers involved, and an estimated 15 to 30 million people participate in Usenet news.

◆ In order to read or post articles, you need to use a program called a *newsreader*. A Web browser often has a newsreader included with it. Internet Explorer (IE), for example, includes a built-in newsreader, Outlook Express. Click on **Tools** in the menu bar, select **Mail and News**, and then select **Read News**. Mozilla and Opera, other browsers mentioned in Chapter 1, also include a newsreader.

Organization of Usenet Articles

All articles belong to one or more newsgroups. Many newsgroups have a charter that states the newsgroup's purpose and the topics discussed within the group. An article is either a follow-up to another article or a new piece on a different topic. Posting an article to more than one newsgroup is called *cross-posting*.

Threads

There may be several articles on the same topic in a single newsgroup. If each of the articles has been posted as a follow-up to some original article, then the collection of these articles is called a *thread*. You'll probably want to have the articles arranged into threads. It really helps to have this sort of organization for a collection of articles in a particular group. You follow a thread by reading the articles one after the other.

Newsgroup Categories

Each newsgroup has a name that gives the topic or topics for the articles in the group. The groups are arranged or named according to a hierarchy. When you look at the name of a newsgroup, you'll see that it usually consists of several words or names separated by periods. The first part of the newsgroup name is the name of the top level of the hierarchy. As you move to the right, the names become more specific. Here is a nice long name:

rec.music.makers.guitar.acoustic

Starting on the left, **rec** is the name of a top-level group; it includes groups that deal with artistic activities, hobbies, or recreational activities. The next name, **music**, indicates that the group addresses topics related to music. The next, **makers**, tells you that this group is about performing or playing music, rather than reviewing music or collecting recordings, for instance. The last two names, **guitar** and **acoustic**, pretty much nail this down as dealing with discussions or other matters related to playing acoustic guitars. To give you a feeling for this naming scheme, here are a few other groups in the **rec.music** hierarchy: **rec.music.makers.piano**, **rec.music.makers.percussion**, **rec.music.marketplace**, **rec.music.reggae**, and **rec.music.reviews**.

There are more than 30,000 newsgroups and several major, top-level categories. We won't list the categories here. A complete list, "Master List of Newsgroup Hierarchies," **http://home.magmacom.com/~leisen/mlnh/index.html**, is maintained by Lewis S. Eisen.

What Is a Newsreader?

A newsreader is the interface between a user and the news itself. It allows you to go through the newsgroups one at a time. Once you've chosen a newsgroup, it allows you to deal with the articles it contains. The newsreader keeps track of the newsgroups you read regularly, as well as the articles you've read in each newsgroup.

Here, we'll talk about using the newsreader included with Internet Explorer, Outlook Express. The newsreader included with other browsers is similar. There are a number of independent newsreaders available. Two popular ones are Free Agent, **http://www.forteinc.com/agent**, and MicroPlanetGravity, **http://sourceforge.net/projects/mpgravity/**.

Starting the Newsreader

After starting Internet Explorer, click on the mail icon (an open envelope) and select **Read News**. If this is the first time you've used it, you'll be presented with an Internet Connection Wizard. You'll be asked for your display name (the name you want to appear on your Usenet posts), an email address (the one people can use to reply to you), and the name of your NNTP Usenet News server. You get the name of the server from your network support group or the company that supplies you with Internet services. After you fill the information in, the wizard will put you into a window from Outlook Express that can handle newsgroups.

If you haven't subscribed to any groups, click on **Newsgroups** and you'll be able to select newsgroups to read. It may take some time—perhaps a few minutes—for the list of all newsgroups to be retrieved from the server. You'll see them in the newsgroup pane as documents and folders; the folders represent the categories in the Usenet hierarchy. Select the ones you'd like to look at regularly by clicking on the newsgroup's name. Why not try the groups **alt.internet.research** and **comp.infosys.search**? Figure 9.4 shows an example of the window Outlook Express presents for reading Usenet news.

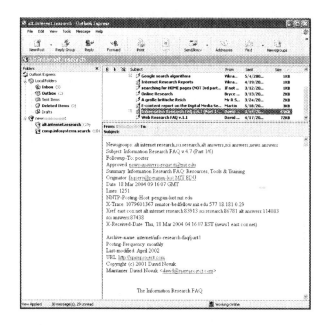

Figure 9.4—Sample Outlook Express Discussion Window—Newsgroup alt.internet.research

Spammers often get lists of email addresses from posts to Usenet. When setting an email address for Usenet, some people use an address that needs to be manually changed before it can be used. For example, if your email address were **chris@here.edu**, you may want to use **NO_chris_SPAM@here.edu**. That way, a person who wants to send you email in regard to a post you've made can figure out what to do, and a program that gathers email addresses automatically will be stymied.

Setting News Preferences

The computer you're using needs to contact a news server (sometimes called an NNTP server) to receive and interact with Usenet news. **NNTP** stands for **Network News Transport Protocol,** the protocol used to exchange Usenet news. Your newsreader needs to have the Internet name or IP address of that computer. This may already be set on your computer, or you may have received instructions about how to set it. If you can read Usenet news, then you don't have to worry about this. If not, click on **Tools** in the menu bar for Outlook Express, select **Accounts,** and then pick the news server. If you're using another newsreader, then check the online help to see how to set the news server.

Posting an Article

Posting an article means composing an article—a message, a question, a great discourse on some deep philosophical or extremely important political topic—and distributing it to a newsgroup. Usenet is a fairly open forum. But some topics are not appropriate for some newsgroups. Before you post anything, read "A Primer on How to Work with the Usenet Community," **ftp:// rtfm.mit.edu/pub/usenet/news.announce.newusers/A_Primer_on_How_to_Work_With_** the_Usenet_Community. You'll also find this posted in **news.announce.newusers**. You post a new article to the current newsgroup by clicking on the icon labeled **New Post** in the toolbar. To post a follow-up to the current article, click on the icon labeled **Reply**.

FAQs

Many newsgroups have volunteers who put together and maintain a collection of common questions and answers. These FAQs can be very informative and useful. You can find them posted either in the newsgroup for which the FAQ was created or posted to **news.answers**.

Be sure to consult the FAQ for information before you post a question to a newsgroup. It may be embarrassing for you if you post a question to a newsgroup and receive several replies (or follow-ups) letting you (and everyone else reading the newsgroup) know that you should read the FAQ before asking other questions. It could also be annoying to other group members to see questions that could be answered with a little research beforehand. A place to look for FAQs (other than the newsgroup) is "Internet FAQ Archives," **http://www.faqs.org/faqs**.

Ways to Locate Newsgroups About Specific Topics

There are thousands of newsgroups. How can you find out which to read or which ones even exist? There are several lists of newsgroups available through Usenet. Keep your eye on the newsgroups **news.answers**, **news.lists.misc**, and **news.groups** so you can read or save these listings when they appear. However, finding a newsgroup is different than reading it; being able to read the newsgroup depends upon whether your server carries it. To find out which groups are available, you select **Newsgroups** from the pull-down menu **Tools** in the menu bar of the news window.

Some Web sites enable you to search for newsgroups. For the sites we'll mention, type in the URL to bring up their Web page. On that page, enter a keyword or phrase, click on a button labeled **Search**, and then work with the results. If a newsgroup is found, click on its name to read articles in the group. Here are the Web sites:

✦ "Harley Hahn's Master List of Usenet Newsgroups," **http://www.harley.com/usenet**. This site allows keyword searching for newsgroups.

✦ "Tile.Net/News," **http://tile.net/news**. Searching here brings up a list of newsgroups. Clicking on the name of a newsgroup takes you to a page that tells about the newsgroup and includes links to documents that are regularly posted there.

Sources of Information About Usenet News on the Web

Some of the best information about Usenet is part of Usenet itself. There are several newsgroups that a beginning or infrequent user should browse. These newsgroups include information about Usenet, FAQ lists for Usenet and several newsgroups, and articles that will help you use Usenet. Here are the newsgroups:

news.announce.newusers	This newsgroup has explanatory and important articles for new or infrequent Usenet users.
news.answers	This newsgroup is where periodic Usenet postings are put. The periodic postings are primarily FAQs. This is often the first place to look when you have a question.
news.newusers.questions	This newsgroup is dedicated to questions from new Usenet users. There is no such thing as a dumb question here. You ought to browse this group to see if others have asked the same question that's been bothering you. Once you get some expertise in using Usenet, you'll want to check this group to see if you can help someone.

The articles you will want to read are posted in **news.announce.newusers**. Here's a list:

- ◆ A Primer on How to Work with the Usenet Community
- ◆ Answers to Frequently Asked Questions About Usenet
- ◆ Hints on Writing Style for Usenet
- ◆ How to Find the Right Place to Post (FAQ)
- ◆ Rules for Posting to Usenet
- ◆ Usenet Software: History and Sources
- ◆ Welcome to news.newusers.questions
- ◆ What Is Usenet?

Links to these articles and other resources about Usenet are available on several different Web pages. Here's a short list of some good general resources:

- ◆ Chapter 5 Usenet—Reading and Writing the News
  http://www.webliminal.com/Lrn-web05.html
- ◆ Usenet Info Center Launch Pad
  http://sunsite.unc.edu/usenet-i/home.html
- ◆ news.newusers.questions Links Page
  http://web.presby.edu/~nnqadmin/nnq/nnqlinks.html

Ways to Search Usenet Archives

One search tool to use to search archives of Usenet news is Google Groups, **http://groups.google.com**. In addition to searching, it allows you to post articles, browse, and find newsgroups. Google Groups keeps archives of Usenet articles back to 1981.

Now we'll do an activity in which we'll search for Usenet news articles using Google Groups.

9.2   SEARCHING USENET NEWS USING GOOGLE GROUPS

OVERVIEW

To use Google Groups to search for Usenet articles on a specific subject, we can enter a search expression, and Google Groups will report back a list of articles. We'll be able to read any of the articles, and we'll note the names of the newsgroups that hold the articles in case we want to read other articles in that group. We'll also see the email address of each article's author; this address is part of every article posted to Usenet. We could send email to the authors if we had questions or comments about what they wrote, thereby taking advantage of their expertise. In this activity, we'll also look at the features and options available to us when we use Google Groups.

We'll search using the terms *dog arthritis*. Why? Well, say you've had a good, faithful dog for some time and the poor thing has developed arthritis. Now you want to know how other pet owners have dealt with this. You want to read what comments they may have about the condition and its treatment.

Here are the steps we'll follow:

1. Go to the home page for Google Groups.

2. Search for articles using the search expression *dog arthritis*.

3. Browse the results.

4. Note the names of newsgroups and authors' email addresses.

5. Explore some of Google Groups's features.

DETAILS

We assume you've already started the Web browser.

1   Go to the home page for Google Groups.

✦ Do It!   Click on the address box, type **http://groups.google.com**, and press **Enter**.

Using this URL, we see the home page for Google Groups.

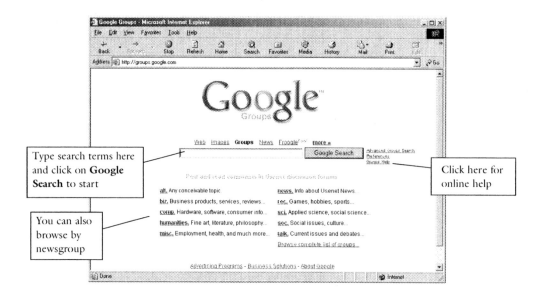

Type search terms here and click on **Google Search** to start

You can also browse by newsgroup

Click here for online help

Figure 9.5—Google Groups Home Page

2   Search for articles using the search expression *dog arthritis*.

✦ Do It!   Type **dog arthritis** in the search box and click on the button labeled Google **Search**.

In Figure 9.5, we've shown where to type in the search expression and where to click to start the search. You'll find that a search looks for articles that contain *all* the words in your search expression, and it searches the Usenet postings. To search using other features or options, click on **Advanced Groups Search**.

3   Browse the results.

Figure 9.6 shows the search results. Because thousands of articles are posted to Usenet daily, it's likely that you'll see different results, so use these as a guide. The relevant articles retrieved from the Google Groups database appear 10 per page sorted by relevance. Click on the hyperlink **Sort by date** to have them listed with the most recent articles first. For each article in the list, we have the subject, the first line or so of the article, a link to the group the article was posted to, the date it was posted, the name of the author, and a link to the thread this article belongs to along with the number of articles in the thread. (The author's email address does appear when you read an article.) For reasons of privacy, we've purposely blurred the portion of the display that shows the poster's name and the portion of the message.

Related newsgroups, ones that are likely to carry articles on this topic, are listed at the top of the page. Click on any of these to see a list of threads (articles on the same subject) listed by date. You may want to browse these groups' articles on similar topics. Click on the hyperlink **Groups Help** for more information about using the results.

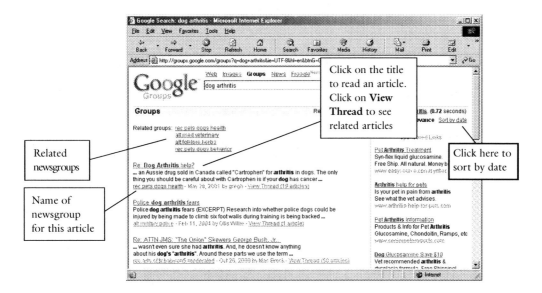

Figure 9.6—Results of Search Using the Search Terms *dog arthritis*

We can read any article by clicking on its title. In this case we'll read an article posted to Usenet by one of the authors. It's not on the topic of dogs and arthritis, but we want to show what an article looks like at Google Groups without invading another's privacy. What you'll see when you click on an article's title will be similar to what we show here.

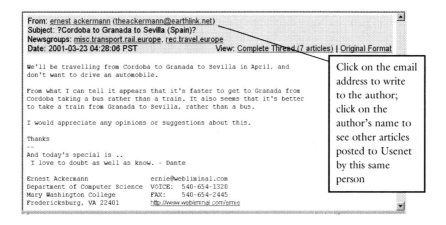

Figure 9.7—Portion of an Article Viewed at Google Groups

If you want to read the article, then you can view this Web page in the same way as any other, using scroll bars as necessary.

Clicking on **Complete Thread** brings up a Web page in which the thread of related articles are represented as hyperlinks. You can read them and follow the discussion of a topic on Usenet. Try this with any article. In some cases, the thread is quite lively. Clicking on **Original Format** shows the article with all its headers.

4 Note the names of newsgroups and authors' email addresses.

As we noted above, several newsgroups with articles related to our search are listed. Clicking on any of these displays the messages for that newsgroup. The listing of articles in Figure 12.6 includes the name of a newsgroup for each article. Clicking the name of a newsgroup listed below the title of an article will display articles in the newsgroup.

You are permitted to post a reply to an article via Google Groups only when you're viewing the articles in a specific newsgroup. You'll see the hyperlink **Post a new message** or **Post a follow-up to this message**. Click on either, and you'll be asked to register for the service or sign in if you already have registered. You'll also see links to information about Usenet etiquette and appropriate uses of this service. There's no fee involved, and Google says it won't use or sell your email address for commercial purposes.

The listing of an article, as in Figure 12.7, also includes the name and email address of the author. Clicking on the email address pops up a window you can use to send the author email. You might want to save the author's email address to write for more information about your topic. Clicking on the name of the author brings up a list of articles posted to Usenet by that person. You may be able to use this to help verify the credibility of the author.

5 Explore some of Google Groups' features.

To see some of the ways you can search the articles at Google Groups, click on the hyperlink **Advanced Groups Search**. You can search by author, newsgroup, subject, and limit results by date, and so on.

You can browse the list of newsgroups archived by clicking on the hyperlink **Browse complete list of groups...** on the home page for Google Groups.

Clicking on the link **Groups Help** brings up a list of frequently asked questions with answers, and several helpful hyperlinks including "Basics of Usenet," **http:// groups.google.com/googlegroups/basics.html**, and "Posting Style Guide," **http:// groups.google.com/googlegroups/posting_style.html**.

Google Groups is, of course, a facet of Google. You can move easily from one to the other, and they use the same syntax rules for searching.

END OF ACTIVITY 9.2

In Activity 9.2, we used Google Groups to search the archives of Usenet articles. When you typed in a keyword or phrase, a list of articles appeared. You then selected articles to read. Google Groups offers several other services, including a good introduction to using Usenet, reading news, and posting articles.

Etiquette in a Discussion Group or a Usenet Newsgroup

RULES	REASONS
Spend some time getting to know the group.	When you first join a discussion group, take a little time to see the types of items discussed and the tone of the discussion. Read the articles in a newsgroup before posting. You may also find that the questions you have are currently being answered.
Write easy-to-read messages.	The material you write to the group should be grammatically correct, concise, and thoughtful. Check your spelling too. It's a lot easier to read something that is well-written, and many group members may not have the time to deal with long-winded, incorrect writing that does not make a clear point. If the posting must go on for several screens, it's a good idea to summarize it and to invite others to ask you for more information.
When responding to something from the group, include only the pertinent portions of the original message.	Let's say that a group member starts a discussion and writes something about 40 lines long. You want to respond, but only to one portion of it. In your follow-up message, include just the portion that's relevant to your response.
When you ask group members any questions, post a summary of the responses you receive.	With this summary, everyone in the group benefits from the responses to your question. Naturally, this applies only if you get several responses and if the answers to the question are of general interest.
Posting or sending a message to the group is a public act.	Everything you write to the group may be distributed to all group members or posted worldwide through Usenet. If the group is moderated, your messages may be read first by the moderator and then passed on to the group. If you're working with a list that isn't moderated (most aren't), your messages go directly to the group. Don't embarrass yourself. A friend, relative, or supervisor may also be a member of the list.
Group members are people like yourself and need to be treated with respect and courtesy.	Respond to messages as if you were talking face-to-face. A member may be from a different culture, may not be familiar with your language, and may have different views and values from your own. Don't respond too quickly to something that upsets you, and don't criticize others too hastily or without good reason. It's better to think before you write than to be sorry afterward.

Avoid sarcasm and be careful with humor.	You are communicating entirely by your words. You don't have the benefit of facial expressions, body language, or tone of voice to let somebody know you're only kidding when you make a sarcastic remark. Group members will appreciate well-written, humorous pieces or responses, but be sure your writing will be interpreted that way.
Think about whether a response to a message should go to the group or to an individual.	Messages to the list should be of general interest. They may be requests on your part for advice or for help in solving a problem. You'll know the email address of the person who made the original request, and you can send a response to that person if it's appropriate.

Table 9.2—Rules for Netiquette

If you're working with an email discussion group, remember to send messages going to the entire group to the list address. Send commands or requests to be interpreted by the software managing the list to the administrative address.

Over the years, several documents have been developed about proper Usenet etiquette. They are posted in **news.announce.newusers**, **news.answers**, or **news.newusers.questions**. Here is a list of some that you ought to read:

+ A Primer on How to Work with the Usenet Community

+ Emily Postnews Answers Your Questions on Netiquette

+ Hints on Writing Style for Usenet

+ How to Find the Right Place to Post (FAQ)

+ Please Read Before Posting

+ Rules for Posting to Usenet

+ A Weekly FAQ on Test Postings

Summary

Both email discussion groups and Usenet news are examples of group communication on the Internet. They're useful and valuable as sources of information for two reasons:

+ The people who participate in them are a ready source of information.

+ The groups often keep archives of files, FAQs, and periodic postings that can sometimes be retrieved and searched.

Email discussion group members communicate via email, with messages broadcast to all group members. In Usenet, people communicate via articles or files that are posted to Usenet newsgroups. Anyone with access to Usenet can access the articles. In both cases, messages can be read, replied to, or posted.

Several thousand discussion groups are available and active on the Internet. They may be called mailing lists, discussion groups, listserv lists, or interest groups. Regardless of the name, each consists of a group of members anywhere on the Internet. This way, communities or collections of people can discuss items related to a common topic, find information about the topic, make announcements to the group, or ask questions and receive help from other group members. The large number of lists guarantees a wide range of topics. The groups are particularly useful to people who want to discuss issues with a large or diverse group. The groups extend any resources beyond a local site.

You send messages to the list by using the list address. Commands and requests for service are usually sent to the administrative address. For example, the list **c-opera**, which deals with topics related to contemporary opera and music theater, has **c-opera@listserv.cuny.edu** as the list address and **listserv@listserv.unb.ca** as the administrative address. You use this second address to join a list, leave or unsubscribe from a list, request archived files from the list, and get a roster of the members of the list. Be sure you use the correct address when you communicate with the group or list. Most lists also have a person designated as the list owner, list administrator, or moderator. That person is in charge of the list, and you send him or her email if you have problems using the list or questions about the operation of the list. Some lists are moderated. Messages sent to these lists first go to moderators, who decide whether to pass the messages on to all group members.

The lists can be thought of as communities. There are generally accepted rules of behavior or etiquette for list members. These include providing appropriate, thoughtful, and concise messages to the group, providing a summary of the responses received in answer to a question, and communicating with other group members in a civil and respectful manner.

Several "lists of lists" and other documents related to using discussion groups are available as part of the World Wide Web. There are also services on the Web that help you find discussion groups and search or retrieve groups' archives.

News is a collection of messages called articles. Each is designated as belonging to one or more newsgroups. These articles are passed from one computer system to another. There are several thousand newsgroups, all arranged into categories. Users at a site can usually select any of the groups that are available and can often reply to, follow up, or post an article. Some estimates put the number of participants at more than 30 million worldwide.

Usenet is a community of users helping each other and exchanging opinions. A code of behavior has developed. The rules are, of course, voluntary, but users are expected to obtain copies of some articles about working with Usenet and to follow the rules. Several newsgroups carry regular postings of articles meant to inform the Usenet community. These are often found in the groups **news.announce.newgroups**, **news.announce.newusers**, and **news.answers**.

You use software called a newsreader to work with the articles and newsgroups in Usenet news. Several different newsreaders are available. The one you use will depend on your preferences and what's available on the system with which you access Usenet.

You'll probably find Usenet a valuable resource for information on a wide array of topics. It can be enjoyable to read and participate in the discussions. Services are available on the World Wide Web to search for newsgroups related to a specific topic and to search for articles that contain keywords or phrases.

Selected Terms Introduced in This Chapter

administrative address

article

cross-posting

discussion group

group address

interest group

list address

listserv

lurking

mailing list

moderator

Network News Transport Protocol

   (NNTP)

newsgroup

newsreader

post

subscribe

thread

unsubscribe

Usenet

Review Questions

Multiple Choice

1. Which of the following is true of a discussion group?
   a. You should not read articles without posting a reply.
   b. You must subscribe to read articles in the list.
   c. You can post a message by sending it to the administrative address.
   d. Past messages are not kept in an archive.

2. The following are part of etiquette in a newsgroup or list except
   a. your messages should be clear and well-written.
   b. you should think before you write your message.
   c. you should not include humor.
   d. you should respond as if you were face-to-face.
   e. All of these are part of list or newsgroup etiquette.

3. You can find names and addresses of discussion groups
   a. at CataList.
   b. at Tile.Net.
   c. in Usenet news postings.
   d. a and b
   e. all of the above

4. In a newsgroup
   a. messages move from computer to computer instead of through email.
   b. you can't post an article without subscribing.
   c. you can not cross-post.
   d. a and b
   e. all of the above

5. The newsgroup where FAQs are regularly posted is
   a. news.announce.newusers
   b. news.questions
   c. news.faqs
   d. news.answers

6. Usenet newsgroup archives can be searched through
   a. AltaVista.
   b. Google Groups.
   c. a and b
   d. Newsgroup archives can't be searched.

True or False

7. T F Usenet newsgroups are also called interest groups or listservs.

8. T F You should save your welcome message that you receive when you subscribe to a discussion list.

9. T F Usenet did not begin as part of the Internet.

10. T F You must subscribe to a Usenet newsgroup in order to read messages.

11. T F To join a discussion list, you must send a message to the administrative address.

12. T F When you reply to a newsgroup message, you should include the whole article to which you are replying to avoid confusion.

13. T F A message to a newsgroup should not include humor.

Completion

14. Observing a discussion or reading discussion group messages without sending messages is known as _____.

15. The address you use to subscribe or to request services from a list is called the _____.

16. _____ is the means of all communication in a discussion group.

17. To leave a discussion group, you need to send a message saying you wish to _____.

18. A(n) _____ is a person who reads discussion group or newsgroup messages and then passes appropriate messages on to the group.

19. A(n) _____ is a collection of articles on a topic in a newsgroup that have been posted in reply to an original article on that topic.

20. Posting an article to more than one newsgroup is known as _____.

Exercises and Projects

Discussion Lists

1. Subscribe to a test discussion list and post a test message.
    a. Send an email to the administrative address **listproc@listproc.umw.edu** with the message

        subscribe test-listproc *your full name*

        In a little while, you should receive an email confirming your addition to the list. Briefly describe the contents of this email.
    b. Lurk for a couple of days. How many messages from this list land in your email inbox each day?
    c. Send a test message to the list address **test-listproc@listproc.umw.edu**. How long did it take to show up in your inbox?
    d. Unsubscribe from the list by following the instructions given in the email you received when you joined.

2. Use one of the two following search services to locate three discussion lists on topics of your choice. List the administrative addresses and list addresses of your three discussion lists.
    a. CataList, the official catalogue of listserv lists
        http://www.lsoft.com/list/listref.html
    b. "TILE.NET/LISTS, the Reference to Internet Discussion & Information Lists"
        http://tile.net/lists

3. Now go to the other search service you did not use in the previous exercise to look for one of your three discussion groups. Compare the two search services – CataList and TILE.NET For each service, describe the type of information it had available. Do you prefer one service? Why?

4. Search the archives of a discussion group in the following ways:
    a. Search using the Web-based services at Classroom Connect, **http://listserv.classroom.com/archives**. Click on the hyperlink "Science," then select the hyperlink **Search the archives**. Search the archives for messages about women and science. Describe what you find.
    b. Search using the Web-based services at **http://listserv.acsu.buffalo.edu/archives**. Select a discussion list based on your interests and do a search. What list did you choose? What did you search for? What were the results of your search?

Usenet Newsgroups

5. Use the following two search services to locate a Usenet newsgroup on any topic of your choice (mythology, creative anachronism, classic cars, your favorite performer/actor, and so on). Choose a topic you are very knowledgeable about so that you will be able to do the exercises that follow! Be sure to use the same search terms when you try out each search service.
   a. "Harley Hahn's Master List of Usenet Newsgroups"
      http://www.harley.com/usenet/
   b. "TILE.NET/LISTS, The Complete Reference to Usenet Newsgroups"
      http://tile.net/news

   Compare the two in terms of their services. Which do you prefer? Why?

6. Locate the FAQ, if there is one, for the newsgroup you found in exercise 5. Search at **http://www.faqs.org/faqs/by-newsgroup**. Read the FAQ. Is it up to date? Formulate a question that the FAQ doesn't answer. What is it? (Don't worry, we'll find you an answer to it in exercise 7!)

7. Use Google Groups to search Usenet for an answer to the question you formulated in exercise 6. If you can't find an answer then post your question to the newsgroup you selected in exercise 5. Follow these steps:
   a. Go to Google Groups, **http://groups.google.com/**, and search the Usenet archives for an answer to your question. Write the search expression you used here. Did you find the answer? What article provided the answer?
   b. If you didn't find an answer then search for the newsgroup you selected in exercise 5 using the advanced groups search form at **http://groups.google.com/advanced_group_search?hl=en**. Once you're on a Web page with a listing of messages click on **Post a new message** to get ready to post a message. If you're not registered at Google Groups, then follow the instructions to register. Now post your question. After a day or so, you'll need to check the newsgroup to see if you've received an answer. Write the name of the newsgroup, your questions, and the date and time you posted the question. When you get an answer, write the date and time it was posted.

8. Use the URL **http://groups.google.com/googlegroups/help.html** to read the Google Groups FAQ.
   a. How do you report abusive or invasive messages posted through Google Groups?
   b. How can you prevent articles you write from appearing in the archives?
   c. How can you remove articles you've posted to Usenet from the Google Groups archives?

SEARCHING ARCHIVES, DOWNLOADING FILES & FTP

The Internet was primarily created so that researchers could exchange ideas and share the results of their work. It stands to reason, then, that one of the basic Internet services would be to enable people to copy files from one computer to another on the Internet. *FTP*, which stands for File Transfer Protocol, is that basic Internet service. It dates back almost to the beginnings of the Internet, the early 1970s, and it's used to share information in any type of file. Most of these files are publicly available through what is called ***anonymous FTP***, since no special password other than *anonymous* is needed to retrieve the files. A computer system that allows others to connect to it through anonymous FTP is called an anonymous FTP site or an ***FTP archive***. The collection of files available at an anonymous FTP site is also called an FTP archive. Other archives of files and software are available on the Web. You can search these for helpful programs and utilities to install on your computer.

This chapter will focus on using FTP and FTP archives as two more facets of doing research on the Web and the Internet. There will also be a brief introduction to using an FTP client (an FTP program on your computer) to upload and download files without using a browser.

The chapter will have the following sections:

♦ Understanding the URL Format for FTP

♦ Downloading a File by Anonymous FTP

♦ Locating FTP Archives and Other Sites for Finding Software

♦ Downloading and Working with Files from Software Archives

♦ Using an FTP Client Program

Web browsers and Web servers using HTTP (Hypertext Transfer Protocol) transfer files across the Internet. Hence, they allow the same sort of sharing as FTP. What is now the World Wide Web wouldn't have been possible without the notions associated with FTP and its use. In fact, one of the first search services available on the Internet (as of 1990) was designed to find files stored in FTP archives. Called Archie (short for *archive,* according to its originators), this service worked by indexing the titles of files in a database built from the entries in many FTP archives. This index, in turn, took the form of a database. When a user supplied a search term, Archie displayed the locations of matching files. When you think about it, you'll see that it works a lot like many of the search engines we've discussed in earlier chapters.

Do we still need to use FTP? Yes. FTP can be used to transfer any type of file. It's commonly used nowadays to distribute software throughout the Internet. Most of these software programs are available as *shareware,* which means that you retrieve (download) the program from an archive, use it, and purchase it if you find the program useful. The concept of distributing software this way was created in 1982 simultaneously by Andrew Fluegleman and Jim Knopf. They each had software, PC-Talk and PC-File that they wanted to sell to others. To bypass the hurdles and costs associated with advertising and marketing their programs, they made them available for others to try at no charge and then asked for a voluntary payment of $25. Some shareware is still distributed that way, but it is also very common for you to have to agree to send in a payment after a trial period, usually 30 days. Software programs known as *freeware* are those that don't require a fee to use, ever. Note that this isn't the same as software being in the public domain. Even if the program is distributed without charge, someone may still be the copyright holder of the work.

FTP is an efficient way to transfer files when you know the exact name and location of the file—and that's all included in its URL. Using FTP, you can also transfer a file from your computer to another. This is called *uploading* a file. When you upload, you usually have to give a login name and password to the other computer system. This turns out to be a good way to work on one computer and transfer your work to another. Some people use this technique to update or create Web pages. They do their work on one computer and then transfer the files to a computer that acts as a Web server.

Understanding the URL Format for FTP

These days, much of the access to files by FTP is through a Web browser. As you know, that means you need to be familiar with the URL format for FTP. Here is the general form of a URL for anonymous FTP:

ftp://name-of-ftp-site/directory-name/file-name

Note the following features:

+ The URL for anonymous FTP starts with **ftp://**.
+ The name of the FTP site follows **//**.
+ The directory name starts with the first single **/** and goes up to, but does not include, the last **/**.
+ The name of the file follows the last **/**.
+ All the slashes (**/**) go in the same direction.

Suppose a friend tells you, "I found this picture of Mars with great detail and colors. You can get it by anonymous FTP at the FTP site for SEDS, **ftp.seds.org**. You'll want to get the file **mars1.gif**. It's in the directory **pub/images/planets/mars**. There are also some animations at the same site in **pub/anim**." You'd like to view the image, and she's told you everything you need to retrieve it. The URL for that file is **ftp://ftp.seds.org/pub/images/planets/mars/mars1.gif**.

Matching this to the general form, we have the following:

ftp://ftp.seds.org/pub/images/planets/mars/mars1.gif

You can also use a URL to refer to a directory. For example, if you enter the URL **ftp://ftp.seds.org/pub/images/planets/**, the Web browser displays a list of all the files or subdirectories in the directory **/pub/images/planets**, as displayed in Figure 10.1. Each file or subdirectory is represented as a hyperlink, and you can view it by clicking on its name. Internet Explorer displays an FTP archive in the same format that Microsoft Windows displays one of your computer's folders or directories.

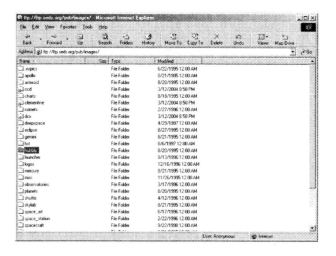

Figure 10.1—FTP Archive Displaying Directory Files

Downloading a File by Anonymous FTP

There are two ways to retrieve a file—that is, to copy it from a remote site to the computer you're using.

Method 1: View the File First, and Then Save It Using the File Menu

If you type a file's URL or if you click on a hyperlink, the file will be transferred to the Web browser. This is useful if you want to view the file before you save it, but the file will be transferred to your computer first. If the browser is configured to display or play a file of that type, you'll see (and hear, if possible) the file's contents in the Web browser window. Some examples of files of this type are text files, Web pages that are text files with HTML commands, or GIF or JPEG image files.

The file may also be displayed in a window created by another program called a *helper application* or *viewer.* If the file is displayed in the browser window, select **Save As** from the **File** pull-down menu in the menu bar. This opens a **Save As** dialog box on the screen. Set the directory or folder name, and then click on the button labeled **Save**. If the file comes up in the window for another application, such as Microsoft Word, save it through the commands for that application. See the tip below to handle a file type that doesn't match any type that your browser can work with.

Method 2: Save the Hyperlink in a File Without Viewing It by Using the Right Mouse Button or Shift and Click

If there is a hyperlink to a file in the Web browser's window and you're at an FTP site, you can save the file without viewing it. Put the mouse pointer on the hyperlink and press the right mouse button. When a menu pops up, choose **Copy to Folder**. This opens a **Browse For Folder** dialog box. Select the folder where you'd like to save the file.

Locating FTP Archives and Other Sites for Finding Software

FTP archives are collections of files available by anonymous FTP in directories arranged according to some scheme. A common arrangement is for the top level to be arranged by the type of computer system (such as Mac, PC, and Unix) and for the levels below that to be ordered according to the type of software (such as games, utilities, and Internet). You start at the home, or root, directory and move or browse through the archive by clicking on hyperlinks that represent folders or directories. Once you've located the file you want, you can download it using one of the methods described in the previous section.

There are several well-established and reliable FTP archives in the world. The following list is representative of general purpose archives. The first has a search form available so you can find files in the archive. The second has a Web page interface that you can use to go through the archives. The last is a more traditional type of listing; the items are well-orga-

✦ T I P ! **What to do when your browser can't display a file**

If you're using Internet Explorer, you'll have the opportunity to save the file to your computer, have another program display the file, cancel the operation, or get more information about downloading files to your computer from IE's online help. You'll want to save it to your computer if you want to copy it to another device for viewing or if you want to view it at another time. Selecting the option **Open** causes Windows to try to open the file. If it can't, another window pops up from which you can specify a program to display the file or to **Use the Web service to find the appropriate program**. Choosing that option causes the browser to search the Web for an appropriate program. If one is found, then select it. If not, then you'll likely see a link to a Web site that lets you search for helper programs based on the file name extension (the part of the name that comes after the last period). A Web site that has a comprehensive list of file name extensions and associated programs is "FILExt—The File Extension Source," **http://filext.com/**.

nized, but you have to find your own way.

- ✦ The public ftp server of ibiblio.org
  ftp://ftp.ibiblio.org/pub/
- ✦ Wuarchive, Washington University in St. Louis
  http://ftp.wustl.edu
- ✦ Garbo archives, University of Vaasa, Finland
  ftp://garbo.uwasa.fi

A better approach is to arrange files in categories according to their function—such as sound files, desktop utilities, games, HTML editors, and so forth—and to annotate each with a description. If there is a way to search the collection by file names and descriptions, then we have a more useful service.

Several of these software directories are available on the Web. Many of the files accessible through these sites are software, programs, or collections of programs and other files that are distributed as shareware. The files are in either executable form (their names end with **.exe**) or compressed form (their names end with **.zip** or **.gz**). We explained these file types in Chapter 2, and we'll show you how to work with them in the next section. Here are a few sources on the Web that list FTP and software or shareware archives:

- ✦ Librarians' Index to the Internet
  http://lii.org, then select **Science, Technology & Computers,**
  then **Computers,** and then **Software**
- ✦ nerd's HEAVEN: The Software Directory
  http://boole.stanford.edu/nerdsheaven.html
- ✦ Yahoo! Computers and Internet: Software: Shareware
  **http://dir.yahoo.com/computers_and_internet/
  software/shareware/**

Downloading and Working with Files from Software Archives

Several services on the Web act as archives and distributors of software in the form of shareware or freeware. Each service supplies links to the programs; when you click on the link, the software is transferred to your computer, essentially by FTP. In other words, you select the software you'd like, and you then use a Web browser to download it to your computer.

Shareware Often Comes in Packages

Most of the files in the archives are packages, or collections of related files. These are in packages because to install, run, and use a single program usually requires several files, such as program libraries, instructions for installing and registering the program, and online help files. When you retrieve shareware, you get all the files you need combined in one file, the package.

The files or packages are processed by a compression program, which reduces the total number of bytes necessary to represent the information in the package. Reducing the size of a file means it takes less time to download the file. Because of this compression, you must do two things to the package after you receive it: uncompress it and extract the individual files from the package.

Compressed files or packages have names that usually end in **.zip**. Two popular compression programs are PKZIP and WinZip (which are both shareware); these are also mentioned in Chapter 2. You will definitely want a copy of either of those utilities. As you might guess, they are both available in compressed format, as packages.

How can we extract the files necessary for those compression programs or similar packages? These and many other packages are in what is called a *self-extracting archive*. The package's file name ends in **.exe**. When you click on the name, it starts extracting its own components. For example, the software for the Mozilla and Opera browsers are in this format.

This compressed format isn't used only with programs. Any single file or collection of files can be compressed and transmitted in that compressed format. In the course of writing this book, we used this technology. Because each chapter has so many images, the files were quite large. We put each chapter and the images into a single package and then compressed it using either PKZIP or WinZip. We used FTP to send the compressed packages to the publisher.

Downloading and Installing Software

Here are the steps involved in downloading and installing shareware or freeware programs and associated files:

◆ Find the program you want to retrieve in a software archive.

◆ Create a folder or directory to hold the program from the archive on your computer.

◆ Click on the hyperlink in the software archive to the program. As soon as you indicate where it should go using a **Save As** dialog box, it will be transferred to your computer.

◆ If the file name ends in **.exe**, then it's likely a self-extracting archive. Locate it using Windows Explorer and double-click on it. It will either install itself—follow the instructions—or it will extract its parts into the current directory.

◆ If the file name ends in **.zip**, then you have to use a program such as PKZIP or WinZip to extract the components. You usually select the folder or directory in which they will go.

◆ In either case, look for a file with a name similar to **Readme** or **Instructions** to see what steps you need to take to install the program or to work with the files in the package. In many cases, the extracted files need to go through some other processing by a program named **Setup** before they are ready to use.

◆ Be sure to check the program and associated files for computer viruses. Many of the archives check files for viruses before making them available to the public, but you ought to check them yourself.

Obtaining a Copy of PKZIP or WinZip

You can see from the above steps that you'll need a copy of PKZIP or WinZip, but you don't need both.

To get a copy of PKZIP, go to the home page for PKWARE, **http://pkware.com**. Spend a little time reading about PKZIP, the way it works, and file compression in general. Click on the hyperlink that takes you through the steps of downloading the software. Store it in a new folder only for PKZIP. Once it has finished downloading, there will be a new application (program) in the folder. Click on it and follow the instructions. It will install itself in a directory or folder. Once it's installed, go to that directory, using Windows Explorer, and read the file named

Readme, which contains information about the files you've installed. The program's name is PKZIP; click on it when you need to use it.

To get a copy of WinZip, go to the home page for WinZip with the URL **http://winzip.com**. Spend a little time reading about WinZip, how it works, and about the topic of file compression. Click on the hyperlink that takes you through the steps of downloading the software. Store it in a new folder only for WinZip. Once it's finished downloading, there will be a new application (program) in the folder. Click on it, and it will lead you through the steps of installing the program in a folder on your computer. The name of the program is WinZip; click on it when you need it.

Acquiring Antivirus Software

You will also want a program that checks files for computer viruses. Several are available, and you can get shareware versions to evaluate and determine which you like best. One, F-PROT, makes its software free to individuals; commercial customers or organizations must pay for using it. Listed with F-PROT are two other sites that offer shareware versions of their antivirus and virus protection software:

- ✦ F-PROT
  http://www.frisk.is/f-prot/download

- ✦ Norton AntiVirus, Symantec
  http://symantec.com/avcenter

- ✦ VirusScan, McAfee
  http://us.mcafee.com/virusInfo/default.asp

If you don't have an antivirus program on your computer, visit one of the sites, download the most recent version, and install it. The antivirus programs from the sites listed above come as compressed packages. Follow the same steps for installing these programs as for almost any other software that you download.

Using Software Archives

In an earlier section of this chapter, we listed the URLs of some lists of software archives or sites in which you can find software to download through FTP. We'll talk about using the archives here, right after we discuss the way the software is distributed. The archives we'll discuss are ones that contain software packages that you can download without charge.

What You'll Find in the Archives

Software archives maintain their own collections of files, and FTP archives have hyperlinks to the files, which are usually stored at the Web site for the person or organization that markets the software. Both types include a search form so you can search the collection for files, and several also have reviews, descriptions, and links to the software arranged into categories so you can browse the items accessible through the archive.

The files are usually arranged in categories according to the type of software, such as games, Internet, utilities, and personal use. Sometimes they are also arranged according to the type of operating system they're designed for, such as Windows 95/98/2000/ME/NT/XP, Mac OS, PDA, or Linux.

Here's a list of a few archives:

Software Archives	URL
CNET Download.com	http://www.download.com
CNET Shareware.com	http://www.shareware.com
IT Pro Downloads	http://itprodownloads.com
WinPlanet	http://www.winplanet.com/
TUCOWS	http://tucows.com
ZDNet Downloads	http://www.zdnet.com/downloads

Before You Download

We're going to demonstrate downloading and installing some software in Activity 10.1. Before you download software, you need to answer a few questions for yourself.

Is the program appropriate for my computer system?

Most of the software archives include a description of the system requirements for the software you'll download. Check that you have enough memory (RAM) to run the program and that you have the correct operating system. Software that's developed for a for a Windows 98/2000 or Windows NT/XP system won't work properly if it's installed on a system running Windows 3.1 or on a Macintosh system.

Do I have enough storage space on my disk to hold the software?

Again, look at the system requirements to see that you have enough disk space to hold the new program along with your other software.

Do I meet the licensing requirements?

Most software is available as shareware to anyone, but some software is available only to educational or nonprofit institutions. The software will likely come with a licensing agreement; you'll need to read this and decide whether to consent to it.

Do I have permission to install the software?

If you're working on your home computer, then there's probably no problem. However, if you're working on a computer that's owned by your school or company—and probably being shared by others—check local policies to see whether you may install new software on the computer.

Do I have the software I need to install the software?

Check to see if you have the proper software, such as PKZIP or WinZip, to extract the parts of the package. Oftentimes, this will be stated in the description of the software. Also look at the name of the package. If it ends with **.zip**, then you'll need a program such as the one we've mentioned to install it.

Will the software have a detrimental impact on other software on my computer?

This isn't always easy to answer until the software is installed, in which case it may be too late. Read as much as you can about the software before installing it to see if it will have a detrimental impact on existing programs or system configuration. Be sure you can check it for viruses before installing it.

Will I be able to "uninstall" the program if things don't go well?

Most software nowadays comes with a program that makes it easy to remove the primary program and all associated files if and when you need to do this.

Now we'll go through some of the details involved in downloading and installing software from an archive.

ACTIVITY

10.1   DOWNLOADING AND INSTALLING SOFTWARE
FROM A SOFTWARE ARCHIVE

OVERVIEW

We've been searching for and finding information on the Web throughout this book. In many instances, we've added some resources to our favorites list. The list has grown and needs some organization and management. We know we can do this through our browser, but we're interested in seeing if there is some software that has better tools for organizing and managing our bookmark or favorites collection. In this activity, we'll go to one of the software archives, find something we'd like to try, check to see that it's appropriate to download and install, and then go through the steps necessary to install it. Here are the steps we'll follow:

1. Go to the home page for Download.com.

2. Search the library for software dealing with managing bookmarks or favorites.

3. Select software to download and check the system requirements.

4. Download the software.

5. Install the software.

Of course, we'll want to try the program at some point, but we won't show that here.

DETAILS

We'll assume that the Web browser is started and displayed on the screen.

1   Go to the home page for Download.com.

✦ Do It!   Click on the address field, type **http://www.download.com**, and press **Enter**.

Download.com is a large, well-organized, and well-maintained software archive. We use the URL for its home page, **http://www.download.com**, to access the software library or archive. A portion of the home page appears in Figure 10.2. We're going to search for software dealing with managing favorites in the next step.

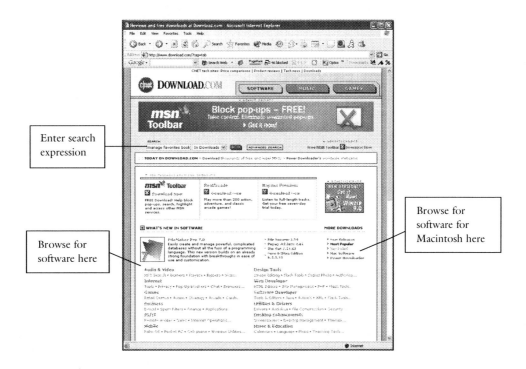

Enter search expression

Browse for software here

Browse for software for Macintosh here

Figure 10.2—Home Page for Download.com

We see from the home page that we can search or browse the archive. You can differentiate between the sponsored links and the others. There are some interesting items on the home page that we couldn't show in Figure 10.2. One is an XML link that takes you to a page where you can get updates of entries to the archive through an RSS feed; these are discussed in Chapter 7. There's also a link to the Help Center for this site. It contains links to a collection of FAQs, the **Beginner's Guide to Downloading**, and other items to use to learn more about downloading and using this archive.

2 Search the library for software dealing with managing favorites or bookmarks.

✦ Do It! Type **manage favorites bookmarks** in the search box, as shown in Figure 10.2, and click on **GO**.

You can search for software by typing a keyword or phrase in the search box and clicking on the button labeled **GO**.

3 Select software to download and check the system requirements.

A portion of the Web page listing the search results appears in Figure 10.3. The first few are sponsored listings, and we'll bypass those. Several of the listings include comments from users. We clicked on the column heading **User rating** to sort the items in descending order by the value of the user rating. That way, we can see which have been rated and choose a popular item to start with. It's worth taking some time clicking on the hyperlinks for some of the packages to read the reviews and ratings. In addition to a link to the review, we see the date the software was added to the archive, the type of license—freeware ("free") or shareware ("free to try" and the amount we have to pay for continued use), and the number of downloads (other folks retrieving the software) listed. To be specific, we'll click on the hyperlink for **JetLinks 1.0**. It is popular, lets us manage favorites or bookmarks from several browsers, and it is free.

✦ Do It!   Click on the hyperlink for **JetLinks 1.0**.

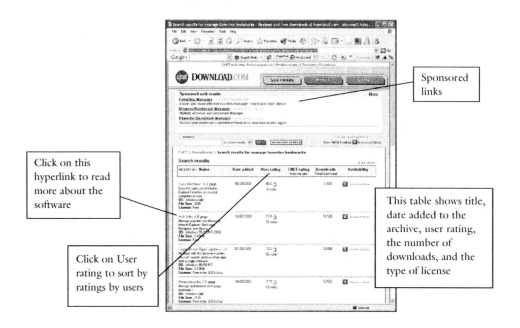

Sponsored links

Click on this hyperlink to read more about the software

This table shows title, date added to the archive, user rating, the number of downloads, and the type of license

Click on User rating to sort by ratings by users

Figure 10.3—Web Page Showing Search Results

A portion of the Web page for JetLinks is shown in Figure 10.4. After reading this page, we see that JetLinks works with both favorites and bookmarks, works with a variety of browsers, is designed to run on a computer that uses a Windows 95/98/NT/2000 operating system, and that in compressed form it takes up roughly 2.41 megabytes. Once it's expanded, we can expect it to take up about twice as much space, and we need to decide if we have enough disk space to install it. We also see a link to the comments of other users. If, after reading the reviews, we feel the software will be useful to us, it is appropriate for our computer, and we have enough space for it, then we can start downloading it.

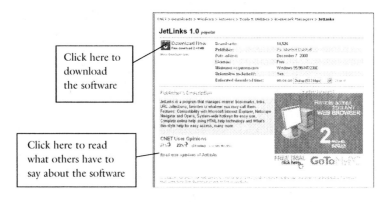

Click here to download the software

Click here to read what others have to say about the software

Figure 10.4—Download.com Information About JetLinks

4 Download the software.

We will save the package in a folder where we can save other items that we download from the Internet. This way, we'll always know where we can find them. We'll be using a folder named **downloads** for this purpose. If it's not already on the computer, then we'll have to create it.

First we'll create a folder to hold the package. We're using Windows XP so we first activate Windows Explorer by clicking on the **Start** button, selecting **All Programs**, and then selecting **Accessories** and choosing **Windows Explorer**. (You can also do this by going to the **Desktop** and clicking on the icon **My Computer**.)

We'll use Windows Explorer to display the contents of Drive C:. Click on **My Computer** in the left pane and select **Local Disk (C:)**. Now click on **File** in the menu bar, select **New**, and then click on **New Folder**.

The window you'll see appears in Figure 10.5.

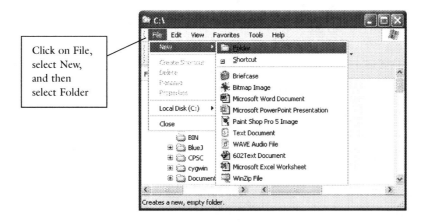

Figure 10.5—Creating a New Folder Using Windows Explorer

A new folder is created. We'll name it **downloads**.

✦ Do It!   Type **downloads** for the folder's name and press **Enter**.

Now we're ready for the second step in the download process. We can use the browser to transfer the file from Download.com to our system. Be sure the Web page like the one in Figure 10.4 is displayed on your computer.

✦ Do It!   Return to the browser window and click on the hyperlink **Download Now**.

The browser will attempt to transfer the file to your computer using FTP. You'll likely get a **File Download** box. We'll click on a button that lets us save the file to disk. A **Save As** dialog box will appear.

Use the controls in the **Save As** dialog box to select the folder **downloads**, as has been done in Figure 10.6. Then click on **Save**.

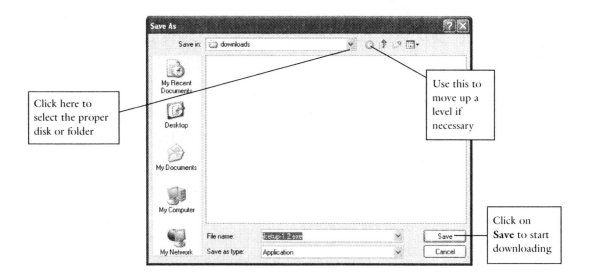

Figure 10.6—Save As Dialog Box with downloads as the Selected Folder

A window pops up on the screen to show the rate at which the file is being transferred and the speed of transfer. If it is possible, the window will also display the time left to download the file. Depending on the speed of your connection, how busy the server is at Download. com, and current Internet traffic, it could take a few seconds or up to several minutes to download the file.

Once the software is downloaded, you have the option to open the file, open the folder that contains the file, or cancel the operation. We're going to open the folder that contains the file.

5   Install the software.

The downloaded file will be in the **downloads** folder we created on Drive C:. If you have anti-virus software installed, this would be a good time to scan the file for viruses. We don't expect any from Download.com, but it is better to be safe. To install the file, we'll have to execute or run the package it came in.

✦ Do It!   Use Windows Explorer to open the folder **downloads**.

The listing indicates that the file is an executable file or an application because its name has the extension **.exe**. All we'll need to do is to double click on the name of the file, and it will start a setup program to take us through the installation. This is similar to the way we installed the Google toolbar for Internet Explorer in Chapter 1.

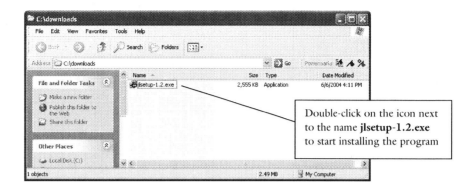

Figure 10.7—View of the Downloaded File

✦ Do It!   Double-click on the icon next to the name **jlsetup-1.2.exe**.

Double clicking on the icon starts a setup program that guides us through the installation. You'll have the opportunity to decide whether to put an icon for the program on the Desktop, to start JetLinks whenever Windows starts, and whether to put an icon for the program in the Quick Start menu, next to the Start button on the taskbar. At a minimum, you'll want to have the installation create an icon for the Desktop. That way, you can start it easily, and the other options may be more difficult for you to remove or customize. At the end of the installation process, you're asked whether you want to start JetLinks. Why not give it a try? Read the online documentation and see if it suits your needs.

If it isn't something you'd like to keep, then you should remove or uninstall the program. There is more to this than removing the files in the folder (**C:\Program Files\JetLinks** in this case) that holds the program and auxiliary files. To uninstall this program, click on **Start** in the taskbar at the lower left of the screen, click on **Control Panel**, and then click on **Add or Remove Programs**. Scroll down the list if necessary, click on the entry for **JetLinks**, and then click on **Change/Remove**. You'll be asked to confirm that you want to remove the program and all of its components (that's why we go through the Control Panel so that everything associated with the program is removed). You can install it again if you wish since we still have the installation package in **c:\downloads**.

Once you've installed the program and decide you want to keep it, you can delete **jlsetup-1.2.exe** in **C:\downloads**. You will also want to delete this file if you uninstall the program and its components as described above.

END OF ACTIVITY 10.1

In Activity 10.1, we downloaded and installed a program from a software archive. The steps we followed were fairly typical, although the details can change, depending on the program downloaded and the software archive used.

Using an FTP Client Program

In the examples and activities discussed so far in this chapter, we have used FTP through the Web browser. That may be all you need to search for and retrieve information from the Web or Internet using FTP. Sometimes, though, you may want to use an FTP program that's separate from the browser. To use an FTP program this way, you'll still need an Internet connection from your computer. The program you run will download files from a server or upload files from your computer to a server. This is the sort of client/server interaction we discussed in Chapter 1. The FTP program you use acts as a client.

When you work with an FTP client to contact another computer (called the *server* or *host*), you'll need to have certain pieces of information. The following list explains what you must know.

You'll need the Internet domain name or address of the server or host.
The client uses the ***domain name*** to contact the server. Earlier in the chapter, in the section "Understanding the URL Format for FTP," we pointed out the domain name portion of a URL that implies the use of FTP.

If you're going to be downloading software, you'll need a user name and a password on the host.
If you're using anonymous FTP, the user name is *anonymous* and the password is your email address. If you're going to download some files from your user account on the server system, you'll use your assigned user name and password.

If you're going to be uploading files to another computer, you'll need a user name and password on the host.
The user name and password enable you to upload files to a directory or folder that isn't necessarily available to the public.

Of course, you'll also need an FTP client for your computer. Several are available as shareware, but one in particular is highly recommended. It's WS_FTP, and it's free for personal use. To get a copy appropriate for your system, go to the download section of FTPplanet.com at **http://www.ftpplanet.com/download.asp** and select **Click here to download WS_FTP LE**. Several very good guides to using WS_FTP are available on the Web. Here's a short list:

- ✦ How to Use WS_FTP
  http://library.albany.edu/internet/ws_ftp.html

- ✦ WS_FTP Tutorials
  http://www.ftpplanet.com/tutorial/index.html

- ✦ How to Use FTP
  http://d-na.com/tryftp.htm

We'll briefly go over how to use WS_FTP, but look at some of these guides for more help when you're ready.

First download and install the appropriate version of the software from FTPplanet.com. Use the same techniques discussed in Activity 10.1.

Once the program is installed, start it by selecting it from the **Start** menu, clicking on an icon on your desktop, or clicking on an icon in a folder. Which one of these you choose depends on how it was installed. When it starts, a session profile pops onto the screen.

Figure 10.8 shows a session profile for connecting to a system with the host name (same as the domain name) **www.mwc.edu**. The user ID or login name for this user is **ernie**. A password isn't typed in here; it will be typed in when the host system is contacted. If a password were saved with this profile, then anyone using the computer could access the files belonging to user

ernie on **www.mwc.edu**. If this were to be an anonymous FTP session, then the box labeled **Anonymous** would be checked. You can select other servers with different profiles by clicking on the button to the right of the profile name.

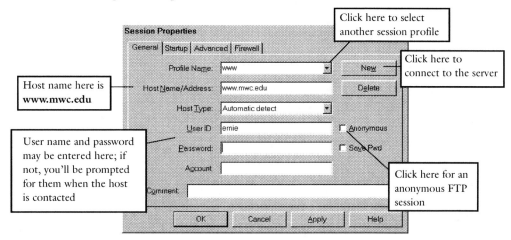

Figure 10.8 —Sample Session Profile for WS_FTP

To contact the host, click on the button labeled **OK**. Acting as a client, WS_FTP attempts to contact the host system. Another window pops up that shows whether the host has been contacted. The user then has control over the transfer of files.

Figure 10.9 shows the window that appears when WS_FTP starts an FTP session with **www.mwc.edu**. The left column lists the files in the current folder of your computer, the client. The right column lists the files in the directory with which you've connected on the host computer.

You can choose a file to transfer by selecting it from the appropriate column. You'll see that there are scroll bars to let you scroll through the list of files and directories on both the client and host computers. In each column, the subdirectories of the current directory are listed in the upper panel and the files are listed in the lower panel.

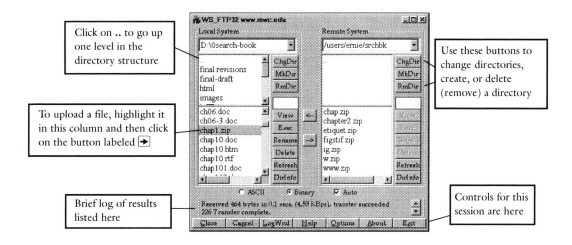

Figure 10.9—Session Window for WS_FTP

Suppose we want to upload the file named **chap1.zip** from the client computer—that's the computer you're using—to the host. We highlight **chap1.zip** as shown in Figure 10.9 and click on the button labeled [➡]. In doing so, we move the file from the client (listed on the left) to the host (listed on the right).

After we click on [➡], another dialog box called **Transfer Status** pops up, showing information about the transfer of the file from one computer to another over the Internet. The items shown include the total number of bytes to transfer, the number transferred so far, the rate of transfer, how much time has been spent so far, and the estimated remaining time. That window will stay on the screen until the transfer is complete. You can stop the transfer by clicking on the **Cancel** button.

To download a file, select the directory on the local system that will hold the file, highlight the name of the file in the list on the right, and click on [⬅].

WS_FTP is one example of an FTP client. It presents a graphical user interface for transferring files between a client and server. Other client programs have a strictly text-based interface. With those, you use a command *get*, as in **get etiquet.zip**, to download a file. You use the command *put*, as in **put chap1.zip**, to upload a file.

Summary

FTP stands for File Transfer Protocol. With FTP, you can share or copy files from one Internet site to another. Anonymous FTP is the term used when you copy a file from one computer to another without giving a login name or a password. Collections of files available by anonymous FTP are called anonymous FTP archives.

To retrieve a file by anonymous FTP through a Web browser, use a URL in the form **ftp://name-of-ftp-site/directory-name/file-name**. One example of such a URL would be **ftp://ftp.seds.org/pub/images/planets/mars/mars1.gif**. To browse a directory, use a URL in the form **ftp://name-of-ftp-site/directory-name**. An example would be **ftp://ftp.seds.org/pub/images/planets**. If the URL is for a file, the Web browser will attempt to display it. You can then save it into a file on your computer. If you give the URL for a directory, the files and subdirectories of that directory will be displayed as hyperlinks. Put the mouse pointer on a hyperlink and press the right mouse button. When a menu pops up, choose **Save Link As**. This opens a **Save As** dialog box on the screen. Set the directory or folder name, and then click on the **Save** button.

Literally trillions of bytes of information, programs, and resources are available by anonymous FTP. Archie, one of the first Internet search programs, is a tool specifically designed for searching anonymous FTP archives. When you supply a keyword, the names of the files, directories, and sites in the database are searched. Several other search services and software libraries search a database that holds descriptions and reviews of software available through anonymous FTP. Some of the software archives also have entries arranged by the type of program (for example, antivirus programs) or by the operating system (for example, Windows 98 or Macintosh).

Transferring a file from another computer to the computer you're using is called downloading. That's what you do when you retrieve a program from an FTP archive. Many of the programs depend on a number of auxiliary files to be run and used effectively, such as online help. These files are put together into a package, and the contents are compressed to allow for easier and faster storage and transfer.

After you retrieve one of these packages of software, you need to process it to extract the components. If the package name ends with **.exe**, then it's a self-extracting archive. Click on the name of the package, and it will unpack itself. If the name ends with **.zip**, you'll need to use a program to decompress it, such as PKZIP or WinZip.

Once the files are extracted, you will run a program (application) to install the program. To be safe, you'll also want to scan the software for computer viruses before you install it. Look for a file with a name such as **Readme**, and read it before you install the program. It may help you decide whether the program is appropriate for you and your computer system. Finally, look for a program—often named **Setup** or **Install**—that you'll run to install the program.

An FTP client program is run on your computer to exchange files with another computer that acts as the host, or server. This program is not usually part of the Web browser. To access another computer through FTP, you need to give the client program the Internet domain name for the host computer. That's the part of the URL that immediately follows **ftp://**. For example, in the URL **ftp://ftp.seds.org/pub/images/planets/mars/mars1.gif**, the domain name is **ftp.seds.org**. Once connected, you can upload files from your computer to the host or download files from the host to your computer. You can do either one by using a graphical interface provided by the client or by using the commands *put* and *get*.

Selected Terms Introduced in This Chapter

anonymous FTP
domain name
freeware
FTP archive
shareware
upload

Review Questions

Multiple Choice

1. The following is an example of the URL format for FTP:
   a. http://ftp.seds.org/pub/images/planets/mars/mars1.gif
   b. http.ftp.seds.org/pub/images/planets/mars/mars1.gif
   c. ftp://ftp.seds.org/pub/images/planets/mars/mars1.gif
   d. ftp:ftp.seds.org/pub/images/planets/mars/mars1.gif

2. Shareware
   a. can be downloaded for free.
   b. often comes in files that need to be unzipped.
   c. is not covered by copyright.
   d. a and b
   e. all of the above

3. Before downloading software from an anonymous FTP site onto your computer, you should
   a. install a virus protection program.
   b. ask for permission.
   c. make sure there is enough space on our computer.
   d. a and b
   e. a and c

4. FTP
   a. can be used without a Web browser.
   b. can only be used by logging in as "anonymous."
   c. is the newest Internet protocol.
   d. a and b
   e. a and c

5. Which of these files is/are in a compressed format?
   a. file.txt
   b. file.zip
   c. file.doc
   d. a and c
   e. all of the above

6. To make use of a compressed file you need to
   a. use an unzipping program.
   b. store it in a folder.
   c. upload it.
   d. keep it on your desktop.

True or False

7. T F The concept of FTP began in the early 1990s.

8. T F With the advent of the Web, FTP is no longer needed.

9. T F The concept of shareware means to download and use a program and to pay for it if you find it useful.

10. T F In a URL for an FTP site, the format is **directory name/file name/server name**.

11. T F Archie is a search tool that allows you to find a server where an FTP file is located.

12. T F You should check every program you download with an anti-virus program.

13. T F An FTP client will allow you to download and upload programs without using a browser.

Completion

14. If no special password is needed to access and download from an FTP site, the process is called _____ FTP.

15. An FTP archive is also known as a(n) _____.

16. The search service specifically for finding FTP files is known as

_____.

17. Software that can be downloaded, used, or distributed without cost is known as

_____.

18. A(n) _____ is a group or collection of related files needed to install, run, and use a program.

19. Downloaded software whose name ends in .exe is a(n) _____.

20. _____ means to transfer a file from your computer to another computer.

Exercises and Projects

This set of exercises and projects is designed to give you practice using anonymous FTP. Along the way, you will see some of the resources available. In some exercises, you'll be asked to find a location, or URL, of similar files or resources. To do that, use any of the search services with which you are familiar.

1. Most Usenet news groups have a FAQ (Frequently Asked Questions) that is archived on an FTP server at the Massachusetts Institute of Technology. Use your Web browser to retrieve the contents of the directory whose URL is **ftp://rtfm.mit.edu/pub/faqs**. Add this URL to your bookmarks or favorites. (Note: RTFM is the place to go when you want to Read The Fine Manual.)
   a. Download the ftp-list FAQ from **ftp://rtfm.mit.edu/pub/faqs/ftp-list/faq**. Under the question "What is Anonymous FTP?" is a list of what is available in FTP archives. What can you find?
   b. Would you say that the FTP FAQ is up-to-date? Explain.

2. Access the Gutenberg Project mirror at the University of Illinois at **ftp://ibiblio.org/pub/docs/books/gutenberg/**.
   a. Write a brief description of what you see at the site. Look at the file named **GUTINDEX.01** and describe the kinds of etexts available via FTP from the Gutenberg Project. List three titles.
   b. Does **ftp://ftp.cdrom.com/pub** have a mirror of the Gutenberg Project? If so, what is its URL? Does **ftp://ftp.cdrom.com/pub** also mirror the Garbo and Simtelnet archives? What are their URLs?
   c. What FTP archives are mirrored at **ftp://mirrors.aol.com**?

3. Retrieve part 1 of the shareware FAQ from **ftp://rtfm.mit.edu/pub/faqs/shareware-faq**. Summarize the rules that govern the use of shareware. What is the difference between shareware and freeware?

4. Go to **http://arachnoid.com**, locate the **Downloadable Programs** link, and download and install on your computer the program AboutTime or another program you find there. Do you need to unzip these programs, or are they self-extracting?

    Take some time to look at this site. The guest book is always busy! Most people would call the software available here freeware, but its author, Paul Lutus, calls it "CareWare." Download his description of CareWare from **http://arachnoid.com/ careware/index.html**, read it, and write a brief description of the concept. Then, do it!

5. People downloading software from the Internet should protect their computer systems from viruses.
    a. Download the computer virus mini-FAQ from **ftp://rtfm.mit.edu/pub/faqs/ computer-virus**. What does the author of this FAQ have to say on the question, "Is there a best antivirus software?"
    b. Download and install an antivirus scanning program from one of the mirrors of **http://www.tucows.com**. Follow the links on the TUCOWS home page to find the appropriate application for your operating system. If you are using WindowsXP, for example, your URL would be something like **http://www.tucows.com/ virus95_default.html**. The next step will ask where you are located so you can access the nearest mirror site to download the program. Explain the steps you follow to download and install the program.

6. Go to **http://shareware.com**
    a. You'll see a list of the week's most popular searches for downloads at shareware.com. What are they?
    b. Use the search feature to find the PKZIP compression program. What did you find?
    c. Use your favorite Web search service to locate the PKZIP compression program. Explain whether it was easier or harder to find PKZIP via a Web search or an FTP search.

7. Have some fun! Download a theme for your desktop and/or a screensaver from **http://www.free-desktop-theme.com/**. Pick a category and choose a theme or choose a screen saver for an upcoming holiday. Follow the directions on that page for downloading the theme and for installation. What did you choose? What protocol moved the file from the server to your machine? HTTP or FTP? How do you know?

8. Download and install the appropriate version of the WS_FTP software from Junod Software, **http://www.ipswitch.com/Products/WS_FTP**. Use the same techniques discussed in the chapter activity.

    Using WS_FTP, download at least two files from different sites mentioned in the chapter or in the previous exercises. (WS_FTP will already be configured to take you to a number of FTP archives.)

    Do you see any advantage to using an FTP client rather than a Web browser for accessing FTP archives? Any disadvantages? Explain.

EVALUATING INFORMATION FOUND ON THE WORLD WIDE WEB

11

Critical thinking skills have always been important to the process of searching for and using information from media such as books, journals, radio broadcasts, television reports, and so forth. With the advent of the Internet and the World Wide Web, these skills have become even more crucial. Traditional books and journal articles need to pass some kind of editorial scrutiny before being published. Web pages, however, can appear without a single person ever reading them through to check for accuracy. Libraries have collection development policies that govern what material they will and will not buy; the Internet and the Web, having no such policies, collect anything. This isn't to say that there isn't information of high quality on the Internet. There are thousands of high-caliber Web pages and well-regarded databases. It is your responsibility to decide whether a page or site is worth selecting and then determine, using well-established guidelines, whether the information is worth using in your research paper, project, or presentation.

In this chapter, we'll look at some issues related to evaluating resources on the World Wide Web. The chapter will include these sections:

◆ Reasons to Evaluate

◆ Guidelines for Evaluation

◆ Information About Evaluating Resources on the World Wide Web

Reasons to Evaluate

We use the information we find on the Internet or Web for a variety of purposes. Sometimes we use it for entertainment, recreation, or casual conversation. When we use it for research, to bolster a belief, or to choose a particular course of action, we have to be sure the information is reliable and authoritative. That puts us in the position of having to verify the information and make judgments about its appropriateness. Reliable information is one of the most important things in life. In order to make decisions and understand our world, we need the most truthful information that we can find.

The nature of the Internet and the World Wide Web makes it easy for almost anyone to create and disperse information. People also have the freedom to design their pages to advertise products or disseminate propaganda unnoticeable within the context of a research report. To think critically about information and its sources means being able to separate fact from opinion. We have to be able to verify information and know its source, we have to determine whether the facts are current, and we need to know why someone offered the information at all. In some situations, we don't have to do all the work ourselves. Some librarians and other information specialists have established virtual libraries on the Web in which the listed sources have been reviewed and evaluated. The following are the major virtual libraries:

- ✦ Academic Info: Your Gateway to Quality Educational Resources
  http://www.academicinfo.net

- ✦ Infomine
  http://infomine.ucr.edu

- ✦ Internet Public Library
  http://www.ipl.org

- ✦ Librarians' Index to the Internet
  http://lii.org

- ✦ Library Spot
  http://libraryspot.com

- ✦ Refdesk.com
  http://www.refdesk.com

- ✦ Resource Directory Network
  http://www.rdn.ac.uk

It's useful to visit these sites to find information that's been reviewed by someone else. Still, when you deal with any information you find on the Web or in a library, it is up to you to be skeptical about it and to assess whether it's appropriate for your purposes. For example, if you want information before buying a CD player, then product announcements from manufacturers will give you some data, but the announcements will probably not be the right source for impartial brand comparisons. If you're researching techniques for advertising electronic consumer products, then the advertisements might be good resource material; if you are writing about the physics involved in producing sound from audio CDs, however, these ads may not be authoritative sources.

Once you find some information, regardless of whether the resource is a book, journal article, Web page, or data from a CD-ROM, a librarian can help you evaluate its usefulness and quality. Librarians, particularly reference librarians, are trained professionals who have lots of experience with evaluating resources. They can usually tell you within seconds if information is relevant, authoritative, and appropriate for your research needs.

Guidelines for Evaluation

After typing an appropriate search expression in a search tool, scan the results. Open a document, and if it isn't readily apparent why that resource has come up in your hit list, activate the Find operation by clicking on **Edit**, choosing **Find in Page**, and typing one of your keywords in the search form. **Find** will take you to the part of the Web page where the word or phrase appears. Sometimes the Find option won't locate the keyword or phrase in the page. This may mean that an earlier version of the page contained the keyword. You'll often discover that the keyword is used in a context that is irrelevant to your research needs. Once you've found a page that appears to be fairly applicable to your topic, you can begin to use the following guidelines for evaluation.

The determination of information quality is not a cut-and-dried process. You can infer quality by clues that will either support or negate your research. Sometimes you need to rely on your intuition or your own previous knowledge about a particular piece of information. Noting this, the following guidelines are just that: guidelines. They are not meant to be absolute rules for evaluating documents found on the Internet and the Web. They are questions that you should ask yourself when looking at Web pages and other Internet sources. After briefly explaining the guidelines, we will indicate how you can apply them to documents and other information that you retrieve from the Web or the Internet.

Who Is the Author or Institution?

✦ If an individual has written the resource, does it offer or give links to biographical information about the author? For example, does it mention educational or other credentials, an occupation, or an institutional affiliation?

✦ What clues does the URL give you about the source's authority? A tilde (~) in the Web page's URL usually indicates that it is a personal page rather than part of an institutional Web site. Also, make a mental note of the domain section of the URL, as follows:

  ✦ **.edu**, educational—can be anything from serious research to zany student pages

  ✦ **.gov**, governmental—government resources

  ✦ **.com**, commercial—may be trying to sell a product

  ✦ **.net**, network—may provide services to commercial or individual customers

- ✦ **.org**, organization—is a nonprofit institution; may be biased
    - ✦ **.mil**, military—U.S. military sites, agencies, and some academies
- ✦ Countries other than the United States use two-letter codes as the final part of their domain names. The United States uses **us** in the domain name when designating state and local government hosts, as well as public schools (**k12** is often used).

Who Is the Audience?

- ✦ Is the Web page intended for the general public, or is it meant for scholars, practitioners, children, and so forth? Is the audience clearly stated?
- ✦ Does the Web page meet the needs of its stated audience?

Is the Content Accurate and Objective?

- ✦ Are there political, ideological, cultural, religious, or institutional biases?
- ✦ Is the content intended to be a brief overview of the topic or an in-depth analysis?
- ✦ If the information is opinion, is this clearly stated?
- ✦ If there are facts and statistics included, are they properly cited?
- ✦ Is it clear how the data was collected, and is it presented in a logical, organized way?
- ✦ Is there a bibliography at the end of the document?
- ✦ If the page is part of a larger institution's Web site, does the institution appear to filter the information that appears at its site? Was the information screened somehow before it was put on the Web?

What Is the Purpose of the Information?

- ✦ Is the purpose of the information to inform, explain, convince, market a product, or advocate a cause?
- ✦ Is the purpose clearly stated?
- ✦ Does the resource fulfill the stated purpose?

How Current Is the Information?

- ✦ Does the Web page have a date that indicates when it was placed on the Web?
- ✦ Is it clear when the page was last updated?
- ✦ Is some of the information obviously out-of-date?
- ✦ Does the page creator mention how frequently the material is updated?

Discussion and Tips

We will now discuss the criteria we have listed and indicate how you can verify information obtained from the Internet.

Who Is the Author or Institution?

If you're not familiar with the author or institution responsible for producing the information, you'll need to do some checking to determine whether the source is reliable and authoritative.

You can't consider a resource reliable if you don't know who wrote it or what institution published it. If a Web page doesn't contain the name of the author or the institution, and if there are no hyperlinks to Web pages that give that information, then you should be suspicious of its content.

Being suspicious doesn't mean that you must disqualify the information. For example, the Web page "Episode 1, 1962–1963: Distortions of Intelligence," **http://www.odci.gov/csi/books/vietnam/epis1.html**, doesn't say who is the author of the information and doesn't give a link to the organization that sponsored the information. But if you look at the URL, you can see that the information is provided through the Web server with the Internet domain name **www.odci.gov**. This indicates that it's supplied by a government organization, which means that it's usually suitable for research purposes. We'll do some more sleuthing in Activity 11.1, starting with this Web page.

✦ T I P ! Look for the name of the author or institution at the top or bottom of a Web page.

✦ T I P ! To find out about the sponsor, go to the home page for the site that hosts the information.

On the other hand, if the information is provided by a commercial site (its URL will contain **.com**, as in **www.apple.com**) or if it's an organization's Web page (its URL will contain **.org**, as in **http://www.ahbfi.org/**), then we may need to do further checking.

Regardless of whether the Web page contains the sponsor's name, we can investigate further by looking for more information about the author or institution. For example, consider the document "CDT Children's Privacy Issues Page," **http://www.cdt.org/privacy/children**. Looking at that Web page, we can see that the Center for Democracy and Technology (CDT) has made it available. There are hyperlinks from that Web page to the home page for

✦ T I P ! To find further information about the institution or author, use a search engine to see what related information is available on the Web.

CDT. You can follow the hyperlinks to find out more about the CDT, or you can go to the home page by typing the URL **http://www.cdt.org** in the address box and pressing **Enter**.

When you can't find your way to a home page or to other information, try using a search engine, directory, or other service to search the Web.

✦ T I P ! Use Google Groups or another tool to search Usenet archives. That way, you can find other information about the author or institution. If an individual is the author, you can see what sorts of articles they've posted on Usenet.

Access Google Groups by using the URL **http://groups.google.com**. Type the author's name in the search form. If a list of articles comes up, click on the titles and read about what the person is interested in.

ACTIVITY

11.1 USING A URL AND SEARCH ENGINES TO INVESTIGATE A RESOURCE

OVERVIEW

In this activity, we'll seek further information about a resource we've come across on the Web. Let's assume that we're doing some research related to the U.S. involvement in Vietnam and we've come across the Web page shown in Figure 11.1. Its title is "Episode 1, 1962–1963: Distortions of Intelligence," but it doesn't contain the name of the author. It appears that the organization providing the information is the Center for the Study of Intelligence, but we're not familiar with that organization. To find more information, we will do the following steps:

1. Use parts of the URL to find further information about this resource.

2. Use a search engine to learn more about this resource.

> Remember that the Web is always changing and that your results may differ from those shown here. Don't let this confuse you. The activities demonstrate fundamental skills. These skills don't change, even though the number of results obtained or the actual screens may look very different.

DETAILS

1 Use parts of the URL to find further information about this resource.

Here is the URL for the Web page shown in Figure 11.1:

http://www.odci.gov/csi/books/vietnam/epis1.html

We can see that the URL for the Web server that makes this document available is **http://www.odci.gov**. The path to the document is **csi/books/vietnam**. Finally, the name of the file containing the document is **epis1.html**.

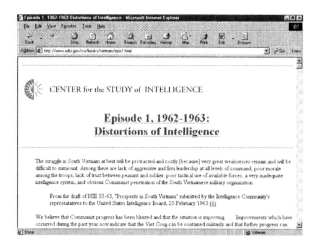

Figure 11.1—Web Page for Episode 1

To obtain more information about the document, we'll first use the URL without the path or file name. That may give us a Web page with links to this document and to other related Web pages.

✦ Do It!   In the address box, type **http://www.odci.gov**, and press **Enter**.

Another way to get the same result is to click on the address box to the right of the URL. The panel will turn blue. Click again so that the cursor is just to the right of the URL (just past **html**). Use b to erase characters until only **http://www.odci.gov** is left, and press **Enter**. The Web page in Figure 11.2 will be displayed in a few seconds.

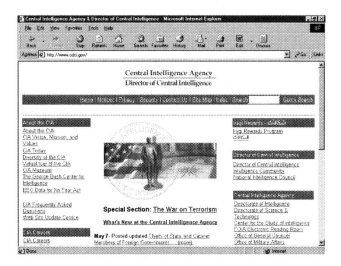

Figure 11.2—Home Page for the Central Intelligence Agency

We see that the URL **http://www.odci.gov** has led us to the home page of the Central Intelligence Agency. The CIA has therefore made the information available. We probably have all heard about the CIA. It is an agency of the U.S. government. To find out more, we'll click on the hyperlink labeled **About the CIA**.

✦ Do It!   Click on the hyperlink **About the CIA**.

Clicking on the hyperlink brings up a Web page describing the CIA. We show the middle of the Web page in Figure 11.3. We read there, "The CIA is an independent agency, responsible to the President through the DCI, and accountable to the American people through the intelligence oversight committees of the U.S. Congress." This indicates that the information we find at this site is authoritative and has likely undergone some review.

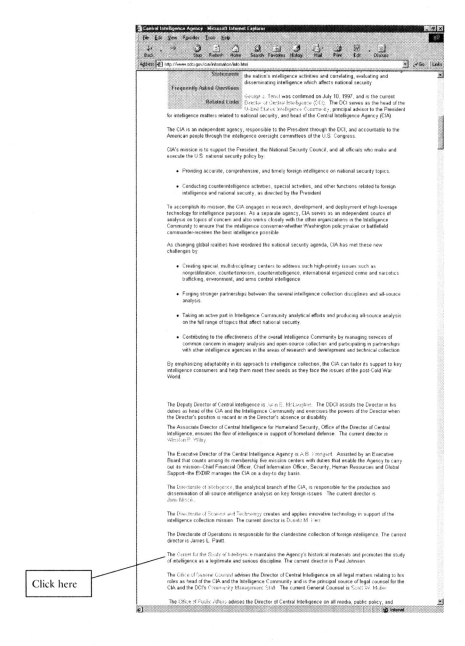

Figure 11.3—The End of the Web Page About the CIA

Now we will try to find out more about the Center for the Study of Intelligence (CSI). The Web page "About the CIA" describes the CSI and includes a hyperlink to the home page for the CSI.

✦ Do It!   Click on the hyperlink **Center for the Study of Intelligence**, as shown in Figure 11.3.

Clicking on this hyperlink takes us to the home page for the CSI; we won't show it here. To find out more about the CSI, we can click on the hyperlink **About CSI**.

✦ Do It!   Click on the hyperlink **About CSI**.

The page "Center for the Study of Intelligence" contains information about the activities and publications of the CSI. There is a hyperlink for publications. We need to click on it.

✦ Do It!   Click on the hyperlink **Publications**.

You'll notice several publications listed by year. Scroll down until you see 1998.

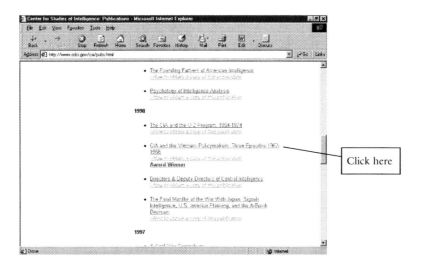

Figure 11.4—Portion of the Web Page "Center for the Study of Intelligence"

✦ Do It!   Click on the hyperlink **CIA and the Vietnam Policymakers: Three Episodes,** as shown in Figure 11.4.

Following that link takes us to a Web page that describes the book *CIA and the Vietnam Policymakers: Three Episodes.* We see on that page that there's a hyperlink to the page we showed in Figure 11.1 and a hyperlink to a Web page that describes the author Harold P. Ford.

✦ Do It!   Click on the hyperlink **Harold P. Ford**.

You can follow other hyperlinks on this page to read more about the book.
Now we know that the Web page we started with is an excerpt from a book by Harold P. Ford, published in 1998 by the Center for the Study of Intelligence, a branch of the CIA. We also read that Mr. Ford has been a professor and an employee of the CIA.

2   Use a search engine to learn more about this resource.

First, we'll see what information we can find on Harold Ford. Teoma is a good choice since it has good coverage and it's easy to use. We'll want to search Mr. Ford's entire name, along with his middle initial. Because Teoma is not case-sensitive, we won't need to capitalize proper nouns if we don't want to.

✦ Do It!   Go to Teoma's home page by typing **http://www.teoma.com** in the address box and pressing **Enter**.

We are now at Teoma's home page, as Figure 11.5 reflects. Enter the search expression by following the next instructions.

✦ Do It!   Type **"Harold p. ford"** in the search form.

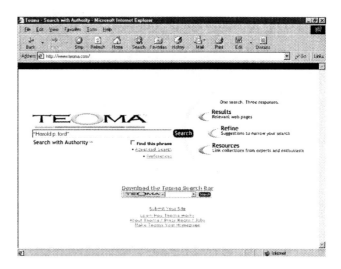

Figure 11.5—Teoma's Home Page with the Search Query Entere

✦ Do It!   Click on **SEARCH**.

Our results appear in Figure 11.6. Yours may differ.

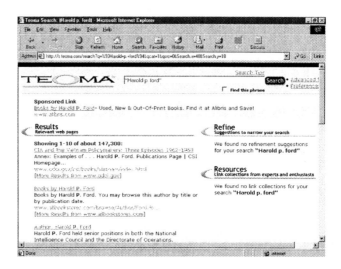

Figure 11.6—A Portion of Teoma's Search Results

Using Teoma for this search gives several results. Several talk about his work with the CIA, some discuss his involvement with that organization during the time the United States was engaged in a war in Vietnam, and some refer to other work he's done. Most state that he is an expert on the topic of the CIA and the U.S. war in Vietnam.

Now we'll use another search engine to see if there's more we can find out related to Mr. Ford's involvement with the CIA's role in Vietnam. We'll search using Vivisimo because it is a metasearch tool and may return results from several different Web databases. This may give us other types of information we can explore if we need to.

✦ Do It!   Go to Vivisimo home page by typing **http:// vivisimo.com** in the address box and pressing **Enter**.

✦ Do It!   Type **"harold p. ford"** in the search form.

The Web page with the search phrase entered appears in Figure 11.7.

Figure 11.7—Teoma's Home Page with the Search Phrase Entered

✦ Do It!   Click on **Search**.

The first few search results appear in Figure 11.8. Note that Vivisimo clusters results on the left into subject categories. Most of the items describe Mr. Ford's writings about U.S. national intelligence and the Vietnam War.

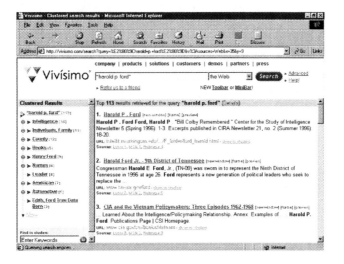

Figure 11.8—Vivisimo's Search Results

We leave it to you to explore and read some of the other links. Remember to think critically about and evaluate the information you find.

END OF ACTIVITY 11.1

In Activity 11.1, we started with a Web page and used its URL to find the organization that published the Web page and to whom we could attribute the text in the Web page. We used Teoma and Vivisimo to find information about the author within the context of this topic.

How Current Is the Information?

In some cases, it's important to know whether the information you're using is up-to-date. This is particularly true when you're using information that contains statistics. If the information is of the type that is frequently updated—for example, a news report or FAQ—then try to be sure you have the most recent information. Check the date on the Web page, and if it's more than a month old, search for a more recent version.

A well-designed Web page indicates when the information was last updated, often at the top or bottom of the page. That will tell you the date of the last modification to the file. Email messages and Usenet news articles usually have the date on which the message was posted. This information is part of the message or it's in the header information.

Who Is the Audience?

Web pages are sometimes written to give information to a specific group: the general public, researchers and scholars, professionals in a specific field, children, potential customers, or others. Try to determine the intended audience, as that may have an impact on whether the information is relevant or appropriate for your purpose. Suppose you are preparing a report on sustainable forest management. An appropriate information resource, whether in print or on the Web, is one that is written for your level of expertise and for the expertise of your audience. The Web page "Strategic Planning and Resource Assessment," by the United States Department of Agriculture, Forest Service, **http://www.fs.fed.us/plan/**, might be useful for a general overview of the issues and principles involved in forest management. On the other hand, the Web page "Alternatives to Methyl Bromide: Research Needs for California," **http://www.cdpr.ca.gov/docs/ dprdocs/methbrom/mb4chg.htm**, is more appropriate for a specialized audience.

Knowing the intended audience can alert you to possible bias. For example, let's say you are looking for information on the anti-acne drug Accutane. You find an in-depth article called "Should Your Teenager Use Accutane?" and learn about both the negatives and positives of this drug, complete with explanations of the possible side effects. By examining the URL and accessing hyperlinks within the document, you find out that the page was published by a well-known pharmaceutical company. Immediately you should realize that the likely intended audience for this page is potential customers. This doesn't mean that you couldn't use the information. But it is important to be aware of bias and hidden persuasion in Web pages.

Is the Content Accurate and Objective?

One of the first things to look for in a Web page is spelling errors. Spelling and grammatical errors not only indicate a lack of editorial control but also undermine the accuracy of the information. It is also extremely important that statistics, research findings, and other claims are documented and cited very carefully. Otherwise, the author could be distorting information or using unreliable data. In the best situations, claims or statistics on Web pages are supported by original research or by hyperlinks or footnotes to the primary sources of the information.

Sometimes, however, you will have to verify the accuracy and objectivity of published information on your own. A good way to do this is by checking to see if the information can be corroborated by other sources. Some researchers promote triangulation: finding at least three sources that agree with the opinions or statistics that the author expounds as fact. If the sources don't agree, you'll need to do more work before you conclude your research. Remember that traditional resources such as books, journal articles, and other material available in libraries may contain more comprehensive information than what is on the Web. You can use those resources as part of the triangulation process as well.

What Is the Purpose of the Information?

When you are evaluating information that you have found on the World Wide Web, on the Internet, or in print, you need to consider its purpose. You need to ask yourself, is this page on the Web to convince, inform, teach, or entertain? Information on the Web can be produced in a variety of formats and styles, and the appearance sometimes gives a clue to its intent. Web pages aimed to market something are often designed in a clever way to catch our attention and emphasize a product. Some Web pages that are primarily oriented toward marketing a product do not clearly distinguish between the informational content of the page and the advertising. It may appear to be an informational page but actually is an advertisement. It's your job, then, to concentrate on the content and to determine the purpose of the information so you'll feel comfortable using it for research or other purposes.

ACTIVITY

11.2   APPLYING GUIDELINES TO EVALUATE A RESOURCE

OVERVIEW

In this activity, we'll apply the guidelines for evaluating information on the Web. If we were researching a topic related to evaluating information on the Internet, we might come across a Web page called "Meeting the Challenge of Critically Evaluating Information on the Internet and the World Wide Web," **http://webliminal.com/khartman/educom98.html**. This is the Web page we'll evaluate in this activity. We'll go through the guidelines by answering each of the following questions:

1. Who is the author or institution?

2. How current is the information?

3. Who is the audience?

4. Is the content accurate and objective?

5. What is the purpose of the information?

In this activity, we'll be able to obtain answers in a rather direct way. It's not always so straightforward, but this is meant to be a demonstration. In your own work, you may have to be more persistent and discerning.

DETAILS

You get to the Web page discussed in this activity by typing in its URL, **http://webliminal.com/khartman/educom98.html**.

1   Who is the author or institution?

Figure 11.9 shows the beginning of the Web page we're considering. The authors' names are at both the beginning and the end of the page, as shown in Figure 11.9. We can see that one author is affiliated with the James Monroe Center Library at Mary Washington College and the other author is affiliated with the computer science department at Mary Washington College. The page has hyperlinks to the authors' home pages and to this college. If we viewed their home pages, we'd see that they have written several books together about searching on the Internet and the Web, and some about more general use of the Internet and the World Wide Web. They each have developed several Web pages to go along with their teaching. Following the links **James Monroe Center Library**, **Department of Computer Science**, and **Mary Washington College**, we'd see that Dr. Ackermann is a professor of computer science and Ms. Hartman was a librarian at a state-supported college in Virginia. These help establish the authors' credentials, which influence our assessment of the resource we're considering.

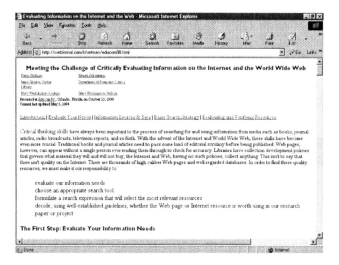

Figure 11.9—Beginning of "Meeting the Challenge" Web Page

We can search the Web for other information about the authors or for hyperlinks to resources that cite their work. One way is to use Google with the search terms "Karen Hartman" and "Ernest Ackermann". When this was tried, Google returned more than 1000 results. Many referred to books and Web pages they have written, several related to courses they have taught, and several were from other sources citing their work.

Another way is to use Google Groups to see what work of hers or his is available on Usenet. You could find any newsgroups to which Ackermann, for example, posts messages by searching the Google Groups archives; you would use "Ernest Ackermann" as the search expression. Type this into the search form and click on **Search**. Then click on one of the articles that appears as described in Activity 11.2. Reading some of the articles he's written and noting the newsgroups to which he posts may give you some clues about whether to consider his work credible.

If you take a look at Ackermann's posting history, you'll see he has posted to a variety of newsgroups including **news.newusers.questions** (if we read those we'll see he's answering questions), **comp.infosystems.www.authoring.html**, **comp.infosystems.search**, and **bit.listserv.nettrain**.

Searching for postings to Usenet tells us that Ackermann is interested in writing Web pages and teaching and training people to use the Internet and the Web. He has posted to discussions about searching. This gives us a positive indication about the resource we've found, as it deals with a related topic—evaluating information on the Internet and the Web.

We can use the URL as a clue to a source's authority. In this case, the URL is **http://webliminal.com/khartman/educom98.html**. The domain name **webliminal.com** ends with **.com**, so the site hosting the page is a commercial entity in the United States.

2 How current is the information?

In Figure 11.9, we see that the material about evaluating information was presented on October 15, 1998, and in Figure 11.10, we see that it was last updated on May 5, 2004. Information related to evaluating information on the Internet and the Web will probably be relevant for several years after the date of publication. The Web page contains several hyperlinks to external sources. As time goes by, those hyperlinks may no longer be relevant or the documents they refer to may have been moved or removed. Unless the authors pay attention to checking the hyperlinks and updating them when necessary, it may be that some of the information may be no longer current after a few years.

3 Who is the audience?

In Figure 11.9, we see the hyperlink **Educom 98**. Following that link takes us to a Web site that describes that conference. Reading through the available information we see this is a national conference aimed at a wide audience including faculty, networking and library professionals, and information technology specialists. (As a side note: Educom and another organization named CAUSE have merged to form an organization named EduCause. The URL for its home page is **http://www.educause.edu**.) From this information and from reading the resource we're considering, we see that the audience consists of information specialists and educators concerned about evaluating information on the Internet.

4 Is the content accurate and objective?

As we read the Web page we're considering, we see that the language is not inflammatory. It is, in fact, rather objective. It lists several references, which may be checked to corroborate the information presented. It also provides links to other Web resources on the same topic. We can conclude that the information presented is accurate and objective.

5 What is the purpose of the information?

The page states that it relates to considering ways to evaluate the quality of information found on the Internet and the World Wide Web. Reading the Web page, which contains recommendations for evaluating resources, we see that this is the case.

Conclusion

The Web page we're considering was written by a librarian and a college professor with experience related to the topic. It's relatively current. Furthermore, it was presented at a conference aimed at faculty, librarians, and other information specialists. We may conclude that it is an authoritative and objective source of information.

END OF ACTIVITY 11.2

In Activity 11.2, we used the guidelines in this chapter to evaluate a Web page. We used a variety of Web and Internet resources to establish the identity and suitability of the authors, and we considered other issues related to whether the information was reliable and appropriate.

Information About Evaluating Resources on the World Wide Web

There are are several good resources on the World Wide Web to help you evaluate information. They give in-depth information about critically examining documents that appear on the Web or in print, and they offer other guidelines and suggestions for assessing Internet and Web resources.

Guides to Evaluating Library Resources

+ "Evaluating What You Have Found," University of Waterloo Library
  http://www.lib.uwaterloo.ca/libguides/1-2.html

+ "How to Critically Analyze Information Sources," Reference Services Division of the Cornell University Library
  http://www.library.cornell.edu/okuref/research/skill26.htm

Brief Guides to Evaluating Web Resources

+ "Viewing Results and Evaluating Quality," Gillian Westera
  http://lisweb.curtin.edu.au/staff/gwpersonal/searchtut/eval.html

+ "Practical Steps in Evaluating Internet Resources," Elizabeth Kirk, Milton S. Eisenhower Library, Johns Hopkins University
  http://milton.mse.jhu.edu:8001/research/education/practical.html

+ "Significance," Iowa State University
  http://www.public.iastate.edu/~CYBERSTACKS/signif.htm

+ "Thinking Critically about World Wide Web Resources," Esther Grassian, UCLA College Library
  http://www.library.ucla.edu/libraries/college/help/critical/index.htm

Extensive Guides to Evaluating Resources on the World Wide Web

+ "Criteria for evaluation of Internet Information Resources," Alastair Smith, Department of Library and Information Studies, Victoria University of Wellington, New Zealand
  http://www.vuw.ac.nz/~agsmith/evaln/index.htm

+ "Evaluating information found on the Internet," Elizabeth Kirk, Milton S. Eisenhower Library, Johns Hopkins University
  http://milton.mse.jhu.edu:8001/research/education/net.html

+ "Kathy Schrock's Guide for Educators—Critical Evaluation Information," Kathleen Schrock
  http://school.discovery.com/schrockguide/eval.html

✦ "Evaluating Web Resources," Jan Alexander and Marsha Tate,
Wolfgram Memorial Library, Widener University
http://www2.widener.edu/Wolfgram-Memorial-Library/webevaluation/webeval.htm

Bibliographies for Evaluating Web Resources

✦ "Bibliography on Evaluating Internet Resources," Nicole Auer,
Virginia Polytechnic Institute and State University
http://www.lib.vt.edu/research/evaluate/evalbiblio.html

✦ "Evaluating Web Sites for Educational Uses: Bibliography and Checklist,"
Carolyn Kotlas, Institute for Academic Technology
http://www.unc.edu/cit/guides/irg-49.html

✦ "Information Quality WWW Virtual Library," T. Matthew Ciolek
http://www.ciolek.com/WWWVL-InfoQuality.html

✦ "Evaluating Web Resources: Bibliography," Jan Alexander and
Marsha Tate, Wolfgram Memorial Library, Widener University
http://www2.widener.edu/Wolfgram-Memorial-Library/webevaluation/webstrbib.htm

Summary

The World Wide Web gives us access to a great variety of information on many different topics. When we want to use the resources we find on the Web for information or research purposes, we need to exercise some care to be sure it's authentic, reliable, and authoritative. We need to be equally cautious when we use other sources.

Print sources that are available to us through a research or academic library have often been put through a screening process by professional librarians. There are several virtual libraries on the Web, and it's useful to consult some of these libraries when doing research. Information in such libraries tends to be evaluated before it's listed. Plus, by consulting these libraries, we can also observe how librarians and other information specialists evaluate resources.

It pays to be skeptical or critical of information we want to use. It's relatively easy to publish information on the Web, and it can be presented in such a way as to hide its intent or purpose. Generally, as we evaluate documents, we also learn more about the topic we're considering. Assessing resources, then, makes us more confident of the information and helps us become better versed in the topic.

We need to use some general guidelines or criteria when evaluating information or resources. In this vein, we should ask the following questions about whatever information we find:

✦ Who is the author or institution?

✦ How current is the information?

✦ Who is the audience?

✦ Is the content accurate and objective?

✦ What is the purpose of the information?

Various strategies will help us find answers to the questions. Here are some of those tips:

✦ Look for the name of the author or institution at
   the top or bottom of a Web page.

✦ Go to the home page for the site hosting the information
   to find out about the organization.

✦ To find further information about the institution or author, use a
   search engine to see what related information is available on the Web.

✦ Use Google Groups to search archives of Usenet articles. This way,
   you can find other information about the author or institution. If
   an individual has written the article, you can see what other articles
   they've posted on Usenet.

✦ Check the top and bottom of a Web page for the date on which
   the information was last modified or updated.

There are a number of Web resources that can help us evaluate information and that discuss issues related to assessing documents.

Review Questions

Multiple Choice

1. You might be suspicious of a Web page that
   a. has an author's name only at the bottom of the page.
   b. does not give the date it was last updated.
   c. uses animations.
   d. all of the above

2. When looking for research information, you'd be safest using a page
   a. that ended in .org.
   b. that had a ~ in its address.
   c. that ended in .gov.
   d. that ended in .com.

3. You can look for information about a Web page's author
   a. by using a search engine to look on the Web.
   b. by looking at newsgroup archives.
   c. by looking him or her up in a print resource.
   d. a and c
   e. all of the above

4. Information in Web pages
   a. is screened by a Web committee.
   b. can be put on the Web by anybody.
   c. must be clearly and accurately stated.
   d. is easily verifiable.

5. In evaluating a Web page, you need to look at
   a. the author of the page.
   b. the currency of the information.
   c. the attractiveness of the page.
   d. a and b
   e. all of the above

6. Looking at the objectivity of a Web page means
   a. to see if the material on a Web page is objectionable.
   b. to see if there are political, cultural, or other biases on the page.
   c. to see if the material is accurate.
   d. to see if the material on the page is up to date.
   e. all of the above

True or False

7. T F Information on a Web page is screened by experts before being posted.

8. T F A ~ (tilde) in a URL means that the page is a personal Web page.

9. T F You should look both at the top and bottom of a Web page to try to find its author.

10. T F If a page doesn't give a date when it was last changed, you can use Internet Explorer to find out when it was last modified.

11. T F A virtual library leads you to sites that have been evaluated by information professionals.

12. T F Thinking critically means to separate facts from opinions.

13. T F A Web page whose author isn't listed is a good source of information for a research paper.

Completion

14. A date on a page is an indication of the _____ of a Web page.

15. It's important to verify information in another source to determine how _____ a Web page is.

16. When you look to see if a Web page is designed to inform or persuade its audience, or to advocate a cause, you are looking for the _____ of the page.

17. A Web page with a domain name ending in .com is a(n) _____ Web page.

18. One way to find out about the sponsoring institution of a Web page is to go to the institution's _____.

19. A government Web page has a domain name that ends in _____.

20. Web pages with domain names ending in _____ may include pages ranging from serious scholarly research to silly personal pages.

Exercises and Projects

1. These pages have to do with immigration. Use the methods discussed in the chapter to evaluate the accuracy and objectivity of each page. Mention the sponsoring organization.

    a. "Texans for Fair Immigration, Inc.: Immigration Facts and Statistics"
        http://www.texansforimmigrationreform.com/
    b. "Migration Dialog"
        http://migration.ucdavis.edu/
    c. "U. S. Citizenship Tutorial"
        http://www.us-immigration.com/citizens.htm
    d. "Why Americans Support Immigration Reform"
        http://209.25.133.193/html/04146710.htm

2. Explore several pages in these sites that are on the subject of alternative medicine. Using the criteria listed in the chapter, evaluate each of these sites for authorship, currency, accuracy, and bias.

    a. "Alternative Medicine Health Updates"
        http://heall.com/body/healthupdates/index.html
    b. "Alternative Medicine for Illness?"
        http://www.imaginemedia.org/gatorbytes/health/layman_guide.htm
    c. "The National Center for Complementary and Alternative Medicine"
        http://nccam.nih.gov/

3. These Web pages all have to do with the issue of sustainable forest management. Write a brief evaluation of each, focusing on whether the information is objective, or is advocating a cause.

    a. "TimberTrek"
        http://www.timbertrek.com.au/education/
    b. "Forestry Facts: An Overview"
        http://www.nafi.com.au/briefings/index.php3?brief=2
    c. "Forest Facts From Owens Forest Products"
        http://www.owensforestproducts.com/forestfacts.html
    d. "Forests: Protection & REstoration"
        http://www.sierraclub.org/forests/

4. Now take a look at the topic of smoking. Which of these two sites do you think gives more accurate, reliable information? Would you use one of them as a source for a research paper? All of them? Why?

    a. "Action on Smoking and Health"
        http://ash.org
    b. "National Smokers Alliance"
        http://www.smokersalliance.org/
    c. "Cigarette Smoking and Cancer"
        http://cis.nci.nih.gov/fact/3_14.htm

5. Let's look at some commercial pages. Explore the following sites. What is the audience and what is the purpose of each of these commercial sites? Is the main purpose informational or to sell a product? Is the information given reliable? What do you think of the mix?

   a. "Better Homes and Gardens Online"
      http://www.bhg.com/
   b. "Michael Flatley's Lord of the Dance"
      http://www.lordofthedance.com
   c. "DeBeers"
      http://www.debeers.com
   d. "Edmunds.com"
      http://www.edmunds.com

6. Look at these pages about home schooling and compare the information. Evaluate each site based on the criteria given in the chapter.

   a. "A Personal Opinion about Home Schooling"
      http://www.adprima.com/homeschooling.htm
   b. "Is Homeschool for You?"
      http://homeschooling.about.com/od/gettingstarted/a/homeschool4you.htm
   c. "Post-secondary Decisions of Public School and Homeschool Graduates"
      http://www.uwstout.edu/lib/thesis/2001/2001lueckeh.pdf

7. Take a look at some other criteria for evaluating Web sites at these pages. Choose one of the following sites, and compare their criteria with those given in the chapter.

   a. "Evaluating Internet Information"
      http://www.library.jhu.edu/elp/useit/evaluate/
   b. "Criteria for Evaluating Internet Sites"
      http://library.websteruniv.edu/webeval.html
   c. "Evaluating Websites"
      http://servercc.oakton.edu/~wittman/eval.htm

8. Design, navigation, and usability can also be important factors to consider when evaluating Web pages or sites. Find some criteria for evaluating a Web page or site for one of these factors. Give the author, title, and URL of the Web page where you find them. (Hint: There are links to many sites about evaluation at Nicole Auer's bibliography at **http://www.lib.vt.edu/research/evaluate/evalbiblio.html**) (Here we are evaluating information on the latest milestone in the history of communication – the Internet and World Wide Web. It's been a long road since those hieroglyphs!)

CITING WEB AND INTERNET SOURCES

12

◆

It is necessary to cite your sources when you write a research report. That way, others who read your work may check the resources you've used. They can check the original sources for accuracy, to see excerpts or ideas in the original context, or to obtain more information. You'll also want to cite resources to let people know where they can find information on the Internet or the Web, whether you're preparing a formal research paper or writing email to a friend. Properly acknowledging your sources gives credit to others whose ideas or expressions you have used in your writing. It is very easy to copy and paste information from the Web, as you saw in Chapter 2, but if you copy material from a source without using quotation marks and present the information as your own work, you are committing an unethical act—plagiarism—and it may have grave consequences. You should also be careful when paraphrasing an author's work—use your own words, don't just rearrange the author's words to make it appear as if it were your own writing.

In this chapter, we'll discuss the formats for different types of URLs and suggest citation styles for various resources. Specifically, this chapter will contain the following sections:

- ◆ Guidelines for Citing Internet and Web Resources
- ◆ Citation Examples
- ◆ Information on the Web about Citing Electronic Resources

Guidelines for Citing Internet and Web Resources

There are several guidelines and styles for citing works correctly. No single uniform style has been adopted or is appropriate in every case.

The styles used for citing electronic works sometimes differ from those for printed works, which have a long tradition of specific formats. Citations for works in print or on the Web have a number of common elements, however. These include the author's name, the work's title, and the date on which the cited work was published or revised.

When you're looking for the proper way to cite resources in a report or research paper, you must first see if there is a required or accepted citation style for your situation. If you're preparing a report or paper for a class, then check with your instructor. If you're writing for a journal, periodical, or some other publication (either in print or electronic form), then see if the editor or publisher has guidelines.

Proper format for citations is determined by several organizations. Three commonly used formats are APA (American Psychological Association) style, MLA (Modern Language Association) style, and the Chicago Manual of Style (University of Chicago). Each of these organizations publishes a handbook or publication guide. In general, researchers in the social sciences use APA format, while humanities scholars use MLA or the Chicago Manual of Style. You will find URLs for these and several other citation style sources later in the chapter in the section entitled "Information on the Web about Citing Electronic Resources."

The following sections will explain some issues and provide tips for solving some of the most common difficulties inherent in citing Web and Internet resources, which are as follows:

◆ URLs, while they are crucial elements of all citations, are often difficult to write or type and may change at any time

◆ Web and Internet resources may be updated or modified at any time

◆ Web resources may not have titles, or the titles may not be descriptive

◆ Web page authors may be difficult to determine

◆ There are differences between the major style guides about the format of citations for Web and Internet items

URL Formats

Unlike citations for printed works, a citation for a Web or Internet resource must have information about how to access it. That's often indicated through the work's URL (Uniform Resource Locator). In addition to telling you where to access a work, a URL serves to retrieve the work. For that reason, we have to be precise about all the symbols in the URL and about capitalization.

Everything on the Web has a URL, indicating where something is located and how to access it. We've seen lots of URLs throughout this text. Here are some examples:

http://www.loc.gov	The home page for The Library of Congress
http://webopedia.internet.com/TERM/v/virus.html	The entry for the term *virus* in PC Webopedia

http://webliminal.com/ khartman/educom98.html	A presentation given at Educom 98 by Karen Hartman and Ernest Ackermann
ftp://ftp.seds.org/pub/images/	The directory of images available from the Students for the Exploration and Development of Space

You'll find it helpful to think of a URL as having the following form:

how-to-get-there://where-to-go/what-to-get

or, in more technical language:

transfer protocol://domain name/directory/subdirectory/ file name.file type

For example, take this URL:

http://webliminal.com/khartman/educom98.html

http is the transfer protocol

webliminal.com is the domain name (also called the host computer name)

khartman is the directory name

educom98 is the file name and **html** is its file type

You probably already know some ways in which URLs are used. For example, all hyperlinks on Web pages are represented as URLs. Entries in bookmark and history files are stored as URLs. You type in a URL when you want to direct your browser to go to a specific Web page. When you cite a resource on the World Wide Web, you include its URL. You'll also want to include the URL when you're telling someone else about a resource, such as in an email message. Here's an example:

> If you haven't already seen this fabulous page, you must look at it. It's called "A Business Researcher's Interests" and is hosted by @BRINT. The URL is: **http://www.brint.com**. It's one of the best subject guides I've ever used.

That way, a friend reading the message could use her browser to go directly to the items you mention.

By providing the name of a Web server and the name of a file or directory holding certain information, a URL tells you how to retrieve the information; from the URL alone, you know which Internet protocol to use when retrieving the information and where it's located. If only a server name is present, as in **http://www.loc.gov**, then a file will still be retrieved. Web servers are configured to pass along a certain file (usually named **index.html** or **index.htm**) when the URL contains only the name of the server or only the name of a directory.

It's important to be precise when you write URLs because a Web browser uses the URL to access something and bring it to your computer. More specifically, the browser sends a request extracted from the information in the URL to a Web server. Remember, we're talking about having one computer communicate with another; as amazing as some computer systems are, they generally need very precise instructions. Therefore, you have to be careful about spaces (generally there aren't blanks in a URL), symbols (interchanging a slash and a period won't give appropriate results), and capitalization.

Here's an example. In Chapter 11 we examined the Web page called "Meeting the Challenge of Critically Evaluating Information on the Internet and the World Wide Web," with the URL **http://webliminal.com/khartman/educom.html**. Inserting a period instead of a slash between **khartman** and **educom.html** and writing the URL as **http://webliminal.com/khartman.educom.html** would cause the browser to give the following response:

```
404 Not Found

The requested URL /khartman.educom98.html was not found on this server.
```

This tells us that either the directory **khartman** or the file named **educom98.html** wasn't present on the Web server **webliminal.com**.

The Dates Are Important

You'll see that the citation examples for citations or references to Web or Internet resources all contain two dates: the date of publication or revision and the date of last access. The reason we need both dates has to do with the nature of digital media as it's made available or published on the Web. Works in print form are different from digital works; printed documents have a tangible, physical form. We all know we can pick up and feel a magazine or journal in our hands, or we can use a book or periodical as a pillow. It's pretty hard to do that with a Web page! This tangible nature of a printed work also gives an edition or revision a permanent nature. It's usually possible to assign a date of publication to a work, and if there are revisions or different editions of a work, it's possible to date and look at the revisions. If a new edition of a printed work exists, that doesn't mean that older editions or versions were destroyed.

The situation is different for Web documents and other items in digital form on the Internet, for several reasons. They don't have a tangible form. It's relatively easy for an author to publish a work (the work usually only needs to be in a certain directory on a computer that functions as a Web server). It's easy to modify or revise a work. Furthermore, when a work is revised, the previous version is often replaced by or overwritten with the new version. Because of this last point, the most recent version may be the only one that exists. The version you cited might not exist anymore. It is therefore necessary to include the date you accessed or read a work listed in a citation or reference. You may also want to keep a copy of the document in a file (save it while browsing) or print a copy of it to provide as documentation if someone questions your sources.

Ways to Find Out When a Page Was Modified

To find the date a work was last revised, see if the date is mentioned as part of the work. You will often see a line like **Last modified: Tuesday, April 27, 2004** in a Web document.

If you don't find this information on the Web page or you want to verify this date, you can download a tool named Page Freshness available at a Web site named "Bookmarklets," **http://www.bookmarklets.com**. The items at the Web site are small programs written in JavaScript. You can add any of them to your favorites list. Once they're in the favorites list, you can use them by clicking on **Favorites** in the navigation toolbar and then clicking on the bookmarklet in the favorites list.

Follow these steps to obtain and use the Page Freshness bookmarklet.

1. Type the URL **http://www.bookmarklets.com/tools/frames.phtml#pgfrshfrm** in the address box and press Enter.

2. Move the mouse pointer over the hyperlink **Page Freshness**, read its description, and click the right mouse button.

3. Select **Add to Favorites** to add the bookmarklet to the favorites list.

Determining Web Page Titles

The title is what shows up as a hyperlink in the search results if you use a search engine. You may also find the title by selecting **View/Page Info**. The title is specified in the HTML source for the page and doesn't necessarily show up in the text of the document as you view it with a browser. There are cases when the title is uninformative or not descriptive. In these situations, the first main heading can be used. Some documents have no title. (If a document doesn't have a title, you can construct one by using the major heading or the first line of text. You should enclose this title in square brackets to show that you created it.)

The following is a portion of the HTML code for a Web page that will be discussed later in the chapter. The exact text of the title of a Web page is surrounded by the tags <TITLE> and </TITLE> in the HTML source for the page. The source for this page begins with:

```
<HTML>
<HEAD>
<TITLE>Karen's home page</TITLE>
</HEAD>
<BODY bgcolor="White" text="Black" background="grnsand.jpg"
 link="Navy" vlink="Maroon">
<h2><center>Welcome to Karen Hartman's home page
</center></h2>
```

Determining the Author of a Web Page

Look for the author's name at the top or the bottom of a document. If it isn't there, there are a few things you may try.

♦ If a document doesn't contain the name of the author or the institution, and there are no hyperlinks to Web pages that give that information, you can manipulate the URL to try to find it. For example, if you found material at the following URL, **http://www.ncrel.org/sdrs/areas/ma0bibp.htm,** and you wanted to quickly find out the name of the publishing body, you could delete the parts of the URL back to the domain section (everything after **org/**) and press **Enter**. This would give you **http://www. ncrel.org**, the home page for this institution, which happens to be the North Central Regional Educational Laboratory.

✦ You may find the author's email address in the document. You can use the browser's **Find** function to locate the @ symbol. If an email address is found, you could send a message and ask the person for more information.

✦ Open the Web page's HTML source information by selecting **View/Source** from your browser's menu. Sometimes the author's name may be viewed there.

Differences Between Styles

While most of the style guides agree to which elements are essential for citation, they all have different ways of formatting the information. Some formats include a URL in angle brackets (< >), and others do not. Some advise including the place of publication if the Web resource is a copy of a printed work. Several say to put the date of last revision and to place in parentheses the date on which you accessed the document, whereas others do not make this recommendation. There is, however, considerable agreement on the basic information to be included in a citation of a Web resource.

✦ T I P ! When you have specific questions about citing Internet and Web sources, check some of the Web resources listed later in this chapter, and be sure to check with whoever is going to be evaluating or editing your work.

Citation Examples

In this section, we will provide citation examples using established citation formats. The styles that we will be using are the Modern Language Association (MLA) for the *Works Cited* part of a paper and the American Psychological Association (APA) for the *References* area of a paper. The types of resources that we will cite are Web pages, email messages, discussion group messages, Usenet newsgroup messages, and FTP resources. The common elements in citations for different types of resources will be listed, and a citation example for each type of included Internet resource will be given in one of the styles. The information provided is general in nature, and it is not meant to cover every situation. We suggest that if you have a specific citation question that is not covered here, you go to one of the citation guides listed in the section entitled "Information on the Web about Citing Electronic Resources" later in the chapter or visit your library. Librarians are usually willing to assist you in locating and using citation style guides as long as you indicate which style you have been instructed to use.

Web Pages

The major citation styles agree that the following elements should be included in a citation for a Web page:

✦ Author's name

✦ Document title

✦ Title of larger or complete work, if relevant

♦ Date of publication or last revision

♦ Date page was accessed

♦ URL

Citation Examples

MLA Style:

> Hartman, Karen. <u>Karen's home page</u>. 1 March 2004. 18 April 2004.
> <http://webliminal.com/khartman>

In the citation, note that the URL is placed in angle brackets. This is a feature of MLA style. APA doesn't require brackets around the URL.

APA Style:

> Hartman, K. (2004, March 1). *Karen's home page*. Retrieved April 18, 2004, from http://webliminal.com/khartman.

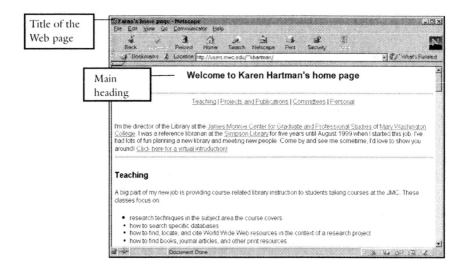

Figure 12.1—Determining the Title of a Web Page

We determined the Web page title by using the title found at the top of the browser window.

Citing a Web Page That Is Part of a Larger or Complete Work

Many Web pages are parts of larger works or projects. In each of these cases, you need to provide not only the author and title of the individual document, but also the title of the larger work, its editor (especially when using MLA style), and the institution that sponsors the site (if applicable). In many instances, you'll want to include information about the complete work in order to put the document in its proper context and to credit the institution that has helped to make the work available. This additional information may help the reader find the Web page again if the URL changes. The following shows how you would cite a page that was part of a larger work.

Citation Examples

MLA Style:

> Bales, Jack. "MWP: Willie Morris (1934-1999)." <u>Mississippi Writers Page</u>. Ed. John Padgett. 25 Jan. 2002. Univ. of Miss. 3 Feb. 2004. <http://www.olemiss.edu/depts/english/ms-writers/dir/morris_willie>

APA Style:

> Bales, J. (2002 January 25). MWP: Willie Morris (1934-1999). In *Mississippi Writers Page*. Retrieved February 3, 2004 from the University of Mississippi Web site: http://www.olemiss.edu/depts./English/ms-writers/dir/morris_willie.

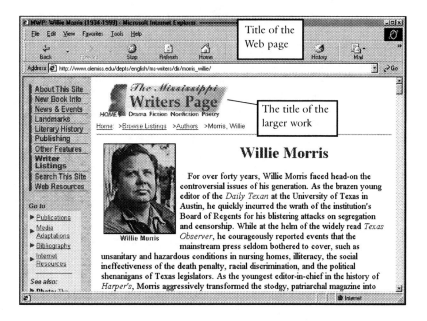

Figure 12.2—A Web Page That Is Part of a Larger Work

In this citation, we determined:

✦ The title of the Web page was found at the top of the browser window. Because MWP is uninformative, we could, if we wished, change the title to simply Willie Morris. If we did so, we would be required to place square brackets around the title, indicating that we had changed it. But in this case, we have decided to leave the Web page title as MWP: Willie Morris (1934-1999). The date range indicates the years Mr. Morris lived.

✦ The writer of this page was found by scrolling down to the end of the article, as shown in Figure 12.3.

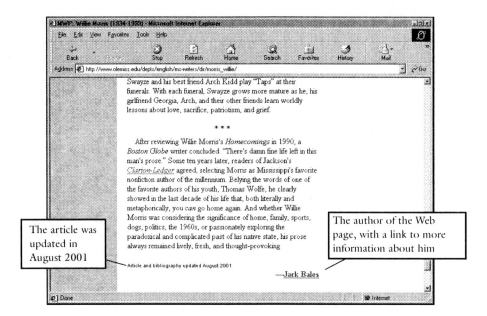

Figure 12.3—Finding the Author of the Willie Morris Page

Determining the date of the last revision proves to be a bit more difficult. Near the author's name there is a statement that the article was updated in August of 2001, but if we scroll down to the end of the page the revision date is listed as January 25, 2002, as shown in Figure 12.4. This is the date we will use.

The editor of the larger work, *Mississippi Writers Page*, is John Padgett. His name is also found at the end of the Web page, as shown in Figure 12.4. Note that MLA requires the editor's name as part of the citation, but APA does not.

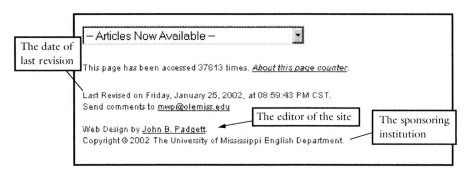

Figure 12.4—Important Information Located at the End of the Web Page

Personal Email Messages

The elements required to cite a personal email message are:

✦ Author's name

✦ Subject of message

✦ Date message was sent

✦ Description and recipient of message

All of these are usually displayed by the software you use to read email and are available as standard headers in a message.

Citation Examples
MLA Style:

> Ackermann, Ernest. "Working on Post-Tenure Review." Email to the author. 31 Jan. 2004.

APA Style:

Personal email messages in APA style are cited within the text of a paper only and should not be included in the References section. Within the text of a document, a personal email message may be cited like this:

> Ernest Ackermann (personal communication, Jan. 31, 2004) stated that the post-tenure review process could be streamlined by using departmental guidelines.

Discussion Group or Listserv Messages

A citation for an email message that was generated in a discussion group or listserv needs to include the discussion group's address. If the message can be retrieved through an archive, the citation needs to include the URL of the Web page that allows access to the archive. The elements usually required to cite discussion group or listserv messages are:

✦ Author's name

✦ Subject of message or title of posting

✦ Date of posting

✦ Description of posting

✦ URL of discussion group or archive

✦ Date of access (MLA only)

Citation Examples
MLA Style:

> Ackermann, Ernest. "Bookmark Files With Netscape 4.0." Online posting. 7 March 2000. Nettrain. 10 Nov. 2002. < http://listserv.buffalo.edu/cgi-bin/wa?S1=nettrain >.

APA Style:

> Ackermann, E. (1999, March 7). Re: Bookmark files with Netscape 4.0. Message posted to Nettrain discussion group, archived at http://listserv.buffalo.edu/cgi-bin/wa?S1=nettrain

Usenet Newsgroup Articles

Usenet news consists of a collection of articles, each of which is part of a specific newsgroup. The articles, as email messages, have headers that give us the information we need for the citation. These are the items to include in the citation of a Usenet article:

- ◆ Author's name
- ◆ Subject of message
- ◆ Name of newsgroup
- ◆ Date message was posted
- ◆ Date of access (MLA only)

Citation Examples

MLA Style:

> Ackermann, Ernest. "Question About Keeping Bay Plant Indoors." Online posting. 3 Dec. 2000. 13 Feb. 2004 <news:rec.gardens>.

APA Style:

> Ackermann, E. (2000, December 3). Question about keeping bay plant indoors. Message posted to news://rec.gardens.

Electronic Journal Articles

An article in an electronic journal can be cited very much like any other Web resource. If you were citing an article in a journal, it would be reasonable to include the journal name, volume, issue, and date. If you were citing a resource from a printed journal, you would also include page numbers, but that doesn't apply in this case. Some citation styles require a paragraph count instead. The URL gives the location of the article. The citation should contain the following elements:

- ◆ Author's name
- ◆ Title of article
- ◆ Title of journal, volume and issue numbers, date of publication
- ◆ Number of paragraphs if possible (not always necessary)
- ◆ Date of last revision, if known and different from date of publication
- ◆ Date accessed
- ◆ URL

Citation Examples

MLA Style:

> Acker, Stephen R. "Approaching Academic Digital Content Management." Syllabus Magazine. May 2002. 1 March 2004. <http://www.syllabus.com/article.asp?id=6334>.

APA Style:

> Acker, S.R. (2002, May). Approaching Academic Digital Content Management. *Syllabus Magazine, May 2002.* Retrieved March 1, 2004 from http://www.syllabus.com/article.asp?id=6334.

Full-text journals that are part of proprietary databases, such as InfoTrac or Lexis-Nexis, will require more information as part of the citation. When in doubt about how to cite a particular online journal, ask a librarian for help.

FTP Resources

FTP stands for File Transfer Protocol. Before Web browsers came into popular use, FTP was the most popular way to retrieve and send files from one computer to another on the Internet. A citation for a file available by FTP usually contains the following elements:

- ✦ Name of author or institution
- ✦ Title of document
- ✦ Size of document, if relevant
- ✦ Date of last revision
- ✦ URL
- ✦ Date accessed

Citation Examples

MLA Style:

> American Civil Liberties Union, Briefing Paper Number 5, Drug Testing in the Work Place. 2 Nov. 1992. 3 Oct. 2003. <ftp://ftp.eff.org/pub/Privacy/Medical/aclu_drug_testing_workplace.faq>

Example of an FTP image file:

> "Meteosat1.jpg" [535K]. 16 Jan 1995. 13 May 2003. <ftp://ftp.estec.esa.nl/pub/photolib/images/panel1/Meteosat1.jpg>

If there is no obvious title for a file, as in the case of a file that holds an image, you may use the file name as the title of the work, or create a descriptive title and enclose it in square brackets.

> [Photograph of Meteosat, 535 K]. 16 Jan. 1995. 13 May 2003. <ftp://ftp.estec.esa.nl/pub/photolib/images/panel1/Meteosat1.jpg>

Note that we have included the size of the file as well.

APA Style:

> American Civil Liberties Union. (1992, November 2). *Briefing Paper Number 5, Drug Testing in the Work Place.* Retrieved October 3, 2003 from ftp://ftp.eff.org/pub/Privacy/Medical/aclu_drug_testing_workplace.faq.

Example of an FTP image file:

> Meteosat1.jpg (1995, January 16). 535K. Photograph of Meteosat 1. Retrieved May 13, 2003 from ftp://ftp.estec.esa.nl/pub/photolib/images/panel1/Meteosat1.jpg.

Recording Citation Information

When doing research on the Internet, it's smart to record the document information by either printing the resource or making it a favorite so that you can return to the resource easily. Keeping a favorites list is a good habit to get into. Making it a Favorite saves the Web page title and URL accurately so you don't have to write it down and risk losing it. Even if you share a computer with others, you can save your favorites to a file on a disk and import them to your computer later.

Information on the Web About Citing Electronic Resources

There are several very good Web pages with information about citing Web and other electronic resources. The following Web pages have links to several other sources on the subject:

- ✦ "Citing Electronic Sources"
  http://www.csbsju.edu/library/internet/citing.html
- ✦ "Citing Electronic Resources," Internet Public Library
  http://www.ipl.org/ref/QUE/FARQ/netciteFARQ.html
- ✦ "LIBRARY & INFORMATION SCIENCE: Citation Guides for Electronic Documents"
  http://www.ifla.org/I/training/citation

The Web pages in this list contain information about specific styles for citations:

- ✦ "Electronic Reference Formats Recommended by the American Psychological Association"
  http://www.apastyle.org/elecref.html
- ✦ "MLA Style," Modern Language Association of America
  http://www.mla.org/ (click on MLA Style)
- ✦ "Citation Styles online!"
  http://www.bedfordstmartins.com/online/citex.html

These two Web pages contain good, thoughtful discussions about citing work from Web or other electronic sources:

◆ "Citing Electronic Information in History Papers,"
Maurice Crouse
http://cas.memphis.edu/~mcrouse/elcite.html

◆ "Electronic Style—What's Here," George H. Hoemann
http://web.utk.edu/~hoemann/whats.html

Summary

Citing references or writing a bibliography is usually part of creating a research report. You provide citations so others may check or examine the resources used in the report. There are several style guides provided by organizations for citing both print and electronic resources. This chapter presents guidelines and tips, with examples from some of these style guides, for documenting or citing information obtained from the Web or the Internet.

Citations for documents and other information found on the Web or the Internet always include the URL (Uniform Resource Locator). A URL includes the names of the Web server and the file or directory holding the information. The URL therefore tells you which Internet protocol to use to retrieve the information and where the information is located. You need to be precise in terms of spelling and capitalization when writing a URL, as a computer will be interpreting it. We listed URL formats for common Web or Internet services.

Most style guidelines suggest that a citation include the author's name, the work's title, the date the information was last revised, the date the information was accessed, and the URL. The date of access is included because it's relatively easy to modify information on the Web and the information may not always be the same as when it was accessed for research. We discussed methods for determining the date of access and the title of a Web document.

The chapter concluded with a list of Web resources that provide more information about citing sources and some suggestions for specific formats.

Review Questions

Multiple Choice

1. In citing a Web resource, you include the following:
   a. The date you accessed the page.
   b. The URL of the page.
   c. The date the page was created or revised.
   d. a and b
   e. all of the above

2. A problem in citing a Web resource is
   a. it may not have a title.
   b. you can't prove that you viewed it.
   c. it may no longer exist.
   d. a and c
   e. all of the above

3. In citing a URL you must include all the following except
   a. the protocol used.
   b. capital letters.
   c. slashes.
   d. All of these are included.

4. URLs are composed in the following fashion:
   a. where to go://what to get/how to get there.
   b. what to get://where to go/how to get there.
   c. how to get there://where to go/what to get.
   d. how to get there://what to get/where to go.

5. In citing an email message to an individual, you include
   a. the name of the sender.
   b. the name of the recipient.
   c. the date the message was received.
   d. a and c
   e. all of the above

6. Why would it be important to include the date you accessed a Web page when you cite it?
   a. Because Web pages are tangible information.
   b. Because Web pages can be changed easily.
   c. To prove that you saw the page.
   d. a and b

True or False

7. T   F   A citation for a Web resource must show how to access it.

8. T   F   All citation styles use the same format when citing a Web resource.

9. T   F   You must be precise in writing a URL for a source you cite.

10. T   F   You should always put the date the source was accessed in parentheses.

11. T   F   Web resources, like books, have a tangible form.

12. T   F   The only date that is important in a citation is the date a page was last revised.

13. T   F   The title of a Web page may not appear in the content area of your browser.

14. T   F   A citation of a newsgroup article includes the name of the newsgroup as the subject of the message.

Completion

15. The major heading that appears when you view a document in a browser is the

_____ .

16. The title that appears in the bar at the top of the browser window (and appears between the title tags in the HTML source) is called the _____ .

17. Social science researchers usually use the _____ format when citing their resources.

18. The difference in citing an individual email and one that was received through a discussion group is that the discussion group citation includes the

_____ .

19. Two major types of citation styles are the _____ and the _____ .

20. When preparing a report for a class, you should check the citation style with

_____ .

Exercises and Projects

1. Write a citation to the document available at **http://www.otterbein.edu/home/ fac/brccbly/general/guide.htm**, using MLA style

2. Go to **http://www.eff.org/pub/Legislation/ecpa.law** and write a citation to the document at that address, using APA style.

3. These two will give you experience citing email messages using MLA Style.
   a. Send yourself an email message with a profound message. (Your philosophy of life? Your grocery list?) Write a citation for the email message as if it were a source in a research paper.)
   b. Ask a friend to send you an email message, and cite that message as well.

4. Suppose you are doing a research project for a mythology class on the significance of the butterfly in Greek mythology. Go to Google at **http://www.google.com** to find resources on your topic. Do a Web search and look at some of the pages retrieved in your results list.
   a. Choose two of the pages in your results list that are relevant to your topic, and write citations for them in MLA format.
   b. Remember that in Google Groups you can search for Usenet newsgroup articles on your topic. From Google's home page, choose Google Groups and perform a search for the same topic and write citations for two relevant newsgroup articles that appear in your results list, also in MLA format.

5. Now return to your results retrieved in question 4, and write citations for those same articles in APA format. (Find a site that gives examples of APA style documentation - You may have luck using "Karla's Guide to Citation Style Guides" at **http://bailiwick.lib.uiowa.edu/journalism/cite.html**)
   a. Write the citations for the two webpages retrieved in question 4a in APA format.
   b. Write the citations for the two newsgroup articles in question 4b in APA format.

6. Access the following site and write a citation for the page in APA format and in MLA format: **http://www.cpc.ncep.noaa.gov/products/hurricane/index.html**.

7. Now we'll try a citation for an online journal article. Access the article at **http://www.educause.edu/pub/er/erm04/erm0441.asp** and write a citation to the article in MLA format.

8. What differences do you see in the requirements for MLA and APA citations of Internet resources? Does one seem more useful than the other? You may want to browse through some other style guides as well. (Go back to Karla's Guide at **http://bailiwick.lib.uiowa.edu/journalism/cite.html** to find other style manuals.)

APPENDIX

A

WAYS TO STAY CURRENT

The content of the World Wide Web is always changing, because tools, resources, and documents are added daily. Many of the tools and resources available for searching and conducting research are very good, but none of them is perfect. You'll want to keep informed of new and improved services. We'll list some ways to do that here. You can regularly visit the Web sites we'll name and read the articles in Usenet newsgroups that carry announcements. We'll also discuss the easy ways you can keep your browser up to date with online updates and keeping your anti-virus software current as well.

Web Sites Listing New Resources

This section contains an annotated list of resources to use to keep track of new Web sites. A Web site that contains links to other sites that will help you keep up with new services and resources of particular interest to information specialists is "Keeping Up with New Web Sites," **http://lii.org/search/file/ newsites** published by the Librarians' Index to the Internet. Several of the sites listed there offer subscription services by email or by RSS.

The Scout Report

The Scout Report lists new and newly discovered resources of interest to researchers and educators. It is a publication of Internet Scout Project, which is part of the computer science department at the University of Wisconsin. The National Science Foundation also supports this project.

Weekly issues of *The Scout Report* contain listings in four categories:

✦ Research and education

✦ General interest

✦ Network tools

✦ In the news

Each listing contains the name of the resource, the URL as a hyperlink, and a written description. Instructions for getting weekly issues through a free email subscription service appear at the end of each issue.

The URL for current issue of *The Scout Report* is **http://scout.wisc.edu/Reports/ ScoutReport/Current/**. To receive the weekly issues by email, visit the Web page with URL **http://scout.wisc.edu/About/subscribe.php** and choose your form of subscription.

What's New Web Sites

Several sites on the Web list new Web sites. Most of these are associated with directories or subject guides and list items that have recently been added.

Here's a short list of "What's New" sites that you may want to check occasionally. You could add them to your bookmark or favorites list.

✦ **Librarians' Index to the Internet: What's New This Week**
An annotated listing of sites added to the index, it's available as the hyperlink **New This Week, http://lii.org/search/ntw,** on the home page at **http://lii.org**

✦ **Net-Happenings**
Archives of the articles posted to the Usenet newsgroup **comp.internet.net-happenings** and the corresponding email discussion group **net-happenings**. Each item lists a resource that's been submitted to the newsgroup or discussion group. Labeled with a category, announcements contain URLs and some descriptive information. To view the archives or to join the list, go to "Educational CyberPlayGround, Net-Happenings Mailing List, Gleason Sackmann," **http://www.edu-cyberpg.com/Community/ nethappenings.html**.

✦ **Research Buzz**
Tara Calishain writes articles about search engines, databases, and online almost daily and posts them to Research Buzz. You can subscribe to this by email or RSS. The URL is **http://www.researchbuzz.com/**.

✦ **Resource Shelf**
Gary Price and his co-editors daily provide an annotated list of resources of particular interest to information professionals. Visit the home page at **http:// www.resourceshelf.com/** for recent listings. You can subscribe to the listings by email or through RSS.

✦ **What's Hot on the Internet**
A weekly annotated list of Web sites selected by the El Dorado County Library, Placerville California. The URL is **http://www.eldoradolibrary.org/thisweek.htm**.

✦ **Yahoo! - What's New**
A listing of new sites added to Yahoo!'s directory. This Web page has links to a list of new sites for each of the past seven days, a list of Yahoo!'s daily picks, and a link to Yahoo!'s weekly picks. The URL is **http://dir.yahoo.com/new/**.

✦ **What's New on the Web**
A monthly listing of new sites and tools on the Web compiled by the University of Queensland Library. Items are selected, reviewed and arranged into the categories

Reference Tools and Services, Social Sciences and Humanities, Biological and Health Sciences, Physical Sciences and Engineering, and Electronic Journals, **http:// www.library.uq.edu.au/internet/new/webnew.html**

Usenet Newsgroups Listing New Web Sites and Resources

Newsgroups for Announcements of New or Changed Web Sites

Two primary Usenet newsgroups announce new Web sites and resources. When people with access to Usenet submit announcements to the groups, the moderators post appropriate announcements. A description of each group follows.

✦ **comp.internet.net-happenings**
Each announcement is tagged with a keyword indicating the type of resource, such as BOOK, COMP, K12, or SOFT. This newsgroup has an associated Web site that includes archives and searching at **http://anduin.eldar.org/~ben/happen.html**.

✦ **news.announce.newgroups**
This is the primary Usenet newsgroup used for announcing new newsgroups. This group also carries discussions related to creating a specific newsgroup. These include requests for discussions (RFD) about new newsgroups and a call for votes (CFV) to determine whether a newsgroup should be established.

Windows Updates

Microsoft regularly issues updates of its operating system software, Internet Explorer, and its other software. Some of these give improvements in performance or add new capabilities, but they also provide security patches as flaws are (regularly) exposed in the browser and related applications. If you've purchased your computer since 2002, it probably uses the Windows XP operating system. With Windows XP you can enable automatic updates, so that you can be notified of software changes or updates automatically. If you're using a fast Internet connection then you'll want to set the update service so the software is downloaded automatically to your computer. With a slower connection, such as a dial-up modem connection, you'll want to choose when the downloads occur. In any case you'll be notified when an update is available. Install critical updates whenever they are available. A note of warning: Don't install updates that supposedly come form Microsoft by email. These usually are viruses or some other harmful software. Microsoft and other operating system companies don't distribute updates by email.

It's easy to set up automatic updating if you're using Windows XP:

1. Click on the **Start** button in the system tray at the lower left of the screen.

2. Click on **Control Panel**.

3. Click on **Performance and Maintenance**, and then click on **System**. If Performance and Maintenance isn't available then click on **System**.

4. Select the tab **Automatic Updates** and set your options. We recommend that you select automatic updates.

If you want to check for updates at any time, or if you're using another version of the Windows operating system, then use Internet Explorer to check for updates by using the URL **http://windowsupdate.microsoft.com.** That takes you to a site that will check to see if there are updates available for your computer system. Click on **scan for updates**. Install any critical updates, and decide whether you want to install others that may be available.

Keeping Antivirus Software Up To Date

You use antivirus software to check existing or new files for known viruses or worms. A file's contents are examined to see if they contain a pattern of code that indicate that it is infected and a potential problem. New viruses and worms must therefore be different than existing ones, and to be able to check for them you need to update the portion of your antivirus software that contains the descriptions of these problems. It is very important that you update your antivirus software.

With a paid subscription service for the antivirus software, you can arrange to have automatic updates. If you don't get updates automatically then regularly check for updates at the antivirus software's Web site. AVG Free Edition for home users on non-networked computers is a free alternative that we've used. It includes the antivirus software and regular updates. Visit "AVG Free Edition," **http://www.grisoft.com/us/us_dwnl_free.php** for more information.

PRIVACY AND SECURITY ON THE INTERNET AND THE WEB

I t's easy to get excited about using the Internet and the World Wide Web. They're vivacious, interesting, and important places to work, learn, do business, and just have fun. The World Wide Web always seems to have something new. You find not only new resources, but also better services and programs, making the Web and the Internet easier to use and more powerful. There's also a great deal of diversity; different cultures, nations, and outlooks are represented on the Web. All these things make for an exciting environment, but we also need to consider the effect of the Internet on our lives, our communities, and society as its use becomes more widespread.

The Internet and the World Wide Web have grown rapidly from a research project into part of the infrastructure of daily life that involves millions of people worldwide. Much of the Internet's usefulness comes from the fact that users and service providers depend on each other and need to support each other. Hopefully, that sort of sharing and respect will continue. Your behavior, your expectations of others, and your activities will make the difference. There are also genuine concerns about privacy and security on the Internet. You'll see that some of the reasons for a lack of privacy and security are based on the nature of the technology that makes up the Internet. In some cases, there are ways you can use technology to give more privacy and security There are also matters of law, ethics, and human behavior that also come into play.

Privacy

You might initially expect the same protection of your privacy on the Internet as you have in your other dealings in society. In some situations, you will find your privacy determined by existing laws and modes of behavior.

When you sign up or register with some services (such as the ones that provide "free" email or a site for your Web pages), you often have to give some information about yourself. Sometimes this is only your name and email address, but some services ask for a mailing address, phone number, zip code, your age, your income, and so on. There are two things to consider here. First, is the service worth the cost of giving information about yourself, and just as important, what will be done with the information. Are you giving away your privacy? Check on these issues before you give out personal information.

Email Privacy

When you send a message by email, the message is separated into packets and the packets are sent out over the Internet. The number of packets depends on the size of the message, since each packet on a particular network has a standard size. Each message has the Internet address of the sender (your address) and the address of the recipient. Packets from a single message may take different routes to the destination, or they may take different routes at different times. This works well for the Internet and for you. Since packets are generally sent through the best path, depending on the traffic load on the Internet, the path doesn't depend on certain systems being in operation, and all you have to give is the address of the destination.

The packets making up an email message may pass through several different systems before reaching their destination. This means there may be some places between you and the destination where the packets could be intercepted and examined. If you're using a computer system shared by others or if the system at the destination is shared by others, there is usually someone (a system administrator) capable of examining all the messages. So, in the absence of codes of ethics or without the protection of law, email could be very public. Needless to say, you shouldn't be reading someone else's email. Most system administrators adopt a code of ethics under which they will not examine email unless they feel it's important to support the system(s) they administer. The truth of the matter is they are generally too busy to bother reading other people's mail.

Who owns your email? If you use an email service, Internet services, or a computer network that's provided for by your employer, then your employer may monitor all of that. Several courts in the United States have ruled that an employer that provides an email service may monitor, read, or save an employee's email. The same holds true for monitoring the use of the Web or other Internet services, or for use of a network. In fact, an employer may do this without notifying the person being monitored. That's not a good way to develop a working relationship, but it is legal. On the other hand, if you are a student (and not an employee) of a college or university, then your email privacy is protected by law as mentioned below.

You need to become familiar with the policies and rules of operations (if they exist) for the organization(s) that provide you with any of the several Internet services.

Electronic Communications Privacy Act

One example of a law to ensure the privacy of email is the Electronic Communications Privacy Act (ECPA) passed in 1986 by Congress. It prohibits anyone from intentionally intercepting, using, and/or disclosing email messages without the sender's permission. The ECPA was passed to protect individuals from having their private messages accessed by government officers or others without legal permission. That bill extended the protections that existed for voice communications to nonvoice communications conveyed through wires or over the airwaves. You can, of course, give your permission for someone to access your email. However, according to the EPCA, law enforcement officials or others cannot access your email in stored form (on a disk or tape) without a warrant, and electronic transmission of your email can't be intercepted or "tapped" without a court order. The ECPA allows a system administrator to access users' email on a computer system if it's necessary for the operation or security of the system. The ECPA then gives the system administrator the responsibility to block access to email passing within or through a system without a court order or warrant. She can and indeed should refuse any requests to examine email unless the proper legal steps are followed.

Other laws, for example the "Patriot Act" of 2001, have amended the ECPA to make it easier for court or law enforcement officials to intercept and monitor email and other electronic communications. Some measure of privacy can be provided for email and other communication on the Internet, but you need to know that absolute privacy isn't guaranteed by the technology or the law.

Encryption

When you send a message by email, it's often transmitted in the same form you typed it. Even though it may be unethical or illegal for someone else to read it, the message is in a form that's easy to read. This is similar to sending a message written on a postcard through the postal service. One way to avoid this is to use encryption to put a message into an unreadable form. The characters in the message can be changed by substitution or scrambling, usually based on some secret code. The message can't be read unless the code and method of encryption are known. The code is called a key. Many messages are encoded by a method called public key encryption. If you encrypt a message and send it on to someone, that person has to know the key to decode your message. If the key is also sent by email, it might be easy to intercept the key and decode the encrypted message.

With public key encryption, there are two keys, one public and the other private. The public key needs to be known. To send a message to a friend, you use her or his public key to encrypt the message. Your friend then uses her or his private key to decode the message after receiving it.

Suppose you want to send an encrypted message to your friend Milo. He tells you his public key; in fact, there's no harm if he tells everybody. You write the message and then encrypt it using Milo's public key. He receives the message and then uses his private key to decode it. It doesn't matter who sent the message to Milo as long as it was encrypted with his public key. Also, even if the message is intercepted, it can't be read without knowing Milo's private key. It's up to him to keep that secret. Likewise, if he wanted to respond, he would use your public key to encrypt the message. You would use your private key to decode it.

You can obtain a version of public key encryption software called PGP, for Pretty Good Privacy. It's freely available to individuals and may be purchased for commercial use. There are some licensing restrictions on the use of the commercial versions in the United States and Canada. Furthermore, U.S. State Department regulations prohibit the export of some versions of this program to other countries. In fact, current restrictions in the United States prohibit the export of most encryption methods, while other countries allow the export of encryption methods and algorithms. Some people feel strongly that these policies should be changed for the sake of sharing information and for the sake of allowing common encryption of sensitive and business messages, but others don't agree.

To read more about PGP, take a look at one or more of these:

+ How PGP Works, **http://www.pgpi.org/doc/pgpintro/**

+ MIT distribution site for PGP, **http://web.mit.edu/network/pgp.html**

+ The comp.security.pgp FAQ, **http://www.cam.ac.uk.pgp.net/pgpnet/pgp-faq**

One issue that needs to be resolved is whether it should be possible for law enforcement or other government officials to decode encrypted messages. Some argue that because of the need to detect criminal action or in the interests of national security, the means to decode any messages should be available to the appropriate authorities. Others argue that individuals have the right to privacy in their communications. In the United States, the issue has been decided in favor of government access in the case of digital telephone communications. The issue hasn't been settled yet for email or other forms of electronic communications.

Here's a list of some extensive resources for information about electronic privacy:

+ 6.805/STS085: Readings on Encryption and National Security
  http://www-swiss.ai.mit.edu/6095/readings-crypto.html

+ 6.805/STS085: Readings on Privacy Implications of Computer Networks
  http://www-swiss.ai.mit.edu/6095/readings-privacy.html

+ EPIC Online Guide to Privacy Resources
  http://www.epic.org/privacy/privacy_resources_faq.html

Privacy on the Web

It's easy to get the impression that we're browsing the Web and using Internet services in an anonymous manner. But that's not the case. Every time you visit a Web site, some information about your computer system is transmitted to the server. When you fill out a form, the information you provide is passed to a server. Some Web sites track the activities of users through the use of *cookies*, information that's passed from the computer that's using a Web browser to a Web server. You also need to be aware of the risks involved with giving out personal information through email, chat groups, and forms. Since it may be difficult to know with whom you are communicating, you need to be very careful about disclosing personal information. Children especially need to know about and be informed of the risks and dangers involved in using the Internet.

What Happens When You Go to a
Web Site—What the Server Knows

When you go to a Web site, either by clicking on a hyperlink or by typing in a URL in the address box, your browser (the client program) sends a request to a Web server. This request includes the IP address of your computer system, the URL of the file or Web page you've requested, the time the request was made, and whether the request was successful. If you clicked on a hyperlink from a Web page, the URL of the Web page is also passed to the server. All of this information is kept in log files on the server. It's possible to have the log files analyzed and track all access to a Web server.

The Trail Left on Your Computer

We've seen that each server keeps log files to identify requests for Web pages. So, in that sense, you leave a trail of your activities on each of the Web servers that you contact. There's also a trail of your activities kept on the computer you use to access the Web. Recently accessed Web pages and a list of the URLs accessed are kept in the cache—a folder or directory that contains recently viewed Web pages, images, and other resources—and the history list. If you're using a public computer, such as in a lab or library, then it's possible for someone to check on your activities.

Cache

Most Web browsers keep copies of recently accessed Web pages, images, and other files. Netscape and other browsers call this the cache; Microsoft Internet Explorer calls these "temporary Internet files." When you return to a Web page you've visited recently, the browser first checks to see if it's available in the cache and retrieves it from your computer rather than retrieving it from a remote site. It's much faster to retrieve a Web page from the cache rather than from a remote site. This is convenient, but it also leaves a record of your activities. It is possible to clear the cache or remove the temporary files:

◆ If you're using Internet Explorer, click on **Tools** in the menu bar, select **Internet Options**, then click on the tab **General** (if it's not already in the foreground). Now click on **Delete Files** in the section titled "Temporary Internet Files."

History List

The Web browser keeps a record of the path you've taken to get to the current location. To see the path and select a site from it, click on **Go** in the menu bar. The browser also keeps a list of all the Web pages visited recently in the history list. This list is kept around for a time period specified in days. You can set the number of days an item may be kept on the list. You can also delete the files from the history list.

◆ If you're using Internet Explorer, click on **Tools** in the menu bar, select **Internet Options**, then click on the tab **General** (if it's not already in the foreground). Set the number of days items are kept in the history list or delete the entire list (click on **Clear History**) here.

Cookies

A cookie is information that's passed to a Web server by a Web browser program. Netscape developed the terms and methods for working with cookies. A Web server requests and/or writes a cookie to your computer only if you access a Web page that contains the commands to do that.

◆ If you're using Internet Explorer, then you can set security zones for different types of Web sites. To set security zones, click on **Tools** in the menu bar, select **Internet Options**, then click on the tab **Security** (if it's not already in the foreground). To customize how cookies are dealt with, click on **Customize**.

Cookies are sometimes viewed as an invasion of privacy, but they are useful to you in some cases. Suppose you want to visit a site frequently that requires you to give a password or a site that you can customize to match your preferences. The protocol HTTP is used when you visit a Web site. When a Web page is requested, a connection is made between the client and the server, the server delivers a Web page, and the connection is terminated. Once the page has been transmitted, the connection is terminated. If you visit a site again, the server, through HTTP, has no information about a previous visit. Cookies can be used to keep track of your password or keep track of the preferences you've set for every visit to that site. That way, you don't have to enter the information each time you visit.

To get more information about cookies, take a look at the Webopedia entry on cookies at **http://webopedia.internet.com/TERM/c/cookie.html**.

Spyware, Adware, Hijacked Web Browsers

Some programs that you use on your computer include code that sends information from your system to another one on the Internet. This code can be used to report your Web activity, such as which sites you visit. That is perfectly legal in the United States, and it can be done without your knowledge, even though most people wouldn't choose to allow that type of activity if they were given a choice. That type of software is called spyware or adware. The included code is often used for marketing purposes, and in that way it's similar to including advertisements with a program or Web site. The same techniques can be used to keep track of all your keystrokes, thus recording and transmitting user names and passwords (that may be illegal!), or they can be used to involve your computer system in some distributed computing effort. In some cases, the options or preferences on your browser may be changed, such as changing the URL for your home page, by visiting a Web site designed to do just that. Scary stuff!

You can learn more about this topic by visiting the Web site "SpywareInfo: What is spyware?," **http://www.spywareinfo.com/articles/spyware/**. More importantly, you'll want to install a program that will detect and remove spyware. There are several good ones available, and like antivirus software, they need to be regularly updated. One of the most highly recommended ones is SpyBot—S&D. It is distributed with no required fee, but if you find it useful, you should make a donation to support the software. The URL to download SpyBot is **http://www.safer-networking.org/en/download/index.html**.

Computer and Network Security

When you use a computer system connected to the Internet, you're able to reach a rich variety of sites and information. By the same token, any system connected to the Internet can be reached in some manner by any of the other computer systems connected to the Internet. Partaking of the material on the Internet also means that you have to be concerned about the security of your computer system and other systems. The reason for the concern about your system is obvious— you don't want unauthorized persons accessing your information or information belonging to others who share your system. You want to protect your system from malicious or unintentional actions that could destroy stored information or halt your system. You don't want others masquerading as you. You need to be concerned about the security of other systems so you can have some faith in the information you retrieve from those systems and so you can conduct business transactions. A lack of security results in damage, theft, and, what may be worse in some cases, a lack of confidence or trust.

Maintaining security becomes more important as we use the Internet for commercial transactions or transmitting sensitive data. There is always the chance that new services introduced to the Internet won't be completely tested for security flaws or that security problems will not be discovered. While it's exciting to be at the cutting edge, there's some virtue in not adopting the latest service or the latest version of software until it has been around for a while. This gives the Internet community a chance to discover problems. Several agencies are dedicated to finding, publicizing, and dealing with security problems. One site that does this is maintained by the U.S. Department of Energy. You can use your Web browser to access the CIAC (Computer Incident Advisory Capability) security Web site by using the URL **http://www.ciac.org/ciac/**.

You don't need to be paranoid about security, but you do need to be aware of anything that seems suspicious. Report any suspicious activity or changes to your directory or files to your system administrator. The system administrator can often take actions to track down a possible break in security. Be suspicious if you're asked for your password at unusual times. You should be asked for it only when you log in. Never give your password to anyone. If a program changes its behavior in terms of requiring more information from you than it did before, an unauthorized user may have replaced the original program with another. This is called a trojan horse because of the similarity of the program to the classic Greek tale. What appears to be benign could hide some malicious actions or threats.

Passwords

If you have to log on to a computer system that is connected to the Internet, then one of your primary defenses against intrusion is your password.

+ Choose a password that will be difficult to guess.

+ Choose a password that's at least six characters long. You'll also want to use a password that contains upper- and lowercase letters and some nonalphabetic characters. Additionally, the password shouldn't represent a word, and it shouldn't be something that's easy to identify with you such as a phone number, room number, birth date, or license number. Some bad choices are **Skippy**, **3451234a**, or **gloria4me**. Better choices might be **All452on**, **jmr!pmQ7**, or **sHo$7otg**. Naturally, you have to choose something you'll remember.

+ Never write down your password; doing that makes it easy to find.

+ In addition to creating a good password, you also need to change it regularly.

Persons who try to gain unauthorized access to a system are called crackers. A cracker will, by some means, get a copy of the password file for a system containing the names of all the users along with their passwords. (In some cases, the permissions on a password file are set so anyone can read it. This is necessary for certain programs to run. Fortunately, the passwords are encrypted.) Once a cracker gets a copy of a password file, she will run a program that attempts to guess the encrypted passwords. If a password is an encrypted version of a word, a word in reverse order, or a word with one numeral or punctuation mark, it is not too difficult for the program to decipher it. If a cracker has one password on a system, she can gain access to that login name and from there possibly go to other portions of the system.

Firewalls

Because connecting a network to the Internet allows access to that network, system administrators and other persons concerned with network security are very concerned about making that connection. One device or part of a network that can help enhance security is called a firewall. A firewall can be a separate computer, a router, or some other network device that allows certain packets into a network. (Remember that all information is passed throughout the Internet as packets.) By using a firewall and configuring it correctly, only certain types of Internet services can be allowed through to the network. Organizations with firewalls often place their Web, FTP, and other servers on one part of their network and put a firewall system between those servers and the rest of the network. The firewall restricts access to the protected internal network by letting through only packets associated with certain protocols. Email can still be delivered, and sometimes Telnet to the internal network is allowed. If you are on the protected portion of the network, behind the firewall, then you can access Internet and Web sites on the Internet, but they may not be able to gain direct access to you. Firewalls also perform logging and auditing functions so that if security is breached, the source of the problem may be determined.

To find out more about firewalls, read "Internet Firewalls: Frequently Asked Questions," **http://www.interhack.net/pubs/fwfaq/**.

If you have a high-speed connection to the Internet in your home, through a cable modem, DSL, or satellite connection, you should consider installing a personal firewall whether you have set up a network or not. That high-speed connection is always (unless the power is off) connected to the Internet, and so your home computer or network is a possible target for others who look for systems they can use for other purposes or systems from which they can steal information. Microsoft offers some good advice about installing and using a firewall at home. It's available at "Protect Your PC," **http://www.microsoft.com/athome/security/protect/default.aspx**.

Viruses and Worms

One type of program that causes problems for Internet users is called a virus. A virus doesn't necessarily copy your data or attempt to use your system. However, it can make it difficult or impossible to use your system. A virus is a piece of code or instructions that attaches itself to existing programs. Just like a biological virus, a computer virus can't run or exist on its own but must be part of an executing program. When these programs are run, the added instructions are also executed. Sometimes the virus does nothing more than announce its presence; in other cases, the virus erases files from your disk. A virus moves from system to system by being part of an executable program. A worm is a program that replicates itself by spreading from one computer on a network to another, usually making many copies of itself. That way, it steals resources from the host system, slowing it down or doing other damage. Viruses and worms are spread as part of some program that infects your computer system, and possibly others on your network, when it is executed. These are often spread through programs that are attachments to email. Sometimes they are disguised as images, word processing documents, or spreadsheets. In any case:

♦ DO NOT CLICK ON AN ATTACHMENT TO AN EMAIL UNLESS YOU ARE EXPECTING THE ATTACHMENT.

✦ Even if you know the person whose email address was used to send an attachment, don't open it unless you are expecting it.

Some viruses or worms, once they infect a computer system, send forged mail with malicious attachments from addresses in the address book of an infected computer to other addresses in the address book. So, never click on or open an attachment unless you know what it is. Seems simple, doesn't it? Still, that is the most common way that viruses are spread.

It is absolutely necessary that you have some antivirus software installed on your computer system. You use that software to scan your system for viruses and to scan incoming mail and programs you load onto your system. Once you have the antivirus software, it is important to keep it up-to-date so new viruses are detected before they infect your computer system. We discussed that in Appendix A.

Getting documents and images from other sites on the Internet won't bring a virus to your system. A virus comes only from running programs on your system. Viruses can exist in executable programs and also have been found in word-processing documents that contain portions of code called macros.

For more information on viruses, check the hyperlinks at "Virus Bulletin Home Page," **http://www.virusbtn.com**.

Other Concerns

There are many other things to be concerned about when we think about security on a computer and a network. If you engage in peer-to-peer networking, then you are likely exchanging files with another computer system. That is similar to the activity in a client-server situation, such as the relationship between a Web browser (the client) and a Web server, but in that situation, files are sent only from the server to the client. In a peer-to-peer relationship, files are exchanged both ways, so that you not only open your system to receive files, but you also allow other computer systems to copy files from your system. Without appropriate controls, private files can be copied from your computer and malicious programs can be installed there. If you use an IM or instant messaging program, then you may be allowing people to send you files or accept files from you as part of a peer-to-peer relationship. You will want to limit that activity to times when you explicitly permit it. Just as in the physical world, the virtual world of the Internet is filled with scams that attempt to swindle people out of money and hoaxes that try to trick people into accepting spyware and viruses. Microsoft does not distribute security patches via email. Don't click on an attachment that claims to be one. Banks, credit card companies, EBay, PayPal, and other commercial or financial organizations don't send email asking you to verify or update your account by providing detailed information involving your bank account number, credit card number, and user names and passwords. Even if it looks like the URL they ask you to click on is legitimate, don't fall for those scams. You need to be aware that people use the Internet to trick others and be careful in your dealings.

Giving Out Information About Yourself and Your Family

There are a number of situations in which you may be asked or tempted to give out personal information. These can range from being asked to fill out a form to download some software or sign up for a service on the Web to being asked for your address or phone number through email or a chat group. Any information you put into a form will be passed to a Web server and find its way into a database. Disclosing your street address to a business sometimes results in your receiving junk mail, and disclosing your email address may result in your getting unsolicited junk email, or spam as it's called. You can't be sure how the information will be used or marketed unless the organization gathering the data makes some explicit guarantees. We hear about and come across situations of fraudulent practices and schemes that swindle money from unsuspecting individuals in the real world, and we're just as likely to come across those types of situations when we're using the Internet. It's relatively easy to create an Internet or Web presence that makes an individual, a company, or an organization appear to be legitimate and trustworthy. Because of this, we need to be all the more skeptical and cautious when conducting personal or commercial dealings on the Internet.

More dangerous situations can arise when we develop a relationship with someone through email or a chat group. These can arise because when we're communicating with someone on the Internet, most of the communication is through text. We don't get to hear the person's voice or see them. We may see a picture, they may tell us about themselves, but we may never know with whom we are communicating. For example, I may be involved in a long series of email messages or have several conversations in a chat room with a person who claims to be my age and gender. The person may even send me a photograph. It could be that the person is totally misrepresenting their true self. So we need to be very careful about giving out any personal information, and we certainly wouldn't make arrangements to meet the person without having the meeting take place in a public location and without taking other precautions.

Children particularly need to discuss these issues with their parents, and they need to understand clearly stated rules about not giving out any personal information or telling someone where they go to school or play.

The Web site "NetSmartz," **http://www.netsmartz.org/**, is a good place to find information about Internet safety issues for children, teens, and parents.

Common sense tells us not to give out personal information, home phone numbers, or home addresses to people we don't know. We're likely not to do that in our daily lives when we don't know the person who is asking for the information, and it is just as important to apply the same rules when we're using the Internet or the World Wide Web. We don't need to be rude or unfriendly, but we do need to be careful, safe, and secure.

INTERNET EXPLORER DETAILS

W e'll cover some of the details of using Internet Explorer in this appendix. We'll also review some of the browser's features that we mentioned in Chapter 1.

Exploring the Web Browser's Window

When you start a Web browser, a window opens on your screen. It's the Web browser's job to retrieve and display a file inside the window. What is in the window will change as you go from site to site, but each window has the same format. The items that help you work with the Web document in the window include the scroll bar, the menu bar, and the toolbar, which are the same every time you use the browser. Figure C-1 shows the browser window with key items labeled.

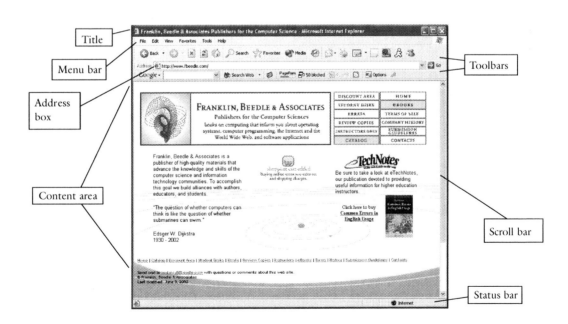

Figure C.1—Internet Explorer Window with Components Labeled

Title

The title of the Web page is created when the page is written. A page's title is not the same as its URL, just as a book's title is different from its library call number.

Menu Bar

The *menu bar* is a list of items each representing a menu from which you can choose an action.

You choose any of these by moving the mouse pointer to the word and clicking on it. You can also activate one of these choices by using the **Alt** key along with the underlined letter. For example, to display the menu associated with **File**, use **Alt**+**F**.

Selecting an item from the menu bar brings up a pulldown menu with several options. For example, if you click on **File**, you see the menu shown to the right.

Select any item in that menu either by clicking on it with the mouse or by pressing the underlined character in its name. To print the current Web page, you can click on **Print** in this menu or you can press **P** (upper- or lowercase). Some items on the menu are followed by **Ctrl+** a letter, such as the following:

Save As...   Ctrl+S

This means that to select the command from the menu, you can either click on **Save As** or use a keyboard shortcut, **Ctrl**+**S**. You use particular command to save a copy of the Web page in a file on your computer.

When you select an item that's followed by ..., as in **Save As...**, it brings up a dialog box. The box will request more information or will ask you to select additional options. If, for example, you select **Save As...**, you will then need to type in or select a file name. When you select an item that's followed by an arrow, as with **New**, it brings up another menu.

☑ T I P ! Giving commands using the keyboard—keyboard shortcuts.

You can access all the commands for using a Web browser by pointing and clicking on a word, icon, or portion of the window, but sometimes you may want to give a command using the keyboard. To do this, use the keys labeled **Ctrl** or **Alt**, along with another key. For example, to print the current Web page, you can select **Print** from a menu or use **Ctrl**+**P**. Using **Ctrl**+**P** means holding down the key labeled **Ctrl**, pressing the key labeled **P**, and then releasing them both. As another example, giving the command **Alt**+**H** will display a menu of items to select for online help. You hold down the key labeled **Alt**, press **H**, and then release them both.

To see a complete list of keyboard shortcuts take a look at "Keyboard Shortcuts for Internet Explorer 6," **http://www.microsoft.com/enable/products/keyboard/keyboardresults.asp?Product=26**. Table C.1 shows some of the commonly used keyboard shortcuts.

Ctrl+A	Select All		**Ctrl**+P	Print the current page
Ctrl+C	Copy page		**Ctrl**+R	Reload the current
Ctrl+V	Paste		**Alt**+H	Display online help menu

Ctrl+X	Cut	**Alt**+◄	Go back one page
Ctrl+F	Find in page	**Alt**+►	Go forward one page
Ctrl+B	Organize favorites	**Alt**+**F4**	Close window
Ctrl+N	Open new window	**F1**	Display
Ctrl+O	Open Address/ Location box	**Esc**	Stop loading the current page

Table C.1—Keyboard Shortcuts

Toolbars

Web browsers, like other Windows software, have one or more rows of icons or items called *toolbars* just below the menu bar. Each item works like a button. When you press it with the mouse, some operation or action takes place. In some cases, a dialog box pops up. For example, if you click on the item to print the current document, you can select a printer and specify whether you want to print the whole document or just a part of it. The icons give you a visual clue to the operation or action they represent. The commands they represent are all available through the items on the menu bar, but the icons give a direct path—a shortcut—to the commands.

Content Area or Document View

The *content area* is the portion of the window that holds the document, page, or other resource as your browser presents it. It can contain text or images. Sometimes the content area is divided into or consists of several independent portions called *frames*. Each frame has its own scroll bar, and you can move through one frame while staying in the same place in others.

The content area holds the Web page you're viewing, which likely contains hyperlinks in text or graphic format. Clicking on a hyperlink with the *left* mouse button allows you to follow the link. Clicking with the *right* mouse button (or holding down the mouse button without clicking if your mouse has only one button) brings up a menu that gives you options for working with a hyperlink.

Scroll Bar

If the document doesn't fit into the window it will be displayed with vertical and/or horizontal *scroll bars*. The horizontal one is at the bottom of the window, and the vertical one is at the right of the window. These scroll bars and their associated arrows help you move through the document. The scroll bars work the same way as those in common Microsoft Windows applications.

Status Bar

When you are retrieving a document, opening a location, or following a hyperlink, the bar along the bottom of the window (the *status bar*) holds the URL that's being used. It also lets you know whether a site is being contacted, if it's responding, and how the transmission is progressing.

Details about the Internet Explorer Window

We'll go over some of the details of the items available through the Internet Explorer window.

Menu Bar

The menu bar near the top of the window includes:

<u>F</u>ile   <u>E</u>dit   <u>V</u>iew   F<u>a</u>vorites   <u>T</u>ools   <u>H</u>elp

Here are some details about each of the pulldown menus:

File

Using the commands in the **File** menu, you can open a new browser window, send an email message, or open a page in an HTML editor (you set this in **Internet Options** from the **Tools** menu). You can also use this menu to open a page in the browser—either a Web page (which you would open by giving its URL) or a file on your computer. You can go in "offline" mode to work with files or messages on your computer without being connected to the Internet. The menu options also allow you to print, mail, save the current document into a file, or create a desktop shortcut to the Web page.

Edit

Use the **Edit** menu to copy items from the current document to other applications, such as a word processor. You can also use **Copy** and **Paste** to copy URLs or email addresses from one window into the address box or address field of a message. In addition, the menu contains the item **Find**, which presents a dialog box that lets you search the current document for a word or phrase.

View

The items on the **View** menu change what you see and how you view those items. You can use this menu to hide any of the toolbars (or to show them if they're not in view) or to change the font size (the size of the letters in the Web page). By choosing an item in the **Explorer Bar**, you split the content area so that a frame is created on the left titled Search, Favorites, History, or Folders.

These windows show the search tools, the favorites list, the history list, or the computer's folders. You also use the **View** menu to reload a copy of the current document; this is useful if there have been some changes to the source page since it was originally loaded or if the images in a document were not loaded automatically. The menu has items to stop the current page from loading. The item **Source** lets you view the source version of the current page so you can see which HTML elements were used to create it. The item **Go To** brings up another menu so you can travel **Back** or **Forward** through the list of the most recently accessed Web pages.

Favorites

This gives quick access to the favorites list. It contains an item to add the current page to the favorites list, and an item to organize or manage the list of folders in the favorites collection.

Tools

This menu gives access to the email and the Usenet newsgroups. There's an item to use to check for updates of Microsoft Software. Another item takes you to related Web sites. The last item,

Internet Options, is what you use to set preferences and options to customize the browser and how its various components work with your computer system.

Help

Choose the **Help** menu to obtain information about using the Web browser. This menu includes a link to online help, an online tutorial to help you use Internet Explorer, and links to other information about this browser.

Toolbars

There are several toolbars in Microsoft Internet Explorer version 6. In this book, we showed the Standard Buttons toolbar and the Address toolbar, which come with the Windows packages, and the Google Toolbar that we installed ourselves (see Chapter 1.)

Standard Buttons

Table C.2 explains the items in the Standard Buttons toolbar.

Name	Explanation
Back, Forward	These two buttons with directional arrows move between documents or Web pages that you've already seen. **Back** takes you to the previous page, and **Forward** can only be used if you've previously used **Back**. To obtain a list of sites to go back to or forward to, put the mouse pointer on either of these icons and click the *right* mouse button.
Stop	This button stops a current Web page from loading. This is useful if it's taking a long time to contact a site or load a page.
Refresh	This button reloads the current Web page from the source. If the page may have changed since you last viewed it, you may want to reload it.
Home	This button takes you to your home page, the one you first saw when you started the browser.
Search	This button opens a frame on the left side of the content area in which you can search the Web. You can select which service to use by clicking **Customize**. To search, you type in one or more keywords and wait for results. Clicking on a listed result opens the page in the main window to the right.

Favorites	This button takes you to your favorites list. A frame opens on the left of the content area showing the items and folders in the favorites list.
Media	This button opens a frame to the left of the content area. You can use items displayed here to play audio or video media found either on the Internet or locally.
History	This item opens the history list in a frame to the left of the content area.
Mail	Use this to access email and Usenet newsgroups with your computer.
Print	This button allows you to print the current document.
Edit	Use this button to edit the current Web page. You'll be editing the Web page on your computer system, not on the Web server that makes the page available on the Web. You can use FTP to transfer what you've edited to a Web server, if you have the proper password and login name.

Table C.2—Items in the Standard Buttons Toolbar

Address Toolbar

The address toolbar shows the URL for the current Web page. Once the Web page is displayed, a Web page icon appears to its left. You can click and drag this icon to add the Web page to the favorites list, to create a shortcut to the page on your desktop, or to add it to the links toolbar. To do that move the mouse pointer to the Web page icon, press the (left) mouse button and hold it down. Now move the mouse pointer to a folder in the favorites folder or to the desktop, and release the mouse button.

You'll see that as you type in a URL the browser shows a list of URLs from the history list that start with the letters you've typed so far. You can save typing by selecting the URL you're intending to type.

Status Bar

The status bar shows information about the page as it is being retrieved and displayed, as well as the progress of that retrieval (shown in the status bar). The item on the right tells what security zone is assigned to the current Web page. Internet Explorer has four predefined security zones—Internet, Local Intranet (pages from your own network or computer), Trusted, and Restricted. These zones are used for security purposes. For more information on using these zones read the sections "Sending Information over the Internet Safely" and "Understanding Security and Privacy on the Internet" in the online help; to access this, press **F1** and click **Contents**.

GLOSSARY

404 error   A response code or error transmitted by a Web server to a client when a requested Web page or file is not present on the server.

acceptable use policy   Within the context of the Internet, a policy that states the proper or acceptable uses of a computer network.

address box   The pane in the browser window of Internet Explorer that holds the current document's URL. You can type a URL in this box and press Enter to access a Web page.

administrative address   The address to use to join an email discussion group or interest group and to send requests for services.

all-in-one search tool   A tool that provides search forms for several search engines and directories all in one site. The tool also provides hyperlinks, which allow you to go to the services directly.

annotated directory   Often referred to as a virtual library, this type of directory has brief summaries, descriptions, ratings, or reviews attached to Web pages and subject guides.

annotation   A brief summary or description of a Web page or of any work listed in a database.

anonymous FTP   A means of using FTP to make files readily available to the public. If you start an FTP session with a remote host, you give the login or user name *anonymous,* and enter your email address as a password. When you use a URL starting with **ftp://** with a Web browser, an anonymous FTP session begins, and you don't have to enter a user name or password.

article   A message or file that is part of a Usenet newsgroup.

attachment   A file that is sent as part of an email message, but that is not part of the main message. Usually images, programs, or word-processing files are sent as attachments, because most email programs allow only plain text in the body of a message.

bibliographic database   An online database that includes citations that describe and identify titles, dates, authors, and other parts of written works. It doesn't contain the full text of the information itself. Some bibliographic databases are annotated, which means there is a brief summary of each work listed.

Boolean searching   Searching that uses Boolean operators (AND, OR, and NOT) in the search expression. Especially helpful in multifaceted or specific topics, Boolean operators help expand or narrow the scope of your search. A search for *rivers OR lakes* returns all documents with both words or either word in them. A search for *rivers AND lakes* returns documents with both words in them. A search for *rivers AND lakes NOT swamps* returns only documents that mention both *rivers* and *lakes* but omits those that also mention *swamps*.

browsing The process of going from one hyperlink to another on the World Wide Web. You can browse indiscriminately, or you can do structured browsing, using a hierarchical subject list in a directory.

cache A portion of memory (either in RAM or on a disk) set aside to hold the items retrieved most recently. For a Web browser, this refers to recent Web pages and images. The cache is used so that items may be retrieved more quickly without going back to the Internet. A browser can be set so that, in case an item hasn't changed, it will retrieve the item from the cache.

case sensitivity The ability of a search tool to distinguish between uppercase and lowercase letters. Some search tools aren't case sensitive; no matter what you type, the tool only picks up lowercase matches. Search engines that are case sensitive will strictly follow the search request; they'll return documents containing the words in the case in which they were entered in the search expression.

certificate authority A company that guarantees the identity of the holder of a digital certificate. A certificate is attached to a message or Web page and can be used to guarantee the authenticity of information.

client/server The interaction between a system that requests information (the client) and another system that provides it (the server). The browser is the client, and a computer at the site that provides the information is the server.

commercial database A database that requires you to pay a subscription cost before accessing it. It is also referred to as a proprietary database.

Communications Decency Act of 1996 Legislation approved by Congress that made it a criminal offense to include potentially indecent or offensive material on the Internet. The U.S. Supreme Court ruled in June of 1997 that this act abridged the freedom of speech that is protected by the First Amendment, and the act was ruled unconstitutional.

compressed file A file that has been processed by a program that applies an algorithm or scheme to compress or shrink a file. A compressed file must first be uncompressed or transformed before it can be read, displayed, or used. Files available through anonymous FTP are often stored in compressed form.

concept searching A feature enabling a search engine to find synonyms in its database. When you type in a word or phrase, the engine automatically searches for the word or phrase you want, plus words or phrases that may mean the same thing. For example, if the word *teenage* were in your search expression, the search engine would also look for the word *adolescent*.

content area The part of a Web browser window that contains the current Web page, including images, text, or hyperlinks.

cookie A relatively small piece of information that is initially placed on a client's computer by a Web server. Once a cookie is present, the same Web server may read or rewrite the cookie. A Web server requests or writes a cookie to your computer only if you access a Web page that contains the commands to do that. Cookies are used to store information such as your login name and password or information about what portions of a Web site were visited on your computer. Sometimes viewed as an invasion of privacy, cookies are useful to you in some cases. Cookies can be used to keep track of your password or keep track of some preferences you've set for every visit to that site. You can set preferences in your browser to accept or reject cookies.

copyright The right to copy or duplicate material such as images, music, and written works. Only the owners of the information can grant this right. Regardless of whether information on the Internet or a Web page is accompanied by a statement asserting copyright, it is still protected by the copyright laws of the United States, the Universal Copyright Convention, or the Berne Union.

cross-posting Posting an article to more than one Usenet newsgroup.

data transfer rate The speed at which a circuit or communications line can transfer information, usually measured in bits per second (bps).

default setting The configuration a search engine uses unless you override the setting by specifying another configuration. For example, in most search engines, the Boolean operator OR is the assumed relationship between two words unless you type AND between the words.

delimited format A format often used to store tables of data. The data fields are separated by commas, tabs, semicolons, or some other delimiter. Spreadsheet programs usually include the facilities to import data that is in delimited format.

Dewey decimal classification system Originated by Melvil Dewey in the late 19th century, this classification system for library materials divides all knowledge into 10 different classes, which are then subdivided into several sets of subclasses. Within these subclasses, decimals reflect still smaller subdivisions. The Dewey decimal classification system is most prevalent today in public libraries, whereas most other types of libraries, including academic ones, use the Library of Congress classification system.

digital certificate A device that is used to encrypt and decrypt information, and to guarantee the identity of the sender and the authenticity of the information.

directory A topical list of Internet resources, arranged hierarchically. Directories are meant to be browsed, but they can also be searched. Directories differ from search engines in one major way—the human element involved in collecting and updating the information.

discussion group A group that discusses a single topic via email messages. An individual subscribes to or joins a discussion group electronically, and all messages sent to the group are distributed to the members by email.

domain name The Internet name for a network or computer system. The name consists of a sequence of characters separated by periods, such as **www.mwc.edu**. The domain name is often the first part of a URL following **://**. For example, the domain name in the URL **http://sunsite.unc.edu/herbmed/culiherb.html** is **sunsite.unc.edu**.

download To transfer or copy a file from another computer (the remote computer) to the computer you're using (the local computer). This term is often applied to the process of retrieving a file from a software library or FTP archive.

duplicate detection An output feature of some search engines and meta-search tools that automatically filters out of your search results any URLs that are duplicated elsewhere in the results.

ECPA (Electronic Communications Privacy Act) The U.S. law that prevents U.S. investigative agencies from intercepting or reading email messages without first obtaining a warrant.

electronic mail (email)   A basic Internet service that allows users to exchange messages electronically.

email discussion group   *See* discussion group.

encryption   A procedure to convert a file or message from its original form to one that can only be read by the intended recipient.

fair use   A provision in most copyright conventions or statutes that makes it possible for individuals to copy portions of a document or other piece of work for short-term use.

FAQ (frequently asked questions)   A list of commonly asked questions and answers on a specific topic. A FAQ is often associated with Usenet newsgroups, but several search tools also include a FAQ file. This, and online help, is usually the first place you should look to find answers.

favorite   A hyperlink that is saved in the favorites list. You can use favorites to keep track of useful or important sites and to return there whenever you are using your browser.

favorites list   The name the Internet Explorer browser gives to the collection of favorites. The browser includes menu bar and toolbar links to the favorites list.

field   Part of a Web page or bibliographic record that is designated for a particular kind of data or text.

field searching   A strategy in which you limit a search to a particular field. In a search engine, you might search only the URL field. In a library catalog, you could search for items by author, title, subject, call number, or any other data element that was designated as a field. By narrowing the scope of searchable items, field searching helps to eliminate the chance of retrieving irrelevant information.

file name extension   The end of a file name in some operating systems where the name of a file ends with a period followed by (usually) two to four letters. The extension is used to associate an application program with the file. For example, the file containing this glossary is named glossary.doc. The file name extension is **.doc**. Clicking on the name of the file automatically opens the file with the Microsoft Word word-processing software.

filter   Software that filters out certain Web sites from the results of a search.

firewall   A security device or system, usually a combination of hardware and software meant to protect a local network from intruders from the Internet.

flame   An email message or article in a Usenet newsgroup that's meant to insult someone or provoke controversy. This term is also applied to messages which contain strong criticism of or disagreement with a previous message or article.

follow-up   An article posted in response to another article. The follow-up has the same subject as the original article.

frame   Some Web pages are divided into rectangular regions called frames. Each frame has its own scroll bar, and in fact, each frame represents an individual Web page.

freeware   A software program that's available for use without any charge. This doesn't mean the program isn't copyrighted. Usually, the originator retains the copyright. Anyone can use it, but the program can't be legally sold or distributed without permission.

frequently asked questions (FAQ)   *See* FAQ.

FTP (File Transfer Protocol)   A means of transferring or sharing files across the Internet from one computer system to another.

FTP archive   A collection of files available through anonymous FTP.

full-text database   A database that contains the full text of the information it describes.

full-text indexing   A search engine feature in which every word, significant or insignificant, is indexed and retrievable through a search.

group address   The address to use to send email to each member of a discussion group, interest group, listserv list, or mailing list.

GUI (graphical user interface)   An interface that uses icons and images in addition to text to represent information, input, and output.

helper application   A program used with a Web browser to display, view, or work with a file that the browser cannot display. For example, a browser can display graphic or image files in GIF or JPEG format. If you accessed an image of another type through a hyperlink, your browser would need a helper application to display it. *See also* plug-in.

hidden Internet   *See* invisible Web.

hierarchy   A list of subjects in a directory. The subjects are organized in successive ranks with the broadest listed first and with more specific aspects or subdivisions listed below.

high precision/high recall   A phenomenon that occurs during a search when you retrieve all the relevant documents in the database and retrieve no unwanted ones.

history list   A list of Internet sites, services, and resources that have been accessed through a Web browser during recent sessions.

hit list   A list of results obtained from an online search.

home page   The first screen or page of a site accessible through a Web browser.

HTML (Hypertext Markup Language)   The format used for writing documents to be viewed with a Web browser. Items in the document can be text, images, sounds, or links to other HTML documents, sites, services, and resources on the Web.

HTTP (Hypertext Transfer Protocol)   The standard protocol that World Wide Web servers and clients use to communicate.

hyperlink   A word, phrase, image, or region of an image that is often highlighted or colored differently and that can be selected as part of a Web page. Each hyperlink represents another Web page; a location in the current Web page; an image, audio, video, or multimedia file; or some other resource on the World Wide Web. When the hyperlink is selected, it activates the resource that it represents.

hypermedia   An extension to hypertext that includes images, audio, and other media.

hypertext   A way of viewing or working with a document in text format that allows you to follow cross-references to other Web resources. By clicking on an embedded hyperlink, the user can choose her own path through the hypertext material.

implied Boolean operator   The characters + and -, which can be used to require or prohibit a word or phrase as part of a search expression. The + acts somewhat like AND, and the - acts as NOT would in a Boolean expression. For example, the Boolean expression rivers AND lakes NOT swamps may be expressed as +rivers +lakes -swamps.

interest group   Group discussion and sharing of information about a single topic carried out via email.

Internet   The collection of networks throughout the world that agree to communicate using specific telecommunication protocols, the most basic being Internet Protocol (IP) and Transmission Control Protocol (TCP), and the services supplied by those networks.

Internet domain name   The Internet name for a network or computer system. The name consists of a sequence of characters separated by periods, such as **www.mwc.edu**. The domain name is often the first part of the URL that follows ://. For example, the domain name in the URL **http://www.ckp.edu/ technical/reference/swftp.html** is **www.ckp.edu**.

invisible Web   Information that is not accessible via search engines. Also referred to as the *hidden Internet.*

IP (Internet Protocol)   The basic protocol used for the Internet. Information is put into a single packet, containing the addresses of the sender and the recipient, and then sent out. The receiving system removes the information from the packet.

IP address   An Internet address in numeric form. It consists of four numerals, each in the range of 0 through 255, separated by periods. An example is 192.65.245.76. Each computer connected to the Internet has an IP address assigned to it. The IP address is sometimes used for authentication.

ISP (Internet service provider)   A usually commercial service that provides access to the Internet. Fees often depend on the amount of time and the maximum possible speed, in bits per second, of access to the Internet.

JPEG (Joint Photographic Experts Group)   A file format used to represent images. It supports more colors than GIF and offers greater compression. However, some detail is lost in the compression.

keyword   A descriptive or significant word in a Web document.

keyword indexing   A feature in which each significant word in the entire document or record is indexed and retrievable by the search engine or computer program being used.

keyword searching   A feature in which the search engine or computer program searches for every occurrence of a particular word in the database, regardless of where it may appear.

LCSH (Library of Congress subject headings)   A list of standardized subject headings that are used to index materials by the Library of Congress. The subject headings are arranged in alphabetical order by the broadest headings, with more precise headings listed under them. Most academic library catalogs are searchable by subject heading as well as by keyword.

Library of Congress classification system   Designed originally for the Library of Congress in the late 19th century, this classification system is used by most academic and special libraries throughout the United States and in many parts of the world. It consists of 21 classes, each designated by a letter of the alphabet. Subdivisions are created by the use of other letters and numbers.

limiting by date   A search tool feature that allows you to limit search results to pages that were indexed after, before, or between certain dates.

list address   *See* group address.

Listserv   The type of software used to manage a listserv list.

listserv list   A type of discussion group, interest group, or mailing list.

low precision/high recall   A phenomenon that occurs during a search when you retrieve a large set of results, including many unwanted documents.

lurking   Reading the email or articles in a discussion group or newsgroup without contributing or posting messages.

mailing list   *See* discussion group.

menu bar   The sequence of pulldown menus across the top of the Web browser window. All browser commands are embedded in the menu bar.

meta-search tool   A tool that allows you to search either more than one search engine or directory simultaneously or a list of search tools that can be accessed from that site. These two major types of meta-search tools are called parallel search tools and all-in-one search tools.

meta-tag   A keyword inserted in the meta-tag portion of the HTML source document by the Web page author. If Web pages don't have much text, meta-tags help them come up in a keyword search.

moderator   A person who manages or administers a discussion group, interest group, listserv list, mailing list, or Usenet newsgroup. In most cases, the moderator is a volunteer. Messages sent to the group are first read by the moderator, who then passes appropriate messages to the group.

modifying search results   Changing an initial search expression to obtain more relevant results. This can involve narrowing the results by field, limiting by date, adding keywords, subtracting keywords, and so forth.

natural language searching   The capability of entering a search expression in the form of a question or statement.

navigation toolbar   Often referred to as the command toolbar, this toolbar contains a sequence of icons or items that represent frequently used commands for navigation and other purposes, such as printing the current Web page.

nested Boolean logic   The use of parentheses in Boolean search expressions. For example, the nested expression *((rivers OR lakes) AND canoeing) NOT camping* will first find resources that contain either the words *rivers* or *lakes* and the term *canoeing,* but not resources that contain the term *camping.*

news aggregator   *See* RSS newsreader.

news server   A computer that is used to hold the collections of articles that make up newsgroups, and to run the programs that pass any new articles posted to its newsgroups on to any other server that carries the same newsgroups.

newsgroup   A collection of Usenet articles arranged by topic. Some are specialized or technical groups (such as **comp.protocols.tcp-ip.domains**—topics related to Internet domain style names), some deal with recreational activities (such as **rec.outdoors.fishing.saltwater**—topics related to saltwater fishing), and one, **news.newusers.questions**, is dedicated to questions from new Usenet users.

newsreader   The software you use to read, reply to, and manage Usenet news. *See also* RSS newsreader.

NNTP (Network News Transport Protocol)   The standard protocol used to distribute Usenet news between computer systems on the Internet in a form that machines can read and computers can access.

offline browsing   Viewing Web pages when you're not connected to the Internet.

OPAC (Online Public Access Catalog)   An electronic catalog of a library's holdings, usually searchable by author, title, subject, keyword, and call number. Thousands of OPACs from libraries all over the world are available on the World Wide Web.

personal home page   A Web page used by an individual to give personal or professional information.

PGP   Pretty Good Privacy, the name given to a public key encryption system for exchanging email in a secure, encrypted format. PGP was developed by Philip R. Zimmerman in 1991.

phrase searching   A search feature supported by most search engines that allows you to search for words that usually appear next to each other. It is possibly the most important search feature.

plug-in An application software that's used along with a Web browser to view or display certain types of files as part of a Web page. Shockwave from Macromedia is a plug-in that allows the browser to display interactive multimedia.

post A message that is sent to an email discussion group or a Usenet newsgroup. Also, to send a message to an email discussion group or Usenet discussion group.

PPP (Point-to-Point Protocol) A standard protocol that allows a computer with a modem to communicate using TCP/IP.

protocol A set of rules for exchanging information between networks or computer systems. The rules specify the format and the content of the information and the procedures to follow during the exchange.

proximity searching A search feature that makes it possible to search for words that are near each other in a document.

public key encryption An encryption method that involves the use of two codes or keys. The two keys, one called the private key and the other called the public key, are assigned to an individual. Using the public key anyone can encrypt a message or file that can only be decrypted or decoded by the use of the corresponding private key.

reference work A resource used to quickly find answers to questions. Traditionally thought of as being in the form of books (such as dictionaries, encyclopedias, quotation directories, manuals, guides, atlases, bibliographies, and indexes), a reference source on the World Wide Web closely resembles its print counterpart. A reference work doesn't necessarily contain hyperlinks to other resources, although it will often have hyperlinks within the document itself.

relevance A measure of how closely a database entry matches a search request. Most search tools on the Web return results based on relevance. The specific algorithm for computing relevance varies from one service to another, but it's often based on the number of times terms in the search expression appear in the document and whether they appear in the appropriate fields.

relevancy ranking A ranking of items retrieved from a database. The ranking is based on the relevancy score that a search engine has assigned.

results per page A feature of some search engines that allows you to designate the number of results listed per page. Search engines usually list 10 results per page.

robot *See* spider.

router A device (hardware) that transfers information between networks.

RSS Really Simple Syndication, RDF Site Summary, or Rich Site Summary. RSS is an XML, or Extensible Markup Language based format for distributing and aggregating Web content.

RSS newsreader Software that allows you to receive, within one page, news sources in XML-based formats, using RSS (Really Simple Syndication) technology. *See also* news aggregator.

scroll bar The rectangular area on the right side of the window that allows you to move up or down in the open document. You move by clicking and dragging it or clicking on the arrows at the bottom and the top of the bar.

search engine A collection of programs that gather information from the Web (*see* spider), index it, and put it in a database so it can be searched. The search engine takes the keywords or phrases you enter, searches the database for words that match the search expression, and returns them to you. The results are hyperlinks to sources that have descriptions, titles, or contents matching the search expression.

search expression   The keywords and syntax that you enter in a search form. With this expression, you ask a search tool to seek relevant documents in a particular way.

search form   The rectangular pane or oblong box that appears on the home pages of most search engines and directories. In this space, you enter a search expression.

shareware   Software that you are allowed to download and try for a specified period free of charge. If you continue to use the program after that time, you are expected to pay a usually modest fee to continue using the product legally.

sorting   An option in some search engines that allows you to determine how you'd like your search results listed—by URL, relevance, domain or location, date, and so on.

spam   Unwanted and unsolicited email. The electronic equivalent of paper junk mail.

special collection   A collection of material, usually a separate collection of a large library, that focuses on a particular topic and covers it in great depth.

special library   A library that focuses on the interests inherent in the institution it serves. Libraries in hospitals, corporations, associations, museums, and other types of institutions are all special libraries. In many cases, they are not open to the public. A special library's collection may be narrow in scope, but it will have depth within the specialty it covers.

specialized database   A self-contained index that is searchable and available on the Web. Items in specialized databases are often not accessible through a keyword search in a search engine.

spider   A computer program that travels the Internet to locate such resources as Web documents, FTP archives, and Gopher documents. It indexes the documents in a database, which is then searched using a search engine (such as AltaVista or Excite). A spider can also be referred to as a robot or wanderer. Each search engine uses a spider to build its database.

status bar   The bar or rectangular region at the bottom of the browser window that displays information regarding the transfer of a Web document to the browser. When the mouse moves over a hyperlink, the status bar shows the hyperlink's URL. When a Web page is requested, the status bar gives information about contacting and receiving information from a server. During transmission, the status bar displays a percentage that reflects how much of the document has been transferred. The status bar also indicates whether transmissions are occurring in a secure manner.

stemming   *See* truncation.

stop word   A word that an indexing program doesn't index. Stop words usually include articles (a, an, and the) and other common words.

streaming media   The method of displaying or playing media such as sound or video as it is being transmitted across the Internet rather than retrieving the entire file before displaying it.

subcategory   A subject category that is more narrowly focused than the broader subject category above it in a hierarchy.

subject catalog   *See* directory.

subject category   A division in a hierarchical subject classification system in a Web directory. You click on the subject category that is likely to contain either the Web pages you want or other subject categories that are more specific.

subject guide   A collection of URLs on a particular topic. Most easily found listed in virtual libraries, they are also referred to as metapages.

subscribe To join a discussion group, interest group, listserv list, or mailing list. You use this term when writing commands to join such a group and to list a Usenet newsgroup on your newsreader.

syntax The rules governing the construction of search expressions in search engines and directories.

tag A code used in HTML that identifies an element so that a Web browser will know how to display it.

TCP/IP (Transmission Control Protocol/ Internet Protocol) A collection of protocols used to provide the basis for Internet and World Wide Web services.

text file A file containing characters in a plain human-readable format. There are no formatting commands such as underlining or displaying characters in boldface or different fonts. It is also called an ASCII file.

thread A collection of articles that all deal with a single posting or email message.

thumbnail A representation of an image in a size that's usually much smaller than its true size. For example, we may represent an image whose size is 100-by-200 pixels as a thumbnail of 25-by-50 pixels.

toolbar The sequence of icons below the menu bar. Clicking on a toolbar icon executes a command or causes an action.

top-level category One of several main subjects in the top of a hierarchy in a directory's list of subjects.

triangulation Finding at least three sources that agree with the opinion or findings that an author expounds as fact. If the sources don't agree, more research is needed.

truncation A process that allows you to search for variant endings of a word. Involved shortening the word and adding a symbol (most databases use the asterisk).

unified search interface A meta-search tool that allow you to use several search engines simultaneously.

unsubscribe To leave, sign off from, or quit a discussion group, interest group, listserv list, or mailing list. You use the term when writing commands to end a relationship with a discussion group or to remove a Usenet newsgroup from the list of those you would regularly read.

upload Transfer a file from the computer system being used to a remote system.

URL (Uniform Resource Locator) A way of describing the location of an item (document, service, or resource) on the Internet and specifying the means by which to access that item.

Usenet A system for exchanging messages called articles arranged according to specific categories called newsgroups. The articles are passed from one system to another, not as email between individuals.

virtual library A directory that contains collections of resources that librarians or cybrarians have carefully chosen and organized in a logical way.

virus A program or executable code that must be part of another executing program. Usually viruses change the configuration or cause havoc with a computer system. The viruses are hidden within some useful or standard program.

Web browser A program used to access the Internet services and resources available through the World Wide Web.

Web hosting service A commercial service (in most cases) that provides a Web server to host a Web site. Fees often depend on the amount of disk space available, monthly traffic measured in bytes, and types of services that are provided.

Web page The information available and displayed by a Web browser as the result of opening a local file or opening a location (URL). The contents and format of the Web page are specified using HTML.

Web server A computer that is running the software and has the Internet connections so that it can satisfy HTTP requests from clients. In other words, it is a properly configured computer system that makes it possible to make Web pages available on the Internet.

Weblog A Web site that is updated on a daily or more frequent basis with new information about a particular subject or range of subjects. Information can be provided by the site owner, taken from other Web sites or outside sources, or contributed by users. Also referred to as a blog.

white page service A Web search service that helps locate email or street addresses for individuals. Similar services for businesses and government agencies are called yellow page services.

wildcard A character that stands in for another character or group of characters. Most search tools use an asterisk for this function. Although the wildcard is most often used in truncation, it can also be used in the middle of words (for example, *wom*n*).

World Wide Web The collection of different services and resources available on the Internet and accessible through a Web browser.

XML Extensible Markup Language is a standard text format for structured documents and data on the Web. XML uses a tag system similar to HTML but where HTML's tags describe how content will be displayed, XML tags define the data in the tagged elements, making information sharing easier.

Yellow page services Web-based business address and telephone directories.

INDEX

403 Forbidden, 15, 23
404 errors, 15, 23, 303

A

address toolbar, 336
Adobe Acrobat, 35
all-in-one search tools, 88–89
    Proteus Internet Search, 88–89
All the Web, 96, 132, 149
    Advanced search mode, 81
    Boolean operators, 79–82
    Boolean searching, 79-82
AltaVista, 77, 116, 127, 135-140, 201, 205, 212
    advanced search mode, 136–138
    Boolean searching, 136–138
    Boolean operators, 136–138
    field searching, 137
    image searching, 205
    search strategy, 135–136
annotated directories, 108
annotations, 99
anonymous FTP, 258
    downloading and
    retrieving files, 260–262
antivirus software, 264
    updating, 320
APA style, 121
    citing resources, 305–316
.asc, 34
.au, 36
audio files, 36
    .au, 36

.mp3, 36
.ra or .ram, 36
.wav, 36

B

basic search strategy, 133
Berners-Lee, Tim, 3
bibliographies
    creating, 301
blogs, *see* weblogs
Boolean operators, 78–79
    implied, 130
Boolean searching, 77–78, 79
    nested, 130
browser, *See* Web browser
bulletin board system (BBS), 241
business addresses
    finding, 179-181

C

cache, 325
case sensitivity, 132
CataList, 17, 238–240
children and Internet safety, 329–330
citing Web and Internet resources, 300–313
    electronic journal articles, 310–311
    email resources, 308–309
    styles, 301
    Usenet articles, 310
    Web pages, 305–308
client/server, 13
.com, 281

company research, 164–168
    finding business
    addresses, 179-181
compressed files, 37, 262
    .gz, 36–37
    PKZIP, 37, 263–264
    WinZip, 37, 263–264
    .zip, 36, 263
content area, 20, 333
cookies, 324, 325–326
copy and paste, 52
copyright, 38, 56, 119, 202–203

D

data files, 35
    .wk1, 35
    .wks, 35
    .xls, 35
.dcr, 36
default settings, 78, 129
Dewey decimal classification system, 214
digital collections, 215
.dir, 36
directories, 63, 64–71, 98–108
    annotations, 99
    browsing, 64–65
    Galaxy, 64, 96
    hierarchy, 64–65
    LookSmart, 64
    Open Directory Project, 65
    searching, 64–65, 101–102
    strengths, 100
    structured browsing, 65, 69
    subject categories, 64, 101–102
    weaknesses, 100–101
    Yahoo!, 69, 100–108
discussion groups (email), 17, 232–240
    administrative address, 252
    CataList, 238–240
    etiquette, 251–252
    finding, 245
    list address, 234
    Listproc, 235–237
    Listserv, 232–235

    lurking, 234
    Majordomo, 235
    moderator, 233, 236
    searching archives, 241
    subscribing, 236
    Tile.Net, 238
    unsubscribing, 236
.doc, 35
Dogpile, 88
domain names, 282
downloading
    files, 37, 43–49, 260–261
    software from software
    archives, 262–271
    tables into documents, 43–54
    using anonymous FTP, 260–263
driving directions
    finding, 179–180
.dxr, 36

E

.edu, 281
Electronic Communications Privacy Act, 323
electronic journals
    citing, 311–312
email
    citing, 308–309
    privacy, 322
email addresses
    finding, 173–174
email and telephone directories, 173–182
    InfoSpace, 174–177
    reverse searches, 178
    white pages services, 173–174
emailing Web pages, 53
encryption, 323–324
error messages, 14–15
evaluating Web and Internet resources, 279–296
    guidelines, 281–283
evaluating Web pages, 279–283
    accuracy or objectivity, 282, 290–291
    audience, 282, 290
    authorship, 281–282
    bibliographies, 295

currency, 282
guidelines, 281–283
purpose, 282, 291
.exe, 262, 263

F

FAQ (frequently asked questions)
    discussion groups, 277
fair use, 38
favorites, 10–11, 18, 22–23, 49–51
    deleting, 50
favorites list, 22, 23
field searching, 131–132, 173–174
fields, 131
file formats, 34–37
File Transfer Protocol,
    See FTP
file types, 34–37
finding words in a Web page, 21–22, 281
FindLaw: Supreme Court
    Opinions, 119, 153, 169–173
firewall, 328
F-PROT, 264
frames, 18, 20, 333
freeware, 259, 267
frequently asked questions, *See* FAQ
FTP (File Transfer Protocol), 14, 17, 258–274
    anonymous, 258–263
    archives, 258–259, 261–271
    client programs, 271–274
    retrieving and
        downloading files, 260–261, 262–271
    search services, 17
    URL formats, 259–260
full-text indexing, 128

G–H

Galaxy, 64, 99
.gif, 35
Google, 6–10, 16, 83–87, 115, 132, 138–142,
    188, 192–195, 203–205, 292
    advanced search, 140–142, 188, 203
    image searching, 203–205
    news searching, 188
    search strategy, 139
    searching within results, 132
    using to find specialized databases, 154
Google Groups, 17, 233, 247–250, 283
.gov, 281
Graphic Interchange Format (.gif), 35
graphical user interface (GUI), 214
.gz, 36
helper applications, 18
hidden Internet, 128, 152
hierarchy, 64–65
high precision/high recall, 129
high precision/low recall, 129
history list, 18, 22, 23, 325
home page, 4
Hoovers.com, 117
HTTP (Hypertext Transfer Protocol), 3, 13
hyperlinks, 3–4
hypermedia, 4
hypertext, 3, 4–5
Hypertext Markup Language
    (HTML), 3, 13

I–K

image files, 35
    .gif, 35
    inserting into
        documents, 54
    .jpg or .jpeg, 35
    searching for, 203–205
    .tif or .tiff, 35
image searching, 203–205
implied Boolean operators, 130
Infomine, 69, 108, 280
InfoSpace, 115, 175–177
Internet, 2
Internet Explorer, *See* Microsoft Internet Explorer
Internet Public Library, 16, 70, 72–75,
    108, 155, 280, 312
    searching, 73–74
Internet safety for children, 329–330
invisible Web, 128, 152, 154
Ixquick, 16, 88, 89–91
.jpeg or .jpg (Joint Photographic
    Expert Group), 35
junk email, *See* spam

keyboard shortcuts, 21–23, 50, 332–333
keyword indexing, 128–129

L

language searching, 132
legal information
    searching for, 169–173
LIBCAT, 215, 216, 222–227
Librarians' Index to the Internet, 16, 70, 108,
    109–113, 155, 156–158, 200–202
Library of Congress
    catalog searching, 216–222
    classification system, 214
    home page, 3–4
    subject headings, 219
library online catalogs, 214–227
    digital collections, 215
    field searching, 215
    finding, 216
    LIBCAT, 215, 216, 222–227
    Libweb, 215, 216–222
library special collections, 222–227
LibrarySpot, 70, 108, 155, 164–165
Libweb, 17, 216–222
limiting by date, 132
link analysis, 127, 139
Listproc, 235–237
Listserv, 17, 232, 235, 237
    citing messages, 309–310
LookSmart, 64, 99
low precision/high recall, 129
lurking, 234
Lycos, 77, 127

M

mailing addresses
    finding, 174–177
Majordomo, 235, 237
map services, 115
maps
    finding, 173–174
medical information
    searching for, 156
MEDLINE, 120, 153, 156–163
    Boolean operators, 159–160

search strategy, 157
menu bar, 332
MetaCrawler, 16, 88
meta-search tools, 16, 61, 63,
    64, 87–91, 143
    Dogpile, 88
    Ixquick, 16, 88, 89–91
    MetaCrawler, 16, 88
    parallel search tools, 87–88
    Proteus Internet Search, 77, 88–89
    Search.com, 88
    unified search
        interfaces, 87–88, 143
    Vivisimo, 16, 143–146
meta-tags, 128–129
Microsoft Internet Explorer, 3–5
    address toolbar, 4, 335, 336
    edit menu, 334
    emailing a Web page, 53
    favorites, 18, 334–335
    file menu, 39, 334
    help menu, 335
    links toolbar, 336
    menu bar, 4, 332–334
    save target as, 43, 52
    standard buttons
        toolbar, 335
        status bar, 336
        tools menu, 334–335
        view menu, 334
.mil, 228
MLA style, 116, 301, 305–312
MP3 or .mp3, 36
modem, 19
modifying search results, 9, 133, 134, 141–142
.mov, 36
Mozilla, 25–28
.mpg or .mpeg (Moving Picture
    Expert Group), 36
multimedia
    searching for, 202–208
multimedia files, 36, 202–203
    .dcr, 36
    .dir, 36
    .dxr, 36

.mov, 36
.mpg or .mpeg, 36
.qt, 36
.ram or .rm, 36

N–O

nested Boolean operators, 130
    logic, 130
    searching, 136, 140
.net, 281
Netscape, 27, 325
Network News Transport Protocol (NNTP), 244
network security, 326–330
newspaper archives on the Web, 189
news aggregation, 194–202
news alerts, 192–194
newspaper directories, 188–189
newsreader, 194–202, 233, 243–244
Next/Sun format, 36
OPAC (online public access catalog), 214
Open Directory Project, 66–68, 99, 155, 190–191
Opera, 3, 25–27
.org, 228
output features, 133
    sorting results, 133

P

parallel search tools, 87–88
.pdf, 34–35
phrase searching, 77, 78–79, 83–87, 130
    Google, 83–87, 140
PKZIP, 263–265
plug-ins, 18–19, 203
Portable Document Format (PDF), 34–35, 154
    Adobe Acrobat, 34–35, 154
PostScript, 34
Pretty Good Privacy, 323–324
printing frames, 53
printing Web pages, 52–53
privacy, 25, 321–330
    children, 283
    and ethics, 178
    policy, 175
Proteus Internet Search, 77, 88–89

protocols, 13
proximity searching, 77–78, 130–131
.ps, 34
PubMed, *see* MEDLINE

Q–R

.qt, 36
QuickTime, 36, 203
.ram or .rm, 36
Readme, 37, 263, 275
RealAudio format, 36
RealVideo, 36
reference works, 70–71, 108–109
relevancy ranking, 133
reverse searches, 178
right mouse button, 20–21
robots, 77, 128
RSS (Really Simple Syndication), 194, 208
RSS newsreaders, 196
.rtf, 35

S

Save As, 40, 46–47, 270, 332
Save Target As, 43, 52
saving
    frames, 53
    image files, 45–47, 54
    Web pages, 40–43, 52
Scout Report, 155, 317–318
search engines, 16, 77–87, 127–146
    All the Web, 127, 145
    AltaVista, 77, 116, 127, 135–138, 205
    basic search strategy, 133–146
    Boolean operators, 78–82, 129–130
    Boolean searching, 79–82, 137–138
    case sensitivity, 132
    default settings, 78
    field searching, 131, 174
    full-text indexing, 128
    Google, 6–10, 16, 83–87, 115, 132,
        138–142, 188, 192–195, 203–205, 292
    high precision/high recall, 129
    high precision/low recall, 129
    image searching, 203–205

implied Boolean operators, 130

keyword indexing, 128–129

limiting by date, 132

link analysis, 127

low precision/high recall, 129

Lycos, 77, 127

meta-tags, 128–129

modifying search results, 9, 133, 134, 141–142

nested Boolean searching, 130, 136, 140

output features, 133

relevancy ranking, 133

robots, 77, 128

spiders, 77, 128

stop words, 128

syntax, 129, 144

search features, 127, 129–130

    phrase searching, 78–79, 83–86

    proximity searching, 78, 130–131,

    truncation, 131

search strategy, basic, 133

Search.com, 88

searching directories, 64–65, 101–102

security information, 326–330

shareware, 49, 259, 262–265,

    antivirus programs, 264

    archives, 264–265

    PKZIP, 36–37

    WinZip, 36–37

Shockwave, 36, 202

software archives, 264–265

    downloading software, 265–271

    searching, 264

sorting results, 138

spam, 178, 244, 330

special library, 214, 215

specialized databases, 17, 28, 63, 71, 109, 114, 152–182,

    bibliographic, 153

    commercial, 153

    fee-based, 154

    finding, 154–155

    FindLaw: Supreme Court Opinions, 153, 169–173

    full-text, 153

    MEDLINE, 153, 156–163

    newspaper archives

        on the Web, 153

    proprietary, 153–154

    U.S. Supreme Court opinions, 169–173

spiders, 77, 99, 122, 128

spreadsheet files, 35, 44

Standard Buttons toolbar, 335–336

status bar, 19, 20, 333, 336

stemming, 131

stop words, 128

stopping a Web page, 22

streaming media, 203

structured browsing,

subject categories, 64–65

subject guides, 70, 109, 113

syntax, 79, 129, 144

T

Tagged Image File Format, 35

Telnet, 214, 328

text files, 34–35

    .asc, 34

    .pdf, 34–35

    .ps, 34

    .txt, 34

thread, 242

.tif or .tiff, 35

Tile.Net, 328, 345

translation services, 132

truncation, 131

.txt, 34

U

unified search interfaces, 88

URL (Uniform Resource Locator), 3, 5, 13–14, 27, 29, 301–303

URL formats, 301–303

Usenet archives

    searching, 17, 247–250

Usenet news, 17, 232–250

    citing, 310

    cross-posting, 242

etiquette, 251–252
FAQ, 245
newsreader, 243–244
posting, 242, 244–245
setting news preferences, 244
thread, 242

V

virtual libraries, 16, 28, 63, 69–76,
    98–122, 155, 280
    Academic Info, 69, 108, 280
    annotated directories, 108
    Infomine, 69, 108, 280
    Internet Public Library, 16, 70,
        72–76, 108, 155, 280
    Librarians' Index to the Internet,
        16, 70, 106, 110–113, 155, 280
    LibrarySpot, 70, 108, 155, 280
    reference works, 70–71, 109–113
    subject guides, 70, 109, 113
    specialized databases, 28, 63, 71,
        109, 114, 155
    World Wide Web Virtual Library, 14, 26
viruses, 328–329
Vivisimo, 16, 88, 138, 143–146, 288–290
    Advanced search mode, 143-144,
    implied Boolean
        operators, 144
    search strategy, 143–146

W

.wav, 36
Web browser,
    content area, 20, 333
    help, 335, 336
    menu bar, 332

preferences, 335
right mouse button, 20–21, 333
scroll bar, 4, 8, 19, 20, 21, 331, 333
status bar, 19, 20, 331, 333, 336
toolbars, 19–20, 331, 333, 335
Web pages, 2
    citing, 305–308
    determining the date of,
        290, 303–304, 305, 308
    the parts of, 132
Web privacy, 324–326
weblogs, 189–192
white pages services, 173–174, 178
    advantages, 174
    disadvantages, 174
    privacy and ethical issues, 178
wildcards, 131
WinZip, 37, 263–264, 275
.wk1, 35
.wks, 35
word-processing files, 35
    .doc, 35
    .rtf, 35
    .wpd, 35
World Wide Web, 2–3
World Wide Web Virtual Library, 14, 26
.wpd, 35
WS_FTP, 272–274

X–Z

.xls, 35
XML, 194–195, 200
Yahoo!, 64, 69, 77, 99, 99–108, 155, 169–173,
    188, 192, 195, 318
    browsing, 103–108, 169–173
.zip, 36–37, 262–263